READINGS IN THE HISTORY OF PHILOSOPHY

SERIES EDITORS:

PAUL EDWARDS, Brooklyn College
RICHARD H. POPKIN, University of California, San Diego

The Volumes and Their Editors:

GREEK PHILOSOPHY: THALES TO ARISTOTLE, Third Edition
Reginald E. Allen

GREEK AND ROMAN PHILOSOPHY AFTER ARISTOTLE
Jason L. Saunders

MEDIEVAL PHILOSOPHY:
ST. AUGUSTINE TO OCKHAM
Father Allan B. Wolter

THE PHILOSOPHY OF THE SIXTEENTH AND
SEVENTEENTH CENTURIES
Richard H. Popkin

EIGHTEENTH-CENTURY PHILOSOPHY
Lewis White Beck

NINETEENTH-CENTURY PHILOSOPHY:
HEGEL TO NIETZSCHE
Peter Koestenbaum

TWENTIETH-CENTURY PHILOSOPHY:
THE ANALYTIC TRADITION
Morris Weitz

Greek and Roman Philosophy after Aristotle

Jason L. Saunders

THE FREE PRESS
New York   London   Toronto   Sydney   Singapore

THE FREE PRESS
A Division of Simon & Schuster Inc.
1230 Avenue of the Americas
New York, NY 10020

Manufactured in the United States of America

1   3   5   7   9   10   8   6   4   2

Library of Congress Catalog Card Number 66–12892

ISBN 0-684-83643-2

TO JULIET, MITCHELL, RACHEL, AND HECUBA

ACKNOWLEDGMENTS

I wish to thank several publishers for their kindness in allowing me to use the following selections in this volume: Penguin Books Ltd., Harmondsworth, Middlesex, for permission to reprint portions of *Lucretius: The Nature of the Universe*, trans. Ronald Latham, copyright © 1951 by Ronald Latham. The Clarendon Press, Oxford, for permission to reprint *The Manual of Epictetus*, trans. P. E. Matheson. The Modern Library, for permission to reprint *Cleanthes' Hymn to Zeus*, trans. by James Adam, from *The Stoic and Epicurean Philosophers*, ed. by Whitney J. Oates, New York, 1940. The following selections from *The Ante-Nicene Fathers*, the Rev. Alexander Roberts and James Donaldson, editors, copyright 1956, Grand Rapids, Michigan, used by permission of the William B. Eerdmans Publishing Co.; portions of *Justin Martyr: Dialogue with Trypho, Address to the Greeks;* Clement of Alexandria: *Stromata;* Origen: *On First Principles*, trans. Rev. Frederick Crombie; and Tertullian: *Prescription against Heretics, On the Soul*, trans. Rev. S. Thewall. Reprinted from *The Enneads*, Third Edition, by Plotinus. (Pantheon Books, a Division of Random House, Inc.). All rights reserved. The Bible text in this publication is from the *Revised Standard Version* of the *Bible*, copyrighted 1946 and 1952 by the Division of Christian Education of the National Council of Churches, and used by permission. The following selections from the Loeb Classical Library, Cambridge, Mass., reprinted by permission of the publishers, Harvard University Press: portions of: Sextus Empiricus, *Outlines of Pyrrhonism*, trans. R. G. Bury, 1933; *Philo*, trans. F. H. Colson and G. H. Whitaker, 1956; *Diogenes Laertius* trans. R. D. Hicks, 1942; Minucius Felix, *Octavius*, trans. Gerald H. Rendall, 1960.

Earlier translations of the original Greek and Latin testimonies of early Stoicism, as these were collected by J. von Arnim, have consisted merely of excerpts. I have offered, in my translations contained in this volume, a wider selection of the more significant materials from the Arnim collection. Since the emphasis of later, Roman, Stoicism was almost entirely on moral philosophy, it seemed worthwhile to include selections showing the philosophical vigor of the earlier, Greek, Stoicism in the areas of metaphysics, epistemology, and logic. I have added letter indications (a, b, c) for ease in locating testimonies listed by Arnim according to number only.

For their unflagging patience, good humor, and for freely giving of their time and energies I wish to thank my students, Tom Andrews, James Groves, John Harris, Hoke Simpson, and Gea Sund, all of the University of California, San Diego.

I should also like to thank Miss Betty Duimstra, Mrs. Paula Hocks, and Mrs. Tressa Miller for their usual kindnesses.

CONTENTS

GREEK AND ROMAN PHILOSOPHY

AFTER ARISTOTLE

INTRODUCTION

WITH THE DEATH OF ARISTOTLE in the year 322 B.C., there came to a close perhaps the greatest period in the long and fruitful history of Western philosophical speculation—the glory that was Athens, its celebrated poets and playwrights, its painters and sculptors, its freedom, pride, and laws. This was the Athens of Socrates, of Plato, and of Aristotle. That the first was put to death by Athens, the first city of Greece, suggests only that the greatest city-state of antiquity became a victim of her own disregard for the justice and freedom of expression, the joyful interplay of ideas, and the celebration of creativity in man and in his artistic human sensitivity. What Athens had given birth to was proudly nurtured until, ignominiously, she punished herself by passing the death sentence on Socrates, the symbol of all her values and the glory of the uniqueness of the Greek heritage. Plato and, after him, Aristotle, and Athens herself continued to exult and to explore, to experience and to understand, and to overreach in their stubborn insistence on the achievement of those very goals and ideals of which Socrates was at once the epitome and the scourge. Their eagerness for life and social pursuits and their reverence for all things both human and divine were as a mirror held up to the world, showing by its momentary image the ceaseless motion and never-ending activity of nature. Such was the Greek world—a world of purpose, of divine order and design, and of fate and human pride. Nature and her struggle for survival, for achievement, and for trial was for the Greeks a living witness to the beauty, truth, and goodness inherent in the processes of life and death, dissolution and rebirth. The inexorable law of its nature was to the Greek world a nature of natures, of things growing in accordance with that Law; it was an ordered and value-laden process of things in motion. The natural world was a world of things becoming and changing; the behavior of the natural world was seen by

1

the Greeks to exemplify an inherent tendency and impulse to strive for perfection, for self-realization.

To move was to act with purpose, and that purpose or goal was viewed as an illustration of the totality of the motions of anything whose *nature* is to act in certain ways. A natural thing is impelled to act as it does by the necessity that governs and orders all things. Even the gods in the Greek Pantheon are restrained by that order and *anangke*. No thing may become or change in opposition to the law of its nature. That the world is orderly and full of motions led the Greeks to believe that there are reasons for all change, that it is intelligent, purposeful motion. The Greeks believed that divinity is reason and that the world is fundamentally knowable. Thus, the name of Socrates was the further reminder, as Plato eulogized him, that the soul of man, which, in man, names the peculiarly human activity, is the reasoning act, the ability to know and to contemplate. Knowledge is thus the achievement of man, but knowledge as process and not as the summation of learning. To know the world, to understand how things are as they are, is to know and understand oneself. "Know thyself" was a maxim for man in a knowable world.

This was the legacy handed down by the Greece of legend and song, passed on in stories, in plays, and in histories. It was celebrated in stone and in monuments. Its remarkable achievement by a remarkable people was exemplified to a very large degree by Greek philosophers, particularly Socrates, Plato, and Aristotle. *Episteme*, knowledge by discovery and demonstration, scientific knowledge, fact and value, was an integral part of this legacy. Its method was dialectic, the interplay of ideas, and the life of the mind. So greatly renowned were the philosophers of Greece that the proximate heirs to the legacy,—the thinkers of the period from the death of Aristotle to the close of the third century of the Christian era—used the word "Greeks" as a synonym for "philosophers."

This period, often referred to as the Hellenistic Age, was an era of marked change to that which had preceded it. The Greek city-state was no more, and Athens was no longer the center of worldly attraction. The glory that was Greece was now to give way to Roman arms and conquest and to the stern but simple piety and lofty grandeur that was to serve as the hallmark of the Roman genius. The emergence of Rome, energetic and impatient, had a profound effect on the world around her. Or, perhaps, its maritime geography placed Rome in a commanding position in a sea of nations whose ruling dynasties had become feeble and dissolute. Commerce had grown large and complex, demanding organization and regularization far beyond the limited and now obsolete means embodied in the earlier system of small and separate city-states, with their petty jealousies and narrow interests. Rome became the great organizer in a world and at a time when such a talent was sadly lacking. The older methods of waging war as well as maintaining the peace were no longer effective as a guarantee of national boundaries.

There is no question that the Periclean Age of Athens represents the heights achieved by the Greek city-states and that the good life is lived in a society so governed that the happiness of its citizens is its chief end. But the march of Alexander of Macedon across the Hellespont and eastward as far as the fabled land of India had in some ways an effect on the world no less important than that of the Athenian glory. The city-state was to be replaced, during the brief and tempestuous rule of Alexander the Great, by larger political units under the dominion of a central court whose rulers were thus at a distance from the affairs of the majority of the people. Such units were deliberately formed to break apart the provincial and local loyalties of the earlier city-states. An important distinction between Greek and barbarian was thus gradually destroyed for the sake of the Empire and imperial loyalty. This, most of all, encouraged the further deterioration of the concept of the free man, resulting in obligation and service to the king and to the state, whose function it was to protect its rule and not the rights of individual citizens. Happiness consisted in submission to the ruler. But the ruler was surrounded by sycophants and those desirous of wresting power for themselves within the widespread disarray of the three kingdoms remaining of the Macedonian conquests. A century of wars, intrigues, and attempts by subject peoples to cast off oppression further weakened the power and strength of these petty overlords.

As the wanton behavior of many such ruling circles increased, a general licentiousness seems to have been accompanied by a falling away from the customs, moral habits, and personal and social conduct earlier upheld. The example of state dignitaries and those in high priestly office was far from an edifying spectacle for increasingly larger numbers of people who came more and more to find a world growing larger, more complex, and more fearsome. The loss of freedom by subject peoples and the lack of moral force behind their obligation to the state or king perhaps played into the hands of Rome and her plans for expansion. By the year 188 before the time of Christ, by means of her skill at diplomacy and the prodigious force of her legions and her navy, the Roman state had converted the seas into a Roman lake. By 146,

Greece, striving to relive its past freedoms and glories, became a protectorate of Rome—at least (and at last) to enjoy the comparative safety of the *pax Romana*. Greece was again at peace, but the power was now in Rome. To be a Roman citizen, to live *with* Rome, promised a stability and vigor not easily found elsewhere. Thus, Rome—eventually to become the first city of the world—carried everywhere its attitudes and its zest for intensely practical ideas as well as a characteristic impatience and lack of interest in accommodation of its native traditions to the older, well-established cultures of Greece and Asia Minor. Indeed, although Greek continued to be the language of literature and the arts, the Latin tongue began to emerge, first as the language of the invading armies and occupying troops together with official state and trade representatives. Roman ways and the Roman penchant for law on Roman terms was not long in making itself felt. The traditions of Rome, as depicted in Vergil for example, came much more slowly to effect literature, rhetoric, grammar, and the arts. And this was because of the great dependence of Roman writers on Greek literary forms and stylistic matters. Nonetheless, the uniquely Roman way of life—ideals, religious practices, and national loyalties—shines through the vestments of so many Roman imitation of Greek modes and slavish copying of Hellenic ideas.

The Hellenistic Age was a time of transition; a new culture was in the making. In part, the legacy of the Greeks was to be enormously influential; and, in part, Rome and its language were to assimilate much that was Greek in thought and in expression, inevitably to graft on to the amalgam the strength and power of its own native tradition. Moralistic and legalistic Rome was to drink deeply from the wellsprings of the Greek glory, but Rome was indelibly to stamp its own mark on the thought and culture of the first several centuries of the new era.

If philosophy may be said to have been born in Greece, then it may be said of its golden age that philosophy flourished brilliantly in the persons and thought of those three men who were to figure importantly in later centuries—Plato, Aristotle, and that symbol of courage and stubborn adherence to truth, the master of dialectic and the epitome of the wise man, Socrates. And if, as Plato would have it, the philosopher is the consummate artist and if philosophic man is a further exemplar of human activity and excellence, it is clear how he could and did flourish in the marketplace and in the affairs of the city-state and why it became increasingly difficult and finally impossible to assume a similar role in the highly organized efficiency of a Roman administration. Opinions were at best one's own business; the affairs of state were regulated by Roman law—the embodiment of the Senate and the Roman people.

The vicissitudes of the earlier centuries of the Hellenistic Age, briefly alluded to above, may easily enough be cast in sharp relief by noticing the shifts and gradual changes taking place in the thought of the philosopher and the direction of his gaze. Maxims of an earlier vintage seemed no longer to command as much attention or to be so widely popular, for example, *the unexamined life is a life not worth living; the ultimate goal of man is contemplation, the life of the mind; philosophy begins in awe and wonder.* For the Greeks, to live well and good was to inquire into the nature of things; knowledge for its own sake alone provided the ultimate value in the life of man.

Such maxims as these were replaced by others vastly different both in tone and substance. These newer slogans and catchwords similarly reflect the very conditions of the world in which they had currency. Knowledge and its pursuit were no longer ends in themselves. The vicissitudes of life in a world struggling to relocate itself called not for human excellence as rational man, for to what avail is pure reason in an impure existence? The call was to sympathy and to resignation; to examine life was to reject or at least to withdraw from most of its implications. Philosophy now tended to become *ars vitae,* a way of life, a way of accommodation for people to whom the human situation no longer appeared as the mirror of a universal calm and ordered existence. Philosophy became a means toward something of value outside itself; and, with its aid, perturbation and the painful experience of dislocation and estrangement widely felt in these times might promise not only an altering of the facts of life and of the world, but also of the affairs of men and particularly of the individual man. Thus, quietude and tranquility, absence of pain, and the withholding of judgment became in many ways the hallmarks of the age. These terms were given wide currency throughout the Hellenistic World, undoubtedly reflecting the beliefs and attitudes, the fears and aspirations of the general population. What was so evident in the ferment and intellectual bruit of the times—the doubts and uncertainties of life, a lack of social, political, and cultural cohesiveness, and a concomitant feeling of alienation—came to the fore in the widespread use of these terms by the philosophers of the various schools of Hellenistic thought. The earlier period—when Athens was the world—found philosophers, among others, looking to the stars and to nature or emphasizing the rational role of man in an ordered universe. The later philosophers, in a different world, sought to preserve a sense of human dignity for the individual man caught up in a web of uncertainties and questionable values.

Happiness and pleasure are not to be found in the exercise of the mind nor in man's role as a free citizen and fraternal member of a local assembly. Nor is it reflected in games and productions that were vivid reminders of communal pride and the loyalty of a common language and tradition. True happiness is found in *withdrawal*, and it is perhaps in Epicureanism that we find this theme most strongly presented—the voice of the ascetic and moral outrage and of dismay. Pleasure, says Epicurus, is the chief end of man, but pleasure meant the absence of bodily pain and a troubled soul. For the Epicurean philosopher, knowledge is to be valued as a means of avoiding entanglement and of providing canons of conduct that reduce the experience of pain and the discomfort of unsure alliances.

Epicureans appear to have lived according to their own teachings: withdrawal from the confusions and activities of the city to the life of the garden. Serenity of mind and an austerity of habit and of attitude pervades much of the thought of Epicurus and his disciples and the lofty lines of Rome's Epicurean poet, Lucretius. Not that these men were unconcerned about asking many of the same kinds of questions raised by Plato and Aristotle; for both Epicurus and Lucretius wondered about the world and the place of man in it.

Epicurus went back to the earliest Greek philosophers for his starting point, as did Plato and Aristotle. Yet, his elaboration of the atomism of Democritus served as a physical basis for the concepts of the freedom of the will and man's responsibility for his actions. The Democritean view that everything is ultimately composed of atomic particles was modified in Epicurean thought so as to provide a path for these atoms that permits deviation of their motions along straight lines. It is in the capacity of the atoms to swerve and thus to collide that the Epicurean hoped to account for occurrences of phenomena. This same capacity is used by them to account for free will, since the collision of the atoms of the soul and the body and the transmission of these motions provides the motive force for human actions. Lucretius faithfully reproduced the views of Epicurus about the nature of the physical world, preserving the essential feature of the doctrine— cosmic order or the undeviating motions or causes of things must be denied to give man freedom. A no less important Epicurean principle is the insistence that understanding of the world can be had without recourse to divine providence; thus inquietude engendered by fear of the gods is eliminated. The doctrine, further requires that sensation be the sole criterion for the attainment of truth. Pleasure and pain are sensations, and sensation represents the mode by which observable procedures of investigation may be carried out. If it is clear that Epicureanism was nobly motivated in its appeal to freedom from fear and superstition, it is also true that many thoughtful people were attracted to its doctrines as a way of escape from the exigencies of their worldly affairs and in the expectation that a life of withdrawal in contemplation would provide contentment, albeit at the sacrifice of responsibility for their fellow men. A rival of such doctrines, Stoicism, provided in many ways a similar program and rule of life. However, the Stoic philosopher was most firmly opposed to disengagement and to retreat from worldly responsibility. Where the Epicurean eschewed involvement, the Stoic urged participation in the affairs of men, so that both philosophies vied for the chief role as physicians of the soul and as the conscience of men everywhere. Each examined the means by which freedom from anxiety might be achieved. Emphasis on moral questions and ethical canons is perhaps less marked in Stoic philosophy, at least in its earlier development. The ideas of the founding fathers of the Stoic school, Zeno, Cleanthes and Chrysippus, include much fundamental re-assessment of logical theory, which the Epicurean philosopher was largely to dismiss as inconsequential. And the Stoic, although in agreement with Epicureans that logic is a tool and not an end in itself, nonetheless found in a formal study of logic much that supported their physical theory and ultimately their ethics. For Stoics were also to argue that all inquiry was for the sole purpose of providing man with a mode of conduct characterized by tranquility of mind and certainty of moral worth.

The Stoics also believed that sensation is the basis of sure and undoubted truths. Their comprehensive presentation implies not only that knowledge is possible, but also that certain knowledge is possible, on the analogy of the incorrigibility of sensate experience. To them, the world is altogether made up of material things, with some notably difficult exceptions, such as meaning. They held that fire, or divine reason, is the ultimate principle in things. Viewing the world as a great machine with all its parts material bodies acting in accordance with fixed rules set by nature, the Stoics nevertheless argued that man is in no way governed but by those same inexorable laws of nature. Fate rules all things, and the world in its motions exhibits a grandeur of orderly arrangement that can only serve as a model of how man might order and regulate his own life. Consequently, the goal of man is to live in accordance with nature, in agreement with the world design. To achieve serenity and tranquility of mind, so pervasive a goal in Hellenistic thought, Stoic moral theory was also based on the physical view that the world is a unity, like a great city. Man becomes a citizen of the world with an obligation and loyalty to all things in that city. He must play an active part in the world, remembering always that virtue is an essential feature of the world.

Moral worth, justice, and duty became the hallmarks of the Stoic philosophy. A certain sternness is found in their ethics, including a well-known denial that the good or wise man need be merciful or show pity, since mercy suggests a deviation from duty and the fated necessity that rules the world. A perplexing problem in Stoic philosophy is how to reconcile the insistence that man is responsible for his acts, and thus that man is free, with the theory of a completely determined universe. Notwithstanding, the loftiness of spirit inherent in Stoic thought and its emphasis on man's essential worth, the theme of universal brotherhood (for *no man is a slave by nature*), and the beneficent workings of divine nature made Stoicism one of the leading philosophic schools of its day.

It was undoubtedly the most influential of the schools from the time of its founding through the first two centuries of the Christian era. It is not at all a coincidence that prominent thinkers, Jew and Christian, Philo Judaeus as well as so many of the early Christian Fathers, should so often argue against Stoic opponents or find agreeable so much of the Stoic doctrine of man's place in the scheme of things. Although Roman Stoicism later became almost entirely concerned with moral philosophy, its doctrine, as originally formulated with some revision, received wide acceptance. Prominent figures in this later period included Marcus Aurelius, an emperor whose *Meditations* is to this day a well-known piece of inspirational literature, and Epictetus, a slave whose thought Arrian, a disciple, has preserved in the *Manual* and the *Discourses*. Seneca (3 B.C.-65 A.D.), an intimate of Nero, was well known for his adherence to Stoicism. Perhaps the greatest of the later Stoic thinkers was Posidonius of Apamaea (135-51 B.C.), who was responsible for the spread of Stoic thought in Rome.

Of ancient Skepticism, it is well to keep in mind that the Platonic Academy went through a period during which a somewhat mild form of Skepticism became a dominant feature in the exposition of Plato's doctrine. Arcesilaus (315-241 B.C), who founded the Middle Academy, and Carneades of Cyrene (213-129 B.C.), the founder of the later New Academy, both held knowledge to be impossible, although the former at least believed that opinions might be distinguished as more or less credible. However, Carneades had worked out a view of probable knowledge, thus permitting the possibility of reasonable choice and not necessarily demanding suspension of judgment.

The other, better-known form of Skepticism is that associated with Pyrrho of Elis, who wrote nothing but was celebrated as the fountainhead of Skeptical beliefs. Our knowledge of this Skepticism is almost entirely that found in the writings of Sextus Empiricus, and the several treatises contained there show the care with which the Skeptics directed their very considerable energies to demolish the arguments of "dogmatic" philosophers. A much favored victim of the Skeptical subtlety of argument was Stoicism, although the Stoics seem to have enjoyed the dispute equally well. Whereas the "dogmatic" philosopher held opinions or beliefs, the Skeptic found no commanding reason to choose one from another, arguing that no more and no less reasonableness could attach to any, and thus one ought to withhold or suspend judgment. Yet, the Skeptic did not find himself unable to make decisions in conducting his affairs; he simply followed the customs of the community. Thus, he believed that his denial of certainty in knowledge would provide him with that quietude and simpler life that the dogmatic holder of opinion could not hope to achieve. There was, as a result, an important connection between what appears to have been the Skeptics' complete preoccupation with theories of knowledge and the practice of life. For Sextus urges over and over again that suspension of judgment is the inevitable outcome of any comparison of the arguments of rival philosophical schools, since their arguments both contradict one another and rest on the most unreliable criteria and evidence. With that suspension of judgment, the goal of the Skeptic—the achievement of a Skeptical way of life—is not different from the goal of his adversary, his "dogmatic" opponent. Together with the Stoics and Epicureans, the Skeptics sought a pathway, a way of life, *ars vitae*, the significance of which would mirror the goals of quietude, surcease, *ataraxia* or tranquility, and the achievement of a euphoric state of mind. Lucian, perhaps the best literary representative of Skeptical themes, pokes fun at the outrageous claims of all those philosophers who claim to have some view about life or knowledge of the world, which pre-empts the possibility that opposing views are not of equal merit.

The philosophers we have been considering seem to reflect a conscious aim of accommodation to a world fraught with unease and extravagance in claim and in practice; Epicurean, Stoic, and Skeptic, in their several ways, appear to have urged means by which the individual might better order his own life and avoid the excesses of human nature that promote the disquieting experience, at the least, of too much involvement. And if these thinkers appeal to an equanimity of mind and the advantages of reasonableness over the use of the emotions and passions, still we have already noted changes in attitude between them and the Athenian philosophers who preceded: rationality and contemplation as the epitome of human excellence had now given way to a more personal, essentially practical, and even a more worldly approach to man's problems.

Earlier philosophers were primarily concerned to understand the natural world and the behavior, the hopes, and the anxieties of men. But now, an additional element was brought forward by the introduction of an important further dimension of human experience—the religious awareness of the meaning of human existence and human history. The hope of salvation was further enhanced by those who came to hold that faith presents a new method for attaining wisdom and truth. Thus, appeals to reason and the senses were supplemented by an increasing emphasis on the efficacy of faith as an imminent aid to man's understanding of himself and his world. The newer religious philosophers struggled to reconcile their beliefs with the older and more familiar methods of the Greek philosophers; philosophy itself was to gain much in this confrontation between reason and faith. This was the formidable task of the philosophers of later antiquity.

One of the earliest members of this group of philosophers was Philo, a Jewish philosopher of Alexandrian background and steeped in the literature of the Old Testament as well as Greek philosophy. At the time of his birth (20 B.C.), Alexandria was the great city of Hellenistic and Jewish culture. Even before the earliest development of a Christian attempt to meet on its own terms the challenge of the wisdom of the Greeks, Philo took on himself the task of reconciling the Judaism of the Scriptures with Platonic philosophy, then in the ascendency at Alexandria. To him, the divine truths of the Old Testament are couched in terms, readily available to all believers, of ordinary sense experience. The imagery of colors and shapes and the appeal to sounds and to the understanding of the relation of father and son serve as but one way of expressing God's law and His will. Scriptural "myths" are also available to reason and to him who seeks as a philosopher to understand. In Philo, we find the culmination at Alexandria of several centuries of Jewish life within a Hellenizing community. Of his many writings, some reflect his purely philosophical training and interests *(Eternity of the World, On Providence)*, and others include historical works *(Life of Moses)* as well as many examples of his allegorical interpretation of Scriptural accounts. One of the fundamental problems of this period in the development of Western thought is treated in considerable detail by Philo in his *On the Account of the World's Creation Given by Moses:* How is it possible that a world created by a perfect God should contain evil?

And if the Platonic philosophy should have been found to be in harmony with a continuing emphasis on an immediacy of internal human experience, such knowledge gained gives direction and purpose to a purely rational account, wholly reliant on the publicity of sensation or the mere exercise of reason—much as the traveler well equipped to travel will need a map or direction lest he wander aimlessly. The congeniality of the Platonic distinction between the world of the senses and the world of Ideas had, by the third century, culminated in an essentially pagan (i.e., neither Jewish nor Christian) synthesis of the metaphysics of Plato with much of the thought predominant in Alexandria. This synthesis is usually referred to as Neoplatonism; its founder and leading thinker was Plotinus. His writings, treatises called *Enneads,* have come down to us, as well as a biography by Porphyry, one of his students.

Plotinus' philosophy is fundamentally one that argues for transcendence and for a world of intelligible forms (the Platonic Ideas) that are exemplars of the perishable things of spacial magnitude and temporality. For the things of sense are characterized by generation and decay, whereas the intelligible world is not in time or space. If not physically separate, the intelligible forms are logically distinct. Thus, Plotinus held that the world of intelligibles further reflects a world beyond them, a world of the *unity* of these essences of things. This unity, which is the source both of the intelligibles and of things in space and time, is called by Plotinus the One. Things are what they are only as unities; they ultimately derive their existence from unity itself, the residuum and source of all particularity, both physical and logical. It is, finally—or better, initially—an aesthetic experience that provides man with his first glimpse of the soul as linked with a world beyond mundane existence. The direction is described as upward, serving to purify the soul of earthly contact. Thus, philosophy, which abstracts from the things of sense and carries one to the world of intelligibles, is for Plotinus the instrument by which the soul's redemption is secured.

The remaining group of philosophers is made up of those thinkers who, as Christians, were also to make the initial move of attempting a rational approach to divine truth as given by revelation. The Platonism and Stoicism of the pagan philosophers of the Hellenistic Age was used by the early Fathers of the Church as a welcomed aid to the formation of Christian doctrine and, more often, as a means by which the marked contrast between the efficacy of faith over that of reason might show both the shortcomings of Greek philosophy and the immediacy of religious experience leading to the supreme knowledge of the truths contained in the Christian Gospel.

The enormous influence of Greek philosophy on the formative years of Christianity, as well as the early Christians distrust of it, are amply illustrated in the works selected for this volume. The account of Saint Paul's meeting with the philosophers in Athens, related in *Acts*, 17, is a classic reminder of the wariness and ill-disguised contempt on both sides. The early Fathers were in disagreement among themselves on such fundamental questions as the origin of evil and God's nature, while even more strongly arguing about the role of philosophy as a guide or detriment to revealed truths. Clement of Alexandria and Tertullian present a vivid portrayal of this conflict of interests and persuasion. Clement, particularly, believed that God had announced, through Greek philosophy, a preparation for the coming of Christ. Origen was also one of those who believed that much of the truth revealed by faith could be understood by reason alone. Tertullian, who had an unremitting hatred for Greek philosophy and considered it a constant danger to the purity and superiority of faith, may be seen to represent a most vigorous exponent of the view that reason is insufficient and that revelation alone will suffice. A milder view of the insufficiency of philosophy is represented in the works of Justin Martyr. Our final author is Minucius Felix, a second-century Christian author whose *Octavius* contains an account of an alternative to the Christian (or Jewish) theme of creation. The alternative is remarkably Epicurean in substance, but a more interesting feature is to be found in the description of the sophisticated pagan philosopher who finds Christianity intolerant and yet amusing.

EPICUREANISM

Epicurean philosophy was perhaps unique in having a lengthy history of popular acceptance for about five centuries following its introduction by Epicurus and yet little or no change or development in doctrine. Of the works of Epicurus, there have come down to us some scattered fragments, three letters (to Herodotus, to Pythocles, and to Menoeceus), and the setting down of the teacher's advice to his followers *(Principal Doctrines)*. Reprinted here are a part of the second letter, the whole of the third, and the *Principal Doctrines*.

The other main source of Epicureanism is found in the celebrated poem *On the Nature of Things (De rerum natura)* by the Roman poet Lucretius (99-55 B.C.). This work in six books contains a complete statement of Epicurean thought as handed down by Epicurus; although written in Latin by a Roman in spirit, the elaboration of ideas about man and the world reflect almost exactly the thought of the revered master, Epicurus, who had lived almost two centuries earlier. Something less than one-sixth of Lucretius' poem is reprinted here, in a freshly written prose version of the original. The selection includes substantial parts of the following: Book I, "Matter and Space"; Book II, "Movement and Shapes of Atoms"; Book III, "Life and Mind"; Book IV, "Sensation (Thought and Will)"; and the first ninety lines of Book V.

Although we know little about the lives of Lucretius and other Epicurean philosophers, Diogenes Laertius gives us an account of Epicurus in *Lives and Opinions of Eminent Philosophers* (Vol. II, Bk. X). Born on the island of Samos, Epicurus, after some years of travel, opened a school outside of Athens in about 306 B.C. The property owned by him contained a garden, and the school located there occasioned the calling of his followers "philosophers of the garden." His association with students was marked by loyalty and the intimacy of close friendship, and his student-disciples revered him, which made the school something akin to a religious sect. At his death, the garden was left to his followers and remained as it was at least until the time of Cicero's visit there, in 78 B.C.

Lucretius
On the Nature of Things

Book I.—MATTER AND SPACE

. . . I will set out to discourse to you on the ultimate realities of heaven and the gods. I will reveal those *atoms* from which nature creates all things and increases and feeds them and into which, when they perish, nature again resolves them. To these in my discourse I commonly give such names as the 'raw material', or 'generative bodies' or 'seeds' of things. Or I may call them 'primary particles', because they come first and everything else is composed of them.

When human life lay grovelling in all men's sight, crushed to the earth under the dead weight of superstition whose grim features loured menacingly upon mortals from the four quarters of the sky, a man of Greece was first to raise mortal eyes in defiance, first to stand erect and brave the challenge. Fables of the gods did not crush him, nor the lightning flash and the growling menace of the sky. Rather, they quickened his manhood, so that he, first of all men, longed to smash the constraining locks of nature's doors. The vital vigour of his mind prevailed. He ventured far out beyond the flaming ramparts of the world and voyaged in mind throughout infinity. Returning victorious, he proclaimed to us what can be and what cannot: how a limit is fixed to the power of everything and an immovable frontier post. Therefore superstition in its turn lies crushed beneath his feet, and we by his triumph are lifted level with the skies.

One thing that worries me is the fear that you may fancy yourself embarking on an impious course, setting your feet on the path of sin. Far from it. More often it is very superstition that is the mother

of sinful and impious deeds. Remember how at Aulis the altar of the
Virgin Goddess was foully stained with the blood of Iphigeneia by
the leaders of the Greeks, the patterns of chivalry. The headband was
bound about her virgin tresses and hung down evenly over both her
cheeks. Suddenly she caught sight of her father standing sadly in front
of the altar, the attendants beside him hiding the knife and her people
bursting into tears when they saw her. Struck dumb with terror, she
sank on her knees to the ground. Poor girl, at such a moment it did not
help her that she had been first to give the name of father to a king.
Raised by the hands of men, she was led trembling to the altar. Not
for her the sacrament of marriage and the loud chant of Hymen. It
was her fate in the very hour of marriage to fall a sinless victim to a
sinful rite, slaughtered to her greater grief by a father's hand, so that
a fleet might sail under happy auspices. Such are the heights of wickedness to which men are driven by superstition. . . .

This dread and darkness of the mind cannot be dispelled by the
sunbeams, the shining shafts of day, but only by an understanding of
the outward form and inner workings of nature. In tackling this theme,
our starting-point will be this principle: *Nothing can ever be created
by divine power out of nothing.* The reason why all mortals are so
gripped by fear is that they see all sorts of things happening on the
earth and in the sky with no discernible cause, and these they attribute to the will of a god. Accordingly, when we have seen that nothing
can be created out of nothing, we shall then have a clearer picture of
the path ahead, the problem of how things are created and occasioned
without the aid of the gods.

First then, if things were made out of nothing, any species could
spring from any source and nothing would require seed. Men could
arise from the sea and scaly fish from the earth, and birds could be
hatched out of the sky. Cattle and other domestic animals and every
kind of wild beast, multiplying indiscriminately, would occupy cultivated and waste lands alike. The same fruits would not grow constantly on the same trees, but they would keep changing: any tree
might bear any fruit. If each species were not composed of its own
generative bodies, why should each be born always of the same kind
of mother? Actually, since each is formed out of specific seeds, it is
born and emerges into the sunlit world only from a place where there
exists the right material, the right kind of atoms. This is why everything cannot be born of everything, but a specific power of generation
inheres in specific objects.

. . . [Again], in order that things might grow, there would be no need of any lapse of time for the accumulation of seed. Tiny tots would turn suddenly into grown men, and trees would shoot up spontaneously out of the earth. But it is obvious that none of these things happens, since everything grows gradually, as is natural, from a specific seed and retains its specific character. It is a fair inference that each is increased and nourished by its own raw material. . . .

The second great principle is this: *nature resolves everything into its component atoms and never reduces anything to nothing.* If anything were perishable in all its parts, anything might perish all of a sudden and vanish from sight. There would be no need of any force to separate its parts and loosen their links. In actual fact, since everything is composed of indestructible seeds, nature obviously does not allow anything to perish till it has encountered a force that shatters it with a blow or creeps into chinks and unknits it. . . .

. . . [That is], because the fastenings of the atoms are of various kinds while their matter is imperishable, compound objects remain intact until one of them encounters a force that proves strong enough to break up its particular constitution. Therefore nothing returns to nothing, but everything is resolved into its constituent bodies. . . .

. . . I have taught you that things cannot be created out of nothing nor, once born, be summoned back to nothing. Perhaps, however, you are becoming mistrustful of my words, because these atoms of mine are not visible to the eye. Consider, therefore, this further evidence of *bodies whose existence you must acknowledge though they cannot be seen.* First, wind, when its force is roused, whips up waves, founders tall ships and scatters cloud-rack. Sometimes scouring plains with hurricane force it strews them with huge trees and batters mountain peaks with blasts that hew down forests. . . .

Then again, we smell the various scents of things though we never see them approaching our nostrils. Similarly, heat and cold cannot be detected by our eyes, and we do not see sounds. Yet all these must be composed of bodies, since they are able to impinge upon our senses. For nothing can touch or be touched except body. . . .

. . . It follows that nature works through the agency of invisible bodies.

On the other hand, things are not hemmed in by the pressure of solid bodies in a tight mass. This is because *there is vacuity in things.* A grasp of this fact will be helpful to you in many respects and will save you from much bewildered doubting and questioning about the universe and from mistrust of my teaching. Well then, by vacuity I mean intangible and empty space. If it did not exist, things could not move at all. For the distinctive action of matter, which is counteraction and obstruction, would be in force always and everywhere. Nothing could proceed, because nothing would give it a starting-point by receding. As it is, we see with our own eyes at sea and on land and high up in the sky that all sorts of things in all sorts of ways are on the move. If there were no empty space, these things would be denied the power of restless movement—or rather, they could not possibly have come into existence, embedded as they would have been in motionless matter. . . .

Again, why do we find some things outweigh others of equal volume? If there is as much matter in a ball of wool as in one of lead, it is natural that it should weigh as heavily, since it is the function of matter to press everything downwards, while it is the function of space on the other hand to remain weightless. Accordingly, when one thing is not less bulky than another but obviously lighter, it plainly declares that there is more vacuum in it, while the heavier object proclaims that there is more matter in it and much less empty space. We have therefore reached the goal of our diligent enquiry: there is in things an admixture of what we call vacuity. . . .

To pick up the thread of my discourse, all nature as it is in itself consists of two things—bodies and the vacant space in which the bodies are situated and through which they move in different directions. The existence of bodies is vouched for by the agreement of the senses. If a belief resting directly on this foundation is not valid, there will be no standard to which we can refer any doubt on obscure questions for rational confirmation. If there were no place and space, which we call vacuity, these bodies could not be situated anywhere or move in any direction whatever. This I have just demonstrated. It remains to show that *nothing exists that is distinct both from body and from vacuity* and could be ranked with the others as a third substance. For whatever *is* must also be something. If it offers resistance to touch, however light and slight, it will increase the mass of body by such amount, great or small, as it may amount to, and will rank with it. If, on the other hand, it is intangible, so that it offers no resistance whatever to anything passing through it, then it will be that empty space which we call vacuity. Besides, whatever it may be in itself, either it will act in some way, or react to other things acting upon it, or else it will be such that things can be and happen in it. But without body nothing can act or react; and nothing can afford a place except emptiness and vacancy. Therefore, besides matter and vacuity, we cannot include in the number of things any third substance that can either affect our senses at any time or be grasped by the reasoning of our minds.

You will find that anything that can be named is either a property or an accident of these two. A *property* is something that cannot be detached or separated from a thing without destroying it, as weight is a property of rocks, heat of fire, fluidity of water, tangibility of bodies, intangibility of vacuum. On the other hand, servitude and liberty, poverty and riches, war and peace, and all other things whose advent or departure leaves the essence of a thing intact, all these it is our practice to call by their appropriate name, *accidents*. . . .

Material objects are of two kinds, atoms and compounds of atoms. The atoms themselves cannot be swamped by any force, for they are preserved indefinitely by their absolute solidity. Admittedly, it is hard to believe that anything can exist that is absolutely solid. The lightning stroke from the sky penetrates closed buildings, as do shouts and other noises. Iron glows molten in the fire, and hot rocks are cracked by untempered scorching. Hard gold is softened and melted by heat; and bronze, ice-like, is liquefied by flame. Both heat and piercing cold seep through silver, since we feel both alike when a cooling shower of water is poured into a goblet that we hold ceremonially in our hands. All these facts point to the conclusion that nothing is really solid. But sound reasoning and nature itself drive us to the opposite conclusion. Pay attention, therefore, while I demonstrate in a few lines that there exist certain bodies that are absolutely solid and indestructible, namely those atoms which according to our teaching are the seeds or prime units of things from which the whole universe is built up.

In the first place, we have found that nature is twofold, consisting of two totally different things, matter and the space in which things happen. Hence each of these must exist by itself without admixture of the other. For, where there is empty space (what we call vacuity), there matter is not; where matter exists, there cannot be a vacuum. Therefore the prime units of matter are solid and free from vacuity.

Again, since composite things contain some vacuum, the surrounding matter must be solid. For you cannot reasonably maintain that anything can hide vacuity and hold it within its body unless you allow that the container itself is solid. And what contains the vacuum in things can only be an accumulation of matter. Hence matter, which possesses absolute solidity, can be everlasting when other things are decomposed.

Again, if there were no empty space, everything would be one solid mass; if there were no material objects with the property of filling the space they occupy, all existing space would be utterly void. It is clear, then, that there is an alternation of matter and vacuity, mutually distinct, since the whole is neither completely full nor completely empty. There are therefore solid bodies, causing the distinction between empty space and full. And these, as I have just shown, can be neither decomposed by blows from without nor invaded and unknit from within nor destroyed by any other form of assault. For it seems that a thing without vacuum can be neither knocked to bits nor snapped nor chopped in two by cutting; nor can it let in moisture or seeping cold or piercing fire, the universal agents of destruction. The more vacuum a thing contains within it, the more readily it yields to these assailants. Hence, if the units of matter are solid and without vacuity, as I have shown, they must be everlasting.

Yet again, if the matter in things had not been everlasting, everything by now would have gone back to nothing, and the things we see would be the product of rebirth out of nothing. But, since I have already shown that nothing can be created out of nothing nor any existing thing be summoned back to nothing, the atoms must be made of imperishable stuff into which everything can be resolved in the end, so that there may be a stock of matter for building the world anew. The atoms, therefore, are absolutely solid and unalloyed. In no other way could they have survived throughout infinite time to keep the world in being. . . .

Here is a further argument. Granted that the particles of matter are absolutely solid, we can still explain the composition and behaviour of soft things—air, water, earth, fire—by their intermixture with empty space. On the other hand, supposing the atoms to be soft, we cannot account for the origin of hard flint and iron. For there would be no foundation for nature to build on. Therefore there must be bodies strong in their unalloyed solidity by whose closer clustering things can be knit together and display unyielding toughness. . . .

Well then, since I have shown that there are completely solid indestructible particles of matter flying about through all eternity, let us elucidate whether or not there is any limit to their number. Similarly, as we have found that there is a vacuum, the place or space in which things happen, let us see whether its whole extent is limited or whether it stretches far and wide into immeasurable depths.

Learn, therefore, that *the universe is not bounded in any direction.* If it were, it would necessarily have a limit somewhere. But clearly a thing cannot have a limit unless there is something outside to limit it, so that the eye can follow it up to a certain point but not beyond. Since you must admit that there is nothing outside the universe, it can have no limit and is accordingly without end or measure. It makes no odds in which part of it you may take your stand: whatever spot anyone may occupy, the universe stretches away from him just the same in all directions without limit. . . .

. . . Things go on happening all the time through ceaseless movement in every direction; and atoms of matter bouncing up from below are supplied out of the infinite. There is therefore a limitless abyss of space, such that even the dazzling flashes of the lightning cannot traverse it in their course, racing through an interminable tract of time. . . .

The universe is restrained from setting any limit to itself by nature, which compels body to be bounded by vacuum and vacuum by body. Thus nature either makes them both infinite in alternation, or else one of them, if it is not bounded by the other, must extend in a pure state without limit. Space, however, being infinite, so must matter be. Otherwise neither sea nor land nor the bright zones of the sky nor mortal beings nor the holy bodies of the gods could endure for one brief hour of time. The supply of matter would be shaken loose from combination and swept through the vastness of the void in isolated particles; or rather, it would never have coalesced to form anything, since its scattered particles could never have been driven into union.

Certainly the atoms did not post themselves purposefully in due order by an act of intelligence, nor did they stipulate what movements each should perform. As they have been rushing everlastingly throughout all space in their myriads, undergoing a myriad changes under the disturbing impact of collisions, they have experienced every variety of movement and conjunction till they have fallen into the particular pattern by which this world of ours is constituted. This world has persisted many a long year, having once been set going in the appropriate motions. From these everything else follows. The rivers replenish the thirsty sea with profuse streams of water. Incubated by the sun's heat, the earth renews its fruits, and the brood of animals that springs from it grows lustily. The gliding fires of ether sustain their life. None of these results would be possible if there were not an ample supply of matter to bounce up out of infinite space in replacement of all that is lost. . . .

There is one belief . . . that you must beware of entertaining—*the theory that everything tends towards what they call 'the centre of the world.'* On this theory, the world stands fast without any impacts from without, and top and bottom cannot be parted in any direction, because everything has been tending towards the centre. . . . But this is an idle fancy of fools who have got hold of the wrong end of the stick. There can be no centre in infinity. . . .

If you take a little trouble, you will attain to a thorough understanding of these truths. For one thing will be illumined by another, and eyeless night will not rob you of your road till you have looked into the heart of nature's darkest mysteries. So surely will facts throw light upon facts.

Book II.—MOVEMENTS AND SHAPES OF ATOMS

What joy it is, when out at sea the stormwinds are lashing the waters, to gaze from the shore at the heavy stress some other man is enduring! Not that anyone's afflictions are in themselves a source of delight; but to realize from what troubles you yourself are free is joy indeed. What joy, again, to watch opposing hosts marshalled on the field of battle when you have yourself no part in their peril! But this is the greatest joy of all: to stand aloof in a quiet citadel, stoutly fortified by the teaching of the wise, and to gaze down from that elevation on others wandering aimlessly in a vain search for the way of life, pitting their wits one against another, disputing for precedence, struggling night and day with unstinted effort to scale the pinnacles of wealth and power. O joyless hearts of men! O minds without vision! How dark and dangerous the life in which this tiny span is lived away! Do you not see that nature is clamouring for two things only, a body free from pain, a mind released from worry and fear for the enjoyment of pleasurable sensations? . . .

Can you doubt then that this power rests with reason alone? All life is a struggle in the dark. As children in blank darkness tremble and start at everything, so we in broad daylight are oppressed at times by fears as baseless as those horrors which children imagine coming upon them in the dark. This dread and darkness of the mind cannot be dispelled by the sunbeams, the shining shafts of day, but only by an understanding of the outward form and inner workings of nature. . . .

If you think that the atoms can stop and by their stopping generate new motions in things, you are wandering far from the path of truth. Since the atoms are moving freely through the void, they must all be kept in motion either by their own weight or on occasion by the impact of another atom. . . .

As a further indication that all particles of matter are on the move, remember that the universe is bottomless: there is no place where the atoms could come to rest. As I have already shown by various arguments and proved conclusively, space is without end or limit and spreads out immeasurably in all directions alike.

It clearly follows that no rest is given to the atoms in their course through the depths of space. Driven along in an incessant but variable movement, some of them bounce far apart after a collision while others recoil only a short distance from the impact. . . .

. . . You must understand that they all derive this restlessness from the atoms. It originates with the atoms, which move of themselves. Then those small compound bodies that are least removed from the impetus of the atoms are set in motion by the impact of their invisible blows and in turn cannon against slightly larger bodies. So the movement mounts up from the atoms and gradually emerges to the level of our senses, so that those bodies are in motion that we see in sunbeams, moved by blows that remain invisible.

And now, as to the rate at which the atoms move, you may gauge this readily from these few indications. First, when dawn sprays the earth with new-born light and the birds, flitting through pathless thickets, fill the neighbourhood according to their kind with liquid notes that glide through the thin air, it is plain and palpable for all to see how suddenly the sun at the moment of his rising drenches and clothes the world with his radiance. But the heat and the bright light which the sun emits do not travel through empty space. Therefore they are forced to move more slowly, cleaving their way as it were through waves of air. And the atoms that compose this radiance do not travel as isolated individuals but linked and massed together. Thus their pace is retarded by one dragging back another as well as by external obstacles. But, when separate atoms are travelling in solitary solidity through empty space, they encounter no obstruction from without and move as single units on the course on which they have embarked. Obviously therefore they must far outstrip the sunlight in speed of movement and traverse an extent of space many times as great in the time it takes for the sun's rays to flash across the sky. . . .

In the face of these truths, some people who know nothing of matter believe that nature without the guidance of the gods could not bring round the changing seasons in such perfect conformity to human needs, creating the crops and those other blessings that mortals are led to enjoy by the guide of life, divine pleasure, which coaxes them through the arts of Venus to reproduce their kind, lest the human race should perish. Obviously, in imagining that the gods established everything for the sake of men, they have stumbled in all respects far from the path of truth. Even if I knew nothing of the atoms, I would venture to assert on the evidence of the celestial phenomena themselves, supported by many other arguments, that the universe was certainly not created for us by divine power: it is so full of imperfections. . . .

In this connexion there is another fact that I want you to grasp. *When the atoms are travelling straight down through empty space by their own weight, at quite indeterminate times and places they swerve ever so little from their course,* just so much that you can call it a change of direction. If it were not for this swerve, everything would fall downwards like rain-drops through the abyss of space. No collision would take place and no impact of atom on atom would be created. Thus nature would never have created anything.

If anyone supposes that heavier atoms on a straight course through empty space could outstrip lighter ones and fall on them from above, thus causing impacts that might give rise to generative motions, he is going far astray from the path of truth. The reason why objects falling through water or thin air vary in speed according to their weight is simply that the matter composing water or air cannot obstruct all objects equally, but is forced to give way more speedily to heavier ones. But empty space can offer no resistance to any object in any quarter at any time, so as not to yield free passage as its own nature demands. Therefore, through undisturbed vacuum all bodies must travel at equal speed though impelled by unequal weights. The heavier will never be able to fall on the lighter from above or generate of themselves impacts leading to that variety of motions out of which nature can produce things. We are thus forced back to the conclusion that the atoms swerve a little—but only a very little, or we shall be caught imagining slantwise movements, and the facts will prove us wrong. For we see plainly and palpably that weights, when they come tumbling down, have no power of their own to move aslant, so far as meets the eye. But who can possibly perceive that they do not diverge in the very least from a vertical course?

Again, if all movement is always interconnected, the new arising from the old in a determinate order—if the atoms never swerve so as to originate some new movement that will snap the bonds of fate, the everlasting sequence of cause and effect—what is the source of the free will possessed by living things throughout the earth? What, I repeat, is the source of that will-power snatched from the fates, whereby we follow the path along which we are severally led by pleasure, swerving from our course at no set time or place but at the bidding of our own hearts? . . . So also in the atoms you must recognize the same possibility: besides weight and impact there must be a third cause of movement, the source of this inborn power of ours, since we see that nothing can come out of nothing. For the weight of an atom prevents its movements from being completely determined by the impact of other atoms. But the fact that the mind itself has no internal necessity to determine its every act and compel it to suffer in helpless passivity —this is due to the slight swerve of the atoms at no determinate time or place. . . .

And now let us turn to a new theme—*the characteristics of the atoms of all substances, the extent to which they differ in shape and the rich multiplicity of their forms*. Not that there are not many of the same shape, but they are by no means all identical with one another. And no wonder. When the multitude of them, as I have shown, is such that it is without limit or count, it is not to be expected that they should all be identical in build and configuration. . . .

Here is a further example. Honey and milk, when they are rolled in the mouth, cause an agreeable sensation to the tongue. But bitter wormwood and astringent centaury screw the mouth awry with their nauseating savour. You may readily infer that such substances as agreeably titillate the senses are composed of smooth round atoms. Those that seem bitter and harsh are more tightly compacted of hooked particles and accordingly tear their way into our senses and rend our bodies by their inroads.

The same conflict between two types of structure applies to everything that strikes the senses as good or bad. You cannot suppose that the rasping stridulation of a screeching saw is formed of elements as smooth as the notes a minstrel's nimble fingers wake from the lyre-strings and mould to melody. . . . Nothing that gratifies the senses is ever without a certain smoothness of the constituent atoms. Whatever, on the other hand, is painful and harsh is characterized by a certain roughness of matter. Besides these there are some things that are not properly regarded as smooth but yet are not jagged with barbed spikes. These are characterized instead by slightly jutting ridges such as tickle the senses rather than hurt them. They include such things as wine-lees and piquant endive. Hot fire, again, and cold frost stab the senses of our body with teeth of a different pattern, as we learn from the different way they affect our sense of touch. For touch and nothing but touch (by all that men call holy!) is the essence of all our bodily sensations, whether we feel something slipping in from outside or are hurt by something born in the body or pleasantly excited by something going out in the generative act of Venus. It is touch again that is felt when the atoms are jarred by a knock so that they are disordered and upset the senses: strike any part of your own body with your hand, and you will experience this for yourself. There must, therefore, be great differences in the shapes of the atoms to provoke these different sensations. . . .

To the foregoing demonstration I will link on another fact which will gain credence from this context: *the number of different forms of atoms is finite*. If it were not so, some of the atoms would have to be of infinite magnitude. Within the narrow limits of any single particle, there can be only a limited range of forms. Suppose that atoms consist of three minimum parts, or enlarge them by a few more. When by fitting on parts at top or bottom and transposing left and right you have exhausted every shape that can be given to the whole body by all possible arrangements of the parts, you are obviously left with no means of varying its form further except by adding other parts. Thence it will follow, if you wish to vary its form still further, that the arrangement will demand still other parts in exactly the same way. Variation in shape goes with increase in size. You cannot believe, therefore, that the atoms are distinguished by an infinity of forms; or you will compel some of them to be of enormous magnitude, which I have already proved to be demonstrably impossible. . . .

To the foregoing demonstration I will link on another fact, which will gain credence from this context: *the number of atoms of any one form is infinite*. Since the varieties of form are limited, the number of uniform atoms must be unlimited. Otherwise the totality of matter would be finite, which I have proved in my verses is not so. I have shown that the universe is kept going by an infinite succession of atoms, so that the chain of impacts from all directions remains unbroken. . . .

. . . Your finite class of atoms, if once you posit such a thing, [will] be scattered and tossed about through all eternity by conflicting tides of matter. They could never be swept together so as to enter into combination; nor could they remain combined or grow by increment. Yet experience plainly shows that both these things happen: objects can be born, and after birth they can grow. It is evident, therefore, that there are infinite atoms of every kind to keep up the supply of everything. . . .

In this connexion there is one fact that you should keep signed and sealed and recorded in the archives of memory: *there is no visible object that consists of atoms of one kind only.* Everything is composed of a mixture of elements. The more qualities and powers a thing possesses, the greater variety it attests in the forms of its component atoms. . . .

It must not be supposed that atoms of every sort can be linked in every variety of combination. If that were so, you would see monsters coming into being everywhere. Hybrid growths of man and beast would arise. Lofty branches would sprout here and there from a living body. Limbs of land-beast and sea-beast would often be conjoined. Chimaeras breathing flame from hideous jaws would be reared by nature throughout the all-generating earth. But it is evident that nothing of this sort happens. We see that everything is created from specific seeds and born of a specific mother and grows up true to type. We may infer that this is determined by some specific necessity. In every individual the atoms of its own kind, derived from all its food, disperse through its limbs and link together so as to set going the appropriate motions. But we see extraneous matter cast back by nature into the earth; and much is expelled from the body, under the impact of blows, in the form of invisible particles which could not link on anywhere or harmonize with the vital motions within so as to copy them.

Do not imagine that these laws are binding on animals alone. The same principle determines everything. As all created things differ from one another by their entire natures, so each one must necessarily consist of distinctive forms of atoms. Not that there is any lack of atoms of the same forms; but objects do not all alike consist of exactly the same components. Since the seeds are not identical, they must differ in their intervals, paths, attachments, weights, impacts, clashes and motions. These do not merely distinguish one animal body from another but separate land from sea and hold the whole sky apart from the earth.

Give ear now to arguments that I have searched out with an effort that was also a delight. Do not imagine that white objects derive the snowy aspect they present to your eyes from white atoms, or that black objects are composed of a black element. And in general do not believe that anything owes the colour it displays to the fact that its atoms are tinted correspondingly. *The primary particles of matter have no colour whatsoever,* neither the same colour as the objects they compose nor a different one. If you think the mind cannot lay hold of such bodies, you are quite wrong. Men who are blind from birth and have never looked on the sunlight have knowledge by touch of bodies that have never from the beginning been associated with any colour. It follows that on our minds also an image can impinge of bodies not marked by any tint. Indeed the things that we ourselves touch in pitch darkness are not felt by us as possessing any colour.

Having proved that colourless bodies are not unthinkable, I will proceed to demonstrate that the atoms must be such bodies.

First, then, any colour may change completely to any other. But the atoms cannot possibly change colour. For something must remain changeless, or everything would be absolutely annihilated. For, if ever anything is so transformed as to overstep its own limits, this means the immediate death of what was before. So do not stain the atoms with colour, or you will find everything slipping back into nothing. . . .

Again, since there can be no colours without light and the atoms do not emerge into the light, it can be inferred that they are not clothed in any colour. For what colour can there be in blank darkness? . . . A peacock's tail, profusely illumined, changes colour as it is turned this way or that. These colours, then, are created by a particular incidence of light. Hence, no light, no colour.

When the pupil of the eye is said to perceive the colour white, it experiences in fact a particular kind of impact. When it perceives black, or some other colour, the impact is different. But, when you touch things, it makes no odds what colour they may be, but only what is their shape. The inference is that the atoms have no need of colour, but cause various sensations of touch according to their various shapes. . . .

Do not imagine that colour is the only quality that is denied to the atoms. *They are also wholly devoid of warmth and cold and scorching heat; they are barren of sound and starved of savour, and emit no inherent odour from their bodies.* . . .

At this stage you must admit that *whatever is seen to be sentient is nevertheless composed of atoms that are insentient.* The phenomena open to our observation do not contradict this conclusion or conflict with it. Rather, they lead us by the hand and compel us to believe that the animate is born, as I maintain, of the insentient.

As a particular instance, we can point to living worms, emerging from foul dung when the earth is soaked and rotted by intemperate showers. Besides, we see every sort of substance transformed in the same way. Rivers, foliage and lush pastures are transformed into cattle; the substance of cattle is transformed into our bodies; and often enough our bodies go to build up the strength of predatory beasts or the bodies of the lords of the air. So nature transforms all foods into living bodies and generates from them all the senses of animate creatures, just as it makes dry wood blossom out in flame and transfigures it wholly into fire. So now do you see that it makes a great difference in what order the various atoms are arranged and with what others they are combined so as to impart and take over motions?

What is it, then, that jogs the mind itself and moves and compels it to express certain sentiments, so that you do not believe that the sentient is generated by the insentient? Obviously it is the fact that a mixture of water and wood and earth cannot of itself bring about vital sensibility. There is one relevant point you should bear in mind: I am not maintaining that sensations are generated automatically from all the elements out of which sentient things are created. Everything depends on the size and shape of the sense-producing atoms and on their appropriate motions, arrangements and positions. None of these is found in wood or clods. And yet these substances, when they are fairly well rotted by showers, give birth to little worms, because the particles of matter are jolted out of their old arrangements by a new factor and combined in such a way that animate objects must result. . . .

Again, pain occurs when particles of matter have been unsettled by by some force within the living flesh of the limbs and stagger in their inmost stations. When they slip back into place, that is blissful pleasure. It follows that the atoms cannot be afflicted by any pain or experience any pleasure in themselves, since they are not composed of any primal particles, by some reversal of whose movements they might suffer anguish or reap some fruition of vitalizing bliss. They cannot therefore be endowed with any power of sensation.

Again, if we are to account for the power of sensation possessed by animate creatures in general by attributing sentience to their atoms, what of those atoms that specifically compose the human race? Pre-

sumably they are not merely sentient, but also shake their sides with
uproarious guffaws and besprinkle their cheeks with dewy teardrops
and even discourse profoundly and at length about the composition of
the universe and proceed to ask of what elements they are themselves
composed. . . .

Here, then, is my first point. In all dimensions alike, on this side or
that, upward or downward through the universe, there is no end. This I
have shown, and indeed the fact proclaims itself aloud and the nature
of space makes it crystal clear. Granted, then, that empty space extends without limit in every direction and that seeds innumerable in
number are rushing on countless courses through an unfathomable universe under the impulse of perpetual motion, *it is in the highest degree
unlikely that this earth and sky is the only one to have been created*
and that all those particles of matter outside are accomplishing nothing.
This follows from the fact that our world has been made by nature
through the spontaneous and casual collision and the multifarious, accidental, random and purposeless congregation and coalescence of
atoms whose suddenly formed combinations could serve on each occasion as the starting-point of substantial fabrics—earth and sea and
sky and the races of living creatures. On every ground, therefore, you
must admit that there exist elsewhere other congeries of matter similar
to this one which the ether clasps in ardent embrace.

When there is plenty of matter in readiness, when space is available
and no cause or circumstance impedes, then surely things must be
wrought and effected. You have a store of atoms that could not be
reckoned in full by the whole succession of living creatures. You have
the same natural force to congregate them in any place precisely as
they have been congregated here. You are bound therefore to acknowledge that in other regions there are other earths and various tribes of
men and breeds of beasts.

Add to this the fact that nothing in the universe is the only one of
its kind, unique and solitary in its birth and growth; everything is a
member of a species comprising many individuals. . . .

Bear this well in mind, and you will immediately perceive that
nature is free and uncontrolled by proud masters and runs the universe
by herself without the aid of gods. For who—by the sacred hearts of the
gods who pass their unruffled lives, their placid aeon, in calm and
peace!—who can rule the sum total of the measureless? Who can hold
in coercive hand the strong reins of the unfathomable? Who can spin
all the firmaments alike and foment with the fires of ether all the fruit-

ful earths? Who can be in all places at all times, ready to darken the clear sky with clouds and rock it with a thunderclap—to launch bolts that may often wreck his own temples, or retire and spend his fury letting fly at deserts with that missile which often passes by the guilty and slays the innocent and blameless? . . .

Book III.—LIFE AND MIND

. . . I have already shown what the component bodies of everything are like; how they vary in shape; how they fly spontaneously through space, impelled by a perpetual motion; and how from these all objects can be created. The next step now is evidently to elucidate in my verses the nature of mind and of life. In so doing I shall drive out neck and crop that fear of Hell which blasts the life of man from its very foundations, sullying everything with the blackness of death and leaving no pleasure pure and unalloyed. . . . The heavier their afflictions, the more devoutly they turn their minds to superstition. Look at a man in the midst of doubt and danger, and you will learn in his hour of adversity what he really is. It is then that true utterances are wrung from the recesses of his breast. The mask is torn off; the reality remains. . . .

First, I maintain that *the mind,* which we often call the intellect, the seat of the guidance and control of life, *is part of a man,* no less than hand or foot or eyes are parts of a whole living creature. There are some who argue that the sentience of the mind is not lodged in any particular part, but is a vital condition of the body, what the Greeks call a *harmony,* which makes us live as sentient beings without having any locally determined mind. Just as good health may be said to belong to the healthy body without being any specific part of it, so they do not station the sentience of the mind in any specific part. In this they seem to me very wide of the mark. . . .

Next, you must understand that *there is also a vital spirit in our limbs* and the body does not derive its sentience from harmony. In the first place, life often lingers in our limbs after a large part of the body has been cut off. On the other hand, when a few particles of heat have dispersed and some air has been let out through the mouth, life forsakes the veins forthwith and abandons the bones. Hence you may infer that all the elements do not hold equal portions of vitality or sustain it equally, but it is chiefly thanks to the atoms of wind and heat that life lingers in the limbs. There is therefore in the body itself a vital breath and heat which forsakes our limbs at death. . . .

Next, I maintain that *mind and spirit are interconnected* and compose between them a single substance. But what I may call the head and the dominant force in the whole body is that guiding principle which we term mind or intellect. This is firmly lodged in the mid-region of the breast. Here is the place where fear or alarm pulsate. Here is felt the caressing touch of joy. Here, then, is the seat of intellect and mind. The rest of the vital spirit, diffused throughout the body, obeys the mind and moves under its direction and impulse. The mind by itself experiences thought and joy of its own at a time when nothing moves either the body or the spirit.

. . . But, when the mind is upset by some more overwhelming fear, we see all the spirit in every limb upset in sympathy. Sweat and pallor break out all over the body. Speech grows inarticulate; the voice fails; the eyes swim; the ears buzz; the limbs totter. Often we see men actually drop down because of the terror that has gripped their minds. Hence you may readily infer a connexion between the mind and the spirit which, when shaken by the impact of the mind, immediately jostles and propels the body.

The same reasoning proves that *mind and spirit are both composed of matter*. We see them propelling the limbs, rousing the body from sleep, changing the expression of the face and guiding and steering the whole man—activities that all clearly involve touch, as touch in turn involves matter. How then can we deny their material nature? You see the mind sharing in the body's experiences and sympathizing with it. When the nerve-racking impact of a spear gashes bones and sinews, even if it does not penetrate to the seat of life, there ensues faintness and a tempting inclination earthwards and on the ground a turmoil in the mind and an intermittent faltering impulse to stand up again. The substance of the mind must therefore be material, since it is affected by the impact of material weapons.

My next task will be to demonstrate to you what sort of matter it is of which this mind is composed and how it was formed. First, I affirm that *it is of very fine texture and composed of exceptionally minute particles*. If you will mark my words, you will be able to infer this from the following facts. It is evident that nothing happens as quickly as the mind represents and sketches the happening to itself.

Therefore the mind sets itself in motion more swiftly than any of those things whose substance is visible to our eyes. But what is so mobile must consist of exceptionally minute and spherical atoms, so that it can be set going by a slight push. . . .

Here is a further indication how flimsy is the texture of the vital spirit and in how small a space it could be contained if it could be massed together. At the instant when a man is mastered by the care-free calm of death and forsaken by mind and spirit, you cannot tell either by sight or by weight that any part of the whole has been filched away from his body. Death leaves everything there, except vital sentience and warmth. Therefore the vital spirit as a whole must consist of very tiny atoms, linked together throughout veins, flesh and sinews—atoms so small that, when all the spirit has escaped from the whole body, the outermost contour of the limbs apepars intact and there is no loss of weight. . . .

It must not be supposed that the stuff of mind or spirit is a single element. The body at death is abandoned by a sort of rarefied wind mixed with warmth, while the warmth carries with it also air. Indeed, heat never occurs without an intermixture of air: because it is naturally sparse, it must have many atoms of air moving in its interstices.

The composition of mind is thus found to be *at least three-fold*. But all these three components together are not enough to create sentience, since the mind does not admit that any of these can create the sensory motions that originate the meditations revolved in the mind. *We must* accordingly *add to these a fourth component,* which is quite nameless. Than this there is nothing more mobile or more tenuous—nothing whose component atoms are smaller or smoother. This it is that first sets the sensory motions coursing through the limbs. Owing to the minuteness of its atoms, it is first to be stirred. Then the motions are caught up by warmth and the unseen energy of wind, then by air. Then everything is roused to movement: the blood is quickened; the impulse spreads throughout the flesh; last of all, bones and marrow are thrilled with pleasure or the opposite excitement. . . .

This *vital spirit,* then, *is present in the whole body.* It is the body's guardian and preserver. For the two are interlocked by common roots and cannot be torn apart without manifest disaster. . . .

Again, body by itself never experiences birth or growth, and we see that it does not persist after death. . . .

If anyone still denies that the body is sentient, and believes it is the spirit interfused throughout the body that assumes this motion which we term sensation, he is fighting against manifest facts. Who can explain what bodily sensation really is, if it is not such as it is palpably presented to us by experience? . . .

Again, it is awkward to maintain that the eyes can see nothing, but the mind peeps out through them as though through open doors. The sense of sight itself leads us the other way, dragging and tugging us right to the eyeballs. Often, for instance, we cannot see bright objects, because our eyes are dazzled by light. This is an experience unknown to doors: the doorways through which we gaze suffer no distress by being flung open. Besides, if our eyes are equivalent to doors, then when the eyes are removed the mind obviously ought to see things better now that the doors are away, doorposts and all. . . .

My next point is this: you must understand that the *minds of living things and the light fabric of their spirits are neither birthless nor deathless*. To this end I have long been mustering and inventing verses with a labour that is also a joy. Now I will try to set them out in a style worthy of your career.

Please note that both objects are to be embraced under one name. When, for instance, I proceed to demonstrate that 'spirit' is mortal, you must understand that this applies equally to 'mind', since the two are so conjoined as to constitute a single substance.

First of all, then, I have shown that spirit is flimsy stuff composed of tiny particles. Its atoms are obviously far smaller than those of swift-flowing water or mist or smoke, since it far outstrips them in mobility and is moved by a far slighter impetus. . . . Now, we see that water flows out in all directions from a broken vessel and the moisture is dissipated, and mist and smoke vanish into thin air. Be assured, therefore, that spirit is similarly dispelled and vanishes far more speedily and is sooner dissolved into its component atoms once it has been let loose from the human frame. When the body, which served as a vessel for it, is by some means broken and attenuated by loss of blood from the veins, so as to be no longer able to contain it, how can you suppose that it can be contained by any kind of air, which must be far more tenuous than our bodily frame?

Again, we are conscious that mind and body are born together, grow up together and together decay. With the weak and delicate frame of wavering childhood goes a like infirmity of judgement. The robust vigour of ripening years is accompanied by a steadier resolve and a maturer strength of mind. Later, when the body is palsied by the potent forces of age and the limbs begin to droop with blunted vigour, the understanding limps, the tongue falters and the mind totters: every-thing weakens and gives way at the same time. It is thus natural that the vital spirit should all evaporate like smoke, soaring into the gusty air, since we have seen that it shares the body's birth and growth and wearies with the weariness of age. . . .

Again, mind and body as a living force derive their vigour and vitality from their conjunction. Without body, the mind alone cannot perform the vital motions. Bereft of vital spirit, the body cannot persist and exercise its senses. As the eye uprooted and separated from the body cannot see, so we perceive that spirit and mind by themselves are powerless. . . .

Moreover, if the spirit is by nature immortal and can remain sentient when divorced from our body, we must credit it, I presume, with the possession of five senses. In no other way can we picture to ourselves departed spirits wandering through the Infernal Regions. So it is that painters and bygone generations of writers have portrayed spirits in possession of their senses. But eyes or nostrils or hand or tongue or ears cannot be attached to a disembodied spirit. Such a spirit cannot therefore be sentient or so much as exist.

. . . Or take for example a snake with flickering tongue, menacing tail and protracted body. Should you choose to hack it in many pieces with a blade, you will see, while the wound is fresh, every severed por-tion separately squirming and spattering the ground with gore, and the foremost part twisting back with its mouth to bite itself in the fierce agony of the wound. Shall we say that in each of these parts there is an entire spirit? But on that hypothesis it would follow that one animate creature had in its body many spirits. Actually, a spirit that was one has been split up along with the body. So both alike must be reckoned mortal, since both alike are split into many parts.

Next, if the spirit is by nature immortal and is slipped into the body at birth, why do we retain no memory of an earlier existence, no impress of antecedent events? If the mind's operation is so greatly changed that all record of former actions has been expunged, it is no long journey, in my judgement, from this experience to annihilation. So you must admit that the pre-existent spirit has died and the one that is now is a new creation. . . .

The further question arises whether or not any atoms of vital spirit are left in a lifeless body. If some are left and lodge there, we are not justified in regarding the spirit as immortal, since it has come away mutilated by the loss of some of its parts. If, on the other hand, it withdraws with its members intact, so that no scrap of it remains in the body, how is it that corpses, when their flesh begins to rot, exude maggots? . . .

. . . If it were immortal and passed from body to body, there would be living things of jumbled characters. Often the hound of Hyrcanian breed would turn tail before the onset of the antlered stag. The hawk would flee trembling through the gusty air at the coming of the dove. Man would be witless, and brute beasts rational. It is an untenable theory that an immortal spirit is modified by a change of body. For whatever changes is disintegrated and therefore destroyed. . . .

From all this it follows that *death is nothing to us* and no concern of ours, since our tenure of the mind is mortal. In days of old, we felt no disquiet when the hosts of Carthage poured in to battle on every side—when the whole earth, dizzied by the convulsive shock of war, reeled sickeningly under the high ethereal vault, and between realm and realm the empire of mankind by land and sea trembled in the balance. So, when we shall be no more—when the union of body and spirit that engenders us has been disrupted—to us, who shall then be nothing, nothing by any hazard will happen any more at all. Nothing will have power to stir our senses, not though earth be fused with sea and sea with sky.

. . . But even in sleep, when mind and body alike are at rest, no one misses himself or sighs for life. If such sleep were prolonged to eternity, no longing for ourselves would trouble us. And yet the vital atoms in our limbs cannot be far removed from their sensory motions at a time when a mere jolt out of sleep enables a man to pull himself together. Death, therefore, must be regarded, so far as we are concerned, as having much less existence than sleep, if anything can have less existence than what we perceive to be nothing. For death is followed by a far greater dispersal of the seething mass of matter: once that icy breach in life has intervened, there is no more waking.

Suppose that Nature herself were suddenly to find a voice and round upon one of us in these terms: 'What is your grievance, mortal, that you give yourself up to this whining and repining? Why do you weep and wail over death? If the life you have lived till now has been a pleasant thing—if all its blessings have not leaked away like water poured into a cracked pot and run to waste unrelished—why then, you silly creature, do you not retire as a guest who has had his fill of life and take your care-free rest with a quiet mind? Or, if all your gains have been poured profitless away and life has grown distasteful, why do you seek to swell the total? The new can but turn out as badly as the old and perish as unprofitably. Why not rather make an end of life and labour? . . . What are we to answer, except that Nature's rebuttal is justified and the plea she puts forward is a true one? . . .

As for all those torments that are said to take place in the depths of Hell, they are actually present here and now, in our own lives.
There is no wretched Tantalus, as the myth relates, transfixed with groundless terror at the huge boulder poised above him in the air. But in this life there really are mortals oppressed by unfounded fear of the gods and trembling at the impending doom that may fall upon any of them at the whim of chance. . . .

Sisyphus too is alive for all to see, bent on winning the insignia of office, its rods and ruthless axes, by the people's vote and embittered by perpetual defeat. To strive for this profitless and never-granted prize, and in striving toil and moil incessantly, this truly is to push a boulder laboriously up a steep hill, only to see it, once the top is reached, rolling and bounding down again to the flat levels of the plain.

By the same token, to be for ever feeding a malcontent mind, filling it with good things but never satisfying it—the fate we suffer when the circling seasons enrich us with their products and their ever-changing charms but we are never filled with the fruits of life—this surely exemplifies the story of those maidens in the flower of life for ever pouring water into a leaking vessel which can never by any sleight be filled. . . .

. . . And the Master himself, when his daylit race was run, Epicurus himself died, whose genius outshone the race of men and dimmed them all, as the stars are dimmed by the rising of the fiery sun. And will *you* kick and protest against your sentence? You, whose life is next-door to death while you are still alive and looking on the light. You, who waste the major part of your time in sleep and, when you are awake, are snoring still and dreaming. You, who bear a mind hag-ridden by baseless fear and cannot find the commonest cause of your distress, hounded as you are, poor creature, by a pack of troubles and drifting in a drunken stupor upon a wavering tide of fantasy.

Men feel plainly enough within their minds, a heavy burden, whose weight depresses them. If only they perceived with equal clearness the causes of this depression, the origin of this lump of evil within their breasts, they would not lead such a life as we now see all too commonly—no one knowing what he really wants and everyone for ever trying to get away from where he is, as though mere locomotion could throw off the load. . . .

What is this deplorable lust of life that holds us trembling in bondage to such uncertainties and dangers? A fixed term is set to the life of mortals, and there is no way of dodging death. In any case the setting of our lives remains the same throughout, and by going on living we do not mint any new coin of pleasure. So long as the object of our craving is unattained, it seems more precious than anything besides. Once it is ours, we crave for something else. So an unquenchable thirst for life keeps us always on the gasp. There is no telling what fortune the future may bring—what chance may throw in our way, or what upshot lies in waiting. By prolonging life, we cannot subtract or whittle away one jot from the duration of our death. The time after our taking off remains constant. However many generations you may add to your store by living, there waits for you none the less the same eternal death. The time of not-being will be no less for him who made an end of life with yesterday's daylight than for him who perished many a moon and many a year before.

Book IV.—SENSATION AND SEX

. . . Now I will embark on an explanation of a highly relevant fact, *the existence of what we call 'images' of things,* a sort of outer skin perpetually peeled off the surface of objects and flying about this way and that through the air. It is these whose impact scares our minds, whether waking or sleeping, on those occasions when we catch a glimpse of strange shapes and phantoms of the dead. Often, when we are sunk in slumber, they startle us with the notion that spirits may get loose from Hades and ghosts hover about among the living, and that some part of us may survive after death when body and mind alike have been disintegrated and dissolved into their component atoms.

I maintain therefore that replicas or insubstantial shapes of things are thrown off from the surface of objects. These we must denote as an outer skin or film, because each particular floating image wears the aspect and form of the object from whose body it has emanated. . . .

We certainly see that many objects throw off matter in abundance, not only from their inmost depths, as we have said before, but from their surfaces in the form of colour. This is done conspicuously by the awnings, yellow, scarlet and maroon, stretched flapping and billowing on poles and rafters over spacious theatres. The crowded pit below and the stage with all its scenery are made to glow and flow with the colours of the canopy. . . . Here then, already definitely established, we have indications of images, flying about everywhere, extremely fine in texture and individually invisible.

Again, the reason why smell, smoke, heat and the like come streaming out of objects in shapeless clouds is that they originate in the inmost depths; so they are split up in their circuitous journey, and there are no straight vents to their channels through which they may issue directly in close formation. When the thin film of surface colour, on the other hand, is thrown off, there is nothing to disrupt it, since it lies exposed right on the outside.

Lastly, the reflections that we see in mirrors or in water or any polished surface have the same appearance as actual objects. They must therefore be composed of films given off by those objects. There exist therefore flimsy but accurate replicas of objects, individually invisible but such that, when flung back in a rapid succession of recoils from the flat surface of mirrors they produce a visible image. That is the only conceivable way in which these films can be preserved so as to reproduce such a perfect likeness of each object. . . .

Let us now consider *with what facility and speed the films are generated* and ceaselessly stream out of objects and slide off their surfaces. For the outermost skin of all objects is always in readiness for them to shed. When this comes in contact with other objects, it may pass through, as it does in particular through glass. When it encounters rough rocks or solid wood, then it is promptly diffracted, so that it cannot reproduce an image. But when it is confronted by something both polished and close-grained, in particular a mirror, then neither of these things happens. The films cannot penetrate, as they do through glass; nor are they diffracted, because the smoothness ensures their preservation. That is why such surfaces reflect images that are visible to us. No matter how suddenly or at what time you set any object in front of a mirror, an image appears. From this you may infer that the surfaces of objects emit a ceaseless stream of flimsy tissues and filmy shapes. Therefore a great many films are generated in a brief space of time, so that their origin can rightly be described as instantaneous. . . .

. . . Here then is proof upon proof that objects emit particles that strike upon the eyes and provoke sight. . . .

Again, when some shape or other is handled in the dark, it is recognized as the same shape that in a clear and shining light is plain to see. It follows that *touch and sight are provoked by the same stimulus.* Suppose we touch a square object and it stimulates our sense in the dark. What can it be that, given light, will strike upon our vision as square, if it is not the film emanating from the object? This shows that the cause of seeing lies in these films and without these nothing can be seen.

. . . Our power of perceiving and distinguishing the distance from us of each particular object is also due to the film. For, as soon as it is thrown off, it shoves and drives before it all the air that intervenes between itself and the eyes. All this air flows through our eyeballs and brushes through our pupils in passing. That is how we perceive the distance of each object: the more air is driven in front of the film and the longer the draught that brushes through our eyes, the more remote the object is seen to be. Of course this all happens so quickly that we perceive the nature of the object and its distance simultaneously. . . .

Let us now consider *why the image is seen beyond the mirror*—for it certainly does appear to be some distance behind the surface. It is just as though we were really looking out through a doorway, when the door offers a free prospect through it and affords a glimpse of many objects outside the house. In this case also the vision is accompanied by a double dose of air. First we perceive the air within the door posts; then follow the posts themselves to right and left; then the light outside and a second stretch of air brushes through the eyes, followed by the objects that are really seen out of doors. A similar thing happens when a mirrored image projects itself upon our sight. On its way to us the film shoves and drives before it all the air that intervenes between itself and the eyes, so that we feel all this before perceiving the mirror. When we have perceived the mirror itslf, then the film that travels from us to it and is reflected comes back to our eyes, pushing another lot of air in front of it, so that we perceive this before the image, which thus appears to lie at some distance from the mirror. Here then is ample reason why we should not be surprised at this appearance of objects reflected in the surface of a mirror, since they involve a double journey with two lots of air.

Now for the question *why our right side appears in mirrors on the left*. The reason is that, when the film on its outward journey strikes the flat surface of a mirror, it is not slewed round intact, but flung straight back in reverse. . . .

Again, mirrors with projecting sides whose curvature matches our own give back to us unreversed images. This may be because the film is thrown from one surface of the mirror to the other and reaches us only after a double rebound. Alternatively, it may be that on reaching the mirror the film is slewed round, because the curved surface gives it a twist towards us. . . .

When we are in the dark we see objects that are in the light for the following reason. The black murky air that lies nearer to us enters first into our open eyes and takes possession of them. It is then closely followed by bright and shining air, which cleanses them and dispels the shadows of the earlier air. For the bright air is many degrees more mobile and many degrees finer-grained and more potent. As soon as this has filled the passages of the eyes with light and opened those that had previously been blockaded by dark air, they are immediately followed by films thrown off from the illuminated objects, and these stimulate our sense of sight. On the other hand, when we look out of light into darkness, we can see nothing: the murky air, of muddier consistency, arrives last and chokes all the inlets of the eyes and blockades their passages, so that they cannot be stirred by the impact of films from any object.

When we see the square towers of a city in the distance, they often appear round. This is because every angle seen at a distance is blunted or even is not seen as an angle at all. Its impact is nullified and does not penetrate as far as our eyes, because films that travel through a great deal of air lose their sharp outlines through frequent collisions with it. When every angle has thus eluded our sense, the result is as though the squared ashlars were rounded off on the lathe—not that they resemble really round stones seen close up, but in a sketchy sort of way they counterfeit them. . . .

If anyone thinks that nothing can be known, he does not know whether even this can be known, since he admits that he knows nothing. Against such an adversary, therefore, who deliberately stands on his head, I will not trouble to argue my case. And yet, if I were to grant that he possessed this knowledge, I might ask several pertinent questions. Since he has had no experience of truth, how does he know the difference between knowledge and ignorance? What has originated the concept of truth and falsehood? Where is his proof that doubt is not the same as certainty?

You will find, in fact, that the concept of truth was originated by the senses and that the senses cannot be rebutted. The testimony that we must accept as more trustworthy is that which can spontaneously overcome falsehood with truth. What then are we to pronounce more trustworthy than the senses? Can reason derived from the deceitful senses be invoked to contradict them, when it is itself wholly derived from the senses? If they are not true, then reason in its entirety is equally false. Or can hearing give the lie to sight, or touch to hearing? Can touch in turn be discredited by taste or refuted by the nostrils or rebutted by the eyes? This, in my view, is out of the question. Each sense has its own distinctive faculty, its specific function. There must be separate discernment of softness and cold and heat and of the various colours of things and whatever goes with the colours; separate functioning of the palate's power of taste; separate generation of scents and sounds. This rules out the possibility of one sense confuting another. It will be equally out of the question for one sense to belie itself, since it will always be entitled to the same degree of credence. Whatever the senses may perceive at any time is all alike true. Suppose that reason cannot elucidate the cause why things that were square when close at hand are seen as round in the distance. Even so, it is better, in default of reason, to assign fictitious causes to the two shapes than to let things clearly apprehended slip from our grasp. This is to attack belief at its very roots—to tear up the entire foundation on which the maintenance of life is built. It is not only reason that would collapse completely. If you did not dare trust your senses so as to keep clear of precipices and other such things to be avoided and make for their opposites, there would be a speedy end to life itself. . . .

Let me now explain briefly *what it is that stimulates the imagination and where those images come from that enter the mind.*

My first point is this. There are a great many flimsy films from the surface of objects flying about in a great many ways in all directions. When these encounter one another in the air, they easily amalgamate, like gossamer or gold-leaf. In comparison with those films that take possession of the eye and provoke sight, these are certainly of a much flimsier texture, since they penetrate through the chinks of the body and set in motion the delicate substance of the mind within and there provoke sensation. So it is that we see the composite shapes of Centaurs and Mermaids and dogs with as many heads as Cerberus, and phantoms of the dead whose bones lie in the embrace of earth. The fact is that the films flying about everywhere are of all sorts: some are produced spontaneously in the air itself; others are derived from various objects and composed by the amalgamation of their shapes. The image of a Centaur, for instance, is certainly not formed from the life, since no living creature of this sort ever existed. But, as I have just explained, where surface films from a horse and a man accidentally come into contact, they may easily stick together on the spot, because of the delicacy and flimsiness of their texture. So also with other such chimerical creatures. . . .

This subject raises various questions that we must elucidate if we wish to give a clear account of it.

The first question is this: Why is it that, as soon as the mind takes a fancy to think about some particular object, it promptly does so? Are we to suppose that images are waiting on our will, so that we have only to wish and the appropriate film immediately impinges on our mind, whether it be the sea that we fancy or the earth or the sky? . . . . . . In one perceptible instant of time, that is, the time required to utter a single syllable, there are many unperceived units of time whose existence is recognized by reason. That explains why, at any given time, every sort of film is ready to hand in every place: they fly so quickly and are drawn from so many sources. And, because they are so flimsy, the mind cannot distinctly perceive any but those it makes an effort to perceive. All the rest pass without effect, leaving only those for which the mind has prepared itself. And the mind prepares itself in the expectation of seeing each appearance followed by its natural sequel. So this, in fact, is what it does see. You must have noticed how even our eyes, when they set out to look at inconspicuous objects, make an effort and prepare themselves; otherwise it is not possible for us to perceive distinctly. And, even when you are dealing with visible objects, you will find that, unless you direct your mind towards them, they have about them all the time an air of detachment and remoteness. What wonder, then, if the mind misses every impression except those to which it surrenders itself? The result is that we draw sweeping conclusions from trifling indications and lead ourselves into pitfalls of delusion. . . .

In this context, there is one illusion that you must do your level best to escape—an error to guard against with all your foresight. You must not imagine that the bright orbs of our eyes were created purposely, so that we might be able to look before us; that our need to stride ahead determined our equipment with the pliant props of thigh and ankle, set in the firm foundation of our feet; that our arms were fitted to stout shoulders, and helpful hands attached at either side, in order that we might do what is needful to sustain life. To interpret these or any other phenomena on these lines is perversely to turn the truth upside down. In fact, *nothing in our bodies was born in order that we might be able to use it, but the thing born creates the use.* There was no seeing before eyes were born, no talking before the tongue was created. The origin of the tongue was far anterior to speech. The ears were created long before a sound was heard. All the limbs, I am well assured, existed before their use. They cannot, therefore, have grown for the sake of being used. . . .

Let me now explain *how it comes about that we can stride forward at will and are empowered to move our limbs* in various ways, and what it is that has learnt to lift along this heavy load of our body. I count on you to mark my words. I will begin by repeating my previous statement that images of walking come to our mind and impinge upon it. Hence comes the will. For no one ever initiates any action without the mind first foreseeing what it wills. What it foresees is the substance of the image. So the mind, when the motions it experiences are such that it wishes to step forward, immediately jogs the vital spirit diffused through every limb and organ of the body. This is easily done, since mind and spirit are interconnected. The spirit in turn then jogs the body. And so bit by bit the whole bulk is pushed forward and set in motion. . . .

Book V.—COSMOLOGY AND SOCIOLOGY

Who has such power within his breast that he could build up a song worthy of this high theme and these discoveries? Who has such mastery of words that he could praise as he deserves the man who produced such treasures from his breast and bequeathed them to us? No one, I believe, whose body is of mortal growth. If I am to suit my language to the majesty of his revelations, he was a god—a god indeed . . . —who first discovered that rule of life that now is called *philosophy*, who by his art rescued life from such a stormy sea, so black a night, and steered it into such a calm and sun-lit haven. Only compare with his achievement those ancient discoveries of other mortals that rank as the work of gods. Ceres, it is said, taught men to use cereals, and Bacchus the juice of the grape; yet without these things we could go on living, as we are told that some tribes live even now. But life could not be well lived till our breasts were swept clean. Therefore that man has a better claim to be called a god whose gospel, broadcast through the length and breadth of empires, is even now bringing soothing solace to the minds of men.

As for Hercules, if you think his deeds will challenge comparison, you will stray farther still from the path of truth. The gaping jaws of that Nemean lion, or the bristly Arcadian boar—what harm could they do us now? Or the Cretan bull and the Hydra with its palisade of venomous snakes, the pest of Lerna? What would it matter to us if Geryon, with the triple strength of his three bodies, still lorded it in farthest Spain, or the foul birds haunted the Stymphalian mere, or Thracian Diomede's horses breathed fire from their nostrils on the

Balkan slopes of Ismara? Or if the scaly, fierce-eyed serpent guarded still the lustrous golden apples of the Hesperides, hugging the tree-trunk with huge coils, there by the forbidding Atlantic shore where none of us ever goes nor even the natives venture? And the other monsters of this sort that met their death—if they had not been mastered, what harm would they do alive? None at all, that I can see. Even now the world swarms with wild beasts, enough and to spare—a thrill of terror lurking in thickets on the mountain side or in the depths of forests. Only, we have little occasion to go near their haunts. But, if our breasts are not swept clean, then indeed what distracting and disruptive forces we must let in! And, when a man harbours these, what sharp stabs of desire with their answering fears tear him to pieces! Pride, meanness, lust, self-indulgence, boredom—what casualties they inflict! The man who has defeated all these enemies and banished them from his mind, by words not by weapons, is surely entitled to a place among the gods. Remember, too, what inspired words he himself has uttered about the immortal gods, and how by his teaching he has laid bare the causes of things.

Treading in his footsteps, I have been running arguments to earth and explaining in my verses the necessity that compels everything to abide by the compact under which it was created. For nothing has power to break the binding laws of eternity. As an instance of this, I have shown that the mind in particular is a natural growth: it is composed of a body that had first to be born, and it cannot remain intact for all time; but we are misled by images in sleep, when we fancy we see someone whose life has left him.

The next stage in the argument is this. I must first demonstrate that the world also was born and is composed of a mortal body. Then I must deal with the concourse of matter that laid the foundation of land, sea and sky, stars and sun and the globe of the moon. I must show what living things have existed on earth, and which have never been born; how the human race began to employ various utterances among themselves for denoting various things; and how there crept into their minds that fear of the gods which, all the world over, sanctifies temples and lakes, groves and altars and images of the gods. After that, I will explain by what forces nature steers the courses of the sun and the journeyings of the moon, so that we shall not suppose that they run their yearly races between heaven and earth of their own free will with the amiable intention of promoting the growth of crops and animals, or that they are rolled round in furtherance of some divine plan. For it may happen that men who have learnt the truth about the carefree existence of the gods fall to wondering by what power the universe is kept going, especially those movements that are seen overhead in the borderland of ether. Then the poor creatures are plunged back into their old superstitions and saddle themselves with cruel masters whom they believe to be all-powerful. All this because they do not know what can be and what cannot: how a limit is fixed to the power of everything and an immovable frontier post. . . .

Epicurus
Letter to Pythocles

Epicurus to Pythocles, greeting.

In your letter to me, of which Cleon was the bearer, you continue to show me affection which I have merited by my devotion to you, and you try, not without success, to recall the considerations which make for a happy life. To aid your memory you ask me for a clear and concise statement respecting celestial phenomena; for what we have written on this subject elsewhere is, you tell me, hard to remember, although you have my books constantly with you. I was glad to receive your request and am full of pleasant expectations. We will then complete our writing and grant all you ask. Many others besides you will find these reasonings useful, and especially those who have but recently made acquaintance with the true story of nature and those who are attached to pursuits which go deeper than any part of ordinary education. So you will do well to take and learn them and get them up quickly along with the short epitome in my letter to Herodotus.

In the first place, remember that, like everything else, knowledge of celestial phenomena, whether taken along with other things or in isolation, has no other end in view than peace of mind and firm conviction. We do not seek to wrest by force what is impossible, nor to understand all matters equally well, nor make our treatment always clear as when we discuss human life or explain the principles of physics in general—for instance, that the whole of being consists of bodies and intangible nature, or that the ultimate elements of things are indivisible, or any other proposition which admits only one explanation of the phenomena to be possible. But this is not the case with celestial phenomena; these at any rate admit of manifold causes for their occurrence and manifold accounts, none of them contradictory of sensation, of their nature.

For in the study of nature we must not conform to empty assumptions and arbitrary laws, but follow the promptings of the facts; for our life has no need now of unreason and false opinion; our one need is untroubled existence. All things go on uninterruptedly, if all be explained by the method of plurality of causes in conformity with the facts, so soon as we duly understand what may be plausibly alleged respecting them. But when we pick and choose among them, rejecting one equally consistent with the phenomena, we clearly fall away from the study of nature altogether and tumble into myth. Some phenomena within our experience afford evidence by which we may interpret what goes on in the heavens. We see how the former really take place, but not how the celestial phenomena take place, for their occurrence may possibly be due to a variety of causes. However, we must observe each fact as presented, and further separate from it all the facts presented along with it, the occurrence of which from various causes is not contradicted by facts within our experience. . . .

Epicurus
Letter to Menoeceus

Epicurus to Menoeceus, greeting.

Let no one be slow to seek wisdom when he is young nor weary in the search thereof when he is grown old. For no age is too early or too late for the health of the soul. And to say that the season for studying philosophy has not yet come, or that it is past and gone, is like saying that the season for happiness is not yet or that it is now no more. Therefore, both old and young ought to seek wisdom, the former in order that, as age comes over him, he may be young in good things because of the grace of what has been, and the latter in order that, while he is young, he may at the same time be old, because he has no fear of the things which are to come. So we must exercise ourselves in the things which bring happiness, since, if that be present, we have everything, and, if that be absent, all our actions are directed toward attaining it.

Those things which without ceasing I have declared unto thee, those do, and exercise thyself therein, holding them to be the elements of right life. First believe that god is a living being immortal and blessed, according to the notion of a god indicated by the common sense of mankind; and so believing, thou shalt not affirm of him ought that is foreign to his immortality or that agrees not with blessedness, but shalt believe about him whatever may uphold both his blessedness and his immortality. For verily there are gods, and the knowledge of them is manifest; but they are not such as the multitude believe, seeing that men do not steadfastly maintain the notions they form respecting them. Not the man who denies the gods worshipped by the multitude, but he who affirms of the gods what the multitude believes about them is truly impious. For the utterances of the multitude about the gods are not true preconceptions but false assumptions; hence it is that the greatest evils happen to the wicked and the greatest blessings happen to the good from the hand of the gods, seeing that they are always favourable to their own good qualities and take pleasure in men like unto themselves, but reject as alien whatever is not of their kind.

Accustom thyself to believe that death is nothing to us, for good and evil imply sentience, and death is the privation of all sentience; therefore a right understanding that death is nothing to us makes the mortality of life enjoyable, not by adding to life an illimitable time, but by taking away the yearning after immortality. For life has no terrors for him who has thoroughly apprehended that there are no terrors for him in ceasing to live. Foolish, therefore, is the man who says that he fears death, not because it will pain when it comes, but because it pains in the prospect. Whatsoever causes no annoyance when it is present, causes only a groundless pain in the expectation. Death, therefore, the most awful of evils, is nothing to us, seeing that, when we are, death is not come, and, when death is come, we are not. It is nothing, then, either to the living or to the dead, for with the living it is not and the dead exist no longer. But in the world, at one time men shun death as the greatest of all evils, and at another time choose it as a respite from the evils in life. The wise man does not deprecate life nor does he fear the cessation of life. The thought of life is no offense to him, nor is the cessation of life regarded as an evil. And even as men choose of food not merely and simply the larger portion, but the more pleasant, so the wise seek to enjoy the time which is most pleasant and not merely that which is longest. And he who admonishes the young to live well and the old to make a good end speaks foolishly, not merely because of the desirableness of life, but because the same exercise at once teaches to live well and die well. Much worse is he who says that it were good not to be born, but when once one is born to pass with all speed through the gates of Hades. For if he truly believes this, why does he not depart from life? It were easy for him to do so, if once he were firmly convinced. If he speaks only in mockery, his words are foolishness, for those who hear believe him not.

We must remember that the future is neither wholly ours nor wholly not ours, so that neither must we count upon it as quite certain to come nor despair of it as quite certain not to come.

We must also reflect that of desires some are natural, others are groundless; and that of the natural some are necessary as well as natural, and some natural only. And of the necessary desires some are necessary if we are to be happy, some if the body is to be rid of uneasiness, some if we are even to live. He who has a clear and certain understanding of these things will direct every preference and aversion toward securing health of body and tranquillity of mind, seeing that this is the sum and end of a blessed life. For the end of all our actions is to be free from pain and fear, and, when once we have attained all this, the tempest of the soul is laid; seeing that the living creature has no need to go in search of something that is lacking, nor to look for anything else by which the good of the soul and of the body will be fulfilled. When we are pained because of the absence of pleasure, then, and then only, do we feel the need of pleasure. Wherefore we call pleasure the alpha and omega of a blessed life. Pleasure is our first and kindred good. It is the starting point of every choice and of every aversion, and to it we come back, inasmuch as we make feeling the rule by which to judge of every good thing. And since pleasure is our first and native good, for that reason we do not choose every pleasure whatsoever, but ofttimes pass over many pleasures when a greater annoyance ensues from them. And ofttimes we consider pains superior to pleasures when submission to the pains for a long time brings us as a consequence a greater pleasure. While therefore all pleasure because it is naturally akin to us is good, not all pleasure is choice-worthy, just as all pain is an evil and yet not all pain is to be shunned. It is, however, by measuring one against another, and by looking at the conveniences and inconveniences, that all these matters must be judged. Sometimes we treat the good as an evil, and the evil, on the contrary, as a good. Again, we regard independence of outward things as a great good, not so as in all cases to use little, but so as to be contented with little if we have not much, being honestly persuaded that they have the sweetest enjoyment of luxury who stand least in need of it, and that whatever is natural is easily procured and only the vain and worthless hard to win. Plain fare gives as much pleasure as a costly diet, when once the pain of want has been removed, while bread and water confer the highest possible pleasure when they are brought to hungry lips. To habituate one's self, therefore, to simple and inexpensive diet supplies all that is needful for health, and enables a man to meet the necessary requirements of life without shrinking, and it places us in a better condition when we approach at intervals a costly fare and renders us fearless of fortune.

When we say, then, that pleasure is the end and aim, we do not mean the pleasures of the prodigal or the pleasures of sensuality, as we are understood to do by some through ignorance, prejudice, or wilful misrepresentation. By pleasure we mean the absence of pain in the body and of trouble in the soul. It is not an unbroken succession of drinking bouts and of revelry, not sexual love, not the enjoyment of the fish and other delicacies of a luxurious table, which produce a pleasant life; it is sober reasoning, searching out the grounds of every choice and avoidance, and banishing those beliefs through which the greatest tumults take possession of the soul. Of all this the beginning and the greatest good is prudence. Wherefore prudence is a more precious thing even than philosophy; from it spring all the other virtues, for it teaches that we cannot lead a life of pleasure which is not also a life of prudence, honor, and justice; nor lead a life of prudence, honor, and justice, which is not also a life of pleasure. For the virtues have grown into one with a pleasant life, and a pleasant life is inseparable from them.

Who, then, is superior in thy judgement to such a man? He holds a holy belief concerning the gods, and is altogether free from the fear of death. He has diligently considered the end fixed by nature, and understands how easily the limit of good things can be reached and attained, and how either the duration or the intensity of evils is but slight. Destiny, which some introduce as sovereign over all things, he laughs to scorn, affirming rather that some things happen of necessity, others by chance, others through our own agency. For he sees that necessity destroys responsibility and that chance or fortune is inconstant; whereas our own actions are free, and it is to them that praise and blame naturally attach. It were better, indeed, to accept the legends of the gods than to bow beneath that yoke of destiny which the natural philsophers have imposed. The one holds out some faint hope that we may escape if we honor the gods, while the necessity of the naturalists is deaf to all entreaties. Nor does he hold chance to be a god, as the world in general does, for in the acts of a god there is no disorder; nor to be a cause, though an uncertain one, for he believes that no good or evil is dispensed by chance to men so as to make life blessed, though it supplies the starting-point of great good and great evil. He believes that the misfortune of the wise is better than the prosperity of the fool. It is better, in short, that what is well judged in action should not owe its successful issue to the aid of chance.

Exercise thyself in these and kindred precepts day and night, both by thyself and with him who is like unto thee; then never, either in waking or in dream, wilt thou be disturbed; but wilt live as a god among men. For man loses all semblance of mortality by living in the midst of immortal blessings.

Epicurus
Principal Doctrines

1. A blessed and eternal being has no trouble himself and brings no trouble upon any other being; hence he is exempt from movements of anger and partiality, for every such movement implies weakness.

2. Death is nothing to us; for the body, when it has been resolved into its elements, has no feeling, and that which has no feeling is nothing to us.

3. The magnitude of pleasure reaches its limit in the removal of all pain. When pleasure is present, so long as it is uninterrupted, there is no pain either of body or of mind or of both together.

4. Continuous pain does not last long in the flesh; on the contrary, pain, if extreme, is present a very short time, and even that degree of pain which barely outweighs pleasure in the flesh does not last for many days together. Illnesses of long duration even permit of an excess of pleasure over pain in the flesh.

5. It is impossible to live a pleasant life without living wisely and well and justly, and it is impossible to live wisely and well and justly without living pleasantly. Whenever any one of these is lacking, when, for instance, the man is not able to live wisely, though he lives well and justly, it is impossible for him to live a pleasant life.

6. In order to obtain security from other men any means whatsoever of procuring this was a natural good.

7. Some men have sought to become famous and renowned, thinking that thus they would make themselves secure against their fellowmen. If, then, the life of such persons really was secure, they attained natural good; if, however, it was insecure, they have not attained the end which by nature's own prompting they originally sought.

8. No pleasure is in itself evil, but the things which produce certain

pleasures entail annoyances many times greater than the pleasures themselves.

9. If all pleasure had been capable of accumulation,—if this had gone on not only by recurrence in time, but all over the frame or, at any rate, over the principal parts of man's nature, there would never have been any difference between one pleasure and another, as in fact there is.

10. If the objects which are productive of pleasures to profligate persons really freed them from fears of the mind,—the fears, I mean, inspired by celestial and atmospheric phenomena, the fear of death, the fear of pain; if, further, they taught them to limit their desires, we should never have any fault to find with such persons, for they would then be filled with pleasures to overflowing on all sides and would be exempt from all pain, whether of body or mind, that is, from all evil.

11. If we had never been molested by alarms at celestial and atmospheric phenomena, nor by the misgiving that death somehow affects us, nor by neglect of the proper limits of pains and desires, we should have had no need to study natural science.

12. It would be impossible to banish fear on matters of the highest importance, if a man did not know the nature of the whole universe, but lived in dread of what the legend tells us. Hence without the study of nature there was no enjoyment of unmixed pleasures.

13. There would be no advantage in providing security against our fellow-men, so long as we were alarmed by occurrences over our heads or beneath the earth or in general by whatever happens in the boundless universe.

14. When tolerable security against our fellow-men is attained, then on a basis of power sufficient to afford support and of material prosperity arises in most genuine form the security of a quiet private life withdrawn from the multitude.

15. Nature's wealth at once has its bounds and is easy to procure; but the wealth of vain fancies recedes to an infinite distance.

16. Fortune but seldom interferes with the wise man; his greatest and highest interests have been, are, and will be, directed by reason throughout the course of his life.

17. The just man enjoys the greatest peace of mind, while the unjust is full of the utmost disquietude.

18. Pleasure in the flesh admits no increase when once the pain of want has been removed; after that it only admits of variation. The limit of pleasure in the mind, however, is reached when we reflect on

the things themselves and their congeners which cause the mind the greatest alarms.

19. Unlimited time and limited time afford an equal amount of pleasure, if we measure the limits of that pleasure by reason.

20. The flesh receives as unlimited the limits of pleasure; and to provide it requires unlimited time. But the mind, grasping in thought what the end and limit of the flesh is, and banishing the terrors of futurity, procures a complete and perfect life, and has no longer any need of unlimited time. Nevertheless it does not shun pleasure, and even in the hour of death, when ushered out of existence by circumstances, the mind does not lack enjoyment of the best life.

21. He who understands the limits of life knows how easy it is to procure enough to remove the pain of want and make the whole of life complete and perfect. Hence he has no longer any need of things which are not to be won save by labor and conflict.

22. We must take into account as the end all that really exists and all clear evidence of sense to which we refer our opinions; for otherwise everything will be full of uncertainty and confusion.

23. If you fight against all your sensations, you will have no standard to which to refer, and thus no means of judging even those judgments which you pronounce false.

24. If you reject absolutely any single sensation without stopping to discriminate with respect to that which awaits confirmation between matter of opinion and that which is already present, whether in sensation or in feelings or in any presentative perception of the mind, you will throw into confusion even the rest of your sensations by your groundless belief and so you will be rejecting the standard of truth altogether. If in your ideas based upon opinion you hastily affirm as true all that awaits confirmation as well as that which does not, you will not escape error, as you will be maintaining complete ambiguity whenever it is a case of judging between right and wrong opinion.

25. If you do not on every separate occasion refer each of your actions to the end prescribed by nature, but instead of this in the act of choice or avoidance swerve aside to some other end, your acts will not be consistent with your theories.

26. All such desires as lead to no pain when they remain ungratified are unnecessary, and the longing is easily got rid of, when the thing desired is difficult to procure or when the desires seem likely to produce harm.

27. Of all the means which are procured by wisdom to ensure hap-

piness throughout the whole of life, by far the most important is the acquisition of friends.

28. The same conviction which inspires confidence that nothing we have to fear is eternal or even of long duration, also enables us to see that even in our limited conditions of life nothing enhances our security so much as friendship.

29. Of our desires some are natural and necessary; others are natural, but not necessary; others, again, are neither natural nor necessary, but are due to illusory opinion. [Epicurus regards as natural and necessary desires which bring relief from pain, as *e.g.* drink when we are thirsty; while by natural and not necessary he means those which merely diversify the pleasure without removing the pain, as *e.g.* costly viands; by the neither natural nor necessary he means desires for crowns and the erection of statues in one's honor.] [1]

30. Those natural desires which entail no pain when not gratified, though their objects are vehemently pursued, are also due to illusory opinion; and when they are not got rid of, it is not because of their own nature, but because of the man's illusory opinion.

31. Natural justice is a symbol or expression of expediency, to prevent one man from harming or being harmed by another.

32. Those animals which are incapable of making covenants with one another, to the end that they may neither inflict nor suffer harm, are without either justice or injustice. And those tribes which either could not or would not form mutual covenants to the same end are in like case.

33. There never was an absolute justice, but only an agreement made in reciprocal intercourse in whatever localities now and again from time to time, providing against the infliction or suffering of harm.

34. Injustice is not in itself an evil, but only in its consequence, viz. the terror which is excited by apprehension that those appointed to punish such offences will discover the injustice.

35. It is impossible for the man who secretly violates any article of the social compact to feel confident that he will remain undiscovered, even if he has already escaped ten thousand times; for right on to the end of his life he is never sure he will not be detected.

36. Taken generally, justice is the same for all, to wit, something found expedient in mutual intercourse; but in its application to particular cases of locality or conditions of whatever kind, it varies under different circumstances.

37. Among the things accounted just by conventional law, whatever

---

1. The bracketed remarks are by an ancient commentator.

in the needs of mutual intercourse is attested to be expedient, is thereby stamped as just, whether or not it be the same for all; and in case any law is made and does not prove suitable to the expediencies of mutual intercourse, then this is no longer just. And should the expediency which is expressed by the law vary and only for a time correspond with the prior conception, nevertheless for the time being it was just, so long as we do not trouble ourselves about empty words, but look simply at the facts.

38. Where without any change in circumstances the conventional laws, when judged by their consequences, were seen not to correspond with the notion of justice, such laws were not really just; but wherever the laws have ceased to be expedient in consequence of a change in circumstances, in that case the laws were for the time being just when they were expedient for the mutual intercourse of the citizens, and subsequently ceased to be just when they ceased to be expedient.

39. He who best knew how to meet fear of external foes made into one family all the creatures he could; and those he could not, he at any rate did not treat as aliens; and where he found even this impossible, he avoided all intercourse, and, so far as was expedient, kept them at a distance.

40. Those who were best able to provide themselves with the means of security against their neighbors, being thus in possession of the surest guarantee, passed the most agreeable life in each other's society; and their enjoyment of the fullest intimacy was such that, if one of them died before his time, the survivors did not lament his death as if it called for commiseration.

STOICISM

Zeno of Citium in Cyprus, founder of the Stoic school, was born in the decades before the death of Aristotle in 322 B.C. With perhaps some exception in the field of logic, Zeno was to establish the framework of Stoic philosophy. Its chief themes were gradually developed by his immediate successors Cleanthes and Chrysippus of the Philosophy of the Stoa or Porch (so named because the school met in a house having a painted porch). Cleanthes, of Assos (*c.* 300-232 B.C.), seems to have been primarily interested in the theology and physics of Stoic doctrine; his famous and revered *Hymn to Zeus* is reprinted here. Chrysippus, of Soli (*c.* 281-201 B.C.), devoted his great energies to the almost complete development and mature expression of the essential features of Stoic logic, ethics, and physics. The selections here are taken from the fragmentary remains of this early and vigorous period in the history of Stoicism, as found in the standard collection by J. von Arnim (see bibliography). The text of the translation is the work of Jason L. Saunders.

The only available continuous text of the early Stoic period available in English may be found in Diogenes Laertius' *Lives* (see bibliography), Book II. *The Manual of Epictetus* (60 A.D.-?) is one of the two works attributed to him by his disciple Arrian, who apparently took them down as lecture notes. (The *Discourses* is the other work).

Early Stoic Logic

THE PARTS OF PHILOSOPHY

SVF I, 45

Philosophical doctrine, say the Stoics, falls into three parts: one physical, another ethical, and the third logical. Zeno of Citium was the first to make this division in his book, *On Doctrine*.

Diogenes Laertius

SVF I, 46

Some Stoics start with logic, go on to physics, and finish with ethics; and among those who do this is Zeno, in his treatise, *On Doctrine*. . . .

Diogenes Laertius

SVF I, 482

Cleanthes makes not three, but six parts of philosophy—dialectic, rhetoric, ethics, politics, physics, theology.

Diogenes Laertius

SVF II, 37

Chrysippus speaks of three specific divisions of philosophy, in the first book of his volume *On Doctrine* and the first book of his *Physics*—physical, ethical and logical. . . .

Diogenes Laertius

SVF II, 38b

Philosophy, they say, is like an animal, logic corresponding to the bones and sinews, ethics to the fleshy parts, physics to the soul. Another simile they use is that of an egg: the shell is logic, next comes the white, ethics, and the yolk in the center is physics. Or again, they liken philosophy to a fertile field: logic being the encircling fence, ethics the crop, physics the soil or the trees. . . .

Diogenes Laertius

SVF II, 42

Chrysippus believes that young students should first learn logic, secondly, ethics, and after these, physics. . . . Now these things having been often said by him, it will suffice to set down what is found in his treatise *On Lives,* Book IV, being thus word for word:

First then, it seems to me, as it has been rightly said by the ancients, that there are three kinds of philosophical speculations, logical, ethical, and physical, and that of these, the logical ought to be placed first, the ethical second, and the physical third; and that part of the physical, the discourse concerning the gods, ought to be the last. . . .

Plutarch

SVF II, 44

The Stoics teach that we should begin with logic, continue with ethics, and place physics last. For first it is necessary to make the mind sure so that it will be an invincible guardian of the teachings. And dialectic serves to make the reason secure. Second we must subscribe to ethics to improve our character, for the study of ethics is without danger to one who has previously mastered logic. And finally we must proceed to physics, for it is more divine and requires more profound attention.

Sextus Empiricus

LOGIC

¶ PRESENTATION

SVF I, 47

Logic, no doubt, was very fully worked out by Chrysippus, but much less was done in it by Zeno than by the older schools.

Cicero

SVF I, 54a

The Wise Man never opines, never regrets, never is mistaken, never changes his mind.

Cicero

SVF I, 54e and f

The Wise Man does not conceive anything weakly, but rather, surely and certainly; therefore also he does not opine. . . . They believe that a rational person . . . neither repents nor is fickle, changeable, or perplexed.

Stobaeus

SVF I, 55

Zeno changed many things in that third part of philosophy, in which first he said some new things concerning the senses themselves, which he considered to be connected by some sort of impulse produced extrinsically, which he called presentation but which we call perception.

Cicero

SVF I, 59b

Arcesilaus perhaps asked Zeno what would happen if the Wise Man could neither perceive anything nor have an opinion. I believe he replied that the Wise Man could never entertain an opinion because there was something which could be perceived. What is it then? Perceptions, no doubt. What sort of perception? Then he defined it as follows: It is an imitation, a seal, an impression from what exists just as it exists. Then it was asked further whether such a true perception was of the same type as a false perception. Here Zeno clearly saw that there was no perception which could be perceived if there could be one arising from that which exists, essentially similar to one arising from that which does not exist. . . .[1]

Cicero

SVF I, 59c

A comprehensive presentation is one which has been stamped and sealed by that which exists and just as it exists in such a way that it could not be produced by what does not exist.

Sextus Empiricus

SVF I, 59g

But let us see what Zeno says. A perception can be grasped and perceived such as has no common characteristic with a false one.

Augustine

---

1. As Arnim says, *SVF I, p. 18*, these passages prove that to Zeno are traced all the elements of the definition of *comprehensive presentation* that are found in the testimony of Sextus Empiricus, given below, SVF I, 59c.

SVF II, 52

It pleased the Stoics to place first their theory of presentation and sensation, because the criterion—by which the truth about things is known—is generically a presentation, and because the theory of assent and of comprehension and thought, the presupposition of everything else, cannot be formulated without involving presentation. For presentation comes first, then articulate thought puts into words what presentation has conveyed.

Diogenes Laertius

SVF II, 53

Presentation is an impression on the soul, the name appropriately taken over from the imprint which a seal makes on wax. Presentations are either comprehensive or noncomprehensive. The comprehensive presentation, which they assert is the criterion of the existence of things, is that which is produced by a real object, resembles the object itself, and is sealed and stamped on the soul. The noncomprehensive presentation either does not come from a real object, or if it does, it does not resemble the object,—nor is it well formed or distinct.

Diogenes Laertius

SVF II, 55

There is a difference between presentation and image. For image is a fancy of the mind, such as occurs in sleep, but presentation is an impression on the soul, i.e., a qualitative change, as Chrysippus held in the second book of his *De Anima*. For one must not take the word *impression* in one sense of "the impression of" a seal, since one cannot hold that many imprints exist at the same spot at the same time.

Diogenes Laertius

SVF II, 60

A presentation is conceived to be that which comes from and resembles a real object and has been stamped, imprinted, and sealed in the soul in such a fashion that it could not have come from an unreal object.

Diogenes Laertius

SVF II, 61

According to the Stoics some presentations are sensible and others are not. The sensible presentations are received through one or more sense organs, the others come through the mind as in the case of the incorporeals and other things received by the reason. Some sensible presentations are from real objects and occur with a yielding and assent, but there are other presentations which are appearances, only seeming to come from a real object. Again, some presentations are rational, others irrational. The rational belong to rational beings, the irrational to irrational animals. The rational presentations are thoughts, but the irrational do not happen to have a name. Some also are the result of skill and others are not. For certainly a statue is regarded in one manner by a trained sculptor and in a different manner by an unskilled person.

Diogenes Laertius

SVF II, 56

Since the Stoic theory remains, let us now discuss it also. These men, then, assert that the comprehensive presentation is the criterion of truth. We shall understand this if first we learn what they conceive as presentation and what its specific differences are. Now, they claim that a presentation is an impression in the soul. But here differences of opinion arise. For Cleanthes understood *impression* as hollows and projections just like the impressions made on wax by a ring. But Chrysippus considers such a view absurd. For first, he said, if the mind should simultaneously present a triangle and quadrangle, this view would require the same body, i.e., the mind at the same time to have in itself the differing shapes of a triangle and a quadrangle, or even a circle also, which is absurd. And if we should have a great many presentations together, the soul also would have a multitude of shapes, which is worse than the previous case. But he conjectured that Zeno had used the word *impression* in the sense of *qualitative change,* so that the definition should be: "Presentation is a qualitative change of the soul," since it is no longer absurd that the same body at the same time, when we have many presentations, should admit a multitude of qualitative changes. For just as the air, when many people are talking at once, admits in one place innumerable differences and contains many vibrations and qualitative changes, so also the ruling part of the soul somewhat analogously will suffer a variety of presentations.

Sextus Empiricus

SVF II, 59

Therefore also they define presentation as an impression in the soul, in fact an impression in the ruling part of the soul. Again they say that either the impression now coming into existence is a presentation, or the one which previously began and still exists. But if it is the one now coming into existence, they would be saying that actual presentation is identical with sensation. For sensation is the beginning of the impression. But presentations occur even apart from actual sensation. But if a presentation is a previously generated impression which still exists, they would be saying that memory is presentation.

Alexander Aphrodisias

SVF II, 63

We must say that a presentation is a certain affection of the living being, bringing into consciousness both itself and the other thing. For example, by looking at something, . . . our sight is affected in a certain manner, and we do not continue in the same condition as we were before looking. Now, by such a change we grasp two things, of which one is the change itself, i.e., the presentation, and the second is that which induced the change, i..e., the thing seen. And similarly with the other senses. Therefore, just as light makes known both itself and all things in it, so also presentation, since it controls a living thing's knowing, must—like light—both reveal itself and indicate that evident object which produced it.

Sextus Empiricus

SVF II, 54a

Chrysippus distinguishes from each other these four expressions: presentation, its—external—object, fictitious image, and fictitious object. Presentation is that affection of the soul which both reveals itself and points to the object by which it is occasioned. For, suppose we see something white. The soul is affected in a particular way through this act of seeing. And in just the same way that this affection or sensation is aroused in the sense organs when the color white is perceived, the soul is affected when it thinks of whiteness; i.e., by receiving within itself an image of what it thinks of. . . . And this object is defined as something whereby a presentation is effected, e.g., something white or something cold or anything else which has the power to produce such an effect on the soul is called its object. Fictitious image is defined as an idle mustering of images, an affection of the soul divorced from any object . . . for while some object underlies the presentation, there is none for the fictitious image. And fictitious object is defined as something that precipitates us into the idle mustering of images in our imagination, but in the way that happens to people who have taken leave of their senses. . . .

Aetius

SVF II, 69

As to what this *comprehensive* presentation is for which we are seeking, those who define it say: "that one coming from a real object, etc." Then again, since everything which is learned definitively is learned from things known, when we inquire as to what a real object is, they turn around and say that a real object is that which produces a comprehensive presentation.

Sextus Empiricus

¶ SENSATION

SVF I, 60

Zeno did not place faith in every perception, but only in those which possess a peculiar mark of those things which are seen; but that perception when it was discerned by virtue of itself, he called *comprehensible*. . . . But after it had been received and approved, he called it *comprehension,* resembling those things which are grasped by the hands—from which analogy he derived this noun, though no one had ever before used this word in this sense; and he also used many new words, for he was speaking of new things. But that which was grasped by sense he called a sensation, and if it was grasped so that it could not be destroyed by reason, he called it knowledge; otherwise he called it ignorance; from which also arises opinion, which is weak and is common to what is false or unknown. But between knowledge and ignorance he placed that comprehension which I mentioned, and counted it neither as right or wrong, but said that it alone was to be believed.

For this reason he placed faith in the senses also, because as I said above, comprehension by the senses seemed to him to be true and trustworthy, not because it grasped everything in the object, but because it missed nothing which could affect it, and because nature had given it to us as a criterion of knowledge and principle of itself from which afterward notions of things might be impressed on our minds from which not only principles, but some wider avenues of approach to rationality are discovered. But error, rashness, ignorance, opinion, and suspicion, and in a word everything foreign to a firm and consistent assent, he removed from virtue and wisdom.

Cicero

SVF I, 61

To these perceptions accepted by the senses Zeno joins the assent of the mind, which he considers to be placed in us and voluntary.

Cicero

SVF II, 71

By sensation the Stoics mean the spirit which stretches from the ruling part of the soul to the senses, and also comprehension by the senses, and also the apparatus of the sense organs, which apparatus some people lack. Furthermore, the activity itself is called sensation.

Diogenes Laertius

SVF II, 74

The Stoics do not place sensation in presentation alone, but make its essence depend on assent. For sensation is assent to a sensible presentation, the assent being in conformity with natural impulse.

Stobaeus

SVF II, 78

The Stoics say that sensations are true, presentations are sometimes true and sometimes false.

Aetius

SVF II, 80

When such difficulties are met with in this matter, the dogmatists . . . are accustomed to say that the external, underlying, sensible object is neither a whole nor a part, but it is we who add the predicate of whole or part to it. For whole is a term of relation, since a whole is considered such with reference to the parts. And the parts are also relative, for they are considered parts with reference to the whole. But relations exist in our recollection and our recollection is in us. Accordingly, the whole and the part are in us, and the external, underlying, sensible object is neither a whole nor a part, but it is the thing of which we predicate our recollection.

Sextus Empiricus

¶ NOTIONS

SVF I, 65a

The *notions* of Zeno, they say, are neither things nor qualities, but are images of the soul, i.e., fictitious objects—like things and like qualities. The ancients called them *ideas*. For the ideas belong among those things subsumed under the notions, as men and horses, or to speak more generally of all living beings and of the other things, of which they say there are ideas. But the Stoic philosophers say that ideas are unreal, and that we share in notions, but that we only chance upon their modifications which they call *common nouns*.

Stobaeus

SVF I, 65c

A notion is an image of reason, neither a real thing nor a quality, but like a real thing and like a quality, as an image of a horse arises even when no horse is present.

Diogenes Laertius

SVF II, 83

The Stoics say: When a man is born, the ruling part of the soul is like a sheet of paper suitable for writing. On this he writes off each single thought. . . . That which comes through the senses is the first thing written down. For those who perceive something, like white, have a memory which comes from it. And when many similar memories have arisen, then we say people have experience, for experience is the manifold of similar presentations. . . . But of thoughts, some arise naturally in the ways already mentioned, without technical skill, while others come by our teaching and conscious effort. These latter are called thoughts only (ἔννοιαι) but the others are also termed *preconceptions*.[2] Now reason, because of which we are called rational, is said to have received all its preconceptions by the time a child is seven years old. And a notion is an image of the mind of a rational living being—for when the image strikes a rational soul, then it is called a notion, taking its name from that of mind.[3] . . . Therefore all those which strike irrational are images only, but those which we or the gods have are both images, generically, and notions, specifically. . . .

Aetius

¶ COMPREHENSION, KNOWLEDGE, AND ART

SVF I, 66

For Zeno denies . . . that you know anything. How is that, you will ask, for we defend the proposition that even a fool comprehends a great many things. But you deny that anyone except the Wise Man can *know* anything. And Zeno illustrated it by a gesture. For when he showed his hand with the fingers extended, he would say, perception is like this. Then when he closed his fingers a little, he would say, assent is like this. Then when he had completely closed his hand and made

---

2. The term προλήψεις (preconceptions), used for primary notions, was introduced into Stoicism by Chrysippus, who borrowed it from Epicurus; ἔννοιαι is used regularly by Zeno.

3. ἐννόημα from νοῦς.

a fist, he would say that that was comprehension.[4] . . . When, finally, he brought his left hand against his right fist and grasped it tightly, he would say that such was knowledge and no one but the Wise Man was capable of it.

Cicero

SVF I, 68b

Ignorance is a changeable and weak assent.

Stobaeus

SVF I, 68c

Knowledge is the assured and certain comprehension which cannot be set aside by argument.

Sextus Empiricus

SVF I, 69

Between knowledge and ignorance Zeno placed comprehension, and he considered it neither as a right nor as a wrong impression.

Cicero

SVF I, 73d

Now every art is a system composed of organized comprehensions directed to an end useful for life. . . .

Sextus

SVF II, 90

The Stoics, i.e., Zeno and Cleanthes say that three things are joined together: knowledge, opinion, and comprehension which stands between them. Knowledge is comprehension which is sure, certain and unchangeable by argument, whereas opinion is a weak and false assent. Comprehension which stands between them is assent to a comprehensive presentation. Now, a comprehensive presentation, according to them, is one that is true in such a way that it cannot become false. They say also that knowledge occurs only in wise men, opinion occurs only in foolish minds, but comprehension is common to both and is the criterion of truth.

Sextus Empiricus

SVF II, 96

Again the Stoics, with reference to goods which concern the soul, say that the virtues are arts. For an art, they say, is a system of organized

---

4. I.e., κατάληψις.

comprehensions, and comprehensions arise in the ruling part of the soul. But it is incomprehensible how a deposit of comprehensions, so numerous as to become an art, could arise in the ruling part of the soul when they assert the soul to be spirit or breath. For since breath or spirit is fluid and is said to be moved as a whole with each impression, each successive impression will erase the one before it.

Sextus Empiricus

¶ THE CRITERION OR STANDARD OF TRUTH

SVF II, 105

According to Chrysippus, in the second book of his *Physics,* the standard of truth, or criterion, is said to be the comprehensive presentation, i.e., that which comes from a real object . . . but [later] in the first book of his treatise *On Doctrine,* he declares that sensation and preconception are the only criteria.

Diogenes Laertius

SVF II, 106

The Stoics asserted that from the senses . . . the mind conceives the notions of those things which they explicate by definition. And hence is developed the whole plan and connection of their learning and teaching.

Augustine

SVF II, 107

Now it is possible to subdivide this rational criterion by saying that one thing is the criterion in the sense of agent, another in the sense of instrument, and the third as occasion or relation. The agent is the man, the instrument is sensation, and the third is the occurrence of the presentation. The man by whom the judgment is made is similar to a craftsman or to one who weighs and measures; sensation and mind resemble the scales or the yardstick, by means of which the elements of the judgment are clarified; and the occurrence of presentation, in accordance with which the man is moved to make a judgment, resembles the relation of the instruments already mentioned.

Sextus Empiricus

SVF II, 108

Celsus teaches something very similar to the Stoics, who destroy intelligible realities when they assert that whatever is grasped is grasped by the senses, and all comprehension is attached to sensation.

Origen

SVF II, 114

The Stoics assert that it is in the nature of things that all things are unique and distinguishable one from the other, and that two or more objects never possess a common character differing in no way whatever.

Cicero

SVF II, 113

It is a Stoic argument—and it is not a very convincing one—that "no hair or grain of sand is in all respects the same as another hair or grain of sand."

[That is, everything is *sui generis,* and nothing is the same as what some other thing is.]

Cicero

SVF II, 115

Now let us discuss briefly assent and approbation. . . . For, when we were explaining the power of the senses, it was made clear that many things are comprehended and perceived by the senses, and this could not occur without assent. Further, since the chief difference between the animate and inanimate is that the animate can do something (for a living being which could do nothing at all is inconceivable), either it must be denied sensation, or else assent, which is in our power, must be allowed to it. . . . These considerations also follow: Without assent, there can be neither memory, concepts, nor arts. And most important of all, though some things may be in our power, nothing is in the power of the man who never assents to anything. Where then will virtue be, if nothing is in our power?

Cicero

SVF II, 116

Moreover it is also clear that there must be set down a principle which wisdom, when it begins to do anything, may follow, and this principle must be consistent with nature. For otherwise, natural disposition, by which we are impelled to act and by which we seek a perception, cannot be set in motion. But that which initiates this motion must first be seen and must be believed in, which cannot take place if that which is

seen cannot be distinguished from a false one. But how can the mind
be moved to natural disposition, if what is seen is not perceived by the
mind to be consistent with or alien to nature?

Furthermore, if it does not occur to the mind what its function is,
it will never do anything at all, never be impelled toward anything,
never be set in motion. But if it is at some time to do something, then
it is necessary that what occurs seems to it to be true.

Cicero

SVF II, 117

Most of all the awareness of virtue proves that many things can be
perceived and comprehended. In these matters alone do we speak of
knowledge. And we believe that knowledge is not just any grasping of
a thing, but it is a stable and unchangeable grasp—in fact it is wisdom,
the art of living, which is its own source of constancy. But if this
constancy had nothing which it perceived or knew, I ask from what
source is it derived and in what manner?

Cicero

SVF II, 118

But the dogmatists[5] in their refutation regularly question the method
by which the skeptic proves there is no criterion. For he argues with the
aid of a criterion or without such aid. If he does not use a criterion, he
will not be trusted; but if he has a criterion he will be self-refuted, and
in saying there is no criterion he will admit adopting a criterion in
order to confirm that assertion.

And again, when we Skeptics argue, "If there is a criterion, either
it is or is not judged by a superior criterion," and then draw one of two
conclusions, viz: an infinite regress or the absurdity that a thing is its
own criterion,—they . . . reply that it is not absurd to consider a thing
as its own criterion. For the straight line is capable of testing both
itself and other lines, and the balance measures the equality of other
things and of itself as well, and light reveals not only other objects
but itself also. Thus the criterion can be established as a criterion of
itself and of other things too.

Sextus Empiricus

SVF II, 121

Suppose the Pyrrhonian suspension of judgment, the idea that nothing
is certain: it is plain that, beginning with itself, it first invalidates

---

5. I.e., the Stoics.

itself. It either grants that something is true, that you are not to suspend your judgment on all things; or it objects in saying that there is nothing true. And it is evident that first it will not be true. For it either affirms what is true or it does not affirm what is true. But if the former, it concedes—though unwillingly—that something is true. If the latter, it leaves true what it wished to do away with. For, in so far as the skepticism which destroys is proved false, so the positions which are being destroyed are proved true (like the dream which says all dreams are false). For in confuting itself, it is confirmatory of the others. And, finally, if it is true, it will make a beginning with itself and not be skepticism of anything else but of itself first. Then if such a man comprehends that he is a man, or that he is skeptical, it is evident that he is not skeptical. . . . For how did he reply to the question? He is evidently no skeptic in respect to this. On the contrary, he affirms even that he does doubt.

And if we according to [the Stoics] suspend judgment in regard to everything, we shall first suspend our judgment in regard to our suspension of judgment itself, whether we are to trust it or not. And if this position is true—that we do not know what is true—then absolutely nothing is allowed to be true by it. But if he will say that even this is questionable—whether we know what is true—by this very statement he grants that truth is knowable, in the very act of appearing not to establish the doubt respecting it.

Then, if a philosophical sect is a leaning toward doctrines or, according to some, a leaning to a number of doctrines which are consistent with one another and with phenomena, tending to a well-lived life; and doctrine is logical comprehension, and comprehension is a state and assent of the mind, not merely skeptics, but every one who makes doctrine is accustomed in certain things to suspend his judgment, either through want or strength of mind, or want of clearness in the things, or equal force in the reasons.

Clement of Alexandria

¶ DIALECTIC

SVF II, 122

Posidonius defines dialectic as the knowledge dealing with truth, falsehood, and that which is neither true nor false, whereas Chrysippus takes its subject to be signs and things signified.

Diogenes Laertius

SVF II, 127

As for disputing on both sides, he, Chrysippus, says that he does not universally reject it, but it ought to be used with caution, as is done in the courts—not with a design really to disprove, but to dissolve their probability. "For to those," he says, "who attempt suspension of judgment concerning all things, it is convenient to do this, and it is an aid to what they desire; but as for those who would work and establish in us a certain knowledge according to which we shall conformably live, they ought, on the contrary, to state the first principles and to direct their new students, who are entered, from the beginning to the end; and, where there is occasion to mention contrary discourses, to dissolve their probability, as is done in the courts."

Plutarch

SVF II, 129

And having said in his book, *Concerning the Use of Reason,* that we ought no more to use the force of reason than of arms . . . Chrysippus adds this: "For it is to be employed for the finding out of truths and for the connection of them, and not for the contrary—though many men do it." By "many men" perhaps he means those who suspend judgment.

Plutarch

SVF II, 130a

The study of dialectic is absolutely necessary and is itself a virtue, embracing other particular virtues under it. . . . Without the study of dialectic the Wise Man cannot guard himself in argument so as never to waver, for it enables him to distinguish between truth and falsehood. . . .

Diogenes Laertius

SVF II, 130b

Such then is the logic of the Stoics, by which they seek to establish their point that the Wise Man is the only dialectician. For all things, they say, are discerned through logical study, including whatever falls within the province of physics, and again whatever belongs to that of ethics.

Diogenes Laertius

SVF II, 132

Some, particularly the Stoics, think that truth differs from the true in three ways, in being, composition, and power; in being, insofar as truth is corporeal, whereas the true is incorporeal. And quite plausibly so, they say, for the true is a proposition and a proposition is an intention of meaning and meaning is incorporeal. On the other hand, truth is corporeal insofar as it is regarded as knowledge declaratory of all true things, and all knowledge is a state or condition of the ruling part of the soul, just as the fist is considered as a state of the hand. The ruling part of the soul is corporeal, according to them, and thus truth is generically corporeal. . . . And truth differs from the true in composition insofar as the true is conceived as something uniform and simple in its nature . . . whereas truth, being composed of knowledge, is on the contrary conceived as a system and collection of many parts. The two differ also in power, since the true is not altogether dependent on knowledge (for even the fool, and the child, and the insane person sometimes say something true, but do not have knowledge of the true) but truth is considered to require knowledge. . . . Hence, the Wise Man, i.e., he who has the knowledge of the true, sometimes says what is false but never speaks falsely because his mind does not assent to the false. . . . Speaking that which is false differs greatly from lying in that the former proceeds from a good intention but lying from bad faith.

Sextus Empiricus

SVF II, 141

The Stoics claim that sound is corporeal and they say it is air vibrating.

Gellius

SVF II, 144a

Sound, speech, and voice are not the same thing. Sound is the result of the sound organs; and speech of the speech organs, which are first the tongue, and then the nose, the lips, and the teeth. But the sound organs are the larynx and the muscles which move it, and the sinews which bring the power to them from the brain. But it was not everything, properly perceptible by hearing, which the ancients called voice, nor was it that only which issues from the mouth, a description which includes crying, whistling, wailing, coughing, and all such thing; but it was only the sound produced by human beings by which communication with one another is possible that they called voice.

Galen

SVF II, 151

. . . For when Chrysippus writes about the inconsistency of speech,

he has as his object to show that like things are denoted by unlike
words and that unlike things are denoted by like words,—which is true.

Varro

SVF II, 152

Chrysippus says that every word is naturally ambiguous, since by the
same word two or more things can be meant. However, Diodorus, whose
surname was Cronos, says that no word is ambiguous, nor does anyone
speak or think ambiguously, nor ought anything seem to be said other
than what he who speaks thinks he is saying.

Gellius

¶ On Meaning

SVF I, 488

Cleanthes and Archedemus call predicates *meanings*.

Clement of Alexandria

SVF II, 166

There was also among the dogmatists another disagreement, for some
located truth and falsity in the thing signified, others in the sound, and
others in the process of thought. The Stoics accepted the first opinion,
asserting that there are three things joined together, the thing signified,
the sign, and the existing object. The sign is the sound, for example the
word "Dion." The thing signified is the matter itself which is indicated
by the sound and which we grasp as it coexists with our thought, but
which the barbarians, although they hear the sound, do not understand.
And the existing object is the external thing, as Dion himself. Of these
three, two are corporeal, the sound and the existing object, and one is
incorporeal, the matter signified and the *meaning*, and it is this that is
true or false. Not every meaning, however, is true or false, for some are
incomplete and others are complete. An illustration of the complete is
what they call a proposition which indeed they define in the statement:
a proposition is that which is either true or false.

Sextus Empiricus

SVF II, 167

Every meaning must be spoken, since this is how it got its class name.[6]
. . . For to speak, as the Stoics themselves say, is to utter the sound
significant of the thing thought.

Sextus Empiricus

---

6. I.e., λεκτόν from λέγεσφαι.

SVF II, 168

By these arguments Aristotle teaches what the things principally and immediately signified by sounds are, and these are thoughts. Through these as means we signify things; and it is not necessary to consider anything else as intermediate between the thought and the thing, as the Stoics do, who assume what they name to be the meaning.

Ammonius

SVF II, 170

Accordingly, the body is not taught, i.e., is not the content of teaching, especially in the Stoic theory. For the things taught are meanings, and meanings are incorporeal.

Sextus Empiricus

¶ INCOMPLETE MEANINGS

SVF II, 181

They say that meaning is that which is suggested in conformity with a rational presentation. And some meanings, say the Stoics, are complete, while others are incomplete. The latter are those whose utterance is unfinished, for example, "writes." For we ask in addition, who? The complete are those whose utterance is finished, as, "Socrates writes."

Diogenes Laertius

SVF II, 183

And so under the heading of incomplete meanings are placed all predicates. . . .

Diogenes Laertius

¶ COMPLETE MEANINGS AND PROPOSITIONS

SVF II, 186

There is a difference between a proposition, a question and an inquiry. . . . For a proposition is that which, when we set it forth in speech, becomes an assertion, and is either false or true; a question is a thing complete in itself like a proposition but demanding an answer, for example, "Is it day?" and this is so far neither true nor false. Thus "It is day" is a proposition; "Is it day?" is a question. An inquiry is something to which we cannot reply by signs, as you can nod "yes" to a question; but you must express the answer in words, "He lives in this or that place.". . .

Diogenes Laertius

SVF II, 194

When I wished to be introduced to the study of logic and instructed in it, it was necessary to take up and learn what the dialecticians call . . . "introductory exercises." Then because at first I had to learn about propositions . . . of necessity I returned to my Greek books. From these I obtained the following Stoic definition of proposition: a *meaning complete in itself and capable of being denied in and by itself.* . . . In general anything which is said in a full and perfect sentence, in such a way that it is necessarily either true or false, is called by the dialecticians [i.e., logicians] a proposition. . . .

Gellius

SVF II, 198

With respect to contradictories relating to the future, the Stoics think the same as they do in the other cases. For they regard future contradictory pairs and their parts just as the contradictories of the present and the past. For either the proposition "it will be" must be true or the proposition "it will not be," if it must be either true or false. And future events are determined in themselves. If there will be a naval battle tomorrow, it is true to say so; if there will not be a battle, it is false to say there will be. Either there will be or there will not be; therefore one part of the contradiction is either true or false.

Simplicius

SVF II, 201a

A probable proposition is that which leads to assent, e.g., "If anything gave birth to something, the former is the mother of the latter." But it is false, because the bird is not the mother of an egg. Again, some propositions are possible, other impossible; and some are necessary, others not necessary. A possible proposition is one capable of being true, if nothing external prevents it from being true, as "Diocles is alive." A proposition is impossible if it is not capable of being true, as "the earth flies." The necessary proposition is that one which is both true and is not capable of being false, or, if capable, is prevented from being false by external circumstances, as, "Virtue is beneficial." Not necessary is that which is true although it can be false even when no external circumstance interferes, as, "Dion is walking about." A plausible proposition is one which has more occasions of being true than false as, "I shall be alive tomorrow." And there are other varieties of propositions. . . .

Diogenes Laertius

SVF II, 202

How can the theory of possible propositions avoid being inconsistent with his theory of fate? For if a possible proposition is not defined as one which is or will be true, as Diodorus says, "but everything capable of coming to pass is possible even if it will not come to pass"—there will be many things possible which are not according to fate. Accordingly, either fate destroys the unconquered, invincible, victorious power of all things or, if fate is as Chrysippus thinks, what is capable of coming to pass will often turn out to be impossible.

Plutarch

Early Stoic Physics

BASIC PHYSICAL THEORY

¶ The Two Principles: Matter and Cause

SVF II, 300

(The Stoics) hold that there are two principles for the universe, the active and the passive. The passive is unqualified reality or matter; the active is the reason inherent in the matter or God. For God is eternal and, present throughout matter, is the artificer of each thing. . . .

Diogenes Laertius

SVF I, 85c

Zeno of Citium says the principles for the universe are God and matter. The former is the active, the latter the passive, and from their combination the four elements arise.

Achilles Tatius

SVF I, 86

Many, however, distinguish between matter and reality, as do Zeno and Chrysippus. Matter, they say, is that which underlies all those things which have qualities, but reality is the primary matter of all things, their most original basis, in its own nature without aspect or form. For example, copper, gold, iron, and other such things are the matter of whatever is made of them; but not their reality. But that which is the cause of the existence both of these things and others as well,—that, they say, is substance.

Chalcidius

SVF I, 87a

The primary matter of all things is reality, is all eternal, and neither increases nor decreases. Its parts, however, are not always arranged in the same way, but are separated and are again conjoined. Throughout, this matter is arranged by the universal reason, which some call fate, and which is similar to the seed in the womb.

Stobaeus

SVF II, 299

They say that the elements differ from the principles. For the latter are ungenerated and indestructible, while the elements are destroyed by the (final) conflagration. The principles are corporeal,[1] but formless as contrasted with the elements we perceive.

Diogenes Laertius

SVF II, 320

[The Stoics] maintain that real beings and the substance in them are bodies only, saying that matter is one, and is the substratum of the elements, and that it is substance; all other things are, as it were, modifications and even the elements are only matter in a certain state. . . . They even say that God himself is only a mode of this matter, and attribute to matter a body which they define as a body without qualities; they also give it magnitude.

Plotinus

SVF II, 332

The genus *that which exists* is general, and has no term superior to it. It is the first term in the classification of *things,* and all things are included under it.

Certain of the Stoics regard the primary genus as even beyond that which exists (mentioned above) . . . and call it the *something.* . . . They say that "in the order of nature some things exist and others do not. And even the things that do not exist are really part of the order of nature. They occur to the mind, as giants, centaurs, and all other figments of unsound reasoning which have begun to take a definite shape, although they have no corporeal consistency."

Seneca

SVF II, 329

The term *something* is a more general one than that of *reality,* for

---

1. The text Arnim uses reads 'αδωμάτους instead of σώματα as in BPF. The preceding context [SVF II, 300] shows that the principles are matter and God.

reality can be used only of corporeal entities, while the genus *something* includes incorporeals. . . .

Alexander Aphrodisias

SVF II, 334

For Manna means *something,* and this is the most generic of all terms.[2]

Philo

SVF II, 330

Moreover, if *something* is taught it will be taught by means either of the genus of *no-things* or the genus of *some-things;* but it is not possible for it to be taught by means of the *no-things,* for these have no reality for the mind according to the Stoics.

Sextus Empiricus

SVF II, 331

. . . The Stoic philosophers supposed time to be incorporeal; for they maintain that of the highest universal, the *some-things,* some are corporeal, others incorporeal, and they enumerate four kinds of incorporeals: meaning, void, place, and time. And from this it is evident that, in addition to supposing time to be incorporeal, they also regard it as a thing conceived as self-existent.

Sextus Empiricus

¶ CAUSES

SVF I, 89

Zeno said that a cause is *that through which;* but that of which it is the cause is an accident. The cause is corporeal, that of which it is the cause is a predicate; and it is impossible for the cause to be present and that of which it is the cause not to occur. The significance of this statement is as follows: A cause is that through which anything occurs, for example through wisdom comes wise deliberation, and by the soul there is life, and through temperance there comes temperate living. For when there is temperance with respect to anything, it is impossible not

2. The τι of the Stoics (i.e., "quiddity") replaces, as the most generic and all-embracing of terms,the Platonic ἕν and the Aristotelian ὄν. Cf. SVF II, 333 (*Anonymi Proleg.* in Aristot. Categ. p. 34b Brandis (Schol. in Aristot.) :

τρία δὲ τὰ καθολικώτατα ὁμώνυμα, ἕν, ὄν, τί. κατὰ πάντων γὰρ τῶν ὄντων φέρεται ταῦτα, κατὰ μὲν Πλάτωνα τὸ ἕν, κατ' Ἀριστοτέλη τὸν ὄν, κατὰ δὲ τοὺς Στωικοὺς τὸ τί.

to have temperate actions, or when there is a soul, not to have life, or wisdom, and not wise results.

Stobaeus

SVF II, 341

The Stoics said that every cause is a corporeal and is a cause to a corporeal of something incorporeal; for example, the scalpel is a corporeal and to the flesh (which is also corporeal) it is the cause of the incorporeal predicate of being cut; and again, fire is a corporeal and to wood (which is also corporeal) it is the cause of the incorporeal predicate of being burned.

Sextus Empiricus

SVF II, 346a

The Stoics believe in only one cause, i.e., the Maker. . . . This collection of causes, as defined by Aristotle and by Plato, comprehends either too much or too little. For if they regard as causes of any object that is to be made everything without which the object cannot be made, they have named too few. Time must be included among the causes, for nothing can be made without time. Time must also include place, for if there be no place where a thing can be made, it will not be made. And motion too, for nothing is either made or destroyed without motion. There is also no art without motion, no change of any kind. Now, however, we are searching for the first, the general cause; this must be simple inasmuch as matter, too, is simple. Do we ask what cause is? It is surely Creative Reason, i.e., God.[3]

Seneca

¶ CORPOREALS AND INCORPOREALS

SVF I, 90

(Zeno) also differed from the same thinkers (i.e., the Peripatetics and Academicians), holding that an incorporeal was incapable of any activity, whereas anything capable of acting or being acted upon in any way could not be incorporeal.

Cicero

---

3. The Stoic view, besides positing the four categories of (1) *substance,* (2) *essential quality,* (3) *accidental quality,* (4) *relation,* regarded material things as the only entities which possessed reality. The Stoics thus differ from Aristotle and Plato in maintaining that nothing is real except matter; besides, they relate everything to one ultimate cause, the acting force or efficient cause, i.e., Creative reason [λόγος σπερματικός], the creative force in nature.

SVF II, 358

A corporeal entity is by nature solid, seeing that it has three dimensions. And what other notion [can there be] of a solid object and a corporeal than that which extends in each direction?

Philo

SVF II, 359

[The Stoics maintain] that that alone exists which can be touched and handled, defining corporeality and reality as identical. . . .

Clement of Alexandria

SVF II, 360

Those Stoics, who are of the school of Zeno, maintain that the *Ideas* are nothing but mere notions [i.e., they are unreal].

Aetius

¶ THE FOUR CATEGORIES AND THE QUALITIES

SVF II, 369

The Stoics reduce [the ten categories of Aristotle, *Cat.* 1b 25], to four, and say that these are: (1) substances (or substrata) [ὑποκείμενα], (2) qualities [ποιά], (3) accidental states [πῶς ἔχοντα], and (4) relative states [πρός τί πως ἔχοντα].[4]

Simplicius

SVF II, 377

The followers of the Stoics said that the qualities and [even] all accidents were corporeal.

Galen

¶ THE ELEMENTS

SVF II, 413a

Of the four elements, fire, air, water, earth (about which Chrysippus has written in his treatise *On Reality*), fire is the chief element; others take their origin in it, and return to it, (and fire appears at the beginning and at the end of [each] cycle). . . .

Stobaeus

---

4. Cf. SVF II, 371 (Plotinus, *Enneads* VI, i, 25) for a similar listing.

SVF II, 413b

From these four elements all things are afterwards formed,—so say the Stoics, Zeno, Cleanthes, and Chrysippus, all of whom took this principle from Empedocles. . . .

Probus

SVF II, 418

And the Stoics say that of the elements, some are active and some passive; the active are air and fire, the passive are earth and water.

Nemesius

SVF II, 421

The Stoics are accustomed to trace all things back to an elemental force of a fiery nature, herein following Heraclitus . . . ; their doctrine is that all force is of the nature of fire, and that, because of this, animate creatures perish when their heat fails; also in every domain of nature a thing is alive and vigorous if it is warm. . . [They say that] there is no animate being contained within the whole universe of nature except fire. . . .

Cicero

SVF II, 423

For some of them, as, for example, the Epicureans, believed that animate things could originate from inanimate things; others held that all animate or inanimate things spring from an animate or living principle, but that, nevertheless, all things, being material or corporeal, spring from a material principle. For the Stoics thought that fire, i.e., one of the four material elements of which this visible world is composed, was both animate and intelligent, the maker of the world and of all things contained in it, that it was in fact God.

Augustine

¶ Spirit, Tension, and Cohesion

SVF II, 449

Chrysippus again in his treatise *On Cohesions* says: "Cohesions are nothing else but (kinds of) air; for bodies are contained by these, and the cause that every one of the bodies contained by cohesion is such as it is, is the containing air, which they call in iron hardness, in stone solidity, in silver whiteness. . . . Yet they everywhere affirm that matter, being of its own nature idle and motionless, is subjected to qualities, and that the qualities being spirits and aerial tensions, give a form and figure to every part of matter to which they adhere."

Plutarch

SVF II, 451[5]

. . . To activate the body, there is an inward motion balanced with an outward motion (which accounts for the tension), thus giving rise to the equilibrium of anything.

Nemesius

SVF II, 458b

For some bodies are endowed with cohesion, others with nature (growth), others with soul, and some with rational soul; for example, stones and wood, which are torn from their kindred materials, He bound together with the most powerful bond of cohesion; and this cohesion is the inclination of the spirit to return to itself. For it begins at the middle and proceeds onwards towards the extremities, and then when it has touched the outermost boundary, it turns back again, until it has again arrived at the same place from which it originally started. This is the continued, unalterable [i.e., incorruptible] course of cohesion. . . . To plants He gave nature, mixing it out of many powers, i.e., the nutritive, the changing, and the power of growth.

And the Creator has made the soul to differ from nature in the following three ways: in sensation, in presentation, and in desire. For plants are destitute of desire and devoid of presentation, and without any participation in sensation. But every animal partakes of all these qualities. . . . Now sensation, . . . in some degree, is a kind of insertion, placing the things that are made apparent to it in the mind; for in the mind, since that is the greatest storehouse and receptacle for all things, everything is placed and treasured up which comes under the operation of the sense of seeing or hearing, or the other organs of sensation. And presentation is an impression in the soul; for of the things which each of the senses has brought in, like a ring or a seal, presentation imprints their own character. And the mind, being like wax, having received the impression, keeps it carefully in itself until forgetfulness, the enemy of memory, has smoothed off the edges of impression, or else has rendered it dim, or perhaps has completely effaced it.

And that which has been visible and has been impressed upon the

---

5. Chrysippus is responsible for the introduction of the notion of tensory motion.

soul at times affects the soul in a way consistent with itself, and at other times in a different way; and this passion to which it is subject is called natural impulse, which in a definition they say is the first motion of the soul. In such important points animals are superior to plants.

Let us now see how man is superior to the rest of the animals. Man has received this one, extraordinary gift, the power of thought, through which he is accustomed to comprehend the nature of all bodies and of all things at the same time; for, as in the body, sight is the leading faculty, and as in the universe the nature of light is pre-eminent, in like manner that part of us which is entitled to the highest rank is the mind. For the mind is the sight of the soul, shining brilliantly with its own rays, by which the great and dense darkness, which ignorance of things shed around, is dissipated.

Philo

¶ MIXTURE

SVF II, 479

According to Chrysippus, in the third book of his *Physics*, the Stoic explanation of the mixture of two substances is that they permeate each other through and through, and that the particles of the one do not merely surround those of the other or lie beside them. Thus, if a small drop of wine is thrown into the sea, it will be equally diffused over the whole sea for awhile, and then will be blended with it.

Diogenes Laertius

¶ INFINITE DIVISION OF BODIES

SVF II, 482

Substance [or matter] can also be acted upon, as Apollodorus says in his *Physics,* for if it were immutable, the things which are produced would never have been produced out of it. Hence the further doctrine that substance is divisible *ad infinitum.* Chrysippus says that the division is not *ad infinitum,* but is itself infinite; for there is nothing infinitely small to which the division can extend. But nevertheless, the division goes on without ceasing. Hence, again, the mixture of two substances is complete. . . .

Diogenes Laertius

¶ Motion

SVF II, 492

They say that motion is the transition of change from place to place, either of the whole body or of the parts of the whole body.

Sextus Empiricus

¶ Place, Void, Space, and Time

SVF II, 501

. . . Just as if there exists *that from which* a thing becomes, and *that by which* a thing becomes, and *that on account of which,* so too there will exist *that in which* a thing becomes. *That from which* a thing becomes, its *matter,* exists, and *that by which,* its cause, and *that on account of which,* its *end,* also exist; therefore, *that in which* a thing becomes, its *place,* exists also. . . . The ancients meant by "chaos" the place which serves to contain all things; for if this had not subsisted, neither earth nor water, nor the remaining elements, nor the universe as a whole, could have been constructed. And even if, in thought, we abolish all things, the place wherein all things were will not be abolished, but remains possessing its three dimensions, length, depth, width. It lacks resistance, however; for this is an attribute peculiar to body.

Sextus Empiricus

SVF II, 502

The Stoics say that there is no void in the world, nor are void and place corporeal.

Galen

SVF II, 505

And the Stoics assert that void is that which is capable of being occupied by an existent thing but is not so occupied. . . . Place is that which is occupied by an existent thing and made equal to that which occupies it. . . . And space, they say, is an interval partly occupied by body and partly unoccupied.

Sextus Empiricus

SVF I, 95c

Outside the world is diffused the infinite void, which is incorporeal. By incorporeal is meant that which, though capable of being occupied by body, is not so occupied. And within the world there is no void.

Diogenes Laertius

SVF II, 511

For time did not exist before there was a world, but began either simultaneously with the world or after it. For since time is the interval of the world's motion or movement, and since movement could not be prior to the object moving, but must of necessity arise either after it or simultaneously with it, it must follow that time also is either coeval with or later born than the world.

Philo

SVF II, 512

God is the creator of time also; for He is the father of its father; and the father of time is the world, which makes its own motion the origin of time.

Philo

SVF II, 514

Most of the Stoics assert that motion itself is the essence of time.

Aetius

SVF II, 518

. . . Chrysippus . . . says that "past and future time are nonexistent, but have subsisted [or will subsist]; only present time exists."

Plutarch

SVF II, 519

It is contrary to common sense that there should be a future time and a past time, but not present time; and that *recently* and *lately* subsist, but *now* is nothing at all. Yet this happens to the Stoics, who admit not the least time between, nor will they allow the present to be indivisible; but whatever anyone thinks to take and understand as present, one part of that, they say, is future, and the other part past.

Plutarch

THE WORLD

¶ THE UNIVERSE AND THE WHOLE (WORLD)

SVF II, 524a

Now the philosophers of the Stoic school suppose that the whole differs
from the universe; for they say that the whole is the world, whereas
the universe is the external void together with the world; and on this
account the whole is finite (for the world is finite), but the universe is
infinite (as is also the void outside the world).

Sextus Empiricus

SVF II, 526

The concept "world" is used by them in three senses: (1) of God himself, who out of the whole reality in a specific way has quality; he is
indestructible and ungenerated, being the creator of this orderly arrangement, who at stated periods of time absorbs into himself the whole
reality and again creates it from himself; (2) and they give the name
of "world" to the orderly arrangement of the heavenly bodies in itself
as such; and (3) in the third sense to that whole of which these two
are parts.

Diogenes Laertius

SVF II, 532

. . . The world is one and has been created; for if it came into being
and is one, it stands to reason that all of its completed separate parts
have the same elementary substances for their substratum, on the principle that the interdependence of the parts is a characteristic of bodies
which constitute a unity.

Philo

SVF II, 534

The world is not infinite but finite, as is evident from its being administered by nature. For there is no nature possible of the infinite,
since it is necessary for nature to hold within its own power that whose
nature it is. That the world has a nature which administers it is evident
first, from the arrangement of the parts of the world, then,. from the
arrangement of those things which are created, thirdly, from the
sympathy of the parts of the world towards each other. . . .

Cleomedes

SVF II, 547

The Stoics say that the world is formed in the shape of a sphere.

Aetius

SVF I, 99

. . . He [Zeno] is satisfied that the whole earth in itself is heavy but, on account of this position, he holds that because it has the middle place, and because bodies of this nature move towards the center, it remains in this place [i.e., where it had been fixed].

Stobaeus

SVF II, 558

The Stoics maintain that the parts of the world are arranged in the following order: the earth is in the middle, as the center; next comes the water, shaped like a sphere, all around it, and concentric with the earth so that the earth is *in* water; after the water comes a spherical layer of air.

Diogenes Laertius

¶ GENERATION, DESTRUCTION, AND
REGENERATION OF THE WORLD

SVF II, 576

And the Stoics . . . held that the world was created and is liable to destruction . . . and that whenever the world came to be, motion must, of necessity, have begun.

Simplicius

SVF II, 580

God, Mind, Fate, and Zeus are all one, and he is called by many other names. Existing in himself from the beginning, he turns all reality into water through air. And just as the seed is surrounded by the seminal fluid, so also he who is the seminal reason of the world remains within the liquid, and with ease fashions matter to his own purposes, with reference to the production of the following stages. Then he first produced the four elements, fire, water, air and earth. . . . The four elements together constitute unqualified reality, or matter. . . . Fire has the uppermost place, and is also called ether; and in it the sphere of the fixed stars is first created. Then comes the sphere of the planets, after that the air, then the water, and lowest of all the earth, which is at the center of all things.

Diogenes Laertius

SVF II, 581

The world comes into being when reality has first been converted from fire through air into an aquaeous solution and then the coarser part of this liquid has condensed as earth, while that whose particles are fine has been turned into air, and this process of rarefaction goes on increasing until it generates fire. And then, out of these elements, plants, living things, and all other natural things are formed by their mixture. . . .

Diogenes Laertius

SVF I, 98

Zeno said the fundamental substance of all existing things is fire, in this following Heraclitus, and the principles of fire were matter and God, here following Plato. But he asserted that they both were corporeal, an active and a passive, whereas Plato said that the primary, active cause was incorporeal. Next, the whole world, at certain fated periods, is dissolved by fire, and then formed again into a world. Now the primary fire is like a kind of seed, containing the reasons of all things and the causes of everything, past, present, and future. Now the union and sequence of these things is an inevitable and unavoidable fate, knowledge, truth, and law of existing things. And in this respect the events of the world are arranged very well, as in a well-governed city.

Eusebius

SVF II, 593

But the stars are of a fiery nature, and for this reason they are nourished by the vapors of the earth, the sea, and the waters, which are raised up by the sun out of the fields which it warms and out of the waters; and when nourished and renewed by these vapors, the stars and the whole ether shed them back again, and then once more draw them up from the same source,—with the loss of none of their matter or only of a very small part, which is consumed by the fire of the stars and the flame of the ether. As a result of which, so our school believe, . . . there will ultimately occur a conflagration of the whole world, because when the moisture has been used up, neither can the earth be nourished nor will the air continue to flow, being unable to rise upward after it has absorbed all the water. Thus, nothing will remain but fire, by which—as a living being and as a god—once again a new world may be created and the ordered universe be restored as before.

Cicero

SVF I, 107

Zeno, Cleanthes, and Chrysippus used to say that reality changes into fire like a seed, and again out of this the same kind of arrangement, such as formerly existed, is achieved.

Stobaeus

SVF I, 109a

Zeno declares that through the conflagration the same things reappear in the same relation. . . .

Tatianus

SVF II, 598

But [the Stoics, Chrysippus and Zeno] admit that there will be a conflagration and purification of this world, the whole of it and its parts as well; and they say its parts will be renewed; and its destruction and the creation of another out of it they call purification.

Hippolytus

SVF II, 606

When, as the Stoics say, the world shall be set on fire, there will then be no evil left, but all will, at that time, become prudent and wise.

Plutarch

SVF II, 607

When animals die, as the Stoics say will occur during the time of the conflagration, there will be no perception if there is no animal, but the object of perception will remain, for there will be fire.

Porphyry

SVF II, 620

Democritus and Epicurus and the greatest number of the Stoic philosophers affirm both the creation and the destructibility of the world, though not all in the same way; for some give a sketch of many worlds, etc. . . . But the Stoics speak of one world only, and assert that God is the cause of its creation, but that the cause of its destruction is no longer God, but [lies in] the power of the unceasingly raging fire which pervades all existing things, dissolving, in the long periods of time, everything into itself; while from it again a regeneration of the world takes place through the providence of the creator. And according to these men, there may be one world spoken of as eternal and another

as destructible, the destructible in reference to the world's present arrangement, yet eternal is the world which in reference to the conflagration is rendered immortal by the regenerations and periodic revolutions
which never cease.

                                                                    Philo

¶ THE WORLD IS A RATIONAL ANIMAL

SVF I, 110

And Plato sets forth virtually the same argument as Zeno. For Zeno
says that the universe is the most beautiful product executed according to nature, and in all probability a living being, endowed with soul,
both intelligent and rational.

                                                        Sextus Empiricus

SVF I, 112

Furthermore, [Zeno] drew a conclusion by analogy, as he often did, in
this manner: "If flutes playing musical tones grew on an olive tree,
would you doubt that some knowledge of flute-playing existed in the
olive tree? If plane trees bore lyres resounding melodiously, you would
also naturally think that music existed in the plane trees. Why, therefore, is the world not considered animate and intelligent, when it produces from itself animate and intelligent beings?"

                                                                   Cicero

SVF I, 114b

Certainly that which contains rational natures is itself completely rational. For it is not possible for the whole to be inferior to the parts.
                                                        Sextus Empiricus

SVF II, 637

And why should you not believe that something of divinity exists in
one who is a part of God? The whole universe which contains us is one,
and is God; we are His associates and His members.

                                                                  Seneca

SVF II, 641

Chrysippus therefore well shows, by the aid of illustrations, that in the
perfected and mature specimen of its kind everything is better [than in
the imperfect and immature], a horse as compared to a foal, a dog vis-
à-vis a puppy, a man as compared to a boy. And similarly, a perfected

and complete being is bound to possess that which is the best thing in all the world. But no being is more perfect than the world, and nothing is better than virtue. Therefore, virtue is an essential attribute of the world. Nor is man's nature more perfect, yet virtue may be realized in man; how much more readily, then, in the world! Therefore, the world possesses virtue; it is all-knowing and consequently God.

Cicero

SVF II, 645

Moreover, they affirm the world to be a city, and the stars like to citizens. . . .

Plutarch

THE HEAVENLY BODIES

¶ THE HEAVENS AND EARTH

SVF I, 115

Zeno of Citium spoke in this fashion: "Heaven is the farthest extremity of the ether; out of which and in which all things are made manifest. For it contains everything except itself; for nothing contains itself but only something else."

Achilles Tatius

SVF II, 650

. . . They hold that the stars are spherical in shape and that the earth is so also, and is at rest [i.e., without motion]; the moon does not shine by its own light, but by the borrowed light of the sun when it shines upon the moon. . . .

Diogenes Laertius

MAN AND ANIMALS

¶ ANIMAL LIFE

SVF II, 714

Of objects that are moved, some are moved by natural impulse and presentation, e.g., animals; and some by transposition, e.g., inanimate objects. And of the latter, plants, they say, are moved by transposition towards growth, if one concedes to them that plants are inanimate objects. Stones, then, have cohesion; plants have nature; and the irrational animals possess natural impulse and presentation, and also the two characteristics already specified. But the reasoning faculty, being peculiar to the human soul, ought not to impel in the same way as is the case with the irrational animals, but ought to discriminate among presentations and not to be carried away by them.

Clement of Alexandria

SVF II, 717

. . . And the Stoics believed that the seminal reasons . . . [which provide the impetus for all animate motions . . .] were imperishable.

Proclus

SVF II, 719

For the Reason of Ultimate Reality, which is the bond of everything, . . . holds all things together, and binds all the parts, and prevents them from being loosened or separated. And the individual soul, so far as it has received power, does not permit any of the parts of the body to be separated or cut off contrary to their nature; but as far as depends upon itself, it preserves everything entire, and conducts the separate parts to a harmony and indissoluble union with one another. . . .

Philo

SVF II, 724

. . . Chrysippus says: "The beasts, meeting the needs of their young, are adapted to them, with the exception of fish, whose young are nourished by themselves." . . . For adaptation seems to be the sensation and perception of that which is proper [to anything].

Plutarch

SVF II, 725

. . . But now it is clear from the determinate inclination of the nature of each animal towards certain kinds of protection, that they possess neither wisdom nor reason, but a natural, constitutional tendency, implanted by reason, towards such things in order to ensure the preservation of the animal.

Origen

¶ THE NATURE OF MAN

SVF I, 124

Zeno of Citium, the founder of the Stoic School, believed that the origin for mankind was established out of a new world, the first men having been generated from the soil, by the aid of the divine fire, that is, the providence of God.

Censorinus

SVF II, 738

For when the nature of man is examined, the theory is usually advanced . . . that through constant changes and cycles in the heavens, a time came which was suitable for sowing the seed of the human race. And when this seed was scattered and sown over the earth, it was granted the divine gift of the soul.

Cicero

SVF I, 158

. . . The Stoics hold that God pervades every substance, and in some part of the world, he is mind, in another, soul or nature, or cohesion.

Themistius

THE NATURE OF THE SOUL

¶ THE SOUL

SVF I, 134a

For Zeno asserted that fire was the nature itself, which for every being produced senses and mind.

Cicero

SVF II, 773a

The theory of the soul is much disputed by nearly all the ancients. For Democritus, and Epicurus, and the whole school of Stoic philosophers assert that the soul is a body. But even these who assert that the soul is a body disagree as to what it really is; for the Stoics say it is a breath hot and fiery.

Nemesius

SVF II, 774

They believe that nature is a fire endowed with skill, proceeding to generate things, and is a fire-like and artistic spirit. And the soul is a perceptive nature, the spirit which is born in us. Therefore, it is a body and endures after death, although it is destructible. But the soul of the whole world is indestructible, of which the souls in living beings are parts.

Diogenes Laertius

¶ The Soul Is Corporeal

SVF I, 136

Some say that the substance of the soul is incorporeal, as Plato said, and others, Zeno and his followers, maintained that it moves bodies. For these people supposed that it is the same thing as the spirit or breath.

Galen

¶ The Mortality of the Soul

SVF II, 809

They say that the soul can be generated and destroyed. It will not be destroyed immediately upon leaving the body, but remains by itself for some time. The souls of the virtuous continue until the dissolution of all things into fire, while the souls of fools endure for an undetermined time. . . .

Arius Didymus

¶ Principal Part of the Soul

SVF II, 836a

The Stoics say that the highest part of the soul is the ruling part, which produces presentation, assent, sensation, and desire; and they call it rational. Aside from the ruling part, there are seven parts which are born of the soul and extend through the body. . . . Five of the seven parts of the soul are the senses: sight, smell, hearing, taste, and touch. Of these, sight is a spirit extending from the ruling part to the eyes [and similarly in the other four cases] . . . Of the remaining

[two], one is the seminal principle, which also is itself a spirit extending from the ruling part to the generative organs; and the other, called by Zeno "vocality," which they also call voice, is a spirit extending from the ruling part to the pharynx, tongue, and the appropriate organs. The ruling part itself, like the sun in the cosmos, dwells in our sphere-shaped head.

Aetius

SVF II, 837

The chief part of the soul is the ruling part, in which presentation and desire arise, and whence speech is sent forth. Its seat is in the heart.

Diogenes Laertius

SVF II, 842

. . . It is acknowledged that the ruling principle resides in one or another of these [i.e., either in the brain or in the heart].[6]

Philo

SVF II, 845

The soul, in my opinion, is endowed with sense. Nothing, therefore, pertaining to the soul, is unconnected with sensation, nothing pertaining to sensation is unconnected with the soul. . . . Now, since it is the soul that imparts the faculty of perception to all things that have sensation, and since it is itself that perceives the senses, not to say properties of them all, how is it likely that it did not itself receive a sense of itself from the beginning? Whence is it to know what is necessary for itself under given circumstances, from the very necessity of natural causes, if it does not know its own property, and what is necessary for it? This we can recognize, indeed, in every soul; I mean, it has a knowledge of itself, without which knowledge of itself no soul could possibly have exercised its own functions. I suppose, too, that it is especially suitable that man, the only rational animal, should have been furnished with such a soul as would make him the rational animal, itself being preeminently rational. Now, how can that soul which makes man a rational animal be itself rational if it be itself ignorant of its rationality, being ignorant of its own very self?

Tertullian

---

6. There seems not to have been any general agreement among the Stoics as to the *place* of the ruling principle, although, for Chrysippus, its seat was thought to be the heart. Both Galen and Philo report a difference of opinion on this subject.

¶ SENSATION AND THE SENSES

SVF II, 850

The Stoics define sensation in the following way: Sensation is the perception or comprehension of an object by means of a sensory organ. There are several ways of expressing what sensation is. It is either a cohesion, a power, an operation, or a presentation which comprehends by means of a sensory organ, according to the ruling principle itself. The sensory organs are intelligent spirits, which from the ruling part extend to all the parts of the body.

Aetius

SVF II, 851

According to the Stoics, the senses have bodies for objects.

Aetius

SVF II, 852

The Stoics name as the general sense that of touch. . . .

Aetius

SVF II, 853

They say that there are five senses, properly so called: seeing, hearing, smelling, tasting, and touching.

Aetius

SVF II, 858

When a man hurts his finger, the pain is in the finger itself, but the sensation of pain is produced . . . in the ruling principle. While the spirit of the part which hurts is different, the principle "senses" it, and the entire soul is affected in the same way. How, then, does this happen? By transmission, the Stoics will say; the part of the spirit which is in the finger is affected first, then it transmits the feeling to the part next to it, and so on, until it reaches the ruling principle.

Plotinus

SVF II, 862

. . . No one of good sense would say that eyes see, but mind sees by means of eyes, nor that ears hear, but the mind by their agency, nor that noses smell, but the ruling principle by using them.

Philo

SVF II, 871

The Stoics say that the causes of seeing are the emission of rays from the eyes to those objects which can be seen, and the simultaneous expansion of the air.

Gellius

SVF II, 872

We are hearing when the air between the sonant body and the organ of hearing suffers concussion, a kind of vibration which spreads spherically and then forms waves and then strikes upon the ears, just as the water in a reservoir forms wavy circles when a stone is thrown in to it.

Diogenes Laertius

FATE, DESTINY, AND PROVIDENCE

¶ DEFINITIONS OF FATE

SVF II, 916a

And Chrysippus the Stoic says that that which is compelled by necessity does not differ from that which is fated, for fate is an ordered, continuous, eternal motion.

Theodoretus

SVF II, 921

Now by fate I mean . . . an order and series of causes wherein cause is connected to cause and each cause of itself produces an effect. That is an immortal truth having its source in all eternity. Therefore, nothing has happened which was not going to happen, and, likewise, nothing is going to happen of which nature does not contain the efficient causes. Consequently, we know that fate is that which is called, not superstitiously, but scientifically [*physice*], "the eternal cause of things, the 'wherefore' of things past, of things present, and of things to come."

Cicero

SVF II, 937c

Nothing . . . either rests or is moved otherwise than according to the reason of Zeus, which is the same thing as fate.

Plutarch

SVF I, 162a

Zeno believes that the law of nature is divine, and that its function is to command what is right and to forbid the opposite.

Cicero

SVF I, 162b

Zeno [calls God] the divine and natural law.

Lactantius

SVF II, 944

Since all things happen by fate, if there were a man whose mind could discern the inner connections of all causes, then surely he would never be mistaken in any prediction he might make. For he who knows the causes of future events necessarily knows what every future event will be. But since no one except God is capable of this, it is left to man to predict the future by means of certain signs which indicate what will follow them. Things which are to be do not suddenly spring into existence, but the evolution of time is like the unwinding of a cable; it creates nothing new but only unfolds each event in its order.

Cicero

¶ AN INFINITE SERIES OF CAUSES

SVF II, 946

Some, when they come to the principle of the universe, deduce all things from it and say that it pervades everything as a cause, not only as the moving causes but as the producing cause of each thing; and this they call the highest cause and fate. It produces the universe, not only all the other things that come into being, but even our thoughts proceed from its motions, just as in an animal each part has a movement which comes not from itself, but from the ruling part of the soul which is in it. And others . . . hold to a mutual interconnection of causes in a descending series, and assert that the consequents always follow the antecedents, that the consequents lead back to those by which they came into being, and that the later are subject to the earlier. Anyone who makes these assertions is obviously introducing fate in a different manner. These people are correctly subdivided into two groups: some make everything depend on one principle, and others do not.

Plotinus

SVF II, 949

For how is it not absurd to say that causes regress to infinity and that there is neither a first nor a last in the series and connection of causes?

. . . According to this argument, even "scientific knowledge" would be impossible, if indeed scientific knowledge[7] is principally the "knowledge" of first causes, and for them there is no first among causes. Not every violation of order is destructive of the frame of reference in which it appears. . . . And if such a thing occurred in the world, that would not absolutely ruin the well-being of the world, any more than some chance recklessness of slaves ruins the well-being of the household and of the master.

Alexander Aphrodisias

SVF II, 951

But inasmuch as there are differences in the natures of men, such that some like sweet things and others slightly bitter; some are licentious . . . while others shrink in horror from such vices as that, . . . since there-fore Chrysippus says there are such differences in human nature, what wonder is it that these dissimilarities are the results of different causes? In thus arguing he fails to see the point at issue, nor in what a cause consists. For it does not follow that if different people have different inclinations on account of natural, antecedent causes, as a consequence, therefore, there are also natural and antecedent causes of our wills and desires. For if that were the case, nothing would be in our power at all. Now indeed we admit that it is not in our power to be quick-witted or stupid, strong or weak. But he who thinks it follows from this that our choice between sitting and walking is not voluntary, does not see what follows what [and fails to understand the true sequence of cause and effect]. For granted clever people and slow people are born like that, owing to antecedent causes, and that the same is true of the strong and the weak, nevertheless it does not follow that their sitting, walking, or doing anything is defined and constituted by principle causes.

Cicero

¶ EVERY PROPOSITION IS EITHER TRUE OR FALSE

SVF II, 952

Chrysippus argues as follows: "If there is a motion without a cause, not every proposition . . . is either true or false; for whatever does not have efficient causes is neither true nor false. However, every proposition is either true or false. Therefore, there is no motion without a cause. If this is so, everything that happens, happens by antecedent causes.

---

7. Scientific knowledge as $\dot{\epsilon}\pi\iota\sigma\tau\dot{\eta}\mu\eta$; "knowledge" as $\gamma\nu\hat{\omega}\sigma\iota\varsigma$.

And if this is so, then everything happens by fate. Therefore, whatever happens, happens by fate." . . . And thus, Chrysippus uses all his powers to prove that every proposition is either true or false. For, just as Epicurus fears that if he grants this, it will also have to be granted that whatever happens, happens by fate . . . so, similarly, Chrysippus fears that if he fails to maintain that every proposition is either true or false, he will not be able to hold that all things happen by fate and by the eternal causes of future events. . . .

Cicero

SVF II, 953

Yet it does not immediately follow from the view[8] that every proposition is either true or false that there are immutable causes, eternally existing, that prevent anything happening otherwise than it will happen. The causes which make true such propositions as "Cato will come into the Senate" are fortuitous causes; they are not inherent in the nature of things and the order of the universe. Nevertheless, "he will come," when true, is as immutable as "he has come" (though we need not on that account fear fate or necessity). And yet this will necessarily be admitted: "If the proposition 'Hortensius will come to the villa near Tusculum' is not true, it follows that it is false." Our opponents do not grant either; which is impossible.

Cicero

SVF II, 954

It is possible that human defects may be due to natural causes, but their eradication and complete removal . . . does not rest with natural causes, but with will, study, and training. And if the power and the existence of fate are proved from a theory of divination, all of these will be done away with. Indeed, if divination exists, what is the nature of the scientific observations . . . which are its source? For I do not believe that those who practice divination dispense entirely with the use of observation in predicting future events, any more than do the other scientific investigators in pursuing their own concerns. Now, here is an example of the observations of the astrologers: "If a man was born at the rising of the Dogstar, he will not die at sea." Watch out, here, Chrysippus, do not leave your position undefended; there is a great contest over it between you and the stalwart logician, Diodorus.[9]

---

8. Carneades is pictured here as arguing against the possible "fatalism" and determinism involved in the statement by Chrysippus.

9. Diodorus, the famed logician, was head of the Megarian school. c. 300 B.C.

For if the conditional proposition "If any man was born at the rising of the Dogstar, he will not die at sea" is true, then the following conditional is also true: "If Fabius was born at the rising of the Dogstar, Fabius will not die at sea." . . . And since that he was born at the rising of the Dogstar is predicated with certainty in the case of Fabius . . . therefore, the proposition "Fabius will die at sea" belongs to the class of impossibilities. Therefore, every false proposition about the future is an impossibility. But this is a view, Chrysippus, that you will not allow at all, and this is the very point about which you are especially at variance with Diodorus. He says that only what either is true or will be true is possible, and whatever will be, he goes on, must necessarily happen, and whatever will not be, cannot possibly happen. You say that things which will not be are still possible, as, for example, it is possible for this gem to be broken even if it never will be, and, again, that the reign of Cypselus at Corinth was not necessary although it had been announced by the oracle of Apollo a thousand years before. But if you are going to sanction divine prophecies of that sort, you will grant false statements as to future events as being in the class of impossibilities. . . . And also, if something is truly stated about the future, and it will be so, you would have to say that it is necessarily so. But the whole of this is the view of Diodorus, which is alien to your school. For if the following is a true conditional proposition, "If you were born at the rising of the Dogstar, you will not die at sea," and if the antecedent in the conditional, "You were born at the rising of the Dogstar," is necessary—for all things true in the past are necessary, as Chrysippus holds, in disagreement with his master Cleanthes, because they are immutable and because what is past cannot turn from true into false—then the consequent also becomes necessary. However, this does not seem to Chrysippus to hold good universally; but all the same, if there is a natural cause why Fabius should not die at sea, it is not possible for Fabius to die at sea.

At this point Chrysippus becomes discomforted and suggests hopefully that the Chaldeans and the rest of the diviners are mistaken, and that they will not use conditional propositions in order to put out their observations in the form "If anyone was born at the rising of the Dogstar he will not die at sea," but rather they will say "It is not the case both that someone was born at the rising of the Dogstar and that that person will die at sea." And how fantastic this is! To avoid falling into the hands of Diodorus, he tries to teach the Chaldeans the proper form in which to set out their observations! For I ask you, if the Chaldeans agree to this procedure of setting forth negations of an infinite number of conjunctions rather than an infinite number of conditionals, why should it not be possible for doctors, geometricians, and other professions to do likewise? . . . What is there that cannot be transferred in that sort of way from the form of a conditional to that of a negated conjunction? And in fact we can express the same thing in other ways. . . . There are many ways of stating a proposition, and none is more twisted around than this one, which Chrysippus hopes that the Chaldeans will accommodate the Stoics by accepting.

. . . For it is not necessary to fear that, if every proposition is either true or false, that all things must necessarily happen through fate. The truth of such a proposition as "Carneades will go down to the Academy" is not due to an eternal stream of natural and necessary causes, and yet nevertheless it is not uncaused, but there is a difference between causes accidentally antecedent and causes intrinsically containing a natural efficiency. . . . And so, those who say that things which are going to be are immutable and that a true future event cannot be changed into a false one, i.e., Diodorus, are not asserting the necessity of fate but explaining the meaning of terms; whereas those who bring in an infinite series of causes, i.e., Chrysippus, rob the human mind of free will and chain it to the necessity of fate.

Cicero

¶ The Confatal (The Lazy Argument)

SVF II, 956

[Chrysippus is being criticized for "lazy reasoning."] If all things are determined, why go to a doctor for your health? If everything is determined by fate, then nothing is possible, and so on.

This argument is criticized by Chrysippus. For some things, he says, are simple, and some are complex. A simple event is: "Socrates will die on that day." Here, whether he does anything or not, the day of his death has been determined. But if it is fated that "Oedipus shall be born to Laius," it will not be possible to add "whether Laius has been with a woman or not"; for this is a complex fact and *confatal*. He calls it this because he thinks it is fated both that Laius will be with his wife and that thus Oedipus will be begotten. Likewise, if it should be said, "Milo will compete in the Olympic games," and someone adds, "Therefore, he will compete whether he has an opponent or not," he would be wrong; for the notion "will compete" is complex because there can be no competition without an opponent. All such captious arguments can be refuted in the same way. "Whether you call in a physician or not, you will be healed" is captious; for it is as much fated that you shall call in a physician as that you shall recover. These connected events, as I have said, are termed by Chrysippus *confatal*.

Cicero

¶ FATE AND POSSIBILITY

SVF II, 959

To say that fate does not rule out the possible and feasible in everything that happens because what nothing prevents from happening is possible even if it does not happen; and to say "effects contrary to things which occur by fate are not prevented from happening, therefore even things which do not happen are none the less possible"; and that our ignorance of what prevents them (although there are such obstacles) supplies a proof of the fact that they are not prevented from happening; for whatever is a cause of their contraries' happening according to fate, is also a cause of their not happening, if indeed, as they say, contrary effects are impossible under identical conditions, but because it is not known to us what they are, therefore they say their occurrence is not prevented. . . .

Alexander Aphrodisias

SVF II, 960

. . . Thus [they preserve] the nature of possibility, as we have pointed out, and on this account they say that not even things which happen by fate, although their occurrence is inviolate, are from necessity, because it is possible for their contrary event to occur, the possibility being thus as stated before.

Alexander Aphrodisias

SVF II, 961

Similarly, one may also say the proposition "there will be a naval battle tomorrow" can be true, but not also necessary. For the necessary is always true, but this will no longer remain true after the battle occurs. But if this is not necessary, neither is the thing signified by the proposition—there will be a battle—of necessity. But if it is to be, though not of necessity (for that there will be a battle is true but not necessary), it is obviously feasible. And if feasible, the feasible is not ruled out by the fact that everything happens according to fate.

Alexander Aphrodisias

SVF II, 1000

Although it is the case that all things are, by fate, forced and connected with a certain necessary and principal reason, yet the dispositions themselves of our minds are, in like manner, liable to punishment by fate, since their proper nature is itself a quality. For if they are made, through nature, originally advantageous and useful, they transmit, in a more uninterrupted and manageable way, any and every force which assails [i.e., by fate] from without. But if, in truth, they are crude, unskilled and rough, and are not strengthened by any means of good arts—even if they should be urged on by little or no impression of the fated misfortune—yet they fall into continual crimes and into errors because of their perverseness and voluntary impulse. This very thing, since it is made in accordance with that reason, this natural and necessary consequence of things produces what is called fate. For it is, by this very origin, as it were, fated and logically consequent, that evil dispositions are not free from sins and errors.

Gellius

¶ FATE AND FREE WILL

SVF II, 974

It seems to me that the ancient philosophers were of two opinions, one group holding that fate so controls everything that it exerts the force of necessity, . . . the other group holding that the voluntary motions of the soul occur without any influence of fate. Chrysippus, however, wished to hold a middle course like an honorary arbiter, but he rather attaches himself to those who believed that the motions of the soul are free from necessity. But by the expressions he uses, he falls back into the same difficulties so that unwillingly he affirms the necessity of fate. Let us see, therefore, how this affects assent. Those ancient philosophers, for whom everything occurs by fate, say that assent is produced by force and necessity. The others, however, who disagree, free assent from fate and assert that if fate rules assent, necessity cannot br avoided. . . . But Chrysippus, since he both rejects necessity and doe: not wish anything to happen without preceding causes, distinguishes two kinds of causes, so that he may escape necessity and retain fate. "For," he says, "perfect and principal causes are one thing, auxiliary and proximate causes are another. For which reason, when we say everything happens by fate and antecedent causes, we do not mean perfect and principal causes, but auxiliary and proximate." And so, the position I argued above, he opposes as follows: "If everything happens by fate, of course it follows that everything happens by preceding causes, but they are not principal and perfect; they are auxiliary and proximate. And if these are not in our power, it does not follow that our appetites are not in our power. But this would follow if we should say everything happens by perfect and principal causes, so that when these causes are not in our power, our appetites are not in our power. For which reason those who so introduce fate as to join necessity with it, must accept that conclusion; but those who do not say that antecedent causes must be perfect and principal escape that conclusion." For as to saying that assent occurs by preceding causes, he thinks it easily explained. For although assent cannot occur without a sense stimulus, yet, since sensation has a proximate and not a principle cause, it has the explanation, as Chrysippus desired, which we gave above; not that something can happen without any external force—for assent requires sense stimulation—but it comes back to his illustration of the cylinder and the top, which cannot begin to move unless an impulse be given them. But when that happens, the top spins and the cylinder revolves according to their own natures. "As therefore," he says, "he who pushes the cylinder gives it a principle of motion, but does not give it a motion of revolution, so an object strikes our sense and as it were stamps its image in the soul, but the assent is in our power, which, as has been said in the case of the cylinder, while put in motion from without, moves for the rest by its own force and nature. But if anything happened without an antecedent cause, it would be false to say that everything happens by fate; but if it is likely that for everything which happens a cause precedes, what reason can be given why we should not admit that everything occurs by fate? Provided it is understood what is the distinction and dissimilarity between causes." . . . For Chrysippus, while admitting that the proximate and adjacent cause of assent is found in sensation, does not concede it to be the necessary cause of giving assent; with the result that if everything occurs by fate, everything occurs by antecedent and necessary causes.

Cicero

SVF II, 975

These men [Chrysippus and Zeno] maintain the universal rule of fate by using the following illustration. Suppose a dog to be tied to a wagon. If he wishes to follow, the wagon pulls him and he follows, so that his own power and necessity unite. But if he does not wish to follow, he will be compelled to anyhow. The same is the case with mankind also. Even if they do not wish to follow, they will be absolutely forced to enter into the fated event.

Hippolytus

SVF II, 993

If, on the one hand, presentations do not arise by fate, [how can fate be the cause] of assent? If, on the other hand, [fate] produces presentations which lead to assent, and assent is said to occur by fate, does not fate oppose itself by producing frequently and in important matters presentations which divert the mind in contrary directions? They say men make mistakes by choosing one alternative and not suspending judgment. [For example] if men yield to what is obscure, they stumble; if to what is false, they are deceived; and if, as usual, to non-comprehensive presentations they are subject to mere opinion. And yet one of the three following propositions must be true: either not every presentation is the work of fate, or every reception of a presentation and every assent is correct, or else fate itself is not blameless. For I do not know how fate can be without reproach when it produces presentations such that, not the resisting or the opposing of them, but the following and yielding to them is blameworthy.

Plutarch

Early Stoic Ethics

¶ THE CHIEF END

SVF I, 179a (I, 552)

This is why Zeno was the first, in his treatise *On the Nature of Man*, to define the end as "life in agreement with nature," which is the same as a virtuous life, virtue being the goal towards which nature guides us. So too Cleanthes in his treatise *On Pleasure.* . . .

Diogenes Laertius

SVF I, 180 (I, 552)

Zeno the Stoic thinks the end to be living according to virtue; and Cleanthes, living agreeably to nature in the right exercise of reason, which he held to consist of the selection of things in accordance with nature.

Clement of Alexandria

SVF I, 181

Zeno, however, who was the originator and first head of the Stoics, set forth that the end of goods is the morally honorable life, and that this is derived from the recommendation of nature.

Cicero

SVF I, 189

So Zeno was mistaken in saying that nothing else but virtue or vice affected even in the smallest degree the attainment of the *summum bonum,* and although other things had no effect whatsoever upon happiness, yet they had some influence upon our desires. . . .

. . . Zeno on the contrary calls nothing good but that which has a peculiar charm of its own that makes it desirable, and no life happy but the life of virtue. . . .

. . . But what can be more inconsistent than their procedure, which is to ascertain the *summum bonum* first, and then to return to nature and demand from her the primary motive of conduct, i.e., of duty?

Cicero

SVF I, 555

By the nature with which our life ought to be in accord, Chrysippus understands both common nature and more particularly the nature of man, whereas Cleanthes takes the common nature alone as that which should be followed, without adding the nature of the individual.

Diogenes Laertius

SVF III, 4

Again, living virtuously is equivalent to living in accordance with experience of the actual course of nature, as Chrysippus says in the first book of his treatise *On Ends;* for our individual natures are parts of the nature of the whole universe. And this is why the end may be defined as life in accordance with nature, or, in other words, in accordance with our own human nature as well as that of the universe, a life in which we refrain from every action forbidden by the law common to all things, i.e., the right reason which pervades all things, and is identical with this Zeus, lord and ruler of all that is. And this very thing constitutes the virtue of the happy man and the smooth current of life, when all actions promote the harmony of the spirit dwelling in the individual man with the will of him who orders the universe.

Diogenes Laertius

SVF III, 12b

For Cleanthes was the first to succeed Zeno in his choice "according to nature" and thus teaching "the end is to live in agreement with nature.". . .

Stobaeus

SVF III, 13

Preceding thinkers, and among them most explicitly Polemo, had explained the *summum bonum* as being 'to live in accordance with nature.' This formula receives from the Stoics three interpretations. The first runs thus, 'to live in the light of a knowledge of the natural sequence of causation,' and they count this conception of the End to be identical with Zeno's, being an explanation of your expression 'to live in agreement with nature.' Their second interpretation is that it means the same as 'to live in the performance of all, or most, of one's inter-

mediate duties.' The Chief Good as thus expounded is not the same as
that of the preceding interpretation, for *that* is right action, and can
be achieved only by the Wise Man, but this belongs to duty merely
inchoate, as it were, and not perfect, which may sometimes be attained
by the foolish. Again, the third interpretation of the formula is 'to live
in the enjoyment of all, or of the greatest, of those things which are in
accordance with nature.' This does not depend solely on our own conduct, for it involves first, a mode of life enjoying virtue, and secondly
a supply of the things which are in accordance with nature but which
are not within our power. But the *summum bonum* as understood in
the third interpretation, and life passed on the basis of the *summum
bonum*, because it is inseparably conjoined to virtue, lie within the
reach of the Wise Man alone; and this is the account of the End of
Goods, as we read in the writings of the Stoics themselves, which was
given by Xenocrates and Aristotle.

Cicero

SVF III, 14

In the case of all the philosophers mentioned, their End of Goods
logically follows: with Aristippus it is simply pleasure; with the Stoics,
harmony with nature, which they interpret as meaning virtuous living,
i.e., the morally good life, and further explain this as meaning to live
with an understanding of the natural course of events, selecting things
that are in accordance with nature and rejecting the opposite.

Thus there are three Ends which do not include moral worth . . .
[and] one theory that is simple, the author of which was Zeno, and
which is based entirely on propriety, that is, on moral worth.

Cicero

SVF III, 16

The end, they say, is to be happy, that for the sake of which everything
is performed, but nothing is done for the sake of itself; to do this first,
viz, to live according to virtue, to live consistently, which is further
this, to live according to nature. Zeno spoke of happiness in this manner: happiness is the "smooth" life. And Cleanthes added to this limit
in his treatises and Chrysippus and others of the Stoic school, saying
that happiness was not different than the happiness of life, but was, they
said, laid open to the public view, the end being that which chances to
be happiness, so that the happy life is this. Therefore, it seems clear
from these considerations, that 'to live according to nature' is of equal
force with: 'to live in accordance with beauty' and 'to live well,' and

again, 'the good and the beautiful' and 'the virtue and the participating virtue;' and that all good is beautiful, in the same way as all the disgraceful is bad; and on this account the Stoic conception of the End is equal to life according to virtue.

Stobaeus

SVF III, 20

Chrysippus, on the other hand, in his survey of the different species of living things, states that in some the body is the principal part, in others the mind, while there are some species which are equally endowed in respect of either; and then proceeds to discuss what constitutes the ultimate good proper to each species. Since he classified man so as to make the mind the principal part in him, he defined the *summum bonum* as to make it appear, not that man is principally mind, but that man is nothing else but mind.

Cicero

SVF III, 21b

There remains therefore one issue to be resolved—pleasure versus moral worth: and on this issue Chrysippus, as far as *I* see, had not much of a struggle. If one should follow the former, many things fall in ruin, and especially fellowship with mankind, affection, friendship, justice, and the rest of the virtues, none of which can exist unless they are disinterested. For virtue driven to duty by pleasure as a sort of pay is not virtue at all but a deceptive sham and pretense of virtue.

Cicero

SVF III, 39

And virtue is a harmonious disposition, choice-worthy for its own sake and not from hope or fear or any external motive. Moreover, it is in virtue that happiness consists; for virtue is the state of mind which tends to make the whole of life harmonious.

Diogenes Laertius

SVF III, 44

... That morality consists in using every means to obtain the things in accordance with nature, and that this endeavor even though unsuccessful is itself the sole thing desirable and the sole good, is actually maintained by the Stoics.

Cicero

¶ GOOD AND EVIL

SVF III, 68

In his treatises in natural philosophy, [Chrysippus] says:

"It is not possible to approach the doctrine of goods and evils, or
the virtues, or happiness, in another or more appropriate way, than
from the common nature and the order of the universe," adding further
on, "for it is necessary to join to these the doctrine concerning goods
and evils, since there is no other better principle or reference for them,
and since physical theory is not received for any other purpose except
for the differentiation between goods and evils."

Plutarch

SVF III, 71

Those of the Old Academy and the Peripatetics, and also the Stoics,
customarily make a distinction by saying that "of existing things some
are good, some evil, some between these two," and these last they term
"indifferent."

Sextus Empiricus

SVF III, 72

Since notions of things are produced in the mind when something has
become known either by experience or combination of ideas or analogy
or logical inference, the fourth and last method in this list is the one
that has given us the conception of Good. For when the mind ascends
by logical inference from the things in accordance with nature, then
finally it arrives at the notion of Good.

At the same time, Good is absolute, and is neither increased nor
diminished; but Good is perceived and called good from its own inherent properties and not by comparison with other things. Just as
honey, although extremely sweet, is yet perceived to be sweet by its own
singular flavor and not by being compared with something else, so this
Good which we are discussing is indeed of superlative value, yet its
value depends on kind and not on quantity. Value is not counted as a
Good nor yet as an Evil; so that however much you increase it in
amount, it will still remain the same in kind. The value of Virtue is
therefore singular and distinct; it depends on kind and not on degree.

Cicero

SVF III, 75

Now the Stoics, holding fast to the "common notions" (as these are
called), define 'good' in this way: "good is utility or not other than

utility," understanding by "utility" virtue and right action, and by "not other than utility" the worthy man and the friend. For virtue, being a certain state of the ruling principle (of mind), and right action, being some kind of activity in accordance with virtue, and precisely utility. And the worthy man, and the friend, belonging also themselves to the class of "goods," cannot be said either to be utility or to be other than utility, for the following reason: the parts, according to the Stoic family, are neither the same as their wholes nor of a different kind from their wholes, just as the hand is neither the same as the whole man (for the hand is not the whole man), nor other than the whole man (for the whole man is conceived as man to include the hand). Since, then, virtue is a part both of the worthy man and of the friend, and the parts are neither the same as their wholes nor other than their wholes, the worthy man and the friend are called "not other than utility." Thus every good thing falls within the definition, whether it is directly "utility" or "not other than utility." Next and by way of a proof, they maintain that 'good' has three senses and each of its implied senses, again, they portray by a separate description. In one sense, 'good,' they say, means "that by which or from which 'utility' can result," this being the most distinguished good and virtue; for from virtue, as from a fountain, all utility naturally springs. And in another sense, 'good' is "that of which utility is an accidental result"; thus not only will the virtues be called "good," but also the actions in accordance with them, inasmuch as utility results also from them. And in the third and last sense, "that which is capable of being useful" is called 'good,' since this description embraces the virtues, virtuous actions, the friends and the worthy men, and both gods and worthy demons.

. . . But the Stoics hold that, in the case of the term 'good,' the second implied sense should be inclusive of the first and the third inclusive of the other two.[1]

. . . There are those who like to argue that if in truth 'good' *is* "that from which utility can result," we must say that generic virtue alone is good (for it is from this alone that utility can result) and that each of the particulars falls *outside* the definition.[2]

. . . But those [i.e., the Stoics] who resist this objection reply as follows: "when we say that 'good' is 'that from which utility results,' this is equivalent to saying 'good' is 'that from which results one of the things useful in life.' " For thus each of the particular virtues also will

---

1. What follows is not in *SVF*.

2. I.e., contrary to the Stoic view, given above and which follows further.

be a good, not as providing utility in general but rather some one of the things useful in life,—one such, being wise, providing the state of being wise, and another, being temperate, providing the state of being temperate.

Sextus Empiricus

SVF III, 84

. . . Do you ask what these questions are? . . . For instance, your question whether the good is corporeal. Now the good is active: for it is beneficial; and what is active is corporeal. The good stimulates the mind and, in a way, molds and embraces that which is essential to the body. The goods of the body are bodily; so therefore must be the goods of the soul. For the soul, too, is corporeal. Ergo, man's good must be corporeal, since man himself is corporeal. His good is a body. . . . Emotions are corporeal . . . [and] evil too. Now all the virtues which I have mentioned are goods, and so are their results. Have you any doubt that whatever can be touched is corporeal? These are bodily. . . . Furthermore, any object that has power to move, force, restrain, or control, is corporeal. . . . In short, any act on our part is performed at the bidding of wickedness or virtue. Only a body can control or forcefully affect another body. The good of the body is corporeal. . . . A man's good is related to his bodily good; therefore, it is bodily.

Seneca

SVF III, 102

And in general there are some mixed goods: e.g., to be happy in one's children or in one's old age. But knowledge is a pure good. Again, some goods are permanent like the virtues, others transitory like joy and walking-exercise.

Diogenes Laertius

SVF III, 107

Goods are either of the nature of ends or they are the means to these ends, or they are at the same time end and means. A friend and the advantages derived from him are means to good, whereas confidence, high spirit, liberty, delight, gladness, freedom from pain, and every virtuous act are of the nature of ends. The virtues (they say) are goods of the nature at once of ends and of means. On the one hand, insofar as they cause happiness they are means, and on the other hand, insofar as they make it complete, and so are themselves part of it, they are ends.

Similarly of evils, some are of the nature of ends and some of means, while others are at once both means and ends. Your enemy and the harm he does you are means; consternation, abasement, slavery, gloom, despair, excess of grief, and every vicious action are of the nature of ends. Vices are evils both as ends and as means, since insofar as they cause misery they are means, but insofar as they make it complete, so that they become part of it, they are ends.

Diogenes Laertius

¶ THINGS INDIFFERENT

SVF I, 191

All other things, Zeno said, were neither good nor bad, but nevertheless some of them were in accordance with nature and others contrary to nature; also among these he counted another interposed or intermediate class of things. He taught that things in accordance with nature were to be chosen and estimated as having a certain value, and their opposites the opposite, while things that were neither he left in the intermediate class, these he declared to possess no motive force whatever.

Cicero

SVF III, 117

Of things that are, some, they say, are good, some are evil, and some neither good nor evil [i.e., morally indifferent]. Neutral [i.e., neither good nor evil] are all those things which neither benefit nor harm a man, such as life, health, pleasure, beauty, strength, wealth, fame, and noble birth . . . For, they say, such things [as life, health and pleasure] are not in themselves goods, but are morally indifferent, though falling under the species or subdivision "things preferred." For as the property of hot is to warm, not to cool, so the property of good is to benefit, not to injure; but wealth and health do no more benefit than injury, therefore neither wealth nor health is good. Further they say that that is not good of which both good and bad use can be made; but of wealth and health both good and bad use can be made; therefore wealth and health are not goods.

Diogenes Laertius

SVF III, 119

The term 'indifferent' has two meanings: in the first it denotes the things which do not contribute either to happiness or to misery, as wealth, fame, health, strength and the like; for it is possible to be

happy without having these, although, if they are used in a certain
way, such use of them tends to happiness or misery. In quite another
sense, those things are said to be indifferent which are without the
power of stirring inclination or aversion; e.g., the fact that the number
of hairs on one's head is odd or even or whether you hold out your
finger straight or bent. But it was not in this sense that the things mentioned above were termed indifferent, they being quite capable of
exciting inclination or aversion. Hence of these latter some are taken
by preference, others are rejected, whereas indifference in the other
sense affords no ground for either choosing or avoiding.

Diogenes Laertius

SVF III, 126

Of things indifferent, as they express it, some are "preferred" other
"rejected." Such as have value are "preferred," while such as have
negative, instead of positive, value are "rejected." Value they define as,
first, any contribution to harmonious living, such as attaches to every
good; secondly, some faculty or use which indirectly contributes to the
life according to nature: which is as much as to say "any assistance
brought by wealth or health towards living a natural life"; thirdly,
value is the full equivalent of an appraiser, as fixed by an expert acquainted with the facts—as when it is said that wheat exchanges for
so much barley with a mule thrown in.

Diogenes Laertius

SVF III, 135

Of things preferred some are preferred for their own sake, some for the
sake of something else, and others again both for their own sake and
for the sake of something else. To the first of these classes belong
natural ability, moral improvement, and the like; to the second, wealth,
noble birth, and the like; to the last, strength, perfect faculties,
soundness of bodily organs. Things are preferred for their own sake
because they accord with nature; not for their own sake, but for the
sake of something else, because they secure not a few utilities. And
similarly with the class of things rejected under the contrary heads.

Diogenes Laertius

SVF III, 151

That which is good makes men good. For example, that which is good
in the art of music makes the musician. But chance events do not
make a good man; therefore, chance events are not good.

That which can fall to the lot of any man, no matter how base or despised he may be, is not a good. But wealth falls to the lot of the pander and the trainer of gladiators; therefore wealth is not a good.

Good does not result from evil. But riches result from greed; therefore, riches are not a good.

That which, while we are desiring to attain it, involves us in many evils, is not a good. But while we are desiring to attain riches, we become involved in many evils; therefore, riches are not a good.

Seneca

SVF III, 154

Pleasure on the contrary, according to most Stoics, is not to be reckoned among the primary objects of natural impulse.

Cicero

SVF III, 155

Epicurus, for example, asserts that pleasure is a good, but he who said [Antisthenes, the Cynic] "I would rather be mad than enjoy pleasure" counted it an evil, while the Stoics say it is indifferent and not preferred; but Cleanthes says that neither is it natural nor does it possess value for life, but, like a cosmetic, has no natural existence.

Sextus Empiricus

SVF III, 166

That which is evil does harm; that which does harm makes a man worse. But pain and poverty do not make a man worse; therefore, they are not evils.

Seneca

¶ APPETITE AND SELECTION

SVF III, 169

Every living thing possessed of reason is inactive if it is not first stirred by some external impression; then the impulse comes, and finally assent confirms the impulse. Now what assent is I shall explain. Suppose that I ought to take a walk: I do walk, but only after uttering the command to myself and approving this opinion of mine.

Seneca

SVF III, 182

It is their view that immediately upon birth (for that is the proper point to start from), a living creature feels an attachment for itself,

and an impulse to preserve itself and to feel affection for its own constitution and for those things which tend to preserve that constitution;
while on the other hand it conceives an antipathy to destruction and
to those things which appear to threaten destruction. In proof of this
opinion, they urge that infants desire things conducive to their health
and reject things that are the opposite before they have ever felt
pleasure or pain; this would not be the case, unless they felt an affection for their own constitution and were afraid of destruction. But it
would be impossible that they should feel desire at all unless they
possessed self-consciousness, and consequently felt affection for themselves. This leads to the conclusion that it is love of self which supplies
the primary impulse to action.

Cicero

SVF III, 188

The initial principle being thus established that things in accordance
with nature are "things to be taken" for their own sake, and their
opposites similarly "things to be rejected," the first "appropriate act,"
[for so I render the Greek *(kathekon)*], is to preserve oneself in one's
natural constitution; the next is to retain those things which are in
accordance with nature and to repel those that are the contrary; then
when this principle of choice and also of rejection has been discovered,
there follows next in order choice conditioned by "appropriate action"; then, such choice becomes a fixed habit; and finally, choice fully
rationalized and in harmony with nature.

Man's first attraction is towards the things in accordance with
nature; but as soon as he has understanding, or rather become capable
of "conception"—in Stoic phraseology *ennoia*—and has discerned the
order and, so to speak, harmony that governs conduct, he therefore
esteems this harmony far more highly than all the things for which he
originally felt an affection, and by exercise of intelligence and reason
infers the conclusion that herein resides the chief good of man, the
thing that is praiseworthy and desirable for its own sake; and that
inasmuch as this consists in what the Stoics term *homologia* and we
"conformity"—inasmuch I say as in this resides that good which is the
end to which all else is a means, moral conduct and moral worth
itself, which alone is counted as a good, although of subsequent development, is nevertheless the sole thing that is for its own efficacy and
value desirable, whereas none of the primary objects of nature is
desirable for its own sake.

Cicero

SVF III, 189

Acts of cognition (which we may term comprehensions or perceptions, or if these words are distasteful or obscure, *katalepseis*)—these are appropriately adopted for their own sake, because they possess an element that so to speak embraces and contains the truth. This can be seen in the case of children, whom we may observe to take pleasure in finding something out for themselves by the use of reason, even though they gain nothing by it.

The sciences also we consider are things to be chosen for their own sake, partly because there is in them something worthy of choice, partly because they consist of acts of cognition and contain an element of fact established by methodical reasoning. The mental assent to what is false is more repugnant to us than all the other things that are contrary to nature.

Cicero

SVF III, 190

And what could be more obvious than that, if we can exercise no choice as between things consonant with and things contrary to nature, prudence is abolished altogether?

Cicero

¶ VIRTUE

SVF I, 199

And whereas his predecessors said that not all virtue resides in the reason, but that certain virtues are perfected by nature or by habit, he placed all the virtues in reason; and whereas they thought that the kinds of virtues that I have stated above can be classed apart, he argued that this is absolutely impossible, and that not merely the exercise of virtue, as his predecessors held, but the mere state of virtue is in itself a splendid thing, although no body possesses virtue without continuously exercising it.

Cicero

SVF III, 200

And besides this, in order that virtue may be perfect, there should be an even temperament and a scheme of life that is consistent with itself throughout; and this result cannot be attained without knowledge of things, and without the art (philosophy) which enables us to understand things human and things divine.

Seneca

SVF III, 200

And what quality is best in man? It is reason; by virtue of reason he surpasses the animals, and is surpassed only by the gods. Perfect reason is therefore the good peculiar to man; all other qualities he shares in some degree with animals and plants. . . .

What then is peculiar to man? Reason. When this is right and has reached perfection, man's felicity is complete. Hence, if everything is praiseworthy and has arrived at the end intended by its nature, when it has brought its peculiar good to perfection, and if man's peculiar good is reason, then, if a man has brought his reason to perfection, he is praiseworthy and has reached the end suited to his nature. This perfect reason is called virtue, and is likewise that which is honorable.

Seneca

SVF III, 214

By nature, we are all born with the seeds of virtue. . . . We must develop them with learning of virtue.

Anecodota Graeca

SVF III, 219

At our birth, nature made us teachable, and gave us reason, not perfect, but capable of being perfected.

Seneca

SVF III, 228

When a rational being is perverted, this is due to the deceptiveness of external pursuits or sometimes to the influence of associates. For the starting-points of nature are never perverse.

Diogenes Laertius

SVF III, 281

To the virtues we have discussed, they also add Dialectic and Physics. Both of these entitle by the name of virtue; the former because it conveys a method that guards us from giving assent to any falsehood or ever being deceived by specious probability, and enables us to retain and to defend the truths that we have learned about good and evil; for without the art of Dialectic they hold that any man may be seduced from truth into error. If therefore rashness and ignorance are in all matters fraught with mischief, the art which removes them is correctly entitled a virtue.

Cicero

SVF III, 282

The same honor is also bestowed (as being called a virtue) with good reason upon knowledge of nature, because he who is to live in accordance with nature must base his principles upon the system and government of the entire world. Nor again can anyone judge truly of things good and evil, save by a knowledge of the whole plan of nature and also of the life of the gods, and of the answer to the question whether the nature of man is or is not in harmony with that of the universe. And no one without knowledge of nature can discern the value (and their value is very great) of the ancient maxims and precepts of the wise men such as to "obey occasion," "follow God," "know thyself," and "moderation in all things." Also this knowledge alone can impart a conception of the power of nature in fostering justice and maintaining friendship and the rest of the affections; nor again without unfolding nature's secrets can we understand the sentiment of piety towards the gods or the degree of gratitude that we owe to them.

Cicero

¶ Law (De Jure et Lege)

SVF III, 308

They say that justice, as well as law and right reason, exists by nature and not by convention: so Chrysippus in his work *On the Morally Beautiful*.

Diogenes Laertius

SVF II, 314

The law of all is the king of things, both human and divine; for it is necessary that law be as a superintendent and a principle and a ruling power both of the good and of the disgraceful, and, because of this, it is the measure both of justice and of injustice. And of those things which by nature are political animals, it commands what ought to be done and prohibits what ought not to be done.

Marcianus

SVF III, 323

For this world is a great city, has one constitution and one law, and this is the reason of nature, commanding what should be done and forbidding what should not be done. Now states which we know about have . . . various constitutions and laws which are by no means identical, for different peoples have different customs and rules of behavior which are . . . extra constructions and additions. The explanation of this is the reluctance of peoples to have fellowship with each other, which is illustrated not only by Greeks to foreigners and foreigners to Greeks, but also is found in each of them separately in dealing with their own kin. And then we find them offering explanations for this which are no real explanations, e.g., poor climate, sterility or poverty of the soil, or the location of a state, whether it is on the coast or inland. . . . They never mention the true explanation, which is their greed and mutual lack of trust, which prevent them from being satisfied with the ordinances of nature, and lead them to give the name of laws to whatever commends itself as advantageous to the communities which hold the same views. So that states which are by nature constitutional are rather an addition to the universal constitution of nature, and the laws of these several states are additions to the right reason of nature . . . for a house is a state compressed into small dimensions, and its management may be called a kind of state management, just as a state is also a great house and statesmanship is the household management.

Philo

SVF III, 326

. . . but listen to him [Chrysippus] who says, in the third book of his treatise *On Gods*: "For it is not possible to discover any principle or any beginning of justice other than from that of the gods and from the common nature. For, on this account, it is necessary for everything to have its principle in this manner, if we wish to discover anything concerning goods and evils."

Plutarch

SVF III, 327

The state is a plurality of human beings governed by law.

Clement of Alexandria

SVF III, 333

They hold that the universe is governed by divine will; it is a city or state of which both men and gods are members, and each one of us is a part of this universe; from which it is a natural consequence that we should prefer the common advantage to our own. For just as the laws set the safety of all above the safety of individuals, so a good, wise and law-abiding man, conscious of his duty to the state, studies the advantage of all more than that of himself or of any single individual. The traitor to his country does not deserve greater reprobation than

the man who betrays the common advantage or security for the sake of
his own advantage or security. This explains why praise is owed to
one who dies for the commonwealth, because it becomes us to love our
country more than ourselves.

Cicero

SVF III, 340

It is held by the Stoics to be important to understand that nature
creates in parents an affection for their children; and parental affection
is the source to which we trace the origin of the association of the
human race in communities. This cannot but be clear in the first place
from the conformation of the body and its members, which by themselves are enough to show that nature's scheme included the procreation
of offspring. Yet it could not be consistent that nature should at once
intend offspring to be born and make no provision for that offspring
when born to be loved and cherished. Even in the lower animals nature's operation can be clearly discerned; when we observe the labor
that they spend on bearing and rearing their young, we seem to be
listening to the actual voice of nature. Hence, as it is manifest that it
is natural for us to shrink from pain, so it is clear that we derive from
nature herself the impulse to love those to whom we have given birth.

From this impulse is developed the sense of mutual attraction which
unites human beings as such; this also is bestowed by nature. The
mere fact of their common humanity requires that one man should feel
another man akin to him.

Cicero

SVF III, 342

And the fact that no one would care to pass his life alone in a desert,
even though supplied with pleasures in unbounded profusion, readily
shows that we are born for society and intercourse, and for a natural
partnership with our fellow men. Moreover, nature inspires us with the
desire to benefit as many people as we can, and especially by imparting
information and the principles of wisdom. Hence it would be hard to
discover anyone who will not impart to another any knowledge that he
may himself possess; so strong is our propensity not only to learn but
also to teach. And just as bulls have a natural instinct to fight with
all their strength and force in defending their calves against lions, so
men of exceptional gifts and capacity for service . . . feel a natural
impulse to be the protectors of the human race. . . . But how inconsistent it would be for us to expect the immortal gods to love and cherish
us, when we ourselves despise and neglect one another! Therefore, just

as we actually use our limbs before we have learnt for what particular useful purpose they were bestowed upon us, so we are united and allied by nature in the common society of the state. Were this not so, there would be no room either for justice or benevolence.

Cicero

SVF III, 351

No one is a slave by nature.

Seneca

SVF III, 367

It is their doctrine that there can be no question of right as between man and the lower animals, because of their unlikeness. Thus Chrysippus in the first book of his treatise *On Justice*.

Diogenes Laertius

SVF III, 369

. . . We are by nature fitted to form unions, societies, and states.

Cicero

¶ FEELINGS AND EMOTIONS

SVF I, 215

For, as Zeno says, even the Wise Man's head will keep its scar long after the wound has healed. He will experience, therefore, certain suggestions and shadows of passion, but from passion itself he will be free.

Seneca

SVF III, 407

. . . Fear is an expectation of evil. . . .

Diogenes Laertius

SVF III, 412

Now from falsehood there results perversion, which extends to the mind; and from this perversion arise many passions or emotions, which are causes of instability. Passion, or emotion, is defined by Zeno as an irrational and unnatural movement in the soul, or again as impulse in excess. The main, or most universal, emotions, according to . . . Zeno in his treatise *On The Passions,* constitute four great classes; grief, fear, desire [or craving], pleasure.

Diogenes Laertius

SVF III, 443

The question has often been raised whether it is better to have moderate emotions, or none at all. Philosophers of our school reject the emotions; the Peripatetics keep them in check.

Seneca

SVF III, 448

They say that the wise man is passionless, because he is not prone to fall into such infirmity. But they add that in another sense the term "apathy" is applied to the bad men, when, that is, it means that he is callous and relentless.

Diogenes Laertius

SVF III, 452

At this point it is pertinent to ask what pity is. For many commend it as a virtue, and call a pitiful man good. But this too is a mental defect.

I know that among the ill-informed, the Stoic school is unpopular on the ground that it is excessively harsh and not at all likely to give good counsel to princes and kings; the cirticism is made that it does not permit a Wise Man to be pitiful, does not permit him to pardon. . . . Pity is the sorrow of the mind brought about by the sight of the distress or sadness caused by the ills of others which it believes come undeservedly. But no sorrow befalls the wise man.

Seneca

SVF III, 453

Let us decide what pardon is, and we shall perceive that the Wise Man ought not to grant it. Pardon is the remission of a deserved punishment. Why a Wise Man ought not to give this is explained more at length by those who make a point of the doctrine; I, to speak briefly as if giving another's opinion, explain it thus: "Pardon is given to a man who ought to be punished; but a Wise Man does nothing which he ought not to do, omits to do nothing which he ought to do; therefore he does not remit a punishment which he ought to exact. But in a more honorable way, he will bestow upon you that which you wish to obtain by pardon; for the wise man will show mercy, be considerate, and rectify. . . ."

Seneca

SVF III, 461

Passions are some kind of judgments of the rational soul itself.

Galen

¶ Moral Actions

SVF I, 230

Now an appropriate act is an act so performed that a reasonable account can be rendered of its performance.

Cicero

SVF III, 497

But since those actions which I have termed "appropriate acts" are based on the primary natural objects, it follows that the former are means to the latter. Hence it may be correctly said that all "appropriate acts" are means to the end of attaining the primary needs of nature. Yet it must not be inferred that their attainment is the ultimate good, inasmuch as moral action is not one of the primary natural attractions, but is an outgrowth of these, a later development, as I have said. At the same time, moral action is in accordance with nature, and stimulates our desire far more strongly than all the objects that attracted us earlier.

Cicero

SVF III, 504

But in the other arts when we speak of an artistic performance, this quality must be considered as in a sense subsequent to and a result of the action; it is what the Stoics term *epigennematikon* (in the nature of an after-growth). Whereas in conduct, when we speak of an act as wise, the term is applied with full correctness from the first inception of the act. For every action that the Wise Man initiates must necessarily be complete forthwith in all its parts; since the thing desirable, as we term it, consists in his activity. As it is a sin to betray one's country . . . where the offense lies in the result of the act, so the passions of fear, grief and lust are sins, even when no extraneous result ensues. The latter are sins not in their subsequent effects, but immediately upon their inception; similarly, actions springing from virtues are to be judged right from their first inception, and not in the successful completion.

Cicero

SVF III, 510

He who makes progress to the extreme performs all beautiful actions, yet his life is not happy. Happiness is added to it when "middle" actions take on some kind of steadiness and particular consistency.

There is a division between the wise and the man who is not yet wise, but is making progress toward it.

Stobaeus

SVF III, 516

[Sextus says that neither will wisdom be an art of life, as it has no artistic work peculiar to itself.]

But in reply to this, they say that although all the works are common to all men, yet they are distinguished by their proceeding either from an artistic or from a nonartistic disposition. For the work of the virtuous man is not that of caring for his parents . . . , but doing this because of wisdom is the act of the virtuous; and just as procuring health is common both to the medical man and to the layman, but to procure health medically is peculiar to the man of art, so also honoring one's parents is common both to the virtuous man and the nonvirtuous, but the honoring of his parents because of wisdom is peculiar to the Wise Man, so that he possesses also an art of life, of which the special work is the performance of each of his actions from the best disposition.

Sextus Empiricus

SVF III, 517

Conduct will not be right unless the will to act is right; for this is the source of conduct. Nor, again, can the will be right without a right attitude of mind; for this is the source of the will. Furthermore, such an attitude of mind will not be found even in the best of men unless he has learned the laws of life as a whole and has worked out a proper judgment about everything, and unless he has reduced facts to a standard of truth.

Seneca

SVF III, 536

It is a tenet of theirs that between virtue and vice there is nothing intermediate, whereas according to the Peripatetics there is, namely, the state of moral improvement. For, say the Stoics, just as a stick may be either straight or crooked, so a man must be either just or unjust. Nor again, are there degrees of justice and injustice; and the same rule applies to the other virtues.

Diogenes Laertius

SVF III, 539

Whereas gradual improvement is good, still, until achieved, man is not good . . . but still evil.

Plutarch

SVF III, 543

He who makes moral progress will take on himself the guilt of everything evil he does or says.

Proclus

¶ THE WISE MAN AND THE FOOL

SVF I, 220

If poverty is an evil, no beggar can be happy, be he as wise as you like. But Zeno dared to say that a wise beggar was not only happy but also wealthy.

Cicero

SVF III, 549

They say that the Wise Man will never form mere opinions, that is to say, he will never give assent to anything that is false.

Diogenes Laertius

SVF III, 551

Especially as you yourselves say that the Wise Man when in a state of frenzy restrains himself from all assent because no distinction between presentations is visible to him.

Cicero

SVF III, 556

The wise are infallible, not being liable to error.

Diogenes Laertius

SVF III, 561

The Wise Man does all things well.

Diogenes Laertius

SVF III, 574

The Wise Man feels no pain; he has physical pains, but is not tortured
by it in his soul—for he does not give in with his soul.

Stobaeus

SVF III, 616

Since we see that man is designed by nature to safeguard and protect
his fellows, it follows from this natural disposition, that the Wise Man
should desire to engage in politics and government, and also to live in
accordance with nature by taking to himself a wife and desiring to
have children by her.

Cicero

SVF III, 628

Nor yet will the Wise Man live in solitude; for he is naturally made
for society and action.

Diogenes Laertius

SVF III, 631

Friendship exists only between the wise and good, by reason of their
likeness to one another. And by friendship they mean a common use of
all that has to do with life, wherein we treat our friends as we should
ourselves. They argue that a friend is worth having for his own sake,
and that it is a good thing to have many friends. But among the bad,
there is no such thing as friendship, and thus no bad man has a friend.

Diogenes Laertius

The Manual of Epictetus[1]

1. Of all existing things some are in our power, and others are not in our power. In our power are thought, impulse, will to get and will to avoid, and, in a word, everything which is our own doing. Things not in our power include the body, property, reputation, office, and, in a word, everything which is not our own doing. Things in our power are by nature free, unhindered, untrammelled; things not in our power are weak, servile, subject to hindrance, dependent on others. Remember then that if you imagine that what is naturally slavish is free, and what is naturally another's is your own, you will be hampered, you will mourn, you will be put to confusion, you will blame gods and men; but if you think that only your own belongs to you, and that what is another's is indeed another's, no one will ever put compulsion or hindrance on you, you will blame none, you will accuse none, you will do nothing against your will, no one will harm you, you will have no enemy, for no harm can touch you.

Aiming then at these high matters, you must remember that to attain them requires more than ordinary effort; you will have to give up some things entirely, and put off others for the moment. And if you would have these also—office and wealth—it may be that you will fail to get them, just because your desire is set on the former, and you will certainly fail to attain those things which alone bring freedom and happiness.

Make it your study then to confront every harsh impression with the words, 'You are but an impression, and not at all what you seem to be'. Then test it by those rules that you possess; and first by this—the chief test of all—'Is it concerned with what is in our power or with what is not in our power?' And if it is concerned with what is not in our power, be ready with the answer that it is nothing to you.

2. Remember that the will to get promises attainment of what you

---

1. This 'handbook' of Epictetus' principles was probably compiled by Arrian, and contains an excellent summary of the master's thought.

will, and the will to avoid promises escape from what you avoid; and he who fails to get what he wills is unfortunate, and he who does not escape what he wills to avoid is miserable. If then you try to avoid only what is unnatural in the region within your control, you will escape from all that you avoid; but if you try to avoid disease or death or poverty you will be miserable.

Therefore let your will to avoid have no concern with what is not in man's power; direct it only to things in man's power that are contrary to nature. But for the moment you must utterly remove the will to get; for if you will to get something not in man's power you are bound to be unfortunate; while none of the things in man's power that you could honourably will to get is yet within your reach. Impulse to act and not to act, these are your concern; yet exercise them gently and without strain, and provisionally.

3. When anything, from the meanest thing upwards, is attractive or serviceable or an object of affection, remember always to say to yourself, 'What is its nature?' If you are fond of a jug, say you are fond of a jug; then you will not be disturbed if it be broken. If you kiss your child or your wife, say to yourself that you are kissing a human being, for then if death strikes it you will not be disturbed.

4. When you are about to take something in hand, remind yourself what manner of thing it is. If you are going to bathe put before your mind what happens in the bath—water pouring over some, others being jostled, some reviling, others stealing; and you will set to work more securely if you say to yourself at once: 'I want to bathe, and I want to keep my will in harmony with nature,' and so in each thing you do; for in this way, if anything turns up to hinder you in your bathing, you will be ready to say, 'I did not want only to bathe, but to keep my will in harmony with nature, and I shall not so keep it, if I lose my temper at what happens'.

5. What disturbs men's minds is not events but their judgements on events. For instance, death is nothing dreadful, or else Socrates would have thought it so. No, the only dreadful thing about it is men's judgement that it is dreadful. And so when we are hindered, or disturbed, or distressed, let us never lay the blame on others, but on ourselves, that is, on our own judgements. To accuse others for one's own misfortunes is a sign of want of education; to accuse oneself shows that one's education has begun; to accuse neither oneself nor others shows that one's education is complete.

6. Be not elated at an excellence which is not your own. If the horse in his pride were to say, 'I am handsome', we could bear with it.

But when you say with pride, 'I have a handsome horse', know that the good horse is the ground of your pride. You ask then what you can call your own. The answer is—the way you deal with your impressions. Therefore when you deal with your impressions in accord with nature, then you may be proud indeed, for your pride will be in a good which is your own.

7. When you are on a voyage, and your ship is at anchorage, and you disembark to get fresh water, you may pick up a small shellfish or a truffle by the way, but you must keep your attention fixed on the ship, and keep looking towards it constantly, to see if the Helmsman calls you; and if he does, you have to leave everything, or be bundled on board with your legs tied like a sheep. So it is in life. If you have a dear wife or child given you, they are like the shellfish or the truffle, they are very well in their way. Only, if the Helmsman call, run back to your ship, leave all else, and do not look behind you. And if you are old, never go far from the ship, so that when you are called you may not fail to appear.

8. Ask not that events should happen as you will, but let your will be that events should happen as they do, and you shall have peace.

9. Sickness is a hindrance to the body, but not to the will, unless the will consent. Lameness is a hindrance to the leg, but not to the will. Say this to yourself at each event that happens, for you shall find that though it hinders something else it will not hinder you.

10. When anything happens to you, always remember to turn to yourself and ask what faculty you have to deal with it. If you see a beautiful boy or a beautiful woman, you will find continence the faculty to exercise there; if trouble is laid on you, you will find endurance; if ribaldry, you will find patience. And if you train yourself in this habit your impressions will not carry you away.

11. Never say of anything, 'I lost it', but say, 'I gave it back'. Has your child died? It was given back. Has your wife died? She was given back. Has your estate been taken from you? Was not this also given back? But you say, 'He who took it from me is wicked'. What does it matter to you through whom the Giver asked it back? As long as He gives it you, take care of it, but not as your own; treat it as passers-by treat an inn.

12. If you wish to make progress, abandon reasonings of this sort: 'If I neglect my affairs I shall have nothing to live on'; 'If I do not punish my son, he will be wicked.' For it is better to die of hunger, so that you be free from pain and free from fear, than to live in plenty and be troubled in mind. It is better for your son to be wicked than for

you to be miserable.[2] Wherefore begin with little things. Is your drop of oil spilt? Is your sup of wine stolen? Say to yourself, 'This is the price paid for freedom from passion, this is the price of a quiet mind.' Nothing can be had without a price. When you call your slave-boy, reflect that he may not be able to hear you, and if he hears you, he may not be able to do anything you want. But he is not so well off that it rests with him to give you peace of mind.

13. If you wish to make progress, you must be content in external matters to seem a fool and a simpleton; do not wish men to think you know anything, and if any should think you to be somebody, distrust yourself. For know that it is not easy to keep your will in accord with nature and at the same time keep outward things; if you attend to one you must needs neglect the other.

14. It is silly to want your children and your wife and your friends to live for ever, for that means that you want what is not in your control to be in your control, and what is not your own to be yours. In the same way if you want your servant to make no mistakes, you are a fool, for you want vice not to be vice but something different. But if you want not to be disappointed in your will to get, you can attain to that.

Exercise yourself then in what lies in your power. Each man's master is the man who has authority over what he wishes or does not wish, to secure the one or to take away the other. Let him then who wishes to be free not wish for anything or avoid anything that depends on others; or else he is bound to be a slave.

15. Remember that you must behave in life as you would at a banquet. A dish is handed round and comes to you; put out your hand and take it politely. It passes you; do not stop it. It has not reached you; do not be impatient to get it, but wait till your turn comes. Bear yourself thus towards children, wife, office, wealth, and one day you will be worthy to banquet with the gods. But if when they are set before you, you do not take them but despise them, then you shall not only share the gods' banquet, but shall share their rule. For by so doing Diogenes and Heraclitus and men like them were called divine and deserved the name.

16. When you see a man shedding tears in sorrow for a child

2. Matheson's translation of παιδα as 'son' here and at the beginning of chapter 12 can hardly be correct. Throughout the whole section it should be rendered as 'slave-boy.' The reading 'son' imposes unnecessarily upon Stoicism a brutality and lack of normal human sympathy and affection which it can ill afford to carry.

abroad or dead, or for loss of property, beware that you are not carried away by the impression that it is outward ills that make him miserable. Keep this thought by you: 'What distresses him is not the event, for that does not distress another, but his judgement on the event.' Therefore do not hesitate to sympathize with him so far as words go, and if it so chance, even to groan with him; but take heed that you do not also groan in your inner being.

17. Remember that you are an actor in a play, and the Playwright chooses the manner of it: if he wants it short, it is short; if long, it is long. If he wants you to act a poor man you must act the part with all your powers; and so if your part be a cripple or a magistrate or a plain man. For your business is to act the character that is given you and act it well; the choice of the cast is Another's.

18. When a raven croaks with evil omen, let not the impression carry you away, but straightway distinguish in your own mind and say, 'These portents mean nothing to me; but only to my bit of a body or my bit of property or name, or my children or my wife. But for me all omens are favourable if I will, for, whatever the issue may be, it is in my power to get benefit therefrom.'

19. You can be invincible, if you never enter on a contest where victory is not in your power. Beware then that when you see a man raised to honour or great power or high repute you do not let your impression carry you away. For if the reality of good lies in what is in our power, there is no room for envy or jealousy. And you will not wish to be praetor, or prefect or consul, but to be free; and there is but one way to freedom—to despise what is not in our power.

20. Remember that foul words or blows in themselves are no outrage, but your judgement that they are so. So when any one makes you angry, know that it is your own thought that has angered you. Wherefore make it your first endeavour not to let your impressions carry you away. For if once you gain time and delay, you will find it easier to control yourself.

21. Keep before your eyes from day to day death and exile and all things that seem terrible, but death most of all, and then you will never set your thoughts on what is low and will never desire anything beyond measure.

22. If you set your desire on philosophy you must at once prepare to meet with ridicule and the jeers of many who will say, 'Here he is again, turned philosopher. Where has he got these proud looks?' Nay, put on no proud looks, but hold fast to what seems best to you, in

confidence that God has set you at this post. And remember that if you abide where you are, those who first laugh at you will one day admire you, and that if you give way to them, you will get doubly laughed at.

23. If it ever happen to you to be diverted to things outside, so that you desire to please another, know that you have lost your life's plan. Be content then always to be a philosopher; if you wish to be regarded as one too, show yourself that you are one and you will be able to achieve it.

24. Let not reflections such as these afflict you: 'I shall live without honour, and never be of any account'; for if lack of honour is an evil, no one but yourself can involve you in evil any more than in shame. Is it your business to get office or to be invited to an entertainment?

Certainly not.

Where then is the dishonour you talk of? How can you be 'of no account anywhere', when you ought to count for something in those matters only which are in your power, where you may achieve the highest worth?

'But my friends,' you say, 'will lack assistance.'

What do you mean by 'lack assistance'? They will not have cash from you and you will not make them Roman citizens. Who told you that to do these things is in our power, and not dependent upon others? Who can give to another what is not his to give?

'Get them then,' says he, 'that we may have them.'

If I can get them and keep my self-respect, honour, magnanimity, show the way and I will get them. But if you call on me to lose the good things that are mine, in order that you may win things that are not good, look how unfair and thoughtless you are. And which do you really prefer? Money, or a faithful, modest friend? Therefore help me rather to keep these qualities, and do not expect from me actions which will make me lose them.

'But my country,' says he, 'will lack assistance, so far as lies in me.'

Once more I ask, What assistance do you mean? It will not owe colonnades or baths to you. What of that? It does not owe shoes to the blacksmith or arms to the shoemaker; it is sufficient if each man fulfils his own function. Would you do it no good if you secured to it another faithful and modest citizen?

'Yes.'

Well, then, you would not be useless to it.

'What place then shall I have in the city?'

Whatever place you can hold while you keep your character for honour and self-respect. But if you are going to lose these qualities in trying to benefit your city, what benefit, I ask, would you have done her when you attain to the perfection of being lost to shame and honour?

25. Has some one had precedence of you at an entertainment or a levee or been called in before you to give advice? If these things are good you ought to be glad that he got them; if they are evil, do not be angry that you did not get them yourself. Remember that if you want to get what is not in your power, you cannot earn the same reward as others unless you act as they do. How is it possible for one who does not haunt the great man's door to have equal shares with one who does, or one who does not go in his train equality with one who does; or one who does not praise him with one who does? You will be unjust then and insatiable if you wish to get these privileges for nothing, without paying their price. What is the price of a lettuce? An obol perhaps. If then a man pays his obol and gets his lettuces, and you do not pay and do not get them, do not think you are defrauded. For as he has the lettuces so you have the obol you did not give. The same principle holds good too in conduct. You were not invited to someone's entertainment? Because you did not give the host the price for which he sells his dinner. He sells it for compliments, he sells it for attentions. Pay him the price then, if it is to your profit. But if you wish to get the one and yet not give up the other, nothing can satisfy you in your folly.

What! you say, you have nothing instead of the dinner?

Nay, you have this, you have not praised the man you did not want to praise, you have not had to bear with the insults of his doorstep.

26. It is in our power to discover the will of Nature from those matters on which we have no difference of opinion. For instance, when another man's slave has broken the wine-cup we are very ready to say at once, 'Such things must happen'. Know then that when your own cup is broken, you ought to behave in the same way as when your neighbour's was broken. Apply the same principle to higher matters. Is another's child or wife dead? Not one of us but would say, 'Such is the lot of man'; but when one's own dies, straightway one cries, 'Alas! miserable am I'. But we ought to remember what our feelings are when we hear it of another.

27. As a mark is not set up for men to miss it, so there is nothing intrinsically evil in the world.

28. If any one trusted your body to the first man he met, you

would be indignant, but yet you trust your mind to the chance comer, and allow it to be disturbed and confounded if he revile you; are you not ashamed to do so?

29.[3] In everything you do consider what comes first and what follows, and so approach it. Otherwise you will come to it with a good heart at first because you have not reflected on any of the consequences, and afterwards, when difficulties have appeared, you will desist to your shame. Do you wish to win at Olympia? So do I, by the gods, for it is a fine thing. But consider the first steps to it, and the consequences, and so lay your hand to the work. You must submit to discipline, eat to order, touch no sweets, train under compulsion, at a fixed hour, in heat and cold, drink no cold water, nor wine, except by order; you must hand yourself over completely to your trainer as you would to a physician, and then when the contest comes you must risk getting hacked, and sometimes dislocate your hand, twist your ankle, swallow plenty of sand, sometimes get a flogging, and with all this suffer defeat. When you have considered all this well, then enter on the athlete's course, if you still wish it. If you act without thought you will be behaving like children, who one day play at wrestlers, another day at gladiators, now sound the trumpet, and next strut the stage. Like them you will be now an athlete, now a gladiator, then orator, then philosopher, but nothing with all your soul. Like an ape, you imitate every sight you see, and one thing after another takes your fancy. When you undertake a thing you do it casually and half-heartedly, instead of considering it and looking at it all round. In the same way some people, when they see a philosopher and hear a man speaking like Euphrates (and indeed who can speak as he can?), wish to be philosophers themselves.

Man, consider first what it is you are undertaking; then look at your own powers and see if you can bear it. Do you want to compete in the pentathlon or in wrestling? Look to your arms, your thighs, see what your loins are like. For different men are born for different tasks. Do you suppose that if you do this you can live as you do now—eat and drink as you do now, indulge desire and discontent just as before? Nay, you must sit up late, work hard, abandon your own people, be looked down on by a mere slave, be ridiculed by those who meet you, get the worst of it in everything—in honour, in office, in justice, in every possible thing. This is what you have to consider: whether you are willing to pay this price for peace of mind, freedom, tranquillity. If not, do not come near; do not be, like the children, first a philosopher,

3. Cf. Epictetus, *Discourses,* III, chap. xv.

then a tax-collector, then an orator, then one of Caesar's procurators. These callings do not agree. You must be one man, good or bad; you must develop either your Governing Principle, or your outward endowments; you must study either your inner man, or outward things—in a word, you must choose between the position of a philosopher and that of a mere outsider.

30. Appropriate acts are in general measured by the relations they are concerned with. 'He is your father.' This means you are called on to take care of him, give way to him in all things, bear with him if he reviles or strikes you.

'But he is a bad father.'

Well, have you any natural claim to a good father? No, only to a father.

'My brother wrongs me.'

Be careful then to maintain the relation you hold to him, and do not consider what he does, but what you must do if your purpose is to keep in accord with nature. For no one shall harm you, without your consent; you will only be harmed, when you think you are harmed. You will only discover what is proper to expect from neighbour, citizen, or praetor, if you get into the habit of looking at the relations implied by each.

31. For piety towards the gods know that the most important thing is this: to have right opinions about them—that they exist, and that they govern the universe well and justly—and to have set yourself to obey them, and to give way to all that happens, following events with a free will, in the belief that they are fulfilled by the highest mind. For thus you will never blame the gods, nor accuse them of neglecting you. But this you cannot achieve, unless you apply your conception of good and evil to those things only which are in our power, and not to those which are out of our power. For if you apply your notion of good or evil to the latter, then, as soon as you fail to get what you will to get or fail to avoid what you will to avoid, you will be bound to blame and hate those you hold responsible. For every living creature has a natural tendency to avoid and shun what seems harmful and all that causes it, and to pursue and admire what is helpful and all that causes it. It is not possible then for one who thinks he is harmed to take pleasure in what he thinks is the author of the harm, any more than to take pleasure in the harm itself. That is why a father is reviled by his son, when he does not give his son a share of what the son regards as good things; thus Polynices and Eteocles were set at enmity with one another by thinking that a king's throne was a good thing. That is why the

farmer, and the sailor, and the merchant, and those who lose wife or children revile the gods. For men's religion is bound up with their interest. Therefore he who makes it his concern rightly to direct his will to get and his will to avoid, is thereby making piety his concern. But it is proper on each occasion to make libation and sacrifice and to offer first-fruits according to the custom of our fathers, with purity and not in slovenly or careless fashion, without meanness and without extravagance.

32. When you make use of prophecy remember that while you know not what the issue will be, but are come to learn it from the prophet, you do know before you come what manner of thing it is, if you are really a philosopher. For if the event is not in our control, it cannot be either good or evil. Therefore do not bring with you to the prophet the will to get or the will to avoid, and do not approach him with trembling, but with your mind made up, that the whole issue is indifferent and does not affect you and that, whatever it be, it will be in your power to make good use of it, and no one shall hinder this. With confidence then approach the gods as counsellors, and further, when the counsel is given you, remember whose counsel it is, and whom you will be disregarding if you disobey. And consult the oracle, as Socrates thought men should, only when the whole question turns upon the issue of events, and neither reason nor any art of man provides opportunities for discovering what lies before you. Therefore, when it is your duty to risk your life with friend or country, do not ask the oracle whether you should risk your life. For if the prophet warns you that the sacrifice is unfavourable, though it is plain that this means death or exile or injury to some part of your body, yet reason requires that even at this cost you must stand by your friend and share your country's danger. Wherefore pay heed to the greater prophet, Pythian Apollo, who cast out of his temple the man who did not help his friend when he was being killed.[4]

Lay down for yourself from the first a definite stamp and style of conduct, which you will maintain when you are alone and also in the society of men. Be silent for the most part, or, if you speak, say only what is necessary and in a few words. Talk, but rarely, if occasion calls you, but do not talk of ordinary things—of gladiators, or horse-races, or athletes, or of meats or drinks—these are topics that arise everywhere—but above all do not talk about men in blame or compli-

---

4. 'Aelian, *Var. Hist.*, tells how three men sent to Delphi had an encounter with robbers. One ran away, another accidentally killed the third in trying to defend him. The Oracle would have nothing to say to the runaway, and absolved the homicide.' (Matheson)

ment or comparison. If you can, turn the conversation of your company by your talk to some fitting subject; but if you should chance to be isolated among strangers, be silent. Do not laugh much, nor at many things, nor without restraint.

Refuse to take oaths, altogether if that be possible, but if not, as far as circumstances allow.

Refuse the entertainments of strangers and the vulgar.[5] But if occasions arise to accept them, then strain every nerve to avoid lapsing into the state of the vulgar. For know that, if your comrade has a stain on him, he that associates with him must needs share the stain, even though he be clean in himself.

For your body take just so much as your bare need requires, such as food, drink, clothing, house, servants, but cut down all that tends to luxury and outward show.

Avoid impurity to the utmost of your power before marriage, and if you indulge your passion, let it be done lawfully. But do not be offensive or censorious to those who indulge it, and do not be always bringing up your own chastity. If some one tells you that so and so speaks ill of you, do not defend yourself against what he says, but answer, 'He did not know my other faults, or he would not have mentioned these alone.'

It is not necessary for the most part to go to the games; but if you should have occasion to go, show that your first concern is for yourself; that is, wish that only to happen which does happen, and him only to win who does win, for so you will suffer no hindrance. But refrain entirely from applause, or ridicule, or prolonged excitement. And when you go away do not talk much of what happened there, except so far as it tends to your improvement. For to talk about it implies that the spectacle excited your wonder.

Do not go lightly or casually to hear lectures; but if you do go, maintain your gravity and dignity and do not make yourself offensive. When you are going to meet any one, and particularly some man of reputed eminence, set before your mind the thought, 'What would Socrates or Zeno have done?' and you will not fail to make proper use of the occasion.

When you go to visit some great man, prepare your mind by thinking that you will not find him in, that you will be shut out, that the doors will be slammed in your face, that he will pay no heed to you. And if in spite of all this you find it fitting for you to go, go and bear what happens and never say to yourself, 'It was not worth all this';

5. I.e., those untrained in philosophy.

for that shows a vulgar mind and one at odds with outward things.

In your conversation avoid frequent and disproportionate mention of your own doings or adventures; for other people do not take the same pleasure in hearing what has happened to you as you take in recounting your adventures.

Avoid raising men's laughter; for it is a habit that easily slips into vulgarity, and it may well suffice to lessen your neighbour's respect.

It is dangerous too to lapse into foul language; when anything of the kind occurs, rebuke the offender, if the occasion allow, and if not, make it plain to him by your silence, or a blush or a frown, that you are angry at his words.

34. When you imagine some pleasure, beware that it does not carry you away, like other imaginations. Wait a while, and give yourself pause. Next remember two things: how long you will enjoy the pleasure, and also how long you will afterwards repent and revile yourself. And set on the other side the joy and self-satisfaction you will feel if you refrain. And if the moment seems come to realize it, take heed that you be not overcome by the winning sweetness and attraction of it; set in the other scale the thought how much better is the consciousness of having vanquished it.

35. When you do a thing because you have determined that it ought to be done, never avoid being seen doing it, even if the opinion of the multitude is going to condemn you. For if your action is wrong, then avoid doing it altogether, but if it is right, why do you fear those who will rebuke you wrongly?

36. The phrases, 'It is day' and 'It is night', mean a great deal if taken separately, but have no meaning if combined. In the same way, to choose the larger portion at a banquet may be worth while for your body, but if you want to maintain social decencies it is worthless. Therefore, when you are at meat with another, remember not only to consider the value of what is set before you for the body, but also to maintain your self-respect before your host.

37. If you try to act a part beyond your powers, you not only disgrace yourself in it, but you neglect the part which you could have filled with success.

38. As in walking you take care not to tread on a nail or to twist your foot, so take care that you do not harm your Governing Principle. And if we guard this in everything we do, we shall set to work more securely.

39. Every man's body is a measure for his property, as the foot is the measure for his shoe. If you stick to this limit, you will keep the

right measure; if you go beyond it, you are bound to be carried away down a precipice in the end; just as with the shoe, if you once go beyond the foot, your shoe puts on gilding, and soon purple and embroidery. For when once you go beyond the measure there is no limit.

40. Women from fourteen years upwards are called 'madam' by men. Wherefore, when they see that the only advantage they have got is to be marriageable, they begin to make themselves smart and to set all their hopes on this. We must take pains then to make them understand that they are really honoured for nothing but a modest and decorous life.

41. It is a sign of a dull mind to dwell upon the cares of the body, to prolong exercise, eating, drinking, and other bodily functions. These things are to be done by the way; all your attention must be given to the mind.

42. When a man speaks evil or does evil to you, remember that he does or says it because he thinks it is fitting for him. It is not possible for him to follow what seems good to you, but only what seems good to him, so that, if his opinion is wrong, he suffers, in that he is the victim of deception. In the same way, if a composite judgement which is true is thought to be false, it is not the judgement that suffers, but the man who is deluded about it. If you act on this principle you will be gentle to him who reviles you, saying to yourself on each occasion, 'He thought it right.'

43. Everything has two handles, one by which you can carry it, the other by which you cannot. If your brother wrongs you, do not take it by that handle, the handle of his wrong, for you cannot carry it by that, but rather by the other handle—that he is a brother, brought up with you, and then you will take it by the handle that you can carry by.

44. It is illogical to reason thus, 'I am richer than you, therefore I am superior to you', 'I am more eloquent than you, therefore I am superior to you.' It is more logical to reason, 'I am richer than you, therefore my property is superior to yours', 'I am more eloquent than you, therefore my speech is superior to yours.' You are something more than property or speech.

45. If a man washes quickly, do not say that he washes badly, but that he washes quickly. If a man drinks much wine, do not say that he drinks badly, but that he drinks much. For till you have decided what judgement prompts him, how do you know that he acts badly? If you do as I say, you will assent to your apprehensive impressions and to none other.

46. On no occasion call yourself a philosopher, nor talk at large of

your principles among the multitude, but act on your principles. For instance, at a banquet do not say how one ought to eat, but eat as you ought. Remember that Socrates had so completely got rid of the thought of display that when men came and wanted an introduction to philosophers he took them to be introduced; so patient of neglect was he. And if a discussion arise among the multitude on some principle, keep silent for the most part; for you are in great danger of blurting out some undigested thought. And when someone says to you, 'You know nothing', and you do not let it provoke you, then know that you are really on the right road. For sheep do not bring grass to their shepherds and show them how much they have eaten, but they digest their fodder and then produce it in the form of wool and milk. Do the same yourself; instead of displaying your principles to the multitude, show them the results of the principles you have digested.

47. When you have adopted the simple life, do not pride yourself upon it, and if you are a water-drinker do not say on every occasion, 'I am a water-drinker.' And if you ever want to train laboriously, keep it to yourself and do not make a show of it. Do not embrace statues. If you are very thirsty take a good draught of cold water, and rinse your mouth and tell no one.

48. The ignorant man's position and character is this: he never looks to himself for benefit or harm, but to the world outside him. The philosopher's position and character is that he always look to himself for benefit and harm.

The signs of one who is making progress are: he blames none, praises none, complains of none, accuses none, never speaks of himself as if he were somebody, or as if he knew anything. And if any one compliments him he laughs in himself at his compliment; and if one blames him, he makes no defence. He goes about like a convalescent, careful not to disturb his constitution on its road to recovery, until it has got firm hold. He has got rid of the will to get, and his will to avoid is directed no longer to what is beyond our power but only to what is in our power and contrary to nature. In all things he exercises his will without strain. If men regard him as foolish or ignorant he pays no heed. In one word, he keeps watch and guard on himself as his own enemy, lying in wait for him.

49. When a man prides himself on being able to understand and interpret the books of Chrysippus, say to yourself, 'If Chrysippus had not written obscurely this man would have had nothing on which to pride himself.'

What is my object? To understand Nature and follow her. I look then for some one who interprets her, and having heard that Chrysippus does I come to him. But I do not understand his writings, so I seek an interpreter. So far there is nothing to be proud of. But when I have found the interpreter it remains for me to act on his precepts; that and that alone is a thing to be proud of. But if I admire the mere power of exposition, it comes to this—that I am turned into a grammarian instead of a philosopher, except that I interpret Chrysippus in place of Homer. Therefore, when some one says to me, 'Read me Chrysippus', when I cannot point to actions which are in harmony and correspondence with his teaching, I am rather inclined to blush.

50. Whatever principles you put before you, hold fast to them as laws which it will be impious to transgress. But pay no heed to what any one says of you; for this is something beyond your own control.

51. How long will you wait to think yourself worthy of the highest and transgress in nothing the clear pronouncement of reason? You have received the precepts which you ought to accept, and you have accepted them. Why then do you still wait for a master, that you may delay the amendment of yourself till he comes? You are a youth no longer, you are now a full-grown man. If now you are careless and indolent and are always putting off, fixing one day after another as the limit when you mean to begin attending to yourself, then, living or dying, you will make no progress but will continue unawares in ignorance. Therefore make up your mind before it is too late to live as one who is mature and proficient, and let all that seems best to you be a law that you cannot transgress. And if you encounter anything troublesome or pleasant or glorious or inglorious, remember that the hour of struggle is come, the Olympic contest is here and you may put off no longer, and that one day and one action determines whether the progress you have achieved is lost or maintained.

This was how Socrates attained perfection, paying heed to nothing but reason, in all that he encountered. And if you are not yet Socrates, yet ought you to live as one who would wish to be a Socrates.

52. The first and most necessary department of philosophy deals with the application of principles; for instance, 'not to lie'. The second deals with demonstrations; for instance, 'How comes it that one ought not to lie?' The third is concerned with establishing and analysing these processes; for instance, 'How comes it that this is a demonstration? What is demonstration, what is consequence, what is contradiction, what is true, what is false?' It follows then that the third department is necessary because of the second, and the second because of the first. The first is the most necessary part, and that in which we

must rest. But we reverse the order: we occupy ourselves with the third, and make that our whole concern, and the first we completely neglect. Wherefore we lie, but are ready enough with the demonstration that lying is wrong.

53. On every occasion we must have these thoughts at hand,

'Lead me, O Zeus, and lead me, Destiny,
Whither ordainèd is by your decree.
I'll follow, doubting not, or if with will
Recreant I falter, I shall follow still.'

Cleanthes

'Who rightly with necessity complies
In things divine we count him skilled and wise.'

Euripides, Fragment 965

'Well, Crito, if this be the gods' will, so be it.'

Plato, *Crito,* 43d

'Anytus and Meletus have power to put me to death,
but not to harm me.'

Plato, *Apology,* 30c

Cleanthes
Hymn to Zeus

O God most glorious, called by many a name,
Nature's great King, through endless years the same;
Omnipotence, who by thy just decree
Controllest all, hail, Zeus, for unto thee
Behoves thy creatures in all lands to call.
We are thy children, we alone, of all
On earth's broad ways that wander to and fro,
Bearing thine image wheresoe'er we go.
Wherefore with songs of praise thy power I will forth show.
Lo! yonder Heaven, that round the earth is wheeled,
Follows thy guidance, still to thee doth yield
Glad homage; thine unconquerable hand
Such flaming minister, the levin brand,
Wieldeth, a sword two-edged, whose deathless might
Pulsates through all that Nature brings to light:
Vehicle of the universal Word, that flows
Through all, and in the light celestial glows
Of stars both great and small. A King of Kings
Through ceaseless ages, God, whose purpose brings
To birth, whate'er on land or in the sea
Is wrought, or in high heaven's immensity;
Save what the sinner works infatuate.
Nay, but thou knowest to make crooked straight:
Chaos to thee is order: in thine eyes
The unloved is lovely, who didst harmonize
Things evil with things good, that there should be
One Word through all things everlastingly.
One Word—whose voice alas! the wicked spurn;
Insatiate for the good their spirits yearn:

Yet seeing see not, neither hearing hear
God's universal law, which those revere,
By reason guided, happiness who win.
The rest, unreasoning, diverse shapes of sin
Self-prompted follow: for an idle name
Vainly they wrestle in the lists of fame:
Others inordinately riches woo,
Or dissolute, the joys of flesh pursue.
Now here, now there they wander, fruitless still,
For ever seeking good and finding ill.
Zeus the all-bountiful, whom darkness shrouds,
Whose lightning lightens in the thunder-clouds,
Thy children save from error's deadly sway:
Turn thou the darkness from their souls away:
Vouchsafe that unto knowledge they attain;
For thou by knowledge art made strong to reign
O'er all, and all things rulest righteously.
So by thee honoured, we will honour thee,
Praising thy works continually with songs,
As mortals should; nor higher meed belongs
E'en to the gods, than justly to adore
The universal law for evermore.

SKEPTICISM

The one main source of Skeptical doctrines is found in the works of Sextus Empiricus, four volumes in the Loeb edition (see bibliography). Though his life is surrounded by obscurity, he may be thought of as the historian of ancient Skepticism. The first volume, *Outlines of Pyrrhonism,* contains the selection here reprinted. The major part of the writings of Sextus consists largely of most interesting amplification of the doctrines and methods found in the *Outlines.* No school of philosophy, no grammarian, and no literary pundit was safe from the Skeptical critique. A glance at the many treatises against the dogmatic philosophers will show the Skeptic to be startlingly modern in his view that the philosopher had no superior insight and no corner on wisdom! Our selections here are intended to reveal the method and temperament of this critic of contemporary institutions and values.

Lucian (120-200 A.D.), a rhetorician and prolific writer, wrote many dialogues showing himself to be a marvelously adept literary representative of Skepticism. One of the more famous examples is reproduced here in *The Sale of Philosophers,* a hilarious but devastating account of philosophers in disarray.

Sextus Empiricus
Outlines of Pyrrhonism
Book I

Chapter I.—OF THE MAIN DIFFERENCE
BETWEEN PHILOSOPHIC SYSTEMS

The natural result of any investigation is that the investigators either discover the object of search or deny that it is discoverable and confess it to be inapprehensible or persist in their search. So, too, with regard to the objects investigated by philosophy, this is probably why some have claimed to have discovered the truth, others have asserted that it cannot be apprehended, while others again go on inquiring. Those who believe they have discovered it are the "Dogmatists," specially so called—Aristotle, for example, and Epicurus and the Stoics and certain others; Cleitomachus and Carneades and other Academics treat it as inapprehensible: the Skeptics keep on searching. Hence it seems reasonable to hold that the main types of philosophy are three— the Dogmatic, the Academic, and the Skeptic. Of the other systems it will best become others to speak: our task at present is to describe in outline the Skeptic doctrine, first premising that of none of our future statements do we positively affirm that the fact is exactly as we state it, but we simply record each fact, like a chronicler, as it appears to us at the moment.

Chapter II.—OF THE ARGUMENTS OF SKEPTICISM

Of the Skeptic philosophy one argument (or branch of exposition) is called "general," the other "special." In the general argument we set forth the distinctive features of Skepticism, stating its purport and principles, its logical methods, criterion, and end or aim; the "Tropes," also, or "Modes," which lead to suspension of judgment, and in what sense we adopt the Skeptic formulae, and the distinction between Skepticism and the philosophies which stand next to it. In the special argument[1] we state our objections regarding the several divisions of so-called philosophy. Let us, then, deal first with the general argument, beginning our description with the names given to the Skeptic School.

Chapter III.—OF THE NOMENCLATURE OF SKEPTICISM

The Skeptic School, then, is also called "Zetetic" from its activity in investigation and inquiry, and "Ephectic" or Suspensive from the state of mind produced in the inquirer after his search, and "Aporetic" or Dubitative either from its habit of doubting and seeking, as some say, or from its indecision as regards assent and denial, and "Pyrrhonean" from the fact that Pyrrho appears to us to have applied himself to Skepticism more thoroughly and more conspicuously than his predecessors.

Chapter IV.—WHAT SKEPTICISM IS

Skepticism is an ability, or mental attitude, which opposes appearances to judgments in any way whatsoever, with the result that, owing to the equipollence of the objects and reasons thus opposed, we are brought firstly to a state of mental suspense and next to a state of "unperturbedness" or quietude. Now we call it an "ability" not in any subtle sense, but simply in respect of its "being able." By "appearances" we now mean the objects of sense perception, whence we contrast them with the objects of thought or "judgments." The phrase "in any way whatsoever" can be connected either with the word "ability," to make us take the word "ability," as we said, in its simple sense, or with the phrase "opposing appearances to judgments"; for inasmuch as we oppose these in a variety of ways—appearances to appearances, or judgments to judgments, or *alternando* appearances to judgments,— in order to ensure the inclusion of all these antitheses we employ the

---

1. Books II and III of the *Outlines*.

phrase "in any way whatsoever." Or, again, we join "in any way what-soever" to "appearances and judgments" in order that we may not have to inquire how the appearances appear or how the thought-objects are judged, but may take these terms in the simple sense. The phrase "op-posed judgments" we do not employ in the sense of negations and affirmations only but simply as equivalent to "conflicting judgments." "Equipollence" we use of equality in respect of probability and im-probability, to indicate that no one of the conflicting judgments takes precedence of any other as being more probable. "Suspense" is a state of mental rest owing to which we neither deny nor affirm anything. "Quietude" is an untroubled and tranquil condition of soul. And how quietude enters the soul along with suspension of judgment we shall explain in 12, "Concerning the End."

Chapter V.—OF THE SKEPTIC

In the definition of the Skeptic system there is also implicitly included that of the Pyrrhonean philosopher; he is the man who participates in this "ability."

Chapter VI.—OF THE PRINCIPLES OF SKEPTICISM

The originating cause of Skepticism is, we say, the hope of attaining quietude. Men of talent, who were perturbed by the contradictions in things and in doubt as to which of the alternatives they ought to accept, were led on to inquire what is true in things and what false, hoping by the settlement of this question to attain quietude. The main basic principle of the Skeptic system is that of opposing to every propo-sition an equal proposition; for we believe that as a consequence of this we end by ceasing to dogmatize.

Chapter VII.—DOES THE SKEPTIC DOGMATIZE?

When we say that the Skeptic refrains from dogmatizing we do not use the term "dogma," as some do, in the broader sense of "approval of a thing" (for the Skeptic gives assent to the feelings which are the necessary results of sense impressions, and he would not, for example, say when feeling hot or cold "I believe that I am not hot or cold"); but we say that "he does not dogmatize" using "dogma" in the sense, which some give it, of "assent to one of the non-evident objects of scientific inquiry"; for the Pyrrhonean philosopher assents to nothing that is non-evident. Moreover, even in the act of enunciating the Skeptic formulae concerning things non-evident—such as the formula "No more (one thing than another)," or the formula "I determine nothing," or any of the others which we shall presently mention, —he does not dogmatize. For whereas the dogmatizer posits the things about which he is said to be dogmatizing as really existent, the Skeptic does not posit these formulae in any absolute sense; for he conceives that, just as the formula "All things are false" asserts the falsity of itself as well as of everything else, as does the formula "Nothing is true," so also the formula "No more" asserts that itself, like all the rest, is "No more (this and that)," and thus cancels itself along with the rest. And of the other formulae we say the same. If then, while the dogmatizer posits the matter of his dogma as substantial truth, the Skeptic enunciates his formulae so that they are virtually cancelled by themselves, he should not be said to dogmatize in his enunciation of them. And, most important of all, in his enunciation of these formulae he states what appears to himself and announces his own impression in an undogmatic way, without making any positive assertion regarding the external realities.

Chapter VIII.—HAS THE SKEPTIC A DOCTRINAL RULE?

We follow the same lines in replying to the question "Has the Skeptic a doctrinal rule?" For if one defines a "doctrinal rule" as "adherence to a number of dogmas which are dependent both on one another and on appearances," and defines "dogma" as "assent to a non-evident proposition," then we shall say that he has not a doctrinal rule. But if one defines "doctrinal rule" as "procedure which, in accordance with appearance, follows a certain line of reasoning, that reasoning indicating how it is possible to seem to live rightly (the word 'rightly' being taken, not as referring to virtue only, but in a wider sense) and tending to enable one to suspend judgment," then we say that he has a doctrinal rule. For we follow a line of reasoning which, in accordance with appearances, points us to a life conformable to the customs of our country and its laws and institutions, and to our own instinctive feelings.

Chapter IX.—DOES THE SKEPTIC DEAL WITH PHYSICS?

We make a similar reply also to the question "Should the Skeptic deal with physical problems?" For while, on the one hand, so far as regards making firm and positive assertions about any of the matters dogmatically treated in physical theory, we do not deal with physics; yet, on the other hand, in respect of our mode of opposing to every proposition an equal proposition and of our theory of quietude we do treat of physics. This, too, is the way in which we approach the logical and ethical branches of so-called "philosophy."

Chapter X.—DO THE SKEPTICS ABOLISH APPEARANCES?

Those who say that "the Skeptics abolish appearances," or phenomena, seem to me to be unacquainted with the statements of our School. For, as we said above, we do not overthrow the affective sense impressions which induce our assent involuntarily; and these impressions are "the appearances." And when we question whether the underlying object is such as it appears, we grant the fact that it appears, and our doubt does not concern the appearance itself but the account given of that appearance,—and that is a different thing from questioning the appearance itself. For example, honey appears to us to be sweet (and this we grant, for we perceive sweetness through the senses), but whether it is also sweet in its essence is for us a matter of doubt, since this is not an appearance but a judgment regarding the appearance. And even if we do actually argue against the appearances, we do not propound such arguments with the intention of abolishing appearances, but by way of pointing out the rashness of the Dogmatists; for if reason is such a trickster as to all but snatch away the appearances from under our very eyes, surely we should view it with suspicion in the case of things non-evident so as not to display rashness by following it.

Chapter XI.—OF THE CRITERION OF SKEPTICISM

That we adhere to appearances is plain from what we say about the criterion of the Skeptic School. The word "criterion" is used in two senses: in the one it means "the standard regulating belief in reality or unreality" (and this we shall discuss in our refutation); in the other it denotes the standard of action by conforming to which in the conduct of life we perform some actions and abstain from others; and it is of the latter that we are now speaking. The criterion, then, of the Skeptic School is, we say, the appearance, giving this name to what is virtually the sense presentation. For since this lies in feeling and involuntary affection, it is not open to question. Consequently, no one, I suppose, disputes that the underlying object has this or that appearance; the point in dispute is whether the object is in reality such as it appears to be.

Adhering, then, to appearances we live in accordance with the normal rules of life, undogmatically, seeing that we cannot remain wholly inactive. And it would seem that this regulation of life is fourfold, and that one part of it lies in the guidance of Nature, another in the constraint of the passions, another in the tradition of laws and customs, another in the instruction of the arts. Nature's guidance is that by which we are naturally capable of sensation and thought; constraint of the passions is that whereby hunger drives us to food and thirst to drink; tradition of customs and laws, that whereby we regard piety in the conduct of life as good, but impiety as evil; instruction of the arts, that whereby we are not inactive in such arts as we adopt. But we make all these statements undogmatically.

Chapter XII.—WHAT IS THE END OF SKEPTICISM?

Our next subject will be the end of the Skeptic system. Now an "end" is "that for which all actions or reasonings are undertaken, while it exists for the sake of none"; or, otherwise, "the ultimate object of appetency." We assert still that the Skeptic's end is quietude in respect of matters of opinion and moderate feeling in respect of things unavoidable. For the Skeptic, having set out to philosophize with the object of passing judgment on the sense impressions and ascertaining which of them are true and which false, so as to attain quietude thereby, found himself involved in contradictions of equal weight, and being unable to decide between them suspended judgment; and as he was thus in suspense there followed, as it happened, the state of quietude in respect of matters of opinion. For the man who opines that anything is by nature good or bad is for ever being disquieted: when he is without the things which he deems good he believes himself to be tormented by things naturally bad and he pursues after the things which are, as he thinks, good; which when he has obtained he keeps falling into still more perturbations because of his irrational and immoderate elation, and in his dread of a change of fortune he uses every endeavor to avoid losing the things which he deems good. On the other hand, the man who determines nothing as to what is naturally good or bad neither shuns nor pursues anything eagerly; and, in consequence, he is unperturbed.

The Skeptic, in fact, had the same experience which is said to have befallen the painter Apelles. Once, they say, when he was painting a horse and wished to represent in the painting the horse's foam, he was so unsuccessful that he gave up the attempt and flung at the picture the sponge on which he used to wipe the paints off his brush, and the mark of the sponge produced the effect of a horse's foam. So, too, the Skeptics were in hopes of gaining quietude by means of a decision regarding the disparity of the objects of sense and of thought, and being unable to effect this they suspended judgment; and they found that quietude, as if by chance, followed upon their suspense, even as a shadow follows its substance. We do not, however, suppose that the Skeptic is wholly untroubled; but we say that he is troubled by things unavoidable; for we grant that he is cold at times and thirsty, and suffers various affections of that k. 'd. But even in these cases, whereas ordinary people are afflicted by two circumstances,—namely, by the affections themselves and, in no less a degree, by the belief that these conditions are evil by nature,—the Skeptic, by his rejection of the added belief in the natural badness of all these conditions, escapes here too with less discomfort. Hence we say that, while in regard to matters of opinion the Skeptic's end is quietude, in regard to things unavoidable it is "moderate affection." But some notable Skeptics have added the further definition "suspension of judgment in investigations."

Chapter XIII.—OF THE GENERAL MODES LEADING TO SUSPENSION OF JUDGMENT

Now that we have been saying that tranquillity follows on suspension of judgment, it will be our next task to explain how we arrive at this suspension. Speaking generally, one may say that it is the result of setting things in opposition. We oppose either appearances to appearances or objects of thought to objects of thought or *alternando*. For instance, we oppose appearances to appearances when we say "The same tower appears round from a distance, but square from close at hand"; and thoughts to thoughts, when in answer to him who argues the existence of providence from the order of the heavenly bodies we oppose the fact that often the good fare ill and the bad fare well, and draw from this the inference that providence does not exist. And thoughts we oppose to appearances, as when Anaxagoras countered the notion that snow is white with the argument, "Snow is frozen water, and water is black; therefore snow also is black." With a different idea we oppose things present sometimes to things present, as in the foregoing examples, and sometimes to things past or future, as, for instance, when someone propounds to us a theory which we are unable to refute, we say to him in reply, "Just as, before the birth of the founder of the School to which you belong, the theory it holds was not as yet apparent as a sound theory, although it was really in existence, so likewise it is possible that the opposite theory to that which you now propound is already really existent, though not yet apparent to us so that we ought not as yet to yield assent to this theory which at the moment seems to be valid."

But in order that we may have a more exact understanding of these antitheses I will describe the Modes by which suspension of judgment is brought about, but without making any positive assertion regarding either their number or their validity; for it is possible that they may be unsound or there may be more of them than I shall enumerate.

Chapter XIV.—CONCERNING THE TEN MODES

The usual tradition amongst the older Skeptics is that the "modes" by which "suspension" is supposed to be brought about are ten in number; and they also give them the synonymous names of "arguments" and "positions." They are these: the first, based on the variety in animals; the second, on the differences in human beings; the third, on the different structures of the organs of sense; the fourth, on the circumstantial conditions; the fifth, on positions and intervals and locations; the sixth, on intermixtures; the seventh, on the quantities and formations of the underlying objects; the eighth, on the fact of relativity; the ninth, on the frequency or rarity of occurrence; the tenth, on the disciplines and customs and laws, the legendary beliefs and the dogmatic convictions. This order, however, we adopt without prejudice.

As superordinate to these there stand three Modes—that based on the subject who judges, that on the object judged, and that based on both. The first four of the ten Modes are subordinate to the Mode based on the subject (for the subject which judges is either an animal or a man or a sense, and existent in some condition): the seventh and tenth Modes are referred to that based on the object judged: the fifth, sixth, eighth and ninth are referred to the Mode based on both subject and object. Furthermore, these three Modes are also referred to that of relation, so that the Mode of relation stands as the highest *genus*, and the three as *species,* and the ten as subordinate *sub-species.* We give this as the probable account of their numbers; and as to their argumentative force what we say is this:

The *First* argument (or *Trope*), as we said, is that which shows that the same impressions are not produced by the same objects owing to the differences in animals. This we infer both from the differences in their origins and from the variety of their bodily structures. Thus, as to origin, some animals are produced without sexual union, others by coition. And of those produced without coition, some come from fire, like the animalcules which appear in furnaces, others from putrid water, like gnats; others from wine when it turns sour, like ants; others from earth, like grasshoppers; others from marsh, like frogs; others from mud, like worms; others from asses, like beetles; others from greens, like caterpillars; others from fruits, like the gall insects in wild figs; others from rotting animals, as bees from bulls and wasps from horses. Of the animals generated by coition, some—in fact the majority —come from homogeneous parents, others from heterogeneous parents, as do mules. Again, of animals in general, some are born alive, like men; others are born as eggs, like birds; and yet others as lumps of flesh, like bears. It is natural, then, that these dissimilar and variant modes of birth should produce much contrariety of sense affection, and that this is a source of its divergent, discordant and conflicting character.

Moreover, the differences found in the most important parts of the body, and especially in those of which the natural function is judging and perceiving, are capable of producing a vast deal of divergence in the sense impressions [owing to the variety in the animals]. Thus, sufferers from jaundice declare that objects which seem to us white are yellow, while those whose eyes are bloodshot call them blood red. Since, then, some animals also have eyes which are yellow, others bloodshot, others albino, others of other colors, they probably, I suppose, have different perceptions of color. Moreover, if we bend down over a book after having gazed long and fixedly at the sun, the letters seem to us to be golden in color and circling round. Since, then, some animals possess also a natural brilliance in their eyes, and emit from them a fine and mobile stream of light, so that they can even see by night, we seem bound to suppose that they are differently affected from us by external objects. Jugglers, too, by means of smearing lampwicks with the rust of copper or with the juice of the cuttle fish make the bystanders appear now copper-colored and now black—and that by just a small sprinkling of extra matter. Surely, then, we have much more reason to suppose that when different juices are intermingled in the vision of animals their impressions of the objects will become different. Again, when we press the eyeball at one side the forms, figures and sizes of the objects appear oblong and narrow. So it is probable that all animals which have the pupil of the eye slanting and elongated—such as goats, cats, and similar animals—have impressions of the objects which are different and unlike the notions formed of them by the animals which have round pupils. Mirrors, too, owing to differences in their construction, represent the external objects at one time as very small—as when the mirror is concave,—at another time as elongated and narrow—as when the mirror is convex. Some mirrors, too, show the head of the figure reflected at the bottom and the feet at the top. Since, then, some organs of sight actually protrude beyond the face owing to their convexity, while others are quite concave, and others again lie in a level plane, on this account also it is probable that their impressions differ, and that the same objects, as seen by dogs, fishes, lions, men and locusts, are neither equal in size nor similar in shape, but vary according to the image of each object created by the particular sight that receives the impression.

Of the other sense organs also the same account holds good. Thus, in respect of touch, how could one maintain that creatures covered with shells, with flesh, with prickles, with feathers, with scales, are all similarly affected? And as for the sense of hearing, how could we say that its perceptions are alike in animals with a very narrow auditory passage and those with a very wide one, or in animals with hairy ears and those with smooth ears? For, as regards this sense, even we ourselves find our hearing affected in one way when we have our ears plugged and in another way when we use them just as they are. Smell also will differ because of the variety in animals. For if we ourselves are affected in one way when we have a cold and our internal phlegm is excessive, and in another way when the parts about our head are filled with an excess of blood, feeling an aversion to smells which seem sweet to everyone else and regarding them as noxious, it is reasonable to suppose that animals too—since some are flaccid by nature and rich in phlegm, others rich in blood, others marked by a predominant excess of yellow or of black gall—are in each case impressed in different ways by the objects of smell. So too with the objects of taste; for some animals have rough and dry tongues, others extremely moist tongues. We ourselves, too, when our tongues are very dry, in cases of fever, think the food proffered us to be earthy and ill flavored or bitter—an affection due to the variation in the predominating juices which we are said to contain. Since, then, animals also have organs of taste which differ and which have different juices in excess, in respect of taste also they will receive different impressions of the real objects. For just as the same food when digested becomes in one place a vein, in another an artery, in another a bone, in another a sinew, or some other piece of the body, displaying a different potency according to the difference in the parts which receive it;—and just as the same unblended water, when it is absorbed by trees, becomes in one place bark, in another branch, in another blossom, and so finally fig and quince and each of the other fruits;—and just as the single identical breath of a musician breathed into a flute becomes here a shrill note and there a deep note, and the same pressure of his hand on the lyre produces here a deep note and there a shrill note;—so likewise it is probable that the external objects appear different owing to differences in the structure of the animals which experience the sense impressions.

But one may learn this more clearly from the preferences and aversions of animals. Thus, sweet oil seems very agreeable to men, but intolerable to beetles and bees; and olive oil is beneficial to men, but when poured on wasps and bees it destroys them; and sea water is a disagreeable and poisonous potion for men, but fish drink and enjoy it. Pigs, too, enjoy wallowing in the most stinking mire rather than in clear and clean water. And whereas some animals eat grass, others eat shrubs, others feed in woods, others live on seeds or flesh or milk; some of them, too, prefer their food high, others like it fresh, and while some prefer it raw, others like it cooked. And so generally, the things which are agreeable to some are to others disagreeable, distasteful and deadly. Thus, quails are fattened by hemlock, and pigs by henbane; and pigs also enjoy eating salamanders, just as deer enjoy poisonous creatures, and swallows gnats. So ants and wood lice, when swallowed by men, cause distress and gripings, whereas the bear, whenever she falls sick, cures herself by licking them up. The mere touch of an oak twig paralyses the viper, and that of a plane leaf the bat. The elephant flees from the ram, the lion from the cock, sea monsters from the crackle of bursting beans, and the tiger from the sound of a drum. One might, indeed, cite many more examples, but—not to seem unduly prolix—if the same things are displeasing to some but pleasing to others, and pleasure and displeasure depend upon sense impression, then animals receive different impressions from the underlying objects.

But if the same things appear different owing to the variety in animals, we shall, indeed, be able to state our own impressions of the real object, but as to its essential nature we shall suspend judgment. For we cannot ourselves judge between our own impressions and those of the other animals, since we ourselves are involved in the dispute and are, therefore, rather in need of a judge than competent to pass judgment ourselves. Besides, we are unable, either with or without proof, to prefer our own impressions to those of the irrational animals. For in addition to the probability that proof is, as we shall show,[2] a non-entity, the so-called proof itself with be either apparent to us or non-apparent. If, then, it is non-apparent, we shall not accept it with confidence; while if it is apparent to us, inasmuch as what is apparent to animals is the point in question and the proof is apparent to us who are animals, it follows that we shall have to question the proof itself as to whether it is as true as it is apparent. It is, indeed, absurd to attempt to establish the matter in question by means of the matter in question, since in that case the same thing will be at once believed and disbelieved,—believed in so far as it purports to prove, but disbelieved in so far as it requires proof,—which is impossible. Consequently we shall not possess a proof which enables us to give our own sense impressions the preference over those of the so-called irrational animals. If, then, owing to the variety in animals their sense impressions differ, and it is impossible to judge between them, we must necessarily suspend judgment regarding the external underlying objects.

By way of super-addition, too, we draw comparisons between mankind and the so-called irrational animals in respect of their sense impressions. For, after our solid arguments, we deem it quite proper to poke fun at those conceited braggarts, the Dogmatists. As a rule, our School compare the irrational animals in the mass with mankind; but since the Dogmatists captiously assert that the comparison is unequal, we—super-adding yet more—will carry our ridicule further and base our

_____
2. Book II, chapter xii, section 12.

argument on one animal only, the dog for instance if you like, which is held to be the most worthless of animals. For even in this case we shall find that the animals we are discussing are no wise inferior to ourselves in respect of the credibility of their impressions.

Now, it is allowed by the Dogmatists that this animal, the dog, excels us in point of sensation: as to smell it is more sensitive than we are, since by this sense it tracks beasts that it cannot see; and with its eyes it sees them more quickly than we do; and with its ears it is keen of perception. Next let us proceed to the reasoning faculty. Of reason one kind is internal, implanted in the soul, the other externally expressed.[3] Let us consider first the internal reason. Now according to those Dogmatists who are, at present, our chief opponents—I mean the Stoics—internal reason is supposed to be occupied with the following matters: the choice of things congenial and the avoidance of things alien; the knowledge of the arts contributing thereto; the apprehension of the virtues pertaining to one's proper nature and of those relating to the passions. Now the dog—the animal upon which, by way of example, we have decided to base our argument—exercises choice of the congenial and avoidance of the harmful, in that it hunts after food and slinks away from a raised whip. Moreover, it possesses an art which supplies what is congenial, namely hunting. Nor is it devoid even of virtue; for certainly if justice consists in rendering to each his due, the dog, that welcomes and guards its friends and benefactors but drives off strangers and evildoers, cannot be lacking in justice. But if he possesses this virtue, then, since the virtues are interdependent, he possesses all the other virtues; and these, say the philosophers,[4] the majority of men do not possess. That the dog is also valiant we see by the way he repels attacks, and intelligent as well, as Homer too testified when he sang how Odysseus went unrecognized by all the people of his own household and was recognized only by the dog Argus, who neither was deceived by the bodily alterations of the hero nor had lost his original apprehensive impression, which indeed he evidently retained better than the men. And according to Chrysippus, who shows special interest in irrational animals, the dog even shares in the far-famed "Dialectic." This person, at any rate, declares that the dog makes use of the fifth complex indemonstrable syllogism when, on arriving at a spot where three ways meet, after smelling at the two roads by which the quarry did not pass, he rushes off at once by the third without stopping to smell. For, says the old writer, the dog im-

---

3. Thought and utterance.
4. I.e., the Stoics.

plicitly reasons thus: "The creature went either by this road, or by that, or by the other: but it did not go by this road or by that: therefore it went by the other." Moreover, the dog is capable of comprehending and assuaging his own sufferings; for when a thorn has got stuck in his foot he hastens to remove it by rubbing his foot on the ground and by using his teeth. And if he has a wound anywhere, because dirty wounds are hard to cure whereas clean ones heal easily, the dog gently licks off the pus that has gathered. Nay more, the dog admirably observes the prescription of Hippocrates: rest being what cures the foot, whenever he gets his foot hurt he lifts it up and keeps it as far as possible free from pressure. And when distressed by unwholesome humors he eats grass, by the help of which he vomits what is unwholesome and gets well again. If, then, it has been shown that the animal upon which, as an example, we have based our argument not only chooses the wholesome and avoids the noxious, but also possesses an art capable of supplying what is wholesome, and is capable of comprehending and assuaging its own sufferings, and is not devoid of virtue, then—these being the things in which the perfection of internal reason consists—the dog will be thus far perfect. And that, I suppose, is why certain of the professors of philosophy have adorned themselves with the title of this animal.[5]

Concerning external reason, or speech, it is unnecessary for the present to inquire; for it has been rejected even by some of the Dogmatists as being a hindrance to the acquisition of virtue, for which reason they used to practice silence during the period of instruction; and besides, supposing that a man is dumb, no one will therefore call him irrational. But to pass over these cases, we certainly see animals— the subject of our argument—uttering quite human cries,—jays, for instance, and others. And, leaving this point also aside, even if we do not understand the utterances of the so-called irrational animals, still it is not improbable that they converse although we fail to understand them; for in fact when we listen to the talk of barbarians we do not understand it, and it seems to us a kind of uniform chatter. Moreover, we hear dogs uttering one sound when they are driving people off, another when they are howling, and one sound when beaten, and a quite different sound when fawning. And so in general, in the case of all other animals as well as the dog, whoever examines the matter carefully will find a great variety of utterance according to the different circumstances, so that, in consequence, the so-called irrational animals may justly be said to participate in external reason. But if they neither

5. The Cynics, or Dog philosophers.

fall short of mankind in the accuracy of their perceptions, nor in internal reason, nor yet (to go still further) in external reason, or speech, then they will deserve no less credence than ourselves in respect of their sense impressions. Probably, too, we may reach this conclusion by basing our arguments on each single class of irrational animals. Thus, for example, who would deny that birds excel in quickness of wit or that they employ external reason? For they understand not only present events but future events as well, and these they foreshow to such as are able to comprehend them by means of prophetic cries as well as by other signs.

I have drawn this comparison (as I previously indicated) by way of super-addition, having already sufficiently proved, as I think, that we cannot prefer our own sense impressions to those of the irrational animals. If, however, the irrational animals are not less worthy of credence than we in regard to the value of sense impressions, and their impressions vary according to the variety of animal,—then, although I shall be able to say what the nature of each of the underlying objects appears to me to be, I shall be compelled, for the reasons stated above, to suspend judgment as to its real nature.

Such, then, is the First of the Modes which induce suspense. The *Second Mode* is, as we said, that based on the differences in men; for even if we grant for the sake of argument that men are more worthy of credence than irrational animals, we shall find that even our own differences of themselves lead to suspense. For man, you know, is said to be compounded of two things, soul and body, and in both these we differ one from another.

Thus, as regards the *body*, we differ in our figures and "idiosyncrasies," or constitutional peculiarities. The body of an Indian differs in shape from that of a Scythian; and it is said that what causes the variation is a difference in the predominant humors. Owing to this difference in the predominant humors the sense impressions also come to differ, as we indicated in our First Argument. So too in respect of choice and avoidance of external objects men exhibit great differences; thus Indians enjoy some things, our people other things, and the enjoyment of different things is an indication that we receive varying impressions from the underlying objects. In respect of our "idiosyncrasies," our differences are such that some of us digest the flesh of oxen more easily than rock fish, or get diarrhea from the weak wine of Lesbos. An old wife of Attica, they say, swallowed with impunity thirty drams of hemlock, and Lysis took four drams of poppy juice without hurt. Demophon, Alexander's butler, used to shiver when he was in the sun or in a hot bath, but felt warm in the shade. Athenagoras the Argive took no hurt from the stings of scorpions and poisonous spiders; and the Psyllaeans, as they are called, are not harmed by bites from snakes and asps, nor are the Tentyritae of Egypt harmed by the crocodile. Further, those Ethiopians who live beyond Lake Meroë on the banks of the river Astapous eat with impunity scorpions, snakes, and the like. Rufinus of Chalcis when he drank hellebore neither vomited nor suffered at all from purging, but swallowed and digested it just like any ordinary drink. Chrysermus the Herophilean doctor was liable to get a heart attack if ever he took pepper; and Soterichus the surgeon was seized with diarrhea whenever he smelled fried sprats. Andron the Argive was so immune from thirst that he actually traversed the waterless country of Libya without needing a drink. Tiberius Caesar could see in the dark; and Aristotle tells of a Thasian who fancied that the image of a man was continually going in front of him.

Seeing, then, that men vary so much in body—to content ourselves with but a few instances of the many collected by the Dogmatists,—men probably also differ from one another in respect of the *soul* itself; for the body is a kind of expression of the soul, as in fact is proved by the science of physiognomy. But the greatest proof of the vast and endless differences in men's intelligence is the discrepancy in the statements of the Dogmatists concerning the right objects of choice and avoidance, as well as other things. Regarding this the poets, too, have expressed themselves fittingly. Thus Pindar says:

> The crowns and trophies of the storm-foot steeds
> Give joy to one; yet others find it joy
> To dwell in gorgeous chambers gold-bedeckt;
> Some even take delight in voyaging
> O'er ocean's billows in a speeding barque.

And the poet says: "One thing is pleasing to one man, another thing to another." Tragedy, too, is full of such sayings; for example:

> Were fair and wise the same thing unto all,
> There had been no contentious quarrelling.

And again:

> 'Tis strange that the same thing abhorr'd by some
> Should give delight to others.

Seeing, then, that choice and avoidance depend on pleasure and displeasure, while pleasure and displeasure depend on sensation and sense impression, whenever some men choose the very things which are avoided by others, it is logical for us to conclude that they are also differently affected by the same things, since otherwise they would all alike have chosen or avoided the same things. But if the same objects affect men differently owing to the differences in the men, then, on this ground also, we shall reasonably be led to suspension of judgment. For while we are, no doubt, able to state what each of the underlying objects appears to be, relatively to each difference, we are incapable of explaining what it is in reality. For we shall have to believe either all men or some. But if we believe all, we shall be attempting the impossible and accepting contradictories; and if so, let us be told whose opinions we are to endorse. For the Platonist will say "Plato's"; the Epicurean, "Epicurus's"; and so on with the rest; and thus by their unsettled disputations they will bring us round again to a state of suspense. Moreover, he who maintains that we ought to assent to the majority is making a childish proposal, since no one is able to visit the whole of mankind and determine what pleases the majority of them; for there may possibly be races of whom we know nothing amongst whom conditions rare with us are common, and conditions common with us rare, —possibly, for instance, most of them feel no pain from the bites of spiders, though a few on rare occasions feel such pain; and so likewise with the rest of the "idiosyncrasies" mentioned above. Necessarily, therefore, the differences in men afford a further reason for bringing in suspension of judgment.

When the Dogmatists—a self-loving class of men—assert that in judging things they ought to prefer themselves to other people, we know that their claim is absurd; for they themselves are a party to the controversy; and if, when judging appearances, they have already given the preference to themselves, then, by thus entrusting themselves with the judgment, they are begging the question before the judgment is begun. Nevertheless, in order that we may arrive at suspension of judgment by basing our argument on one person—such as, for example, their visionary "Sage"[6]—we adopt the Mode which comes Third in order.

This *Third Mode* is, we say, based on differences in the senses. That the senses differ from one another is obvious. Thus, to the eye paintings seem to have recesses and projections, but not so to the touch. Honey, too, seems to some pleasant to the tongue but unpleasant to the eyes;

6. The ideal "Wise Man" of the Stoics.

so that it is impossible to say whether it is absolutely pleasant or un-pleasant. The same is true of sweet oil, for it pleases the sense of smell but displeases the taste. So too with spurge:[7] since it pains the eyes but causes no pain to any other part of the body, we cannot say whether, in its real nature, it is absolutely painful or painless to bodies. Rain water, too, is beneficial to the eyes but roughens the wind-pipe and the lungs; as also does olive oil, though it mollifies the epidermis. The cramp fish, also, when applied to the extremities produces cramp, but it can be applied to the rest of the body without hurt. Consequently we are unable to say what is the real nature of each of these things, al-though it is possible to say what each thing at the moment appears to be.

A longer list of examples might be given, but to avoid prolixity, in view of the plan of our treatise, we will say just this. Each of the phenomena perceived by the senses seems to be a complex; the apple, for example, seems smooth, odorous, sweet and yellow. But it is non-evident whether it really possesses these qualities only; or whether it has but one quality but appears varied owing to the varying structure of the sense organs; or whether, again, it has more qualities than are apparent, some of which occlude our perception. That the apple has but one quality might be argued from what we said above regarding the food absorbed by bodies, and the water sucked up by trees, and the breath in flutes and pipes and similar instruments; for the apple likewise may be all of one sort but appear different owing to differences in the sense organs in which perception takes place. And that the apple may possibly possess more qualities than those apparent to us we argue in this way. Let us imagine a man who possesses from birth the senses of touch, taste and smell, but can neither hear nor see. This man, then, will assume that nothing visible or audible has any exis-tence, but only those three kinds of qualities which he is able to appre-hend. Possibly, then, we also, having only our five senses, perceive only such of the apple's qualities as we are capable of apprehending; and possibly it may possess other underlying qualities which affect other sense organs, though we, not being endowed with those organs, fail to ap-prehend the sense objects which come through them.

"But," it may be objected, "nature made the senses commensurate with the objects of sense." What kind of "nature"? we ask, seeing that there exists so much unresolved controversy amongst the Dogmatists concerning the reality which belongs to nature. For he who decides the question as to the existence of nature will be discredited by them if he

7. A species of plants with acrid, milky juice.

is an ordinary person, while if he is a philosopher he will be a party to
the controversy and therefore himself subject to judgment and not a
judge. If, however, it is possible that only those qualities which we
seem to perceive subsist in the apple, or that a greater number subsist,
or, again, that not even the qualities which affect us subsist, then it
will be non-evident to us what the nature of the apple really is. And the
same argument applies to all the other objects of sense. But if the
senses do not apprehend external objects, neither can the mind apprehend them; hence, because of this argument also, we shall be driven,
it seems, to suspend judgment regarding the external underlying
objects.

In order that we may finally reach suspension by basing our argument on each sense singly, or even by disregarding the senses, we
further adopt the *Fourth Mode* of suspension. This is the Mode based,
as we say, on the "circumstances," meaning by "circumstances" conditions or dispositions.[8] And this Mode, we say, deals with states that are
natural or unnatural, with waking or sleeping, with conditions due to
age, motion or rest, hatred or love, emptiness or fulness, drunkenness or
soberness, predispositions, confidence or fear, grief or joy. Thus, according as the mental state is natural or unnatural, objects produce
dissimilar impressions, as when men in a frenzy or in a state of ecstasy
believe they hear daemons' voices, while we do not. Similarly they
often say that they perceive an odour of storax or frankincense, or
some such scent, and many other things, though we fail to perceive
them. Also, the same water which feels very hot when poured on inflamed spots seems lukewarm to us. And the same coat which seems of
a bright yellow color to men with blood-shot eyes does not appear so
to me. And the same honey seems to me sweet, but bitter to men with
jaundice. Now should anyone say that it is an intermixture of certain
humors which produces in those who are in an unnatural state improper
impressions from the underlying objects, we have to reply that, since
healthy persons also have mixed humors, these humors too are capable
of causing the external objects—which really are such as they appear
to those who are said to be in an unnatural state—to appear other than
they are to healthy persons. For to ascribe the power of altering the
underlying objects to those humors, and not to these, is purely fanciful;
since just as healthy men are in a state that is natural for the healthy
but unnatural for the sick, so also sick men are in a state that is unnatural for the healthy but natural for the sick, so that to these last

8. I.e. the mental or physical state of the subject at the moment of perception.

also we must give credence as being, relatively speaking, in a natural state.[9]

Sleeping and waking, too, give rise to different impressions, since we do not imagine when awake what we imagine in sleep, nor when asleep what we imagine when awake; so that the existence or non-existence of our impressions is not absolute but relative, being in relation to our sleeping or waking condition. Probably, then, in dreams we see things which to our waking state are unreal, although not wholly unreal; for they exist in our dreams, just as waking realities exist although non-existent in dreams.

Age is another cause of difference. For the same air seems chilly to the old but mild to those in their prime; and the same color appears faint to older men but vivid to those in their prime; and similarly the same sound seems to the former faint, but to the latter clearly audible. Moreover, those who differ in age are differently moved in respect of choice and avoidance. For whereas children—to take a case—are all eagerness for balls and hoops, men in their prime choose other things, and old men yet others. And from this we conclude that differences in age also cause different impressions to be produced by the same underlying objects.

Another cause why the real objects appear different lies in motion and rest. For those objects which, when we are standing still, we see to be motionless, we imagine to be in motion when we are sailing past them.

Love and hatred are a cause, as when some have an extreme aversion to pork while others greatly enjoy eating it. Hence too, Menander said:

> Mark now his visage, what a change is there
> Since he has come to this! How bestial!
> 'Tis actions fair that make the fairest face.

Many lovers, too, who have ugly mistresses think them most beautiful.

Hunger and satiety are a cause; for the same food seems agreeable to the hungry but disagreeable to the sated.

Drunkenness and soberness are a cause; since actions which we think shameful when sober do not seem shameful to us when drunk.

Predispositions are a cause; for the same wine which seems sour to those who have previously eaten dates or figs, seems sweet to those

9. This is aimed against the Stoic view that only the healthy, or normal, is "natural."

who have just consumed nuts or chick peas; and the vestibule of the bathhouse, which warms those entering from outside, chills those coming out of the bathroom if they stop long in it.

Fear and boldness are a cause; as what seems to the coward fearful and formidable does not seem so in the least to the bold man.

Grief and joy are a cause; since the same affairs are burdensome to those in grief but delightful to those who rejoice.

Seeing then that the dispositions also are the cause of so much disagreement, and that men are differently disposed at different times, although, no doubt, it is easy to say what nature each of the underlying objects appears to each man to possess, we cannot go on to say what its real nature is, since the disagreement admits in itself of no settlement. For the person who tries to settle it is either in one of the aforementioned dispositions or in no disposition whatsoever. But to declare that he is in no disposition at all—as, for instance, neither in health nor sickness, neither in motion nor at rest, of no definite age, and devoid of all the other dispositions as well—is the height of absurdity. And if he is to judge the sense impressions while he is in some one disposition, he will be a party to the disagreement, and, moreover, he will not be an impartial judge of the external underlying objects owing to his being confused by the dispositions in which he is placed. The waking person, for instance, cannot compare the impressions of sleepers with those of men awake, nor the sound person those of the sick with those of the sound; for we assent more readily to things present, which affect us in the present, than to things not present.

In another way, too, the disagreement of such impressions is incapable of settlement. For he who prefers one impression to another, or one "circumstance" to another, does so either uncritically and without proof or critically and with proof; but he can do this neither without these means (for then he would be discredited) nor with them. For if he is to pass judgment on the impressions he must certainly judge them by a criterion; this criterion, then, he will declare to be true, or else false. But if false, he will be discredited; whereas, if he shall declare it to be true, he will be stating that the criterion is true either without proof or with proof. But if without proof, he will be discredited; and if with proof, it will certainly be necessary for the proof also to be true, to avoid being discredited. Shall he, then, affirm the truth of the proof adopted to establish the criterion after having judged it or without judging it? If without judging, he will be discredited; but if after judging, plainly he will say that he has judged it by a criterion; and of that criterion we shall ask for a proof, and of that proof again a criterion. For the proof always requires a criterion to confirm it, and the criterion also a proof to demonstrate its truth; and neither can a proof be sound without the previous existence of a true criterion nor can the criterion be true without the previous confirmation of the proof. So in this way both the criterion and the proof are involved in the circular process of reasoning, and thereby both are found to be untrustworthy; for since each of them is dependent on the credibility of the other, the one is lacking in credibility just as much as the other. Consequently, if a man can prefer one impression to another neither without a proof and a criterion nor with them, then the different impressions due to the differing conditions will admit of no settlement; so that as a result of this Mode also we are brought to suspend judgment regarding the nature of external realities.

The *Fifth Argument* (or *Trope*) is that based on positions, distances, and locations; for owing to each of these the same objects appear different; for example, the same porch when viewed from one of its corners appears curtailed, but viewed from the middle symmetrical on all sides; and the same ship seems at a distance to be small and stationary, but from close at hand large and in motion; and the same tower from a distance appears round but from a near point quadrangular.

These effects are due to distances; among effects due to locations are the following: the light of a lamp appears dim in the sun but bright in the dark; and the same oar bent when in the water but straight when out of the water; and the egg soft when inside the fowl but hard when in the air; and the jacinth fluid when in the lynx but hard when in the air; and the coral soft when in the sea but hard when in the air; and sound seems to differ in quality according as it is produced in a pipe, or in a flute, or simply in the air.

Effects due to positions are such as these: the same painting when laid flat appears smooth, but when inclined forward at a certain angle it seems to have recesses and prominences. The necks of doves, also, appear different in hue according to the differences in the angle of inclination.

Since, then, all apparent objects are viewed in a certain place, and from a certain distance, or in a certain position, and each of these conditions produces a great divergency in the sense-impressions, as we mentioned above, we shall be compelled by this Mode also to end up in suspension of judgment. For in fact anyone who purposes to give the preference to any of these impressions will be attempting the impossible. For if he shall deliver his judgment simply and without proof, he will be discredited; and should he, on the other hand, desire to adduce proof, he will confute himself if he says that the proof is false, while if he asserts that the proof is true he will be asked for a proof of its truth, and again for a proof of this latter *ad infinitum.* But to produce proofs to infinity is impossible; so that neither by the use of proofs will he be able to prefer one sense impression to another. If, then, one cannot hope to pass judgement on the afore-mentioned impressions either with or without proof, the conclusion we are driven to is suspension; for while we can, no doubt, state the nature which each object appears to possess as viewed in a certain position or at a certain distance or in a certain place, what its real nature is we are, for the foregoing reasons, unable to declare.

The *Sixth Mode* is that based on admixtures, by which we conclude that, because none of the real objects affects our senses by itself but always in conjunction with something else, though we may possibly be able to state the nature of the resultant mixture formed by the external object and that along with which it is perceived, we shall not be able to say what is the exact nature of the external reality in itself. That none of the external objects affects our senses by itself but always in conjunction with something else, and that, in consequence, it assumes a different appearance, is, I imagine, quite obvious. Thus, our own complexion is of one hue in warm air, of another in cold, and we should not be able to say what our complexion really is, but only what it looks like in conjunction with each of these conditions. And the same sound appears of one sort in conjunction with rare air and of another sort with dense air; and odors are more pungent in a hot bathroom or in the sun than in chilly air; and a body is light when immersed in water but heavy when surrounded by air.

But to pass on from the subject of external admixture,—our eyes contain within themselves both membranes and liquids. Since, then, the objects of vision are not perceived apart from these, they will not be apprehended with exactness; for what we perceive is the resultant mixture, and because of this the sufferers from jaundice see everything yellow, and those with bloodshot eyes reddish like blood. And since the same sound seems of one quality in open places, of another in narrow and winding places, and different in clear air and in murky air, it is probable that we do not apprehend the sound in its real purity; for the ears have crooked and narrow passages, which are also befogged by vaporous effluvia which are said to be emitted by the regions of the head. Moreover, since there reside substances in the nostrils and in the organs of taste, we apprehend the objects of taste and of smell in conjunction with these and not in their real purity. So that, because of these admixtures, the senses do not apprehend the exact quality of the external real objects.

Nor yet does the mind apprehend it, since, in the first place, its guides, which are the senses, go wrong; and probably, too, the mind itself adds a certain admixture of its own to the messages conveyed by the senses; for we observe that there are certain humors present in each of the regions which the Dogmatists regard as the seat of the "Ruling Principle" whether it be the brain or the heart, or in whatever part of the creature one chooses to locate it. Thus, according to this Mode also we see that, owing to our inability to make any statement about the real nature of external objects, we are compelled to suspend judgment.

The *Seventh Mode* is that based, as we said, on the quantity and constitution of the underlying objects, meaning generally by "constitution" the manner of composition. And it is evident that by this Mode also we are compelled to suspend judgment concerning the real nature of the objects. Thus, for example, the filings of a goat's horn appear white when viewed simply by themselves and without combination, but when combined in the substance of the horn they look black. And silver filings appear black when they are by themselves, but when united to the whole mass they are sensed as white. And chips of the marble of Taenarum seem white when planed, but in combination with the whole block they appear yellow. And pebbles when scattered apart appear rough, but when combined in a heap they produce the sensation of softness. And hellebore if applied in a fine and powdery state produces suffocation, but not so when it is coarse. And wine strengthens us when drunk in moderate quantity, but when too much is taken it paralyses the body. So likewise food exhibits different effects according to the quantity consumed; for instance, it frequently upsets the body with indigestion and attacks of purging because of the large quantity taken. Therefore in these cases, too, we shall be able to describe the nature of the shaving of the horn and of the compound made up of many shavings, and that of the particle of silver and of the compound of many particles, and that of the sliver of Taenarean marble and of the compound of many such small pieecs, and the relative natures of the pebbles, the hellebore, the wine and the food,—but when it comes to the independent and real nature of the objects, this we shall be unable to describe because of the divergency in the sense-impressions which is due to the combinations.

As a general rule, it seems that wholesome things become harmful when used in immoderate quantities, and things that seem hurtful when taken to excess cause no harm when in minute quanties. What we observe in regard to the effects of medicines is the best evidence in support of our statement: for there the exact blending of the simple drugs makes the compound wholesome, but when the slightest oversight is made in the measuring, as sometimes happens, the compound is not only unwholesome but frequently even most harmful and deleterious. Thus the argument from quantities and compositions causes confusion as to the real nature of the external substances. Probably, therefore, this Mode also will bring us round to suspension of judgment, as we are unable to make any absolute statement concerning the real nature of external objects.

The *Eighth Mode* is that based on relativity; and by it we conclude that, since all things are relative, we shall suspend judgment regarding their independent and real essence. But this point we must notice—that here as elsewhere we use the term "are" for the term "appear," and what we virtually mean is "all things appear relative." And this statement is twofold, implying, firstly, relation to the thing which judges (for the external object which is judged appears in relation to that thing), and, in a second sense, relation to the accompanying percepts, for instance the right side in relation to the left. Indeed, we have already argued that all things are relative—for example, with respect to the thing which judges, it is in relation to some one particular animal or man or sense that each object appears, and in relation to such and such a circumstance; and with respect to the concomitant percepts, each object appears in relation to some one particular admixture or mode or combination or quantity or position.

There are also special arguments to prove the relativity of all things, in this way: Do things which exist "differentially" differ from relative things or not? If they do not differ, then they too are relative; but if they differ, then, since everything which differs is relative to something (for it has its name from the relation to that from which it differs), things which exist differentially are relative. Again,—of existing things some, according to the Dogmatists,[10] are *summa genera*, others *infimae species*, others both genera and species; and all these are relative; therefore all things are relative. Further, some existing

10. Including the Peripatetics, as well as the Stoics. A *summum genus* (e.g. "Being") may be divided into *genera* (e.g. "Animals," "Minerals"), and these subdivided into *species* (e.g. "Men," "Dogs," etc.), down to the *infimae species* (e.g. "Negroes") which cannot be further subdivided. The intermediate species (e.g. "Men") are both *genera* (in relation to their subspecies) and *species* (in relation to higher genera).

things are fully evident, as they say, others non-evident; and the apparent things are signifying, but the non-evident signified by the apparent; for according to them "the things apparent are the vision of the non-evident." But the significant and the signified are relative; therefore all things are relative. Moreover, some existent things are similar, others dissimilar, and some equal, others unequal; and these are relative; therefore all things are relative. And even he who asserts that not all things are relative confirms the relativity of all things, since by his arguments against us he shows that the very statement "not all things are relative" is relative to ourselves, and not universal.

When, however, we have thus established that all things are relative, we are plainly left with the conclusion that we shall not be able to state what is the nature of each of the objects in its own real purity, but only what nature it appears to possess in its relative character. Hence it follows that we must suspend judgment concerning the real nature of the objects.

The *Mode* which, as we said, comes *Ninth* in order is based on constancy or rarity of occurrence, and we shall explain it as follows. The sun is, of course, much more amazing than a comet; yet because we see the sun constantly but the comet rarely we are so amazed by the comet that we even regard it as a divine portent, while the sun causes no amazement at all. If, however, we were to conceive of the sun as appearing but rarely and setting rarely, and illuminating everything all at once and throwing everything into shadow suddenly, then we should experience much amazement at the sight. An earthquake also does not cause the same alarm in those who experience it for the first time and those who have grown accustomed to such things. How much amazement, also, does the sea excite in the man who sees it for the first time! And indeed the beauty of a human body thrills us more at the first sudden view than when it becomes a customary spectacle. Rare things too we count as precious, but not what is familiar to us and easily got. Thus, if we should suppose water to be rare, how much more precious it would appear to us than all the things which are accounted precious! Or if we should imagine gold to be simply scattered in quantities over the earth like stones, to whom do we suppose it would then be precious and worth hoarding?

Since then, owing to the frequency or rarity of their occurrence, the same things seem at one time to be amazing or precious and at another time nothing of the sort, we infer that though we shall be able perhaps to say what nature appears to belong to each of these things in virtue of its frequent or rare occurrence, we are not able to state what nature absolutely belongs to each of the external objects. So because of this Mode also we suspend judgment regarding them.

There is a *Tenth Mode,* which is mainly concerned with Ethics, being based on rules of conduct, habits, laws, legendary beliefs, and dogmatic conceptions. A rule of conduct is a choice of a way of life, or of a particular action, adopted by one person or many—by Diogenes, for instance, or the Laconians. A law is a written contract amongst the members of a State, the transgressor of which is punished. A habit or custom (the terms are equivalent) is the joint adoption of a certain kind of action by a number of men, the transgressor of which is not actually punished; for example, the law proscribes adultery, and custom with us forbids intercourse with a woman in public. Legendary belief is the acceptance of unhistorical and fictitious events, such as, amongst others, the legends about Cronos; for these stories win credence with many. Dogmatic conception is the acceptance of a fact which seems to be established by analogy or some form of demonstration, as, for example, that atoms are the elements of existing things, or homoeomeries, or *minima,* or something else.

And each of these we oppose now to itself, and now to each of the others. For example, we oppose habit to habit in this way: some of the Ethiopians tattoo their children, but we do not; and while the Persians think it seemly to wear a brightly dyed dress reaching to the feet, we think it unseemly; and whereas the Indians have intercourse with their women in public, most other races regard this as shameful. And law we oppose to law in this way: among the Romans the man who renounces his father's property does not pay his father's debts, but among the Rhodians he always pays them; and among the Scythian Tauri it was a law that strangers should be sacrificed to Artemis, but with us it is forbidden to slay a human being at the altar. And we oppose rule of conduct to rule of conduct, as when we oppose the rule of Diogenes to that of Aristippus or that of the Laconians to that of the Italians. And we oppose legendary belief to legendary belief when we say that whereas in one story the father of men and gods is alleged to be Zeus, in another he is Oceanos—"Ocean sire of the gods, and Tethys the mother that bare them." And we oppose dogmatic conceptions to one another when we say that some declare that there is one element only, others an infinite number; some that the soul is mortal, others that it is immortal; and some that human affairs are controlled by divine providence, others without providence.

And we oppose habit to the other things, as for instance to law when we say that amongst the Persians it is the habit to indulge in intercourse with males, but amongst the Romans it is forbidden by law to do so; and that, whereas with us adultery is forbidden, amongst the Massagetae it is traditionally regarded as an indifferent custom, as Eudoxus of Cnidos relates in the first book of his *Travels;* and that, whereas intercourse with a mother is forbidden in our country, in Persia it is the general custom to form such marriages; and also among the Egyptians men marry their sisters, a thing forbidden by law amongst us. And habit is opposed to rule of conduct when, whereas most men have intercourse with their own wives in retirement, Crates did it in public with Hipparchia; and Diogenes went about with one shoulder bare, whereas we dress in the customary manner. It is opposed also to legendary belief, as when the legends say that Cronos devoured his own children, though it is our habit to protect our children; and whereas it is customary with us to revere the gods as being good and immune from evil, they are presented by the poets as suffering wounds and envying one another. And habit is opposed to dogmatic conception when, whereas it is our habit to pray to the gods for good things, Epicurus declares that the Divinity pays no heed to us; and when Aristippus considers the wearing of feminine attire a matter of indifference, though we consider it a disgraceful thing.

And we oppose rule of conduct to law when, though there is a law which forbids the striking of a free or well-born man, the pancratiasts strike one another because of the rule of life they follow; and when, though homicide is forbidden, gladiators destroy one another for the same reason. And we oppose legendary belief to rule of conduct when we say that the legends relate that Heracles in the house of Omphale "toiled at the spinning of wool, enduring slavery's burden," and did things which no one would have chosen to do even in a moderate degree, whereas the rule of life of Heracles was a noble one. And we oppose rule of conduct to dogmatic conception when, whereas athletes covet glory as something good and for its sake undertake a toilsome rule of life, many of the philosophers dogmatically assert that glory is a worthless thing. And we oppose law to legendary belief when the poets represent the gods as committing adultery and practicing intercourse with males, whereas the law with us forbids such actions; and we oppose it to dogmatic conception when Chrysippus says that intercourse with mothers or sisters is a thing indifferent, whereas the law forbids such things. And we oppose legendary belief to dogmatic conception when the poets say that Zeus came down and had intercourse with mortal women, but amongst the Dogmatists it is held that such a thing is impossible; and again, when the poet relates that because of

his grief for Sarpedon Zeus "let fall upon the earth great gouts of
blood," whereas it is a dogma of the philosophers that the deity is
impassive; and when these same philosophers demolish the legend of
the hippocentaurs, and offer us the hippocentaur as a type of unreality.

We might indeed have taken many other examples in connexion
with each of the anthitheses above mentioned; but in a concise account
like ours, these will be sufficient. Only, since by means of this Mode
also so much divergency is shown to exist in objects, we shall not be
able to state what character belongs to the object in respect of its real
essence, but only what belongs to it in respect of this particular rule
of conduct, or law, or habit, and so on with each of the rest. So because
of this Mode also we are compelled to suspend judgment regarding the
real nature of external objects. And thus by means of all the Ten
Modes we are finally led to suspension of judgment.

Book II

Chapter IX.—DOES ANYTHING TRUE REALLY EXIST?

Seeing, then, that there is a controversy amongst the Dogmatists
regarding "the true," since some assert that something true exists,
others that nothing true exists, it is impossible to decide the controversy, because the man who says that something true exists will not
be believed without proof, on account of the controversy; and if he
wishes to offer proof, he will be disbelieved if he acknowledges that his
proof is false, whereas if he declares that his proof is true he becomes
involved in circular reasoning and will be required to show proof of
the real truth of his proof, and another proof of that proof, and so on
ad infinitum. But it is impossible to prove an infinite series; and so it
is impossible also to get to know that something true exists.

Moreover, the "something," which is, they declare, the highest
genus of all, is either true or false or neither false nor true or both false
and true. If, then, they shall assert that it is false they will be confessing that all things are false. For just as it follows because "animal"
is animate that all particular animals also are animate, so too if the
highest genus of all ("something") is false all the particulars also will
be false and nothing true. And this involves also the conclusion that

nothing is false; for the very statements "all things are false," and "something false exists," being themselves included in the "all," will be false. And if the "something" is true, all things will be true; and from this again it follows that nothing is true; since this statement itself (I mean that "nothing is true") being "something" is true. And if the "something" is both false and true, each of its particulars will be both false and true. From which we conclude that nothing is really true; for that which has its real nature such that it is true will certainly not be false. And if the "something" is neither false nor true, it is acknowledged that all the particulars also, being declared to be neither false nor true, will not be true. So for these reasons it will be non-evident to us whether the true exists.

Furthermore, the true things are either apparent only, or non-evident only, or in part non-evident and in part apparent; but none of these alternatives is true, as we shall show; therefore nothing is true. If, however, the true things are apparent only, they will assert either that all or that some of the apparent are true. And if they say "all," the argument is overthrown; for it is apparent to some that nothing is true. If, again, they say "some," no one can assert without testing that these phenomena are true, those false, while if he employs a test or criterion he will say either that this criterion is apparent or that it is non-evident. But it is certainly not non-evident; for it is now being assumed that the apparent objects only are true. And if it is apparent, since the matter in question is what apparent things are true and what false, that apparent thing which is adopted for the purpose of judging the apparent objects will itself in turn require an apparent criterion, and this again another, and so on *ad infinitum*. But it is impossible to judge an infinite series; and hence it is impossible to apprehend whether the true things are apparent only.

Similarly also he who declares that the non-evident only are true will not imply that they are all true (for he will not say that it is true that the stars are even in number and that they are also odd); while if some are true, whereby shall we decide that these non-evident things are true and those false? Certainly not by an apparent criterion; and if by a non-evident one, then since our problem is which of the non-evident things are true and which false, this non-evident criterion will itself also need another to judge it, and this again a third, and so on *ad infinitum*. Neither, then, are the true things non-evident only.

The remaining alternative is to say that of the true some are apparent, some non-evident; but this too is absurd. For either all the apparent and all the non-evident are true, or some of the apparent and some of the non-evident. If, then, we say "all," the argument will again be overthrown, since the truth is granted of the statement "nothing is true," and the truth will be asserted of both the statements "the stars are even in number" and "they are odd." But if some of the apparent are true and some of the non-evident, how shall we judge that of the apparent these are true but those false? For if we do so by means of an apparent thing, the argument is thrown back *ad infinitum;* and if by means of a thing non-evident, then, since the non-evidents also require to be judged, by what means is this non-evident thing to be judged? If by an apparent thing, we fall into circular reasoning; and if by a thing non-evident, into the regress *ad infinitum.* And about the non-evident we must make a similiar statement; for he who attempts to judge them by something non-evident is thrown back *ad infinitum,* while he who judges by a thing apparent or with the constant assistance of a thing apparent falls back *ad infinitum,* or, if he passes over to the apparent, is guilty of circular reasoning. It is false, therefore, to say that of the true some are apparent, some non-evident.

If, then, neither the apparent nor the non-evident alone are true, nor yet some apparent and some non-evident things, nothing is true. But if nothing is true, and the criterion seems to require the true for the purpose of judging, the criterion is useless and vain, even if we grant, by way of concession, that it possesses some subtantial reality. And if we have to suspend judgment as to whether anything true exists, it follows that those who declare that "dialectic is the science of things true and false and neither" speak rashly.

And since the criterion of truth has appeared to be unattainable, it is no longer possible to make positive assertions either about those things which (if we may depend on the statements of the Dogmatists) seem to be evident or about those which are non-evident; for since the Dogmatists suppose they apprehend the latter from the things evident, if we are forced to suspend judgement about the evident, how shall we dare to make pronouncements about the non-evident? . . .

Lucian
The Sale of Philosophers[1]

Zeus. You there, set the seats out and get the place ready for people to come in! You—bring the specimens in and stand them in a row! But clean them up a bit first; make them worth looking at, so that they'll attract lots of attention. Hermes—you make the proclamation.

Hermes. Buyers! Into the sale room now, and good luck to you! Philosophers for sale! All shapes and sizes! Assorted doctrines! Cash down or twelve months' credit on security!

Zeus. Plenty of customers. Don't waste time—can't keep them waiting. Let's go.

Hermes. Which do you want to put up first?

Zeus. This long-haired fellow, the Ionian. He looks pretty formidable.

Hermes. Pythagoras! Step down off the platform and let the customers have a look at you.

Zeus. Well, tell them about him.

Hermes. One philosopher going—no superior, very impressive. Who's for him? Who wants to be Superman? Who wants to understand the cosmic harmony? Or live another life?

Buyer. Looks all right—what does he specialize in?

---

1. The Greek title literally means "The Sale of Lives"; βίος, "life," can also mean "biography," as in Plutarch's *Lives.* Here the predominant notion is of specimen characters of philosophers; the word is variously translated. Lucian protests in *The Fisher* (a sequel to this piece, which seems to have aroused hostility) that he was not criticizing individuals, but in fact several of the figures he uses are readily recognizable, and are here represented by their own names and not by the names of the schools associated with them (e.g., Socrates, not Socratic)....

From *Lucian: Selected Works,* translated by Bryan P. Reardon, copyright © 1965 by The Bobbs-Merrill Company, Inc., reprinted by permission of the Liberal Arts Press Division of the Bobbs-Merrill Company, Inc.

Hermes. Arithmetic, astronomy, magic, geometry, music, sorcery. First-class fortuneteller you're looking at.

Buyer. Can I ask him questions?

Hermes. Go ahead, and good luck to you.

Buyer. Where are you from?

Pythagoras. Samos.[2]

Buyer. Education?

Pythagoras. Egypt: local sages.

Buyer. Tell me, what will you teach me if I buy you?

Pythagoras. I shan't *teach* you anything; I'll remind you.[3]

Buyer. How will you remind me?

Pythagoras. I'll purify your soul first, and wash the dirt off it.

Buyer. All right, say I'm purified. How do you go about this reminding?

Pythagoras. The first thing is a long silence. Not a word for five years; not a sound.

Buyer. My dear man, you'd be a good teacher for Croesus' son.[4] I'm a chatterbox, I don't want to be a statue. Never mind—what comes after the five years' silence?

Pythagoras. You'll learn music and geometry.

Buyer. A delicious road to wisdom—learn to play the lyre!

Pythagoras. Then counting next.

Buyer. But I *can* count.

Pythagoras. How do you count?

Buyer. One, two, three, four——

Pythagoras. See? What you call four is ten, a perfect triangle— what we swear by.[5]

Buyer. Well, by your almighty Four, I never heard anything more divine or sacred!

Pythagoras. Then, my friend, you'll learn about earth and air and fire and water—their courses, shapes, and motions.

Buyer. Shapes? Fire and air and water?

Pythagoras. Very distinct shapes. Nothing can move without shape

---

2. Pythagoras here, and later Heraclitus and Democritus, are represented as speaking in the Ionic dialect.

3. The theory of *anamnesis;* see Plato, *Meno.*

4. Who was dumb; see Herodotus, I. 34 and 85.

5. $1 + 2 + 3 + 4 = 10$; the triangle is $\begin{smallmatrix} & & \bullet & & \\ & \bullet & & \bullet & \\ \bullet & & \bullet & & \bullet \end{smallmatrix}$.

and form. Besides that, you'll learn that God is Number and Mind and Harmony.

Buyer. Would you believe it!

Pythagoras. And on top of what I've said, you'll learn that though you think you're a unity, in fact you're one thing in appearance and another in reality.

Buyer. What? I'm somebody else? Not the man who's speaking to you?

Pythagoras. You are now. But once you appeared in another body, with another name; and you'll change again hereafter.[6]

Buyer. You mean I'm going to take lots of shapes and never die? But that's enough of that. What are your views on food?

Pythagoras. I eat nothing living, but anything else. Except beans.[7]

Buyer. Why not beans? Don't you like them?

Pythagoras. It isn't that. They're sacred; their nature's a mystery. In the first place, they're pure seed. If you peel one while it's still green, you can see it's built like a man's privates. And if you boil one and expose it in the moonlight for a determined number of nights, you get blood. More important still, the Athenians always use them to choose their officials with.[8]

Buyer. Excellent arguments: very reverent. Now strip; I want to see you naked too. Ye gods, he's got a golden thigh! He must be a god, not a mortal! Oh, I must have him. What do you want for him?

Hermes. Ten minas.

Buyer. I'll take him at that.

Zeus. Take the customer's name and address.

Hermes. He's from Italy, I should think—round about Croton or Tarentum or one of those Greek towns.[9] But he hasn't bought him for himself; he's acting for a syndicate—must be three hundred of them.

Zeus. They can take him away! Next lot!

Hermes. You want this scruffy one from the Black Sea?

Zeus. Yes, all right.

Hermes. Hey, you! You with the knapsack and the sleeveless cloak![10] Come on down and walk round the room! Next lot, one manly

---

6. The theory of transmigration of the soul.

7. Cf. Lucian, *The Cock* 4-5 and 18. Lucian embroiders Pythagoras' doctrine slightly in the present passage.

8. Beans were used as lots in Athenian elections.

9. Magna Graecia; see Lucian *The Cock* 18.

10. A garment typical of the Cynic philosopher; cf. Lucian, various *Dialogues of the Dead.*

specimen! Spirited, independent—splendid fellow! What am I bid?

Buyer. Independent? Are you selling a free man?[11]

Hermes. That's right.

Buyer. Aren't you afraid he might have you up for kidnapping? He might even take you to the Areopagus.[12]

Hermes. Oh, he doesn't mind being sold. He feels completely free.

Buyer. But what use would he be? Look at the dreadful state he's in—he's filthy! He'd do for digging or for fetching water, I suppose.

Hermes. Not only that—put him to guard your house and he'll be much more reliable than any dog. In fact Dog's actually his name.[13]

Buyer. Where's he from? What does he claim to do?

Hermes. Better ask him that.

Buyer. I'm scared of him; he looks sullen and moody. He might bark at me if I go near him—or even bite me. See how he's got his stick up? Look at the way he scowls—and that nasty threatening look in his eyes!

Hermes. Oh, don't be frightened—he's tame.

Buyer. Well—to start with, where are you from, my good man?

Diogenes. Everywhere.

Buyer. What do you mean?

Diogenes. You see before you a citizen of the world.

Buyer. Who's your ideal?

Diogenes. Hercules.

Buyer. Well, you've got a club like him. Why not wear a lionskin too?

Diogenes. My cloak's my lionskin. I'm a soldier as he was—pleasure's what I'm fighting. I'm a volunteer, not a conscript. My purpose is to purify people's lives.

Buyer. That's a splendid purpose! But what's your line, particularly? What's your method?

Diogenes. I liberate mankind by treating their passions. Briefly, I aim to be a spokesman for Truth and Candor.

Buyer. All right, spokesman; if I buy you, how will you handle me?

Diogenes. The first thing I'll do if I take you in hand will be to strip your easy life off you. I'll shut you up with Want and give you a

---

11. There is a play on ἐλεύθερος, which means both "free" and "independent" in the sense of "aggressively self-reliant."

12. Roughly equivalent to "Supreme Court."

13. This is a play on words; the Greek κύων, from which "Cynic" is derived, means "dog."

coarse cloak to wear. Then I'll make you work till you drop. You'll sleep on the ground and drink water and fill your belly with what you can get. If you have any money you'll go and throw it in the sea under my regime. You won't bother about marriage or children or homeland; all that will be stuff and nonsense to you. You'll leave your own home and live in a funeral vault or an abandoned tower or even a jar.[14] Your knapsack will be full of lupines[15] and books packed to the covers with writing. You live like that and you'll say you're happier than the King of Persia. Whipping and torture won't bother you a bit.

Buyer. Won't bother me? Won't feel any pain if I'm whipped? What do you think I am—a tortoise? A crab?

Diogenes. You'll put that line of Euripides into practice—with a slight adjustment.

Buyer. What line?

Diogenes. "Your mind will hurt, the tongue will feel no pain."[16] These are the essentials: go ahead boldly and be abusive to everybody alike, king or commoner. Don't be timid about it; it'll make them take notice of you, they'll think you tough. Use rough language and a harsh tone; snarl like a veritable dog. Scowl, and let your gait suit your scowl. Behave like a savage beast, in fact, all the time. Have no shame, and don't bother about decency and moderation. Wipe the blush right off your face. Make for places where the crowds are thickest, and when you find them, fix your mind on a solitary existence. Have nothing to do with anybody; don't let anybody near you, friend or stranger—that would destroy your authority. And what people don't do even in privacy, you do boldly where everybody can see you—go for the laughs in your love life. And finally, if you feel like it, swallow a raw squid or cuttlefish and die.[17] That's the kind of happiness we'll fix you up with.

Buyer. Well, I don't want it. Ugh! What a nasty unnatural life!

Diogenes. But look you, it's so simple; anybody can live it, it's there for the taking. You don't need education or any rubbishy theories; this is a short cut to fame. Even if you're an ignoramus—a

---

14. Diogenes lived in a jar, not a tub, as is usually supposed; cf. Lucian, *Dialogues of the Dead*, 11. 3.

15. Seeds of the pea family, traditional philosophers' fare; cf. Lucian, *Dialogues of the Dead*, 1. 1.

16. Euripides, *Hippolytus* 612, "My tongue has sworn, my mind remains unsworn."

17. As Diogenes was said to have done; cf. Lucian, *A Trip to Hades* 7, n. 6.

tanner or fishmonger or joiner or money-changer—there's nothing to
stop you from becoming famous. All you need is a thick skin and a
brass neck and a good sound course in how to be abusive.

Buyer. Well, I don't want you for that kind of thing. You might
make a sailor, though, in a pinch, or a gardener, but only if he'll let
you go cheap—two obols at most.

Hermes. He's yours. Take him. We'll be glad to be rid of him.
He's just a general nuisance, the way he shouts and insults everybody
alike with his foul tongue.

Zeus. Call another one. The Cyrenaic—that one with the purple
robe and the wreath on his head.

Hermes. Attention please, gentlemen! This lot's expensive—cost you
real money. A sweet specimen going! An ecstatic specimen! Who's
eager for a soft life? Any bids for a hedonist?[18]

Buyer. Here, you, come and tell me what you can do. I'll buy you
if you're any use.

Hermes. Don't bother him with questions, sir; he's drunk. He can't
answer anyway—his tongue's lost its foothold, as you can see.

Buyer. Who in his right sense would buy such a moral wreck?
What a wanton wretch! What a smell of scent off him, too! Can't
walk without staggering and falling over! Hermes, you tell me what
he's like. What's his specialty?

Hermes. Well, briefly, he's good company, he can put away his
share of liquor, he's very good for a spree with a flute girl—just the
thing for a dissolute, lascivious master. And then he's a connoisseur of
cakes and a highly experienced cook; a real expert in easy living. He
was educated at Athens and also served tyrants in Sicily; they thought
the world of him. His doctrine, in a nutshell, is to depise everything,
make use of everything, and draw pleasure from everywhere.

Buyer. You'd better look for somebody else—somebody with plenty
of money. I'm not up to buying a gay character.

Hermes. Looks as if we've got this one on our hands, Zeus. Can't
sell him.

Zeus. Put him on one side and bring on another. No—these two,
better—the laughing one from Abdera and the weeping one from
Ephesus.[19] I'll sell them as a pair.

---

18. According to the Cyrenaics, pleasure was the highest good. Details are con-
tributed to the following sketch by Aristippus, the founder of the Cyrenaic school.

19. Democritus of Abdera founded the "atomist" theory of matter; Heraclitus
of Ephesus held that fire was the primary substance of the universe and that everything was in a state of flux, and was nicknamed "the obscure" for his enigmatic
assertions.

Hermes. Come on, you two, down here! An excellent pair going! What am I bid for the cleverest pair you'll find?

Buyer. Heavens, aren't they different? One of them can't stop laughing, and the other's crying his heart out—looks as if he's in mourning! You there! What's up? What's the joke?

Democritus. What's the joke? You make me laugh, you and all your goings on; that's the joke.

Buyer. What's that you say? You're laughing at us all? You think our life's nothing?

Democritus. That's right. It's empty and meaningless, just atoms moving in the infinite.

Buyer. Oh no it isn't. It's you that's infinitely empty—that's the truth of it. Damn your insolence, wipe that grin off your face!—And you, my dear sir—I'd be much better talking to you, I think. Why are you crying?

Heraclitus. I am considering the human situation, my friend. It calls for tears and lamentation; we are doomed from the start. Wherefore I pity man and mourn for him. Of the present I take no great account, but what will be hereafter is grief unmitigated; I mean conflagration and universal disaster. For this I sorrow, and because nothing abides; all things are stirred together as into porridge. Pleasure is one with pain, knowledge with ignorance, great with small; up and down they go, around and about, changing places, the sport of time.

Buyer. What then is time?

Heraclitus. A child at play, quarreling, agreeing at the checkerboard.

Buyer. And what are men?

Heraclitus. Mortal gods.

Buyer. And gods?

Heraclitus. Immortal men.

Buyer. Talking in riddles, eh? Composing puzzles? You're as bad as Apollo's oracle—quite incomprehensible.[20]

Heraclitus. I am not interested in you.

Buyer. Then nobody in his right mind's going to buy you.

Heraclitus. Young or old, buy me or buy me not, the hell with the lot of you.

Buyer. This poor devil's not far from the nuthouse. I'm not buying either of them.

Hermes. They stay unsold too.

Zeus. Put another one up.

Hermes. That Athenian? The chatterbox?

---

20. Cf. Lucian, *Zeus Rants* 31.

Zeus. Yes, all right.

Hermes. You there! Come here! Going, one virtuous, intelligent specimen. Any bids for his holiness?

Buyer. Tell me, what do you specialize in?

Socrates. I'm a lover of youth. I know all about love.[21]

Buyer. Expect me to buy you? It's a tutor for my boy I want—and he's a handsome lad!

Socrates. What better companion than me could you find for a handsome lad? I'm not a lover of the body; it's the soul I find beautiful. Nothing to worry about; even if they lie under the same cloak with me, you won't hear them complain about the way I treat them.

Buyer. I don't believe you. A lover of youth, and you don't mess around with anything but the soul? Despite the opportunities when you're under the same cloak?

Socrates. Why, I swear by the dog and the plane tree, that's the truth of it!

Buyer. Ye gods! What a funny oath!

Socrates. What's funny about it? Don't you think the dog's a god? Look at the fuss they make of Anubis in Egypt! And what about the Dog Star in the heavens, and Cerberus in the underworld?

Buyer. All right, I was wrong. Well, what's your way of life?

Socrates. I live in a state I fashioned for myself, under an original constitution and my own laws.[22]

Buyer. Tell me one of your decrees.

Socrates. All right, I'll tell you my decree about women; it's the principal one. No woman belongs to one man: they're available to anyone who wants them.

Buyer. What's that? The laws of adultery are swept away?

Socrates. Heavens, yes, and all the pusillanimous arguments on that subject, in a word.

Buyer. What's your doctrine about handsome boys, then?

Socrates. Their kisses will be the prize for excellence, for splendid, spirited deeds.

Buyer. Very generous, aren't you? What's the principal thing in your philosophy?

Socrates. Forms of reality, patterns. Everything you see—earth,

21. Socrates expounds his views on love in Plato's *Symposium;* see 219 there for his relations with young men.

22. I.e., "Plato's" Republic (cf. Lucian, *A True Story* II. 17), the inspiration for which came to some degree from Socrates. In the figure of Socrates, Lucian is also sketching Plato and the Academics, his descendants.

what's on it, sky, sea—all of these have invisible images outside the universe.

Buyer. Where?

Socrates. Nowhere. If they were anywhere they wouldn't exist.

Buyer. I can't see these patterns you talk about.

Socrates. Of course you can't; you're spiritually blind. *I* can see the patterns of everything—an invisible you, another me—two of everything, in fact.

Buyer. What good eyes you've got! You're a clever fellow—I must have you. Look, what do you want for him?

Hermes. Give me two talents.

Buyer. I'll buy him at that. But I'll pay you later.

Hermes. What's your name?

Buyer. Dion of Syracuse.[23]

Hermes. There you are—take him, and good luck to you. You, the Epicurean—you're up next! Any bids for this one? He's a pupil of the two that were up for sale a minute ago, the laughing one and the drunken one.[24] But he has one more feature—he's more impious. Otherwise he's a sweet specimen: quite a gourmet.

Buyer. How much does he cost?

Hermes. Two minas.

Buyer. There you are. But hold on a minute—what does he like to eat?

Hermes. Sweet things—anything with honey in it. Dried figs best of all.

Buyer. That's easy enough. I'll buy him some Carian fruitcakes.

Zeus. Call another. That one there—that close-cropped, sullen one, the Stoic.

Hermes. Good idea. It looks as if there's quite a mob of city men waiting for him to come up.[25] Pure virtue for sale! The perfect way of life for sale! Who wants to be the only know-it-all?

Buyer. Don't follow you.

Hermes. This chap's the only wise man, the only handsome man,

---

23. A disciple of Plato and a minister of Dionysius; after the latter's overthrow as tyrant of Syracuse in 345 B.C., Dion in fact tried to found a state built on Platonic lines.

24. Epicurean atomism is derived from Democritus, and Epicurean hedonism from the Cyrenaics.

25. Stoicism was very popular among men of affairs; it proved particularly congenial to the Roman temperament. The Stoics are Lucian's favorite target; with this sketch, cf. Lucian, *Hermotimus*.

the only just man, brave man, king, orator, rich man, lawgiver, et cetera, et cetera.[26]

Buyer. Is he the only cook, then? And the only tanner and carpenter and so on?

Hermes. I suppose so.

Buyer. Here, you, sir, come here; I think I'll buy you. Tell me what you're like. Don't you mind being sold as a slave?

Stoic. No. That's beyond human control, and what's beyond human control is indifferent.

Buyer. I don't understand you.

Stoic. Don't you? Don't you understand that in such matters some are preferred and some, on the other hand, are not-preferred?[27]

Buyer. I still don't understand.

Stoic. I don't suppose you do. You're not used to our technical terms, and you're incapable of conceptual representation.* The real philosopher, the man who's learned logic properly, knows not only this but the nature of complete and incomplete predicates too, and the degree of difference between them.

Buyer. In philosophy's name, don't be mean—at least tell me what they are, complete and incomplete predicates. They sound very impressive somehow, the way they roll off the tongue.

Stoic. Of course I'll tell you. Suppose a lame man suddenly hurts his lame foot on a rock; then the lameness—which he had to start with, you see—is a complete predicate; now he's got an incomplete predicate, namely his wound, as well.

Buyer. How very subtle! What else do you specialize in?

Stoic. Verbal snares. I trap people who talk to me and stop their mouths and make them shut up—I muzzle them, in fact. This is called the power of renowned syllogism.

Buyer. Heavens! That sounds powerful! I'll bet you always win.

Stoic. Well, take an example. Have you a child?

Buyer. Suppose I have?

Stoic. If your child wanders near a river, and a crocodile sees him

---

26. I.e., by Stoic definitions of wisdom, justice, etc., the possession of these virtues necessitated a Stoic attitude.

27. As they helped or hindered the virtuous life. Lucian's satire here and in the following passage is directed against the Stoic concern with technical logic rather than morality.

*More accurately, and to correspond with the translation of the Stoic fragments, φαντασία καταληπτική should be rendered "comprehensive presentation" rather than "conceptual representation."—*Ed.*

and catches him, and then promises to give him back to you if you can tell him correctly what he has decided to do, give the child back or not—what would you say he'd decided to do?

Buyer. That's a tricky question. I don't know what I'd say to get the child back. For heaven's sake, *you* answer and save my child—quick, before the crocodile swallows him!

Stoic. Don't worry! I'll teach you stranger things than that.

Buyer. Such as?

Stoic. The Reaper, the Master,[28] and above all Electra and the Hooded Man.

Buyer. Hooded Man? Electra?

Stoic. The Electra—Agamemnon's daughter. She knew and didn't know the same thing. Orestes was standing beside her before she recognized him; she knew that Orestes was her brother, but didn't know that this was Orestes. But the Hooded Man—that really is a wonderful argument for you. Tell me, do you know your own father?

Buyer. Yes.

Stoic. Well, if I put a hooded man beside you and asked you if you knew him, what would you say?

Buyer. No, of course.

Stoic. But this hooded man *is* your father all the time. So if you don't know this man, clearly you don't know your father.

Buyer. Oh, no. I'd take his hood off and find out who he was. But never mind—tell me, what's the purpose of philosophy? What will you do when you've reached the peak of virtue?

Stoic. Then I'll apply myself to the chief natural goods, wealth, health, and so on. But there's a lot of hard work to do first, sharpening the sight on closely written books, collecting scholarly comments, and filling myself up with wrong usages and strange words. And the main thing is, you can't be a philosopher unless you go out of your mind and take the cure three times running.[29]

Buyer. A very noble, manly program. But how about your Stoic habit of moneylending, like Gnipho? Does that show you've been cured and are perfectly virtuous?

Stoic. Yes. At least, only the philosopher is fit to be a moneylender. For since he specializes in drawing conclusions, and lending money and drawing interest on it are obviously not very different from drawing

---

28. Fallacies, the details of which are unknown.

29. As Chrysippus, Cleanthes' successor as the head of the Stoic school in the third century B.C., was said to have done; cf. Lucian, *A True Story* II. 18.

conclusions,[30] what applies to the one applies to the other—only the real philosopher can do it. And draw not just simple interest like other people, but interest on interest; you know that there's first interest and second interest, a sort of second generation of the first?[31] And of course you follow the reasoning of the syllogism, "If he gets the first interest, he will get the second; but he *will* get the first, therefore he *will* get the second."

Buyer. Are we to say the same, then, of the fees that you get from young men for teaching them philosophy? Clearly only the real philosopher can get money for his virtue.

Stoic. That's right. I take money not for myself, you see, but for the giver's own sake. For some men are outgiving and others are intaking. I'm training myself to be intaking and my students to be outgiving.

Buyer. No! The other way around! The student should be intaking. You're the only rich man, so you should be outgiving.

Stoic. You're joking, sir. Take care I don't shoot you down with my indemonstrable syllogism.

Buyer. What's dangerous about that?

Stoic. It'll put you out and strike you dumb and dislocate your intellect. But best of all, I can turn you into a stone right now if I like.

Buyer. A stone? My dear chap, you aren't Perseus.

Stoic. Just you listen. Is a stone a substance?

Buyer. Yes.

Stoic. Isn't an animate being a substance?

Buyer. Yes.

Stoic. And you're an animate being?

Buyer. I suppose so.

Stoic. Then you're a substance, so you're a stone.

Buyer. Stop it! Analyze me properly, for heaven's sake, and make me a man again!

Stoic. Easy. Be a man again. Tell me, is every substance an animate being?

Buyer. No.

Stoic. Is a stone an animate being?

Buyer. No.

Stoic. Are you a substance?

---

30. In the Greek, the verb used for "to draw conclusions" is a compound of the simple verb λογίζεσθαι, "to draw interest."

31. τόκος, "interest," means literally "offspring."

Buyer. Yes.

Stoic. You're a substance, but still an animate being?

Buyer. Yes.

Stoic. Then if you're an animate being, you're not a stone.

Buyer. Thanks very much. I felt like Niobe—my legs were getting cold and stiff already. I'll buy you. How much is he?

Hermes. Twelve minas.

Buyer. There you are.

Hermes. Are you sole buyer?

Buyer. Heavens, no! There are all these men here.

Hermes. Well, there are plenty of them, broad-shouldered fellows —just right for the Reaper.

Zeus. Don't waste time. Call another—the Peripatetic.[32]

Hermes. You there—that fine fellow, that rich fellow! Now, gentlemen, buy my wise man! Knows simply everything!

Buyer. What's he like?

Hermes. Restrained, decent, agreeable company. Best of all, there are two of him.

Buyer. Two? How come?

Hermes. One aspect outside, another inside. So remember, if you buy him, one of him's called Exoteric and the other Esoteric.[33]

Buyer. What's his particular intellectual line?

Hermes. That there are three kinds of good—spiritual, physical, and external.

Buyer. That's a doctrine one can grasp. How much is he?

Hermes. Twenty minas.

Buyer. That's a lot.

Hermes. Oh, no, my dear fellow. He seems to have a bit of money himself, you see. You buy him while there's time. He'll teach you lots more things right away—how long a gnat lives, how far down sunlight goes in the sea, and what an oyster's soul's like.

Buyer. Heavens, what a scholarly mind!

Hermes. Ah, but if you heard some of his other ideas! Much more penetrating than these. All about generation and birth and the forma-

---

32. The following sketch touches on some Aristotelian logical doctrine and scientific experiments.

33. A reference to the traditional division of Aristotle's works into "popular" ("exoteric") and "for the initiated" ("esoteric"). Aristotle himself uses the former to mean "common" or "standard," of philosophical arguments, and does not use the latter at all.

tion of the embryo in the womb, and how man is a creature that laughs, whereas an ass is a creature that doesn't laugh or build houses or sail ships either.

Buyer. Very impressive, all that knowledge. Very useful too. Twenty, you say? All right, I'll have him.

Hermes. Right.

Zeus. Who's left?

Hermes. This Skeptic here. Hey, Coppernob![34] Come here and be auctioned! Hurry up! Not many to sell you to; most of them are drifting off now. Still—any bids for this one?

Buyer. Yes, me. But tell me first, what do you know?

Pyrrhias. Nothing.

Buyer. How do you mean, nothing?

Pyrrhias. I don't think there *is* anything at all.

Buyer. Aren't *we* something?

Pyrrhias. I'm not even sure of that.

Buyer. Nor even that you're somebody?

Pyrrhias. I'm much more doubtful still about that.

Buyer. What a state to be in! Well, what's the idea of these scales?

Pyrrhias. I weigh arguments in them. I balance them till they're equal, and when I see they're exactly alike and exactly the same weight, then—ah, then!—I don't know which is the sounder.

Buyer. What are you good at apart from that?

Pyrrhias. Everything except catching a runaway slave.

Buyer. And why can't you do that?

Pyrrhias. My good man, I can't apprehend anything.[35]

Buyer. I don't suppose you can. You seem slow and stupid. Well, what's the end of your knowledge?

Pyrrhias. Ignorance, deafness, and blindness.

Buyer. You'll be unable to see or hear, you say?

Pyrrhias. And unable to judge or feel either. No better than a worm, in fact.

Buyer. I must buy you for that. How much shall we say for him?

Hermes. One Attic mina.

Buyer. There you are. Well now, you—I've bought you, eh?

Pyrrhias. I'm not sure.

Buyer. Nonsense! I *have* bought you, and I've paid my money.

---

34. Pyrrhias ("Coppernob") is named after Pyrrho, the founder of the Skeptic philosophy here sketched; its principal tenet was the impossibility of knowledge.

35. This is a pun on the Greek καταλαμβάνω, meaning both "seize" and "conceive."

Pyrrhias. I defer judgment; I'm considering the matter.

Buyer. Look, you come with me—you're my slave.

Pyrrhias. Who can tell whether what you say is true?

Buyer. The auctioneer can. My mina can. These people here can.

Pyrrhias. Is there anybody here?

Buyer. I'm going to put you on the treadmill, then. I'll show you I'm boss—the hard way!

Pyrrhias. Suspend decision on it.

Buyer. Oh ye gods! Look, I've already told you my decision.

Hermes. Stop dillydallying, you, and go with him—he's bought you. Gentlemen, we invite you to come tomorrow; we'll be putting up ordinary people, workmen and tradesmen.

PHILO (JUDAEUS) OF ALEXANDRIA

Although a large quantity of his writings has survived, we know relatively little of his life. He was born in about 20 B.C. in the great port city of Alexandria. As a distinguished member of the Jewish community, he was the leader of a delegation to address the Emperor Caligula (39 A.D.) seeking leniency in the Romans' treatment of the Jews; we know unfortunately that he was unsuccessful. A substantial illustration of his use of allegory is contained here in his treatise *On the Account of the World's Creation Given by Moses,* an excellent example of Philo's dual loyalties; for, to him, Plato was an Athenian image of Moses.

On the Account of the World's Creation Given by Moses

I. While among other lawgivers some have nakedly and without embellishment drawn up a code of the things held to be right among their people, and others, dressing up their ideas in much irrelevant and cumbersome matter, have befogged the masses and hidden the truth under their fictions, Moses, disdaining either course, the one as devoid of the philosopher's painstaking effort to explore his subject thoroughly, the other as full of falsehood and imposture, introduced his laws with an admirable and most impressive exordium. He refrained, on the one hand, from stating abruptly what should be practiced or avoided, and on the other hand, in face of the necessity of preparing the minds of those who were to live under the laws for their reception, he refrained from inventing myths himself or acquiescing in those composed by others. His exordium, as I have said, is one that excites our admiration in the highest degree. It consists of an account of the creation of the world, implying that the world is in harmony with the Law, and the Law with the world, and that the man who observes the law is constituted thereby a loyal citizen of the world, regulating his doings by the purpose and will of Nature, in accordance with which the entire world itself also is administered.

Now it is true that no writer in verse or prose could possibly do justice to the beauty of the ideas embodied in this account of the creation of the kosmos. For they transcend our capacity of speech and of hearing, being too great and august to be adjusted to the tongue or ear of any mortal. Nevertheless they must not on this account be passed over in silence. Nay, for the sake of the God-beloved author we must be venturesome even beyond our power. We shall fetch nothing from our own store, but, with a great array of points before us, we shall mention only a few, such as we may believe to be within reach of the human mind when possessed by love and longing for wisdom.

The minutest seal takes in under the graver's hand the contours of colossal figures. So perchance shall the beauties of the world's creation recorded in the Laws, transcendent as they are and dazzling as they do by their bright gleams the souls of readers, be indicated by delineations minute and slight. But first we must draw attention to a matter which ought not to be passed over in silence.

II. There are some people who, having the world in admiration rather than the Maker of the world, pronounce it to be without beginning and everlasting, while with impious falsehood they postulate in God a vast inactivity; whereas we ought on the contrary to be astonished at His powers as Maker and Father, and not to assign to the world a disproportionate majesty. Moses, both because he had attained the very summit of philosophy, and because he had been divinely instructed in the greater and most essential part of Nature's lore, could not fail to recognize that the universal must consist of two parts, one part active Cause and the other passive object; and that the active Cause is the perfectly pure and unsullied Mind of the universe, transcending virtue, transcending knowledge, transcending the good itself and the beautiful itself; while the passive part is in itself incapable of life and motion, but, when set in motion and shaped and quickened by Mind, changes into the most perfect masterpiece, namely this world. Those who assert that this world is unoriginate unconsciously eliminate that which of all incentives to piety is the most beneficial and the most indispensable, namely providence. For it stands to reason that what has been brought into existence should be cared for by its Father and Maker. For, as we know, it is a father's aim in regard of his offspring and an artificer's in regard of his handiwork to preserve them, and by every means to fend off from them aught that may entail loss or harm. He keenly desires to provide for them in every way all that is beneficial and to their advantage: but between that which has never been brought into being and one who is not its Maker no such tie is formed. It is a worthless and baleful doctrine, setting up anarchy in the well-ordered realm of the world, leaving it without protector, arbitrator, or judge, without anyone whose office it is to administer and direct all its affairs.

Not so Moses. That great master, holding the unoriginate to be of a different order from that which is visible, since everything that is an object of sensible perception is subject to becoming and to constant change, never abiding in the same state, assigned to that which is invisible and an object of intellectual apprehension the infinite and undefinable as united with it by closest tie; but on that which is an object of the senses he bestowed "genesis," "becoming," as its appropriate name. Seeing then that this world is both visible and perceived by the senses, it follows that it must also have had an origin. Whence it was entirely to the point that he put on record that origin, setting forth in its true grandeur the work of God.

III. He says that in six days the world was created, not that its Maker required a length of time for His work, for we must think of God as doing all things simultaneously, remembering that "all" includes with the commands which He issues the thought behind them. Six days are mentioned because for the things coming into existence there was need of order. Order involves number, and among numbers by the laws of nature the most suitable to productivity is 6, for if we start with 1 it is the first perfect number, being equal to the product of its factors (*i.e.* $1 \times 2 \times 3$), as well as made up of the sum of them (*i.e.* $1 + 2 + 3$), its half being 3, its third part 2, its sixth part I. We may say that it is in its nature both male and female, and is a result of the distinctive power of either. For among things that are it is the odd that is male, and the even female. Now of odd numbers 3 is the starting-point, and of even numbers 2, and the product of these two is 6. For it was requisite that the world, being most perfect of all things that have come into existence, should be constituted in accordance with a perfect number, namely six; and, inasmuch as it was to have in itself beings that sprang from a coupling together, should receive the impress of a mixed number, namely the first in which odd and even were combined, one that should contain the essential principle both of the male that sows and of the female that receives the seed.

Now to each of the days He assigned some of the portions of the whole, not including, however, the first day, which He does not even call "first," lest it should be reckoned with the others, but naming it "one." He designates it by a name which precisely hits the mark, for He discerned in it and expressed by the title which He gives it the nature and appellation of the unit, or the "one."

IV. We must recount as many as we can of the elements embraced in it. To recount them all would be impossible. Its pre-eminent element is the intelligible world, as is shown in the treatise dealing with the "One." For God, being God, assumed that a beautiful copy would never be produced apart from a beautiful pattern, and that no object of perception would be faultless which was not made in the likeness of an original discerned only by the intellect. So when He willed to create this visible world He first fully formed the intelligible world, in order that He might have the use of a pattern wholly God-like and incorporeal in producing the material world, as a later creation, the very image of an earlier, to embrace in itself objects of perception of as many kinds as the other contained objects of intelligence.

To speak of or conceive that world which consists of ideas as being in some place is illegitimate; how it consists (of them) we shall know if we carefully attend to some image supplied by the things of our world. When a city is being founded to satisfy the soaring ambition of some king or governor, who lays claim to despotic power and being magnificent in his ideas would fain add a fresh lustre to his good fortune, there comes forward now and again some trained architect who, observing the favourable climate and convenient position of the site, first sketches in his own mind wellnigh all the parts of the city that is to be wrought out, temples, gymnasia, town-halls, market-places, harbours, docks, streets, walls to be built, dwelling-houses as well as public buildings to be set up. Thus after having received in his own soul, as it were in wax, the figures of these objects severally, he carries about the image of a city which is the creation of his mind. Then by his innate power of memory, he recalls the images of the various parts of this city, and imprints their types yet more distinctly in it: and like a good craftsman he begins to build the city of stones and timber, keeping his eye upon his pattern and making the visible and tangible objects correspond in each case to the incorporeal ideas.

Just such must be our thoughts about God. We must suppose that, when He was minded to found the one great city, He conceived beforehand the models of its parts, and that out of these He constituted and brought to completion a world discernible only by the mind, and then, with that for a pattern, the world which our senses can perceive.

V. As, then, the city which was fashioned beforehand within the mind of the architect held no place in the outer world, but had been engraved in the soul of the artificer as by a seal; even so the universe that consisted of ideas would have no other location than the Divine Reason, which was the Author of this ordered frame. For what other place could there be for His powers sufficient to receive and contain, I say not all but, any one of them whatever uncompounded and untempered?

Now just such a power is that by which the universe was made, one that has as its source nothing less than true goodness. For should one conceive a wish to search for the cause, for the sake of which this whole was created, it seems to me that he would not be wrong in saying, what indeed one of the men of old did say, that the Father and Maker of all is good; and because of this He grudged not a share in his own excellent nature to an existence which has of itself nothing fair and lovely, while it is capable of becoming all things. For of itself it was without order, without quality, without soul, (without likeness); it was full of inconsistency, ill-adjustment, disharmony: but it was capable of turning and undergoing a complete change to the best, the very contrary of all these, to order, quality, life, correspondence, identity, likeness, perfect adjustment, to harmony, to all that is characteristic of the more excellent model.

VI. Now God, with no counsellor to help Him (who was there beside Him?) determined that it was meet to confer rich and unrestricted benefits upon that nature which apart from Divine bounty could obtain of itself no good thing. But not in proportion to the greatest of His own bounties does He confer benefits—for these are without end or limit—but in proportion to the capacities of the recipients. For it is not the nature of creation to receive good treatment in like manner as it is the nature of God to bestow it, seeing that the powers of God are overwhelmingly vast, whereas creation, being too feeble to entertain their abundance, would have broken down under the effort to do so, had not God with appropriate adjustment dealt out to each his due portion.

Should a man desire to use words in a more simple and direct way, he would say that the world discerned only by the intellect is nothing else than the Word of God when He was already engaged in the act of creation. For (to revert to our illustration) the city discernible by the intellect alone is nothing else than the reasoning faculty of the architect in the act of planning to found the city. It is Moses who lays down this, not I. Witness his express acknowledgement in the sequel, when setting on record the creation of man, that he was moulded after the image of God (Gen. i. 27). Now if the part is an image of an image, it is manifest that the whole is so too, and if the whole creation, this entire world perceived by our senses (seeing that it is greater than any human image) is a copy of the Divine image, it is manifest that the archetypal seal also, which we aver to be the world descried by the mind, would be the very Word of God.

VII. Then he says that "in the beginning God made the heaven and the earth," taking "beginning" not, as some think, in a chronological sense, for time there was not before there was a world. Time began either simultaneously with the world or after it. For since time is a measured space determined by the world's movement, and since movement could not be prior to the object moving, but must of necessity arise either after it or simultaneously with it, it follows of necessity that time also is either coeval with or later born than the world. To venture to affirm that it is elder born would be to do violence to philosophic sense. And since the word "beginning" is not here taken as the chronological beginning, it would seem likely that the numerical order is indicated, so that "in the beginning He made" is equivalent to "He made the heaven first": for it is indeed reasonable that it should come into existence first, being both best of created things and made from the purest of all that is, seeing that it was destined to be the most holy dwelling-place of manifest and visible gods. For, even if the Maker made all things simultaneously, order was none the less an attribute of all that came into existence in fair beauty, for beauty is absent where there is disorder. Now order is a series of things going on before and following after, in due sequence, a sequence which, though not seen in the finished productions, yet exists in the designs of the contrivers; for only so could these things be fashioned with perfect accuracy, and work without leaving their path or clashing with each other.

First, then, the Maker made an incorporeal heaven, and an invisible earth, and the essential form of air and void. To the one he gave the name of "Darkness," since the air when left to itself, is black. The other he named "abyss," for the void is a region of immensity and vast depths. Next (He made) the incorporeal essence of water and of life-breath and, to crown all, of light. This again, the seventh in order, was an incorporeal pattern, discernible only by the mind, of the sun and of all luminaries which were to come into existence throughout heaven.

VIII. Special distinction is accorded by Moses to life-breath and to light. The one he entitles the "breath" of God, because breath is most life-giving, and of life God is the author, while of light he says that it is beautiful pre-eminently (Gen. i. 4): for the intelligible as far surpasses the visible in the brilliancy of its radiance, as sunlight assuredly surpasses darkness and day night, and mind, the ruler of the entire soul, the bodily eyes. Now that invisible light perceptible only by mind has come into being as an image of the Divine World Who brought it within our ken: it is a supercelestial constellation, fount of the constellations obvious to sense. It would not be amiss to term it "all-brightness," to signify that from which sun and moon, as well as fixed stars and planets draw, in proportion to their several capacity, the light befitting each of them: for that pure and undiluted radiance is bedimmed so soon as it begins to undergo the change that is entailed by the passage from the intelligible to the sensibly discerned, for no object of sense is free from dimness.

IX. Right too is his statement that "darkness was above the abyss"

(Gen. i. 2). For in a sense the air is over the void, inasmuch as it has spread over and completely filled the immensity and desolation of the void, of all that reaches from the zone of the moon to us. After the kindling of the intelligible light, which preceded the sun's creation, darkness its adversary withdrew: for God, in His perfect knowledge of their mutual contrariety and natural conflict, parted them one from another by a wall of separation. In order, therefore, to keep them from the discord arising from pereptual clash, to prevent war in place of peace prevailing and setting up disorder in an ordered universe, He not only separated light and darkness, but also placed in the intervening spaces boundary-marks, by which He held back each of their extremities: for, had they been actual neighbours, they were sure to produce confusion by engaging with intense and never-ceasing rivalry in the struggle for mastery. As it was, their assault on one another was broken and kept back by barriers set up between them. These barriers are evening and dawn. The latter, gently restraining the darkness, anticipates the sunrise with the glad tidings of its approach; while evening, supervening upon sunset, gives a gentle welcome to the oncoming mass of darkness. We must, however, place these, dawn and evening I mean, in the category of the incorporeal and intelligible: for there is in these nothing whatever patent to the senses, but they are simply models and measuring-rules and patterns and seals, all of these being incorporeal and serving for the creation of other bodies. When light had come into being, and darkness had moved out of its way and retired, and evening and dawn had been fixed as barriers in the intervals between them, as a necessary consequence a measure of time was forthwith brought about, which its Maker called Day, and not "first" day but "one," an expression due to the uniqueness of the intelligible world, and to its having therefore a natural kinship to the number "One."

X. The incorporeal world, then, was now finished and firmly settled in the Divine Reason, and the world patent to sense was ripe for birth after the pattern of the incorporeal. And first of its parts, best of them all, the Creator proceeded to make the Heaven, which with strict truth he entitled firmament, as being corporeal: for the body is naturally solid, seeing that it has a threefold dimension. What else indeed do we conceive a solid object and a body to be, but that which extends in each direction? Fitly then, in contradistinction to the incorporeal and purely intelligible, did He call this body-like heaven perceived by our senses "the solid firmament." After so designating it He went on forthwith to speak of it as "heaven." He did so with unerring propriety, either because it is the "boundary" of all things, or because it came into being first of things "visible." When the heaven had been created he names a second day, thus assigning to heaven the whole space and interval of a day. He does this by reason of the position of dignity which heaven occupies among the objects of sense. . . .

XIII. Now in the original creation of all things, as I have said already, God caused all shrubs and plants to spring out of the earth perfect, having fruits not unripe but at their prime, to be perfectly ready for the immediate use and enjoyment of the animals that were forthwith to come into being. God then enjoins the earth to give birth to all these, and the earth, as though it had been long pregnant and in travail, brings forth all kinds of things sown, all kinds of trees, and countless kinds of fruits besides. But not only were the several fruits nourishment for animals, but also a provision for the perpetual reproduction of their kind, containing within them the seed-substances. Hidden and imperceptible in these substances are the principles or nuclei of all things. As the seasons go round these become open and manifest. For God willed that Nature should run a course that brings it back to its starting-point, endowing the species with immortality, and making them sharers of eternal existence. For the sake of this He both led on the beginning speedily towards the end, and made the end to retrace its way to the beginning. For it is the case both that the fruit comes out of the plants, as an end out of a beginning, and that out of the fruit again, containing as it does the seed in itself, there comes the plant, a beginning out of an end.

XIV. On the fourth day, the earth being now finished, he ordered the heaven in varied beauty. Not that He put the heaven in a lower rank than the earth, giving precedence to the inferior creation, and accounting the higher and more divine worthy only of the second place; but to make clear beyond all doubt the mighty sway of His sovereign power. For being aware beforehand of the ways of thinking that would mark the men of future ages, how they would be intent on what looked probable and plausible, with much in it that could be supported by argument, but would not aim at sheer truth; and how they would trust phenomena rather than God, admiring sophistry more than wisdom; and how they would observe in time to come the circuits of sun and moon, on which depend summer and winter and the changes of spring and autumn, and would suppose that the regular movements of the heavenly bodies are the causes of all things that year by year come forth and are produced out of the earth; that there might be none who owing either to shameless audacity or to overwhelming ignorance should venture to ascribe the first place to any created thing, 'let them,' said

He, 'go back in thought to the original creation of the universe, when, before sun or moon existed, the earth bore plants of all sorts and fruits of all sorts; and having contemplated this let them form in their minds the expectation that hereafter too shall it bear these at the Father's bidding, whensoever it may please Him.' For He has no need of His heavenly offspring on which He bestowed powers but not independence: for, like a charioteer grasping the reins or a pilot the tiller, He guides all things in what direction He pleases as law and right demand, standing in need of no one besides: for all things are possible to God. . . .

XVII. The aforesaid numeral [4], then, having been deemed worthy of such high privilege in nature, it was a matter of course that its Maker arrayed the heaven on the fourth day with a most divine adornment of perfect beauty, namely the light-giving heavenly bodies; and, knowing that of all things light is best, He made it the indispensable means of sight, the best of the senses; for what the intellect is in the soul, this the eye is in the body; for each of them sees, one the things of the mind, the other things of sense; and they have need, the mind of knowledge, that it may become cognisant of incorporeal objects, the eye of light, for the apprehending of bodily forms.

Light has proved itself the source of many other boons to mankind, but pre-eminently of philosophy, the greatest boon of all. For man's faculty of vision, led upwards by light, discerned the nature of the heavenly bodies and their harmonious movement. He saw the well-ordered circuits of fixed stars and planets, how the former moved in unchanging orbit and all alike, while the latter sped round in two revolutions out of harmony with each other. He marked the rhythmic dances of all these, how they were marshalled by the laws of a perfect music, and the sight produced in his soul an ineffable delight and pleasure. Banqueting on sights displayed to it one after another, his soul was insatiate in beholding. And then, as usually happens, it went on to busy itself with questionings, asking What is the essence of these visible objects? Are they in nature unoriginate, or had they a beginning of existence? What is the method of their movement? And what are the principles by which each is governed? It was out of the investigation of these problems that philosophy grew, than which no more perfect good has come into the life of mankind.

XVIII. It was with a view to that original intellectual light, which I have mentioned as belonging to the order of the incorporeal world, that He created the heavenly bodies of which our senses are aware. These are images divine and exceeding fair, which He established in heaven as in the purest temple belonging to corporeal being. This He did that they might serve many purposes. One purpose was to give light; another to be signs; a third duly to fix seasons of the year; and lastly for the sake of days, months, years, which (as we all know) have served as measures of time and given birth to number. The kind of useful service rendered by each of the bodies mentioned is self-evident; yet that the truth may be more precisely apprehended it may not be out of place to follow it step by step in a reasoned account.

All time having been divided into two portions, day and night, the Father assigned the sovereignty of the day to the sun, as to a great king, and that of the night to the moon and the host of the other stars. The greatness of the sway and government pertaining to the sun finds its clearest proof in what has been already mentioned: one and alone it has by itself separately had day apportioned to it, half of the whole of time; while all the rest with the moon have had allotted to them the other half, which has received the name of night. And when the sun has risen, all that multitude of stars which were visible but now is not merely dimmed but becomes actually invisible through the pouring forth of its light; and upon its setting they begin all of them to shine out in their own true characters.

XIX. The purpose of their existence is, as the Lord Himself pronounced, not only to send forth light upon the earth, but also to give timely signs of coming events. For either by their risings or settings or eclipses, or again by the seasons of their appearance or disappearance, or by other alterations in their movements, men conjecture future issues, good harvests and bad, increase and decay of animal life, fair weather and foul, gales and calms, floodings and shrinkings of rivers, seas smooth and rough, irregularities of the seasons, either wintry summers, or scorching winters, or springs like autumn, or autumns like spring. Indeed it has happened that, by conjecture based on the movements of the heavenly bodies, men have notified in advance a disturbance and shaking of the earth, and countless other unusual occurrences, proving the complete truth of the words, "the stars were made for signs."

It is added, moreover, "and for appointed times" (Gen. i. 14). By "appointed times" Moses understood the four seasons of the year, and surely with good reason. For what idea does "appointed time" convey but "time of achievement"? Now the four seasons of the year bring about achievement by bringing all things to perfection, all sowing and planting of crops, and the birth and growth of animals.

The heavenly bodies were created also to furnish measures of time: for it is by regular revolutions of sun, moon, and the other bodies that days and months and years were constituted. This in itself involved the showing of their most useful service of all; I mean number as part of the world's order, time by its mere lapse indicating it. For out of one day came "one," out of two "two," out of three "three," out of a month "thirty," out of a year the number equivalent to the days made up of twelve months, and out of infinite time came (the conception of) infinite number.

So many and so essential are the benefits within the scope of the constitutions and movements of the heavenly bodies. To how vast a number of other operations of nature, methinks, do they extend! Operations obscure to us—for all things are not within the ken of mortals— yet working together for the permanence of the whole; operations which are invariably carried out under ordinances and laws which God laid down in His universe as unalterable.

XX. Earth and heaven having been equipped with the array appropriate to either—earth on the third day, heaven, as has been recounted, on the fourth—the Creator took in hand to form the races of mortal creatures, beginning with aquatic creatures on the fifth day, deeming that there is no kinship so close as that between animals and the number 5. For living creatures differ from those without life in nothing more than in ability to apprehend by the senses; and sense has a fivefold division, into sight, hearing, taste, smell, touch; and to each of these their Maker assigned special aspects of matter, and an individual faculty of testing it, with which to assay objects coming under its notice. Colours are tested by sight, sounds by hearing, savours by taste, perfumes by smell, while touch assays the softness and hardness of various substances, their smoothness and roughness, and recognizes things hot or cold.

So then he bids all kinds of fish and sea-monsters to take shape, creatures differing in their habitats and their sizes and qualities; for different seas produce to some extent different fish; not eveywhere were all kinds formed. This is as we should have expected, for some kinds delight in a lagoon and not in a really deep sea, some in harbours and roadsteads. These can neither crawl up on to the land, nor swim far out from the land; and those that haunt the depths of the open seas avoid jutting headlands or islands or rocks. Some thrive in calm unruffled waters, others in those that are stormy and broken by waves; for, through the exercise of bearing their constant blows and of thrusting back their onset by sheer force, they put on flesh and grow lusty.

Directly after these He made all kinds of birds, as sister kinds to those in the waters, both being things that float. And He left incomplete no form of creature that travels in air.

XXI. Water and air having now duly received as a sort of lot of their own the living creatures appropriate to them, He again called upon the earth for the production of the portion that had been left out. When the plants had been created the land-animals had been wanting. So He saith "Let the earth bring forth cattle and wild beasts and creeping things after each kind" (Gen. i. 24). The earth forthwith puts forth, as it was bidden, creatures all differing in build and in the varying strength and capacity to hurt or to serve that was inherent in them.

To crown all he made man, in what way I will say presently, when I have first pointed out the exceeding beauty of the chain of sequence which Moses has employed in setting forth the bringing in of life. For of the forms of animal life, the least elaborately wrought has been allotted to the race of fish; that worked out in greatest detail and best in all respects to mankind; that which lies between these two to creatures that tread the earth and travel in the air. For the principle of life in these is endowed with perceptions keener than that in fishes, but less keen than that in men. Wherefore, of the creatures that have life, fishes were the first which he brought into being, creatures in whose being the body predominates over the soul or life-principle. They are in a way animals and not animals; lifeless beings with the power of movement. The seed of the principle of life has been sown in them adventitiously, with a view only to the perpetuation of their bodies, just as salt (we are told) is added to flesh that it may not easily decay.

After the fishes He made the birds and land-creatures; for, when we come to these, we find them with keener senses and manifesting by their structure far more clearly all the qualities proper to beings endowed with the life-principle.

To crown all, as we have said before, He made man, and bestowed on him mind *par excellence,* life-principle of the life-principle itself, like the pupil in the eye: for of this too those who investigate more closely than others the nature of things say that it is the eye of the eye.

XXII. At that time, indeed, all things took shape simultaneously. But, though all things took shape together, the fact that living organisms were afterwards to come into existence one out of another rendered necessary an adumbration of the principle of order in the narrative. Now in particular creatures the order we find is this, that they begin at what is lowest in its nature, and end in the best of all; what this best of all is we must go on to show. Now seed is the original starting-point of living creatures. That this is a substance of a very low order, resembling foam, is evident to the eye. But when it has been deposited in the womb and become solid, it acquires movement, and at once enters upon natural growth. But growth is better than seed, since in created things movement is better than quiescence. But nature, or growth, like an artificer, or (to speak more properly) like a consummate art, forms living creatures, by distributing the moist substance to the limbs and different parts of the body, the substance of life-breath to the faculties of the soul, affording them nourishment and endowing them with perception. We must defer for the present the faculty of reasoning, out of consideration for those who maintain that it comes in from without, and is divine and eternal.

Well, then, natural growth started from so poor a thing as seed, but it ended in that which is of greatest worth, the formation of the living creature and of man. Now we find that this selfsame thing has occurred in the case of the creation of the universe also. For when the Creator determined to form living creatures, those first in order were inferior, if we may so speak, namely fishes, while those that came last in order were best, namely men; and coming between the two extremes, better than those that preceded them, but inferior to the others, were the rest, namely land creatures and birds of the air.

XXIII. After all the rest, as I have said, Moses tells us that man was created after the image of God and after His likeness (Gen. i. 26). Right well does he say this, for nothing earth-born is more like God than man. Let no one represent the likeness as one to a bodily form; for neither is God in human form, nor is the human body God-like. No, it is in respect of the Mind, the sovereign element of the soul, that the word "image" is used; for after the pattern of a single Mind, even the Mind of the Universe as an archetype, the mind in each of those who successively came into being was moulded. It is in a fashion a god to him who carries and enshrines it as an object of reverence; for the human mind evidently occupies a position in men precisely answering to that which the great Ruler occupies in all the world. It is invisible while itself seeing all things, and while comprehending the substances of others, it is as to its own substance unperceived; and while it opens by arts and sciences roads branching in many directions, all of them great highways, it comes through land and sea investigating what either element contains. Again, when on soaring wing it has contemplated the atmosphere and all its phases, it is borne yet higher to the ether and the circuit of heaven, and is whirled round with the dances of planets and fixed stars, in accordance with the laws of perfect music, following that love of wisdom which guides its steps. And so, carrying its gaze beyond the confines of all substance discernible by sense, it comes to a point at which it reaches out after the intelligible world, and on descrying in that world sights of surpassing loveliness, even the patterns and the originals of the things of sense which it saw here, it is seized by a sober intoxication, like those filled with Corybantic frenzy, and is inspired, possessed by a longing far other than theirs and a nobler desire. Wafted by this to the topmost arch of the things perceptible to mind, it seems to be on its way to the Great King Himself; but, amid its longing to see Him, pure and untempered rays of concentrated light stream forth like a torrent, so that by its gleams the eye of the understanding is dazzled.

And, since images do not always correspond to their archetype and pattern, but are in many instances unlike it, the writer further brought out his meaning by adding "after the likeness" to the words "after the image," thus showing that an accurate cast, bearing a clear impression, was intended.

XXIV. One may not unfitly raise the question what reason there could be for his ascribing the creation in the case of man only not to one Creator as in the case of the rest but, as the words would suggest, to several. For he represents the Father of the universe as speaking thus, "Let us make man after our image and likeness." 'Can it be,' I would ask, 'that He to whom all things are subject, is in need of anyone whatever? Or can it be that when He made the heaven and the earth and the seas, he required no one to be his fellow-worker, yet was unable apart from the co-operation of others by His own unaided power to fashion a creature so puny and perishable as man?' The full truth about the cause of this it must needs be that God alone knows, but the cause which by probable conjecture seems plausible and reasonable we must not conceal. It is this. Among existences some partake neither of virtue nor of vice, like plants and animals devoid of reason; the one sort because they are without animal life and furnished with a nature incapable of consciously receiving impressions; the other sort because from them mind and reason have been eliminated: for mind and reason are as it were the dwelling-place of vice and virtue, which are by nature constituted to make their abode in them. Others again have partnership with virtue only, and have no part or lot in vice. Such are the heavenly bodies; for these are said to be not only living creatures but living creatures endowed with mind, or rather each of them a mind in itself, excellent through and through and unsusceptible of any evil. Others are of mixed nature, as man, who is liable to contraries, wisdom and folly, self-mastery and licentiousness, courage and cowardice, justice and injustice, and (in a word) to things good and evil, fair and foul, to virtue and vice. Now it was most proper to God the universal Father to make those excellent things by Himself alone, because of their kinship to Him. To make those which are neither good nor bad was not alien to Him, since those too are free from vice which is hateful to Him. To make those of mixed nature was in one respect proper to Him, in another not so; proper, so far as the better principle which forms an ingredient in them is concerned, alien, in virtue of the contrary and worse principle. So we see why it is only in the instance of man's creation that we are told by Moses that God said "Let us make," an expression which plainly shows the taking with Him of others as fellow-workers. It is to the end that, when man orders his course aright, when his thoughts and deeds are blameless, God the universal Ruler may be owned as their Source; while others from the number of His subordinates are held responsible for thoughts and deeds of a contrary sort: for it could not be that the Father should be the cause of an evil thing to His offspring: and vice and vicious activities are an evil thing.

And when Moses had called the genus "man," quite admirably did he distinguish its species, adding that it had been created "male and female," and this though its individual members had not yet taken shape. For the primary species are in the genus to begin with, and reveal themselves as in a mirror to those who have the faculty of keen vision.

XXV. It is obvious to inquire why man comes last in the world's creation; for, as the sacred writings show, he was the last whom the Father and Maker fashioned. Those, then, who have studied more deeply than others the laws of Moses and who examine their contents with all possible minuteness, maintain that God, when He made man partaker of kinship with Himself in mind and reason best of all gifts, did not begrudge him the other gifts either, but made ready for him beforehand all things in the world, as for a living being dearest and closest to Himself, since it was His will that when man came into existence he should be at a loss for none of the means of living and of living well. The means of living are provided by the lavish supplies of all that makes for enjoyment; the means of living well by the contemplation of the heavenly existences, for smitten by their contemplation the mind conceives a love and longing for the knowledge of them. And from this philosophy took its rise, by which man, mortal though he be, is rendered immortal. Just as givers of a banquet, then, do not send out the summonses to supper till they have put everything in readiness for the feast; and those who provide gymnastic and scenic contests, before they gather the spectators into the theatre or the stadium, have in readiness a number of combatants and performers to charm both eye and ear; exactly in the same way the Ruler of all things, like some provider of contests or of a banquet, when about to invite man to the enjoyment of a feast and a great spectacle, made ready beforehand the material for both. He desired that on coming into the world man might at once find both a banquet and a most sacred display, the one full of all things that earth and rivers and sea and air bring forth for use and for enjoyment, the other of all sorts of spectacles, most impressive in their substance, most impressive in their qualities, and circling with most wondrous movements, in an order fitly determined always in accordance with proportion of numbers and harmony of revolutions. In all these one might rightly say that there was the real music, the original and model of all other, from which the men of subsequent ages, when they had painted the images in their own souls, handed down an art most vital and beneficial to human life.

XXVI. Such is the first reason for which apparently man was created after all things: but we must mention a second that is not improbable. Directly he came into existence man found there all provisions for life. This was for the instruction of future generations. Nature seemed almost to cry aloud in so many words that like the first father of the race they were to spend their days without toil or trouble surrounded by lavish abundance of all that they needed. And this will be so if irrational pleasures do not get control of the soul, making their assaults upon it through greediness and lust, nor the desires for glory or wealth or power arrogate to themselves the control of the life, nor sorrows lower and depress the mind; and if fear, that evil counsellor, do not dispel high impulses to noble deeds, nor folly and cowardice and injustice and the countless host of other vices assail him. For in sooth as things now are, when all these evils which have been recounted have won the day, and men have flung themselves unrestainedly into the indulgence of their passions and left uncontrolled their guilty cravings, cravings which it were sinful even to name, a fitting penalty is incurred, due punishment of impious courses. That penalty is difficulty in obtaining the necessaries of life. For men plough the prairies and irrigate it from spring and river; they sow and plant; and through the livelong year unweariedly take up by day and night the ever renewed toil of the tiller of the earth; and yet they are hard put to it to gather in their requisite supplies, and these at times of poor quality and barely sufficient, having suffered injury from many causes: either they were ravaged by recurring rainfalls, or beaten down in masses by the weight of hail that fell on them, or half frozen by snow, or torn up roots and all by violent winds; for water and air can in many ways change the fruitfulness of crops into barrenness. But if the unmeasured impulses of men's passions were calmed and allayed by self-mastery, and their earnestness and eager striving after the infliction of wrongs were checked by righteousness; if, in a word, the vices and the fruitless practices to which they prompt were to give place to the virtues and their corresponding activities, the warfare in the soul, of all wars veritably the most dire and most grievous, would have been abolished, and peace would prevail and would in quiet and gentle ways provide good order for the exercise of our faculties, and there would be hope that God, being the Lover of virtue and the Lover of what is good and beautiful and also the Lover of man, would provide for our race good things all coming forth spontaneously and all in readiness. For it is clear that it is easier without calling in the husbandman's art to supply in abundance the yield of growths already existing than to bring into being things that were non-existent.

XXVII. Let what has been said suffice for an account of the second reason. A third is this. God, being minded to unite in intimate and loving fellowship the beginning and end of created things, made heaven the beginning and man the end, the one the most perfect of imperishable objects of sense, the other the noblest of things earthborn and perishable, being, in very truth, a miniature heaven. He bears about within himself, like holy images, endowments of nature that correspond to the constellations. He has capacities for science and art, for knowledge, and for the noble lore of the several virtues. For since the corruptible and the incorruptible are by nature contrary the one to the other, God assigned the fairest of each sort to the beginning and the end, heaven (as I have said) to the beginning, and man to the end.

XXVIII. Finally, this is suggested as a cogent reason. Man was bound to arise after all created things, in order that coming last and suddenly appearing to the other animals he might produce consternation in them; for they were sure, as soon as they saw him, to be amazed and do homage to him as to a born ruler or master: and so on beholding him they were all tamed through all their kinds, those who were most savage in their natures at the first sight of him becoming at once most manageable, displaying their untamed pugnacity one against another, but to man and man alone showing gentleness and docility. On this account too the Father, when he had brought him into existence as a living being naturally adapted for sovereignty, not only in fact, but by express mandate appointed him king of all creatures under the moon, those that move on land and swim in the sea and fly in the air. For all things mortal in the three elements of land and water and air did He make subject to men, but exempted the heavenly beings as having obtained a portion more divine. The clearest proof of man's rule is afforded by what goes on before our eyes. Sometimes vast numbers of cattle are led by one quite ordinary man neither wearing armour nor carrying an iron weapon nor anything with which to defend himself, with nothing but a sheepskin to cover him and a staff wherewith to show them which way to go and to lean on should he grow weary on his journeys. See, there is a shepherd, a goatherd, a cowherd leading flocks of sheep and goats, and herds of kine. They are men not even strong and lusty in body, unlikely, so far as healthy vigour goes, to create consternation in those who see them. And all the prowess and strength of all those well-armed animals, who possess the equipment which nature provides and use it in self-defence, cower before him like slaves before a master, and do his bidding. Bulls are harnessed to plough the land, and cutting deep furrows all day long, sometimes all night as well, accomplish a long bout with some farm-hand to direct them: rams laden with thick fleeces of wool, when spring-time comes, stand peacefully or even lie down quietly at the shepherd's bidding, and offer their wool to the shears, growing accustomed, just as cities do, to render their yearly tribute to him whom nature has given them for king. Nay, even the horse, most spirited of all animals, is easily controlled by the bit to prevent his growing restive and running away. He hollows his back, making it a convenient seat, takes his rider on it and bearing him aloft gallops at a great pace intent on bringing himself and his rider to the destination which the latter is eager to reach. As for his rider, firmly seated on him, without trouble and in much composure, he gets through his journey using the body and feet of another.

XXIX. Anyone who wished to enlarge on the subject would have plenty more to say tending to prove that nothing whatever has been emancipated and withdrawn from the domination of men: this is sufficiently indicated by what has been said. There is a point, however, as to which ignorance must be avoided. The fact of having been the last to come into existence does not involve an inferiority corresponding to his place in the series. Drivers and pilots are evidence of this. The former, though they come after their team and have their appointed place behind them, keep hold of the reins and drive them just as they wish, now letting them fall into a sharp trot, now pulling them up should they go with more speed than is necessary. Pilots again, taking their way to the stern, the hindmost place in the ship, are, one may say, superior to all on board, for they hold in their hands the safety of the ship and those on board it. So the Creator made man after all things, as a sort of driver and pilot, to drive and steer the things on earth, and charged him with the care of animals and plants, like a governor subordinate to the chief and great King.

XXX. Now when the whole world had been brought to completion in accordance with the properties of six, a perfect number, the Father invested with dignity the seventh day which comes next, extolling it and pronouncing it holy; for it is the festival, not of a single city or country, but of the universe, and it alone strictly deserves to be called "public" as belonging to all people and the birthday of the world. I doubt whether anyone could adequately celebrate the properties of the number 7, for they are beyond all words. Yet the fact that it is more wondrous than all that is said about it is no reason for maintaining silence regarding it. Nay, we must make a brave attempt to bring out at least all that is within the compass of our understandings, even if it be impossible to bring out all or even the most essential points. . . .

XXXIII. So august is the dignity inherent by nature in the number 7, that it has a unique relation distinguishing it from all the other numbers within the decade: for of these some beget without being begotten, some are begotten but do not beget, some do both these, both beget and are begotten: 7 alone is found in no such category. We must establish this assertion by giving proof of it. Well then, 1 begets all the subsequent numbers while it is begotten by none whatever: 8 is begotten by twice 4, but begets no number within the decade: 4 again holds the place of both, both of parents and of offspring; for it begets 8 by being doubled, and is begotten by twice 2. It is the nature of 7 alone, as I have said, neither to beget nor to be begotten. For this reason other philosophers liken this number to the motherless and virgin Nikè, who is said to have appeared out of the head of Zeus, while the Pythagoreans liken it to the chief of all things: for that which neither begets nor is begotten remains motionless; for creation takes place in movement, since there is movement both in that which begets and in that which is begotten, in the one that it may beget, in the other that it may be begotten. There is only one thing that neither causes motion nor experiences it, the original Ruler and Sovereign. Of Him 7 may be fitly said to be a symbol. Evidence of what I say is supplied by Philolaus in these words: "There is, he says, a supreme Ruler of all things, God, ever One, abiding, without motion, Himself (alone) like unto Himself, different from all others." . . .

XLI. The objects which are distinguished by sight, the noblest of the senses, participate in the number of which we are speaking, if classified by their kinds: for the kinds which are seen are seven—body, extension,[1] shape, size, colour, movement, quiescence, and beside these there is no other. . . .

XLIII. These and yet more than these are the statements and reflections of men on the number 7, showing the reasons for the very high honour which that number has attained in Nature, the honour in which it is held by the most approved investigators of the science of Mathematics and Astronomy among Greeks and other peoples, and the special honour accorded to it by that lover of Virtue, Moses. He inscribed its beauty on the most holy tables of the Law, and impressed it on the minds of all who were set under him, by bidding them at intervals of six days to keep a seventh day holy, abstaining from other work that has to do with seeking and gaining a livelihood, and giving their time to the one sole object of philosophy with a view to the improvement of character and submission to the scrutiny of conscience. Conscience, established in the soul like a judge, is never abashed in administering reproofs, sometimes employing sharper threats, sometimes gentler admonitions; threats, where the wrongdoing appeared to be deliberate; admonitions, to guard against a like lapse in the future, when the misconduct seemed unintentional and the result of want of caution.

XLIV. In his concluding summary of the story of creation he says: "This is the book of the genesis of heaven and earth, when they came into being, in the day in which God made the heaven and the earth and every herb of the field before it appeared upon the earth, and all grass of the field before it sprang up" (Gen. ii. 4, 5). Is he not manifestly describing the incorporeal ideas present only to the mind, by which, as by seals, the finished objects that meet our senses were moulded? For before the earth put forth its young green shoots, young verdure was present, he tells us, in the nature of things without material shape, and before grass sprang up in the field, there was in existence an invisible grass. We must suppose that in the case of all other objects also, on which the senses pronounce judgement, the original forms and measures, to which all things that come into being owe shape and size, subsisted before them; for even if he has not dealt with everything in detail but in the mass, aiming as he does at brevity in a

1. I.e., "of how many dimensions." The word may, perhaps, mean "distance" or "separation," i.e., from other bodies.

high degree, nevertheless what he does say gives us a few indications of universal Nature, which brings forth no finished product in the world of sense without using an incorporeal pattern.

XLV. Keeping to the sequence of the creation and carefully observing the connexion between what follows and what has gone before, he next says: "and a spring went up out of the earth and watered all the face of the earth" (Gen. ii. 6). Other philosophers say that all water is one of the four elements out of which the world was made. But Moses, wont as he is with keener vision to observe and apprehend amazingly well even distant objects, does indeed regard the great sea as an element, a fourth part of the whole, which his successors, reckoning the seas we sail to be in size mere harbours compared to it, call Ocean; but he distinguished sweet drinkable water from the salt water, assigning the former to the land and looking on it as part of this, not of the sea. It is such a part, for the purpose already mentioned, that by the sweet quality of the water as by a uniting glue the earth may be bound and held together: for had it been left dry, with no moisture making its way in and spreading by many channels through the pores, it would have actually fallen to pieces. It is held together and lasts, partly by virtue of the life-breath that makes it one, partly because it is saved from drying up and breaking off in small or big bits by the moisture. This is one reason, and I must mention another which is a guess at the truth. It is of the nature of nothing earth-born to take form apart from wet substance. This is shown by the depositing of seeds, which either are moist, as those of animals, or do not grow without moisture: such are those of plants. From this it is clear that the wet substance we have mentioned must be a part of the earth which gives birth to all things, just as with women the running of the monthly cleansings; for these too are, so physical scientists tell us, the bodily substance of the *fetus*. And what I am about to say is in perfect agreement with what has been said already. Nature has bestowed on every mother as a most essential endowment teeming breasts, thus preparing in advance food for the child that is to be born. The earth also, as we all know, is a mother, for which reason the earliest men thought fit to call her 'Demeter,' combining the name of 'mother' with that of 'earth'; for, as Plato[2] says, earth does not imitate woman, but woman earth. Poets quite rightly are in the habit of calling earth All-mother,' and 'Fruit-bearer' and 'Pandora' or 'Give-all,' inasmuch as she is the originating cause of existence and continuance in existence to all animals and plants alike. Fitly therefore on earth also, most ancient and most

2. *Menexenus* 238 A.

fertile of mothers, did Nature bestow, by way of breasts, streams of rivers and springs, to the end that both the plants might be watered and all animals might have abundance to drink.

XLVI. After this he says that "God formed man by taking clay from the earth, and breathed into his face the breath of life" (Gen. ii. 7). By this also he shows very clearly that there is a vast difference between the man thus formed and the man that came into existence earlier after the image of God: for the man so formed is an object of sense-perception, partaking already of such or such quality, consisting of body and soul, man or woman, by nature mortal; while he that was after the (Divine) image was an idea or type or seal, an object of thought (only), incorporeal, neither male nor female, by nature incorruptible.

It says, however, that the formation of the individual man, the object of sense, is a composite one made up of earthly substance and of Divine breath: for it says that the body was made through the Artificer taking clay and moulding out of it a human form, but that the soul was originated from nothing created whatever, but from the Father and Ruler of all: for that which He breathed in was nothing else than a Divine breath that migrated hither from that blissful and happy existence for the benefit of our race, to the end that, even if it is mortal in respect of its visible part, it may in respect of the part that is invisible be rendered immortal. Hence it may with propriety be said that man is the borderland between mortal and immortal nature, partaking of each so far as is needful, and that he was created at once mortal and immortal, mortal in respect of the body, but in respect of the mind immortal. . . .

LII. Quite excellently does Moses ascribe the bestowal of names also to the first man (Gen. ii. 19): for this is the business of wisdom and royalty, and the first man was wise with a wisdom learned from and taught by Wisdom's own lips, for he was made by divine hands; he was, moreover, a king, and it befits a ruler to bestow titles on his several subordinates. And we may guess that the sovereignty with which that first man was invested was a most lofty one, seeing that God had fashioned him with the utmost care and deemed him worthy of the second place, making him His own viceroy and lord of all others. For men born many generations later, when, owing to the lapse of ages, the race had lost its vigour, are none the less still masters of the creatures that are without reason, keeping a safe torch (as it were) of sovereignty and dominion passed down from the first man.

So Moses says that God brought all the animals to Adam, wishing to see what appellations he would assign to them severally. Not that he was in any doubt—for to God nothing is unknown—but because He knew that He had formed in mortal man the natural ability to reason of his own motion, that so He Himself might have no share in faulty action. No, He was putting man to the test, as a teacher does a pupil, kindling his innate capacity, and calling on him to put forth some faculty of his own, that by his own ability man might confer titles in no wise incongruous or unsuitable, but bringing out clearly the traits of the creatures who bore them. For the native reasoning power in the soul being still unalloyed, and no infirmity or disease or evil affection having intruded itself, he received the impressions made by bodies and objects in their sheer reality, and the titles he gave were fully apposite, for right well did he divine the character of the creatures he was describing, with the result that their natures were apprehended as soon as their names were uttered. So greatly did he excel in all noble traits, thus attaining the very limit of human happiness.

LIII. But since no created thing is constant, and things mortal are necessarily liable to changes and reverses, it could not but be that the first man too should experience some ill fortune. And woman becomes for him the beginning of blameworthy life. For so long as he was by himself, as accorded with such solitude, he went on growing like to the world and like God, and receiving in his soul the impressions made by the nature of each, not all of these, but as many as one of mortal composition can find room for. But when woman too had been made, beholding a figure like his own and a kindred form, he was gladdened by the sight, and approached and greeted her. She, seeing no living thing more like herself than he, is filled with glee and shamefastly returns his greeting. Love supervenes, brings together and fits into one the divided halves, as it were, of a single living creature, and sets up in each of them a desire for fellowship with the other with a view to the production of their like. And this desire begat likewise bodily pleasure, that pleasure which is the beginning of wrongs and violation of law, the pleasure for the sake of which men bring on themselves the life of mortality and wretchedness in lieu of that of immortality and bliss.

LIV. While the man was still leading a life of solitude, the woman not having been yet formed, a park or pleasaunce, we are told, was planted by God, quite unlike the pleasaunces with which we are familiar (Gen. ii. 8 f.): for in them the wood is soulless; they are full of trees of all sorts, some ever-blooming to give uninterrupted joy to the eye, some bursting forth with young life every spring: some again bearing cultivated fruit for man, not only for use by way of necessary nourishment, but also for his superfluities, for the enjoyment of a life of luxury; while others yield a different kind of fruit, supplied to the wild beasts to satisfy their actual needs. But in the divine park or pleasaunce all plants are endowed with soul or reason, bearing the virtues for fruit, and beside these insight and discernment that never fail, by which things fair and ugly are recognized, and life free from disease, and incorruption, and all that is of a like nature.

This description is, I think, intended symbolically rather than literally; for never yet have trees of life or of understanding appeared on earth, nor is it likely that they will appear hereafter. No, Moses evidently signifies by the pleasaunce the ruling power of the soul which is full of countless opinions, as it might be of plants; and by the tree of life he signifies reverence toward God, the greatest of the virtues, by means of which the soul attains to immortality; while by the tree that is cognisant of good and evil things he signifies moral prudence, the virtue that occupies the middle position, and enables us to distinguish things by nature contrary the one to the other.

LV. Having set up these standards in the soul, He watched, as a judge might, to see to which it would tend. And when He saw it inclining to wickedness, and making light of holiness and godly fear, out of which comes the winning of immortal life, He cast it forth, as we might expect, and drove it from the pleasaunce, giving the soul which committed offences that defy the healer's skill, no hope of a subsequent return, inasmuch as the reason given for their deception was in a high degree blameworthy. This we must not leave unexplained. It is said that in olden time the venomous earthborn crawling thing could send forth a man's voice, and that one day it approached the wife of the first man and upbraided her for her irresoluteness and excessive scrupulosity in delaying and hesitating to pluck a fruit most beauteous to behold and most luscious to taste, and most useful into the bargain, since by its means she would have power to recognize things good and evil. It is said that she, without looking into the suggestion, prompted by a mind devoid of steadfastness and firm foundation, gave her consent and ate of the fruit, and gave some of it to her husband; this instantly brought them out of a state of simplicity and innocence into one of wickedness: whereat the Father in anger appointed for them the punishments that were fitting. For their conduct well merited wrath, inasmuch as they had passed by the tree of life immortal, the consummation of virtue, from which they could have gathered an existence long and happy. Yet they chose that fleeting and mortal existence which is not an existence but a period of time full of misery.

LVI. Now these are no mythical fictions, such as poets and sophists delight in, but modes of making ideas visible, bidding us resort to allegorical interpretation guided in our renderings by what lies beneath the surface. Following a probable conjecture one would say that the serpent spoken of is a fit symbol of pleasure, because in the first place he is an animal without feet sunk prone upon his belly; secondly because he takes clods of earth as food; thirdly because he carries in his teeth the venom with which it is his nature to destroy those whom he has bitten. The lover of pleasure is exempt from none of these traits, for he is so weighted and dragged downwards that it is with difficulty that he lifts up his head, thrown down and tripped up by intemperance: he feeds not on heavenly nourishment, which wisdom by discourses and doctrines proffers to lovers of contemplation, but on that which comes up out of the earth with the revolving seasons, and which produces drunkenness, daintiness, and greediness. These, causing the cravings of the belly to burst out and fanning them into flame, make the man a glutton, while they also stimulate and stir up the stings of his sexual lusts. For he licks his lips over the labour of caterers and confectioners, and twisting his head about all round strains to catch some of the steam and savour of the delicacies. Whenever he beholds a richly spread table, he flings down his whole person and tumbles upon the dishes set out, eager to devour all at once. His aim is not to sate his hunger, but to leave nothing that has been set before him undevoured. Hence we see that no less than the serpent he carries his poison in his teeth. These are the agents and ministers of excess, cutting and chewing all eatable, handing them over first to the tongue, the judge of savours, for its decision, then to the gullet. Immoderate eating is by its nature deadly and poisonous, for what is eaten has no chance of being assimilated, owing to the rush of the fresh viands which takes place before those already swallowed have been digested. Again the serpent is said to emit a human voice. This is because pleasure employs ten thousand champions and defenders, who have undertaken to look after her and stand up for her, and who dare to spread the doctrine that she has assumed universal sovereignty over small and great, and that no one whatever is exempt therefrom.

LVII. And certainly the first approaches of the male to the female have pleasure to guide and conduct them, and it is through pleasure that begetting and the coming of life is brought about, and the offspring is naturally at home with nothing sooner than pleasure, delighting in it and feeling distress at pain its contrary. This is why the infant when born actually weeps aloud, chilled most likely by the cold all round it; for when, leaving a place of fiery warmth in the womb, which for a long time it has tenanted, it suddenly issues into the air, a cold and unaccustomed place, it is taken aback and utters cries, a most clear sign of its pain and its annoyance at suffering. And they tell us that every living creature hastens after pleasure as its most necessary and essential end, and man above all: for while other creatures seek pleasure only through taste and the organs of reproduction, man does so through the other senses as well, pursuing with ears and eyes all such sights and sounds as can afford delight. A very great deal more is said in praise of pleasure, and of the great closeness of its connexion and kinship with living creatures.

LVIII. But what has now been said is enough to show why the serpent seemed to utter a human voice. It is for this reason, I think, that even in the detailed laws, where the lawgiver writes about animals, laying down which may be eaten and which may not, he especially praises the "snake-fighter" as it is called (Lev. xi. 22). This is a reptile with legs above its feet, with which it springs from the ground and lifts itself into the air like a grasshopper. For the snake-fighter is, I think, nothing but a symbolic representation of self-control, waging a fight that never ends and a truceless war against intemperance and pleasure. Self-control welcomes beyond measure simplicity and abstemiousness and so much as is requisite for a severe and lofty mode of life; intemperance gives a like welcome to superfluity and extravagance, which induce softness and voluptuousness in soul and body, and these result in the culpable life, the life that in the view of right-minded people is worse than death.

LIX. Pleasure does not venture to bring her wiles and deceptions to bear on the man, but on the woman, and by her means on him. This is a telling and well-made point: for in us mind corresponds to man, the senses to woman; and pleasure encounters and holds parley with the senses first, and through them cheats with her quackeries the sovereign mind itself: for when each sense has been subjugated to her sorceries, delighting in what she proffers, the sense of sight in variegated colours and shapes, that of hearing in harmonious sounds, that of taste in delicate savours, and that of scent in the fragrance of perfumes which it inhales, then all of them receive the gifts and offer them like handmaids to the Reason as to a master, bringing with them Persuasion to plead that it reject nothing whatever. Reason is forthwith ensnared and becomes a subject instead of a ruler, a slave instead of a master, an alien instead of a citizen, and a mortal instead of an immortal. In a word we must never lose sight of the fact that Pleasure, being a courte-

san and a wanton, eagerly desires to meet with a lover, and searches
for panders, by whose means she shall get one on her hook. It is the
senses that act as panders for her and procure the lover. When she has
ensnared these she easily brings the Mind under her control. To it,
dwelling within us, the senses convey the things seen without, reporting
them fully and making them manifest, impressing on it the forms of
the several objects, and producing in it the corresponding affection. For
it resembles wax, and receives the images that reach it through the
senses, by which it apprehends material substances, being incapable, as
I have said before, of doing this by itself.

LX. Those who were the first to become slaves to a passion grievous and hard to heal at once had experience of the wages paid by
Pleasure. The woman incurred the violent woes of travail-pangs, and
the griefs which come one after another all through the remainder of
life. Chief among them are all those that have to do with children at
birth and in their bringing up, in sickness and in health, in good fortune and evil fortune. In the next place she tasted deprivation of
liberty, and the authority of the husband at her side, whose commands
she must perforce obey. The man, in his turn, incurred labours and
distress in the unceasing sweat of his brow to gain the necessaries of
life. He was without those good things which the earth had been
taught to bear of itself independently of all skill in the husbandman.
His life was spent in unbroken toils in the pursuit of food and livelihood to save him from perishing by famine. For I imagine that, just as
sun and moon always give their light after once for all being bidden to
do so when the universe was first created, and continue to keep the
divine ordinance for no other reason than that evil has been sent into
exile far away from heaven's frontiers; even so would earth's deep and
fertile soil, unaided by the skill of agricultural labourers, bear rich
abundance as the seasons come round. As it is, when evil began to get
the better of the virtues, the ever-flowing springs of the bounties of
God were closed, that they might not brings supplies to those felt to be
undeserving of them. If the human race had had to undergo the fitting
penalty, it must needs have been wiped out by reason of its ingratitude
to God its benefactor and preserver. But He being merciful took pity
on it and moderated the punishment, suffering the race to continue, but
no longer as before supplying it with food ready to its hand, that men
might not, by indulging the twin evils of idleness and satiety, wax
insolent in wrong-doing.

LXI. Such is the life of those who at the outset are in enjoyment of
innocence and simplicity of character, but later on prefer vice to virtue.

By his account of the creation of the world of which we have spoken Moses teaches us among many other things five that are fairest and best of all.

Firstly that the Deity is and has been from eternity. This with a view to atheists, some of whom have hesitated and have been of two minds about His eternal existence, while the bolder sort have carried their audacity to the point of declaring that the Deity does not exist at all, but that it is a mere assertion of men obscuring the truth with myth and fiction.

Secondly, that God is one. This with a view to the propounders of polytheism, who do not blush to transfer from earth to heaven mob-rule, that worst of evil polities.

Thirdly, as I have said already, that the world came into being. This because of those who think that it is without beginning and eternal, who thus assign to God no superiority at all.

Fourthly, that the world too is one as well as its Maker, who made His work like Himself in its uniqueness, who used up for the creation of the whole all the material that exists; for it would not have been a whole had it not been formed and consisted of parts that were wholes. For there are those who suppose that there are more worlds than one, while some think that they are infinite in number. Such men are themselves in very deed infinitely lacking in knowledge of things which it is right good to know.

Fifthly, that God also exercises forethought on the world's behalf. For that the Maker should care for the thing made is required by the laws and ordinances of Nature, and it is in accordance with these that parents take thought beforehand for children.

He that has begun by learning these things with his understanding rather than with his hearing, and has stamped on his soul impressions of truths so marvellous and priceless, both that God is and is from eternity, and that He that really *is* is One, and that He has made the world and has made it one world, unique as Himself is unique, and that He ever exercises forethought for His creation, will lead a life of bliss and blessedness, because he has a character moulded by the truths that piety and holiness enforce.

PLOTINUS

Plotinus (205-270 A.D.) was educated in cosmopolitan Alexandria and is said to have traveled to India and Persia in order to learn more of philosophies akin to his own. He probably owes the chief principles of his system to the inspiration and instruction he received from Ammonius Saccas in Alexandria. Plotinus established his school in Rome, where he developed his later, mature doctrines. He wrote fifty-four treatises that his student and disciple, Porphyry, rearranged after the death of his master into six groupings of nine chapters each. They are thus called *Enneads*, the Greek word for nine. The selection here, is taken from the celebrated translation by McKenna (see bibiliography) and is ordered in such a way as to make a reading of these very difficult treatises less so. It may be useful to keep in mind that, for Plotinus, philosophy as rationality is a necessary step on the path to the mystical union of the soul with the One.

Ennead I
Sixth Tractate — Beauty

1. Beauty addresses itself chiefly to sight; but there is a beauty for the hearing too, as in certain combinations of words and in all kinds of music, for melodies and cadences are beautiful; and minds that lift themselves above the realm of sense to a higher order are aware of beauty in the conduct of life, in actions, in character, in the pursuits of the intellect; and there is the beauty of the virtues. What loftier beauty there may be, yet, our argument will bring to light.

What, then, is it that gives comeliness to material forms and draws the ear to the sweetness perceived in sounds, and what is the secret of the beauty there is in all that derives from Soul?

Is there some One Principle from which all take their grace, or is there a beauty peculiar to the embodied and another for the bodiless? Finally, one or many, what would such a Principle be?

Consider that some things, material shapes for instance, are gracious not by anything inherent but by something communicated, while others are lovely of themselves, as, for example, Virtue.

The same bodies appear sometimes beautiful, sometimes not; so that there is a good deal between being body and being beautiful.

What, then, is this something that shows itself in certain material forms? This is the natural beginning of our inquiry.

What is it that attracts the eyes of those to whom a beautiful object is presented, and calls them, lures them, towards it, and fills them with joy at the sight? If we possess ourselves of this, we have at once a standpoint for the wider survey.

Almost everyone declares that the symmetry of parts towards each other and towards a whole, with, besides, a certain charm of colour, constitutes the beauty recognized by the eye, that in visible things, as indeed in all else, universally, the beautiful thing is essentially symmetrical, patterned.

But think what this means.

Only a compound can be beautiful, never anything devoid of parts; and only a whole; the several parts will have beauty, not in themselves, but only as working together to give a comely total. Yet beauty in an aggregate demands beauty in details: it cannot be constructed out of ugliness; its law must run throughout.

All the loveliness of colour and even the light of the sun, being devoid of parts and so not beautiful by symmetry, must be ruled out of the realm of beauty. And how comes gold to be a beautiful thing? And lightning by night, and the stars, why are these so fair?

In sounds also the simple must be proscribed, though often in a whole noble composition each several tone is delicious in itself.

Again since the one face, constant in symmetry, appears sometimes fair and sometimes not, can we doubt that beauty is something more than symmetry, that symmetry itself owes its beauty to a remoter principle?

Turn to what is attractive in methods of life or in the expression of thought; are we to call in symmetry here? What symmetry is to be found in noble conduct, or excellent laws, in any form of mental pursuit?

What symmetry can there be in points of abstract thought?

The symmetry of being accordant with each other? But there may be accordance or entire identity where there is nothing but ugliness: the proposition that honesty is merely a generous artlessness chimes in the most perfect harmony with the proposition that morality means weakness of will; the accordance is complete.

Then again, all the virtues are a beauty of the Soul, a beauty authentic beyond any of these others; but how does symmetry enter here? The Soul, it is true, is not a simple unity, but still its virtue cannot have the symmetry of size or of number: what standard of measurement could preside over the compromise or the coalescence of the Soul's faculties or purposes?

Finally, how by this theory would there be beauty in the Intellectual-Principle, essentially the solitary?

2. Let us, then, go back to the source, and indicate at once the Principle that bestows beauty on material things.

Undoubtedly this Principle exists; it is something that is perceived at the first glance, something which the Soul names as from an ancient knowledge and, recognizing, welcomes it, enters into unison with it.

But let the Soul fall in with the Ugly and at once it shrinks within itself, denies the thing, turns away from it, not accordant, resenting it.

Our interpretation is that the Soul—by the very truth of its nature, by its affiliation to the noblest Existents in the hierarchy of Being—when it sees anything of that kin, or any trace of that kinship, thrills with an immediate delight, takes its own to itself, and thus stirs anew to the sense of its nature and of all its affinity.

But, is there any such likeness between the loveliness of this world and the splendours in the Supreme? Such a likeness in the particulars would make the two orders alike: but what is there in common between beauty here and beauty There?

We hold that all the loveliness of this world comes by communion in Ideal-Form.

All shapelessness whose kind admits of pattern and form, as long as it remains outside of Reason and Idea, is ugly by that very isolation from the Divine-Thought. And this is the Absolute Ugly: an ugly thing is something that has not been entirely mastered by pattern, that is by Reason, the Matter not yielding at all points and in all respects to Ideal-Form.

But where the Ideal-Form has entered, it has grouped and co-ordinated what from a diversity of parts was to become a unity: it has rallied confusion into co-operation: it has made the sum one harmonious coherence: for the Idea is a unity and what it moulds must come to unity as far as multiplicity may.

And on what has thus been compacted to unity, Beauty enthrones itself, giving itself to the parts as to the sum: when it lights on some natural unity, a thing of like parts, then it gives itself to that whole. Thus, for an illustration, there is the beauty, conferred by craftsmanship, of all a house with all its parts, and the beauty which some natural quality may give to a single stone.

This, then, is how the material thing becomes beautiful—by communicating in the thought (Reason, Logos) that flows from the Divine.

3. And the Soul includes a faculty peculiarly addressed to Beauty—one incomparably sure in the appreciation of its own, when Soul entire is enlisted to support its judgement.

Or perhaps the Soul itself acts immediately, affirming the Beautiful where it finds something accordant with the Ideal-Form within itself, using this Idea as a canon of accuracy in its decision.

But what accordance is there between the material and that which antedates all Matter?

On what principle does the architect, when he finds the house standing before him correspondent with his inner ideal of a house, pronounce it beautiful? Is it not that the house before him, the stones apart, is the inner idea stamped upon the mass of exterior matter, the indivisible exhibited in diversity?

So with the perceptive faculty: discerning in certain objects the Ideal-Form which has bound and controlled shapeless matter, opposed in nature to Idea, seeing further stamped upon the common shapes some shape excellent above the common, it gathers into unity what still remains fragmentary, catches it up and carries it within, no longer a thing of parts, and presents it to the Ideal-Principle as something concordant and congenial, a natural friend: the joy here is like that of a good man who discerns in a youth the early signs of a virtue consonant with the achieved perfection within his own soul.

The beauty of colour is also the outcome of a unification: it derives from shape, from the conquest of the darkness inherent in Matter by the pouring-in of light, the unembodied, which is a Rational-Principle and an Ideal-Form.

Hence it is that Fire itself is splendid beyond all material bodies, holding the rank of Ideal-Principle to the other elements, making ever upwards, the subtlest and sprightliest of all bodies, as very near to the unembodied; itself alone admitting no other, all the others penetrated by it: for they take warmth but this is never cold; it has colour primally; they receive the Form of colour from it: hence the splendour of its light, the splendour that belongs to the Idea. And all that has resisted and is but uncertainly held by its light remains outside of beauty, as not having absorbed the plenitude of the Form of colour.

And harmonies unheard in sound create the harmonies we hear and wake the Soul to the consciousness of beauty, showing it the one essence in another kind: for the measures of our sensible music are not arbitrary but are determined by the Principle whose labour is to dominate Matter and bring pattern into being.

Thus far of the beauties of the realm of sense, images and shadow-pictures, fugitives that have entered into Matter—to adorn, and to ravish, where they are seen.

4. But there are earlier and loftier beauties than these. In the sense-bound life we are no longer granted to know them, but the Soul, taking no help from the organs, sees and proclaims them. To the vision of these we must mount, leaving sense to its own low place.

As it is not for those to speak of the graceful forms of the material world who have never seen them or known their grace—men born blind, let us suppose—in the same way those must be silent upon the beauty of noble conduct and of learning and all that order who have never cared for such things, nor may those tell of the splendour of virtue who have never known the face of Justice and of Moral-Wisdom beautiful beyond the beauty of Evening and of Dawn.

Such vision is for those only who see with the Soul's sight—and at the vision, they will rejoice, and awe will fall upon them and a trouble deeper than all the rest could ever stir, for now they are moving in the realm of Truth.

This is the spirit that Beauty must ever induce, wonderment and a delicious trouble, longing and love and a trembling that is all delight. For the unseen all this may be felt as for the seen; and this the Souls feel for it, every Soul in some degree, but those the more deeply that are the more truly apt to this higher love—just as all take delight in the beauty of the body but all are not stung as sharply, and those only that feel the keener wound are known as Lovers.

5. These Lovers, then, lovers of the beauty outside of sense, must be made to declare themselves.

What do you feel in presence of the grace you discern in actions, in manners, in sound morality, in all the works and fruits of virtue, in the beauty of Souls? When you see that you yourselves are beautiful within, what do you feel? What is this Dionysiac exultation that thrills through your being, this straining upwards of all your soul, this longing to break away from the body and live sunken within the veritable self?

These are no other than the emotions of Souls under the spell of love.

But what is it that awakens all this passion? No shape, no colour, no grandeur of mass: all is for a Soul, something whose beauty rests upon no colour, for the moral wisdom the Soul enshrines and all the other hueless splendour of the virtues. It is that you find in yourself, or admire in another, loftiness of spirit; righteousness of life; disciplined purity; courage of the majestic face; gravity, modesty that goes fearless and tranquil and passionless; and, shining down upon all, the light of god-like Intellection.

All these noble qualities are to be reverenced and loved, no doubt, but what entitles them to be called beautiful?

They exist: they manifest themselves to us: anyone that sees them must admit that they have reality of Being; and is not Real-Being really beautiful?

But we have not yet shown by what property in them they have wrought the Soul to loveliness: what is this grace, this splendour as of Light, resting upon all the virtues?

Let us take the contrary, the ugliness of the Soul, and set that against its beauty: to understand, at once, what this ugliness is and how it comes to appear in the Soul will certainly open our way before us.

Let us then suppose an ugly Soul, dissolute, unrighteous: teeming with all the lusts; torn by internal discord; beset by the fears of its cowardice and the envies of its pettiness; thinking, in the little thought it has, only of the perishable and the base; perverse in all its impulses; the friend of unclean pleasures; living the life of abandonment to bodily sensation and delighting in its deformity.

What must we think but that all this shame is something that has gathered about the Soul, some foreign bane outraging it, soiling it, so that, encumbered with all manner of turpitude, it has no longer a clean activity or a clean sensation, but commands only a life smouldering dully under the crust of evil; that, sunk in manifold death, it no longer sees what a Soul should see, may no longer rest in its own being, dragged ever as it is towards the outer, the lower, the dark?

An unclean thing, I dare to say; flickering hither and thither at the call of objects of sense, deeply infected with the taint of body, occupied always in Matter, and absorbing Matter into itself; in its commerce with the Ignoble it has trafficked away for an alien nature its own essential Idea.

If a man has been immersed in filth or daubed with mud, his native comeliness disappears and all that is seen is the foul stuff besmearing him: his ugly condition is due to alien matter that has encrusted him, and if he is to win back his grace it must be his business to scour and purify himself and make himself what he was.

So, we may justly say, a Soul becomes ugly—by something foisted upon it, by sinking itself into the alien, by a fall, a descent into body, into Matter. The dishonour of the Soul is in its ceasing to be clean and apart. Gold is degraded when it is mixed with earthly particles; if these be worked out, the gold is left and is beautiful, isolated from all that is foreign, gold with gold alone. And so the Soul; let it be but cleared of the desires that come by its too intimate converse with the body, emancipated from all the passions, purged of all that embodiment has thrust upon it, withdrawn, a solitary, to itself again—in that moment the ugliness that came only from the alien is stripped away.

6. For, as the ancient teaching was, moral-discipline and courage and every virtue, not even excepting Wisdom itself, all is purification.

Hence the Mysteries with good reason adumbrate the immersion of the unpurified in filth, even in the Nether-World, since the unclean loves filth for its very filthiness, and swine foul of body find their joy in foulness.

What else is Sophrosyny, rightly so-called, but to take no part in the pleasures of the body, to break away from them as unclean and unworthy of the clean? So too, Courage is but being fearless of the death which is but the parting of the Soul from the body, an event which no one can dread whose delight is to be his unmingled self. And Magnanimity is but disregard for the lure of things here. And Wisdom is but the Act of the Intellectual-Principle withdrawn from the lower places and leading the Soul to the Above.

The Soul thus cleansed is all Idea and Reason, wholly free of body, intellective, entirely of that divine order from which the wellspring of Beauty rises and all the race of Beauty.

Hence the Soul heightened to the Intellectual-Principle is beautiful to all its power. For Intellection and all that proceeds from Intellection are the Soul's beauty, a graciousness native to it and not foreign, for only with these is it truly Soul. And it is just to say that in the Soul's becoming a good and beautiful thing is its becoming like to God, for from the Divine comes all the Beauty and all the Good in beings.

We may even say that Beauty *is* the Authentic-Existents and Ugliness is the Principle contrary to Existence: and the Ugly is also the primal evil; therefore its contrary is at once good and beautiful, or is Good and Beauty: and hence the one method will discover to us the Beauty-Good and the Ugliness-Evil.

And Beauty, this Beauty which is also The Good, must be posed as The First: directly deriving from this First is the Intellectual-Principle which is pre-eminently the manifestation of Beauty; through the Intellectual-Principle Soul is beautiful. The beauty in things of a lower order—actions and pursuits for instance—comes by operation of the shaping Soul which is also the author of the beauty found in the world of sense. For the Soul, a divine thing, a fragment as it were of the Primal Beauty, makes beautiful to the fullness of their capacity all things whatsoever that it grasps and moulds.

7. Therefore we must ascend again towards the Good, the desired of every Soul. Anyone that has seen This, knows what I intend when I say that it is beautiful. Even the desire of it is to be desired as a Good. To attain it is for those that will take the upward path, who will set all their forces towards it, who will divest themselves of all that we have put on in our descent: so, to those that approach the Holy Celebrations of the Mysteries, there are appointed purifications and the laying aside of

the garments worn before, and the entry in nakedness—until, passing, on the upward way, all that is other than the God, each in the solitude of himself shall behold that solitary-dwelling Existence, the Apart, the Unmingled, the Pure, that from Which all things depend, for Which all look and live and act and know, the Source of Life and of Intellection and of Being.

And one that shall know this vision—with what passion of love shall he not be seized, with what pang of desire, what longing to be molten into one with This, what wondering delight! If he that has never seen this Being must hunger for It as for all his welfare, he that has known must love and reverence It as the very Beauty; he will be flooded with awe and gladness, stricken by a salutary terror; he loves with a veritable love, with sharp desire; all other loves than this he must despise, and disdain all that once seemed fair.

This, indeed, is the mood even of those who, having witnessed the manifestation of Gods or Supernals, can never again feel the old delight in the comeliness of material forms: what then are we to think of one that contemplates Absolute Beauty in Its essential integrity, no accumulation of flesh and matter, no dweller on earth or in the heavens—so perfect Its purity—far above all such things in that they are non-essential, composite, not primal but descending from This?

Beholding this Being—the Choragus of all Existence, the Self-Intent that ever gives forth and never takes—resting, rapt, in the vision and possession of so lofty a loveliness, growing to Its likeness, what Beauty can the Soul yet lack? For This, the Beauty supreme, the absolute, and the primal, fashions Its lovers to Beauty and makes them also worthy of love.

And for This, the sternest and the uttermost combat is set before the Souls; all our labour is for This, lest we be left without part in this noblest vision, which to attain is to be blessed in the blissful sight, which to fail of is to fail utterly.

For not he that has failed of the joy that is in colour or in visible forms, not he that has failed of power or of honours or of kingdom has failed, but only he that has failed of only This, for Whose winning he should renounce kingdoms and command over earth and ocean and sky, if only, spurning the world of sense from beneath his feet, and straining to This, he may see.

8. But what must we do? How lies the path? How come to vision of the inaccessible Beauty, dwelling as if in consecrated precincts, apart from the common ways where all may see, even the profane?

He that has the strength, let him arise and withdraw into himself, foregoing all that is known by the eyes, turning away for ever from the material beauty that once made his joy. When he perceives those shapes of grace that show in body, let him not pursue: he must know them for copies, vestiges, shadows, and hasten away towards That they tell of. For if anyone follow what is like a beautiful shape playing over water —is there not a myth telling in symbol of such a dupe, how he sank into the depths of the current and was swept away to nothingness? So too, one that is held by material beauty and will not break free shall be precipitated, not in body but in Soul, down to the dark depths loathed of the Intellective-Being, where, blind even in the Lower-World, he shall have commerce only with shadows, there as here.

'Let us flee then to the beloved Fatherland': this is the soundest counsel. But what is this flight? How are we to gain the open sea? For Odysseus is surely a parable to us when he commands the flight from the sorceries of Circe or Calypso—not content to linger for all the pleasure offered to his eyes and all the delight of sense filling his days.

The Fatherland to us is There whence we have come, and There is The Father.

What then is our course, what the manner of our flight? This is not a journey for the feet; the feet bring us only from land to land; nor need you think of coach or ship to carry you away; all this order of things you must set aside and refuse to see: you must close the eyes and call instead upon another vision which is to be waked within you, a vision, the birth-right of all, which few turn to use.

9. And this inner vision, what is its operation?

Newly awakened it is all too feeble to bear the ultimate splendour. Therefore the Soul must be trained—to the habit of remarking, first, all noble pursuits, then the works of beauty produced not by the labour of the arts but by the virtue of men known for their goodness: lastly, you must search the souls of those that have shaped these beautiful forms.

But how are you to see into a virtuous Soul and know its loveliness?

Withdraw into yourself and look. And if you do not find yourself beautiful yet, act as does the creator of a statue that is to be made beautiful: he cuts away here, he smoothes there, he makes this line lighter, this other purer, until a lovely face has grown upon his work. So do you also: cut away all that is excessive, straighten all that is crooked, bring light to all that is overcast, labour to make all one glow of beauty and never cease chiselling your statue, until there shall shine out on you from it the godlike splendour of virtue, until you shall see the perfect goodness surely established in the stainless shrine.

When you know that you have become this perfect work, when you are self-gathered in the purity of your being, nothing now remaining that can shatter that inner unity, nothing from without clinging to the authentic man, when you find yourself wholly true to your essential nature, wholly that only veritable Light which is not measured by space, nor narrowed to any circumscribed form nor again diffused as a thing void of term, but ever unmeasurable as something greater than all measure and more than all quantity—when you perceive that you have grown to this, you are now become very vision: now call up all your confidence, strike forward yet a step—you need a guide no longer —strain, and see.

This is the only eye that sees the mighty Beauty. If the eye that adventures the vision be dimmed by vice, impure, or weak, and unable in its cowardly blenching to see the uttermost brightness, then it sees nothing even though another point to what lies plain to sight before it. To any vision must be brought an eye adapted to what is to be seen, and having some likeness to it. Never did eye see the sun unless it had first become sunlike, and never can the Soul have vision of the First Beauty unless itself be beautiful.

Therefore, first let each become godlike and each beautiful who cares to see God and Beauty. So, mounting, the Soul will come first to the Intellectual-Principle and survey all the beautiful Ideas in the Supreme and will avow that this is Beauty, that the Ideas are Beauty. For by their efficacy comes all Beauty else, by the offspring and essence of the Intellectual-Being. What is beyond the Intellectual-Principle we affirm to be the nature of Good radiating Beauty before it. So that, treating the Intellectual-Cosmos as one, the first is the Beautiful: if we make distinction there, the Realm of Ideas constitutes the Beauty of the Intellectual Sphere; and The Good, which lies beyond, is the Fountain at once and Principle of Beauty: the Primal Good and the Primal Beauty have the one dwelling-place and, thus, always, Beauty's seat is There.

Ennead IV
Eighth Tractate—the Soul's Descent into Body

1. Many times it has happened: lifted out of the body into myself; becoming external to all other things and self-encentred; beholding a marvellous beauty; then, more than ever, assured of community with the loftiest order; enacting the noblest life, acquiring identity with the divine; stationing within It by having attained that activity; poised above whatsoever within the Intellectual is less than the Supreme: yet, there comes the moment of descent from intellection to reasoning, and after that sojourn in the divine, I ask myself how it happens that I can now be descending, and how did the Soul ever enter into my body, the Soul which, even within the body, is the high thing it has shown itself to be.

Heraclitus, who urges the examination of this matter, tells of 'compulsory alternation from contrary to contrary', speaks of ascent and descent, says that 'change reposes', and that 'it is weariness to keep toiling at the same things and to be always overcome by them'; but he seems to teach by metaphor, not concerning himself about making his doctrine clear to us, probably with the idea that it is for us to seek within ourselves as he sought for himself and found.

Empedocles—where he says that it is law for faulty souls to descend to this sphere, and that he himself was here because he turned 'a deserter, wandered from God, in slavery to a raving discord'—reveals neither more nor less than Pythagoras and his school seem to me to convey on this as on many other matters; but in his case, versification has some part in the obscurity.

We have to fall back on the illustrious Plato, who uttered many noble sayings about the Soul, and has in many places dwelt upon its entry into body, so that we may well hope to get some light from him.

What do we learn from this philosopher?

We will not find him so consistent throughout that it is easy to discover his mind.

Everywhere, no doubt, he expresses contempt for all that is of sense, blames the commerce of soul with body as an enchainment, an entombment, and upholds as a great truth the saying of the Mysteries that the Soul is here a prisoner. In the Cavern of Plato and in the Cave of Empedocles, I discern this universe, where the 'breaking of the fetters' and the 'ascent' from the depths are figures of the wayfaring towards the Intellectual Realm.

In the Phaedrus he makes a failing of the wings the cause of the entry to this realm: and there are Periods which send back the Soul after it has risen; there are judgements and lots and fates and necessities driving other souls down to this order.

In all these explanations he finds guilt in the arrival of the Soul at body. But treating, in the Timaeus, of our universe he exalts the Cosmos and entitles it 'a blessed god', and holds that the Soul was given by the goodness of the Creator to the end that the total of things might be possessed of intellect, for thus intellectual it was planned to be, and thus it cannot be except through soul. There is a reason, then, why the Soul of this All should be sent into it from God: in the same way the Soul of each single one of us is sent, that the universe may be complete; it was necessary that all beings of the Intellectual should be tallied by just so many forms of living creatures here in the realm of sense.

2. Inquiring, then, of Plato as to our own soul, we find ourselves forced to inquire into the nature of soul in general—to discover what there can be in its character to bring it into partnership with body, and, again, what this Cosmos must be in which, willing, unwilling or in any way at all, soul has its activity.

We have to face also the question as to whether the Creator has planned well, or whether the World-Soul, it may be, resembles our human souls which, in governing their inferior, the body, must sink deeper and deeper into it if they are to control it.

No doubt the individual body—though in all cases appropriately placed within the universe—is of itself in a state of dissolution, always on the way to its natural terminus, demanding much irksome forethought to save it from every kind of outside assailant, always gripped by need, requiring every help against constant difficulty: but the body inhabited by the World-Soul—complete, competent, self-sufficing, exposed to nothing contrary to its nature—this needs no more than a brief word of command, while the governing soul is undeviatingly what its nature makes it wish to be, and, amenable neither to loss nor to addition, knows neither desire nor distress.

This is how we come to read that our soul, entering into association with that complete soul and itself thus made perfect, 'walks the lofty ranges, administering the entire Cosmos', and that as long as it does not secede and is neither inbound to body nor held in any sort of servitude, so long it tranquilly bears its part in the governance of the All, exactly like the World-Soul itself; for in fact it suffers no hurt whatever by furnishing body with the power to existence, since not every form of care for the inferior need wrest the providing soul from its own sure standing in the highest.

The Soul's care for the universe takes two forms: there is the supervising of the entire system, brought to order by deedless command in a kingly presidence, and there is that over the individual, implying direct action, the hand to the task, one might say, in immediate contact: in the second kind of care the agent absorbs much of the nature of its object.

Now in its comprehensive government of the heavenly system, the Soul's method is that of an unbroken transcendence in its highest phases, with penetration by its lower power: at this, God can no longer be charged with lowering the All-Soul, which has not been deprived of its natural standing and from eternity possesses and will unchangeably possess that rank and habit which could never have been intruded upon it against the course of nature but must be its characteristic quality, neither failing ever nor ever beginning.

Where we read that the souls of stars stand to their bodily forms as the All-Soul to the body of the All—for these starry bodies are declared to be members of the Soul's circuit—we are given to understand that the star-souls also enjoy the blissful condition of transcendence and immunity that becomes them.

And so we might expect: commerce with the body is repudiated for two only reasons, as hindering the Soul's intellective act and as filling it with pleasure, desire, pain; but neither of these misfortunes can befall a soul which has never deeply penetrated into the body, is not a slave but a sovereign ruling a body of such an order as to have no need and no shortcoming and therefore to give ground for neither desire nor fear.

There is no reason why it would be expectant of evil with regard to such a body nor is there any such preoccupied concern, bringing about a veritable descent, as to withdraw it from its noblest and most blessed vision; it remains always intent upon the Supreme, and its governance of this universe is effected by a power not calling upon act.

3. The Human Soul, next:

Everywhere we hear of it as in bitter and miserable durance in body, a victim to troubles and desires and fears and all forms of evil, the body its prison or its tomb, the Cosmos its cave or cavern.

Now this does not clash with the first theory (that of the impassivity of soul as in the All); for the descent of the human Soul has not been due to the same causes (as that of the All-Soul).

All that is Intellectual-Principle has its being—whole and all—in the place of Intellection, what we call the Intellectual Cosmos: but there exist, too, the intellective powers included in its being, and the separate intelligences—for the Intellectual-Principle is not merely one; it is one and many. In the same way there must be both many souls and one, the one being the source of the differing many just as from one genus there rise various species, better and worse, some of the more intellectual order, others less effectively so.

In the Intellectual-Principle a distinction is to be made: there is the Intellectual-Principle itself, which like some huge living organism contains potentially all the other forms; and there are the forms thus potentially included now realized as individuals. We may think of it as a city which itself has soul and life, and includes, also, other forms of life; the living city is the more perfect and powerful, but those lesser forms, in spite of all, share in the one same living quality: or, another illustration, from fire, the universal, proceed both the great fire and the minor fires; yet all have the one common essence, that of fire the universal, or, more exactly, participate in that from which the essence of the universal fire proceeds.

No doubt the task of the Soul, in its more emphatically reasoning phase, is intellection: but it must have another as well, or it would be undistinguishable from the Intellectual-Principle. To its quality of being intellective it adds the quality by which it attains its particular manner of being: it ceases to be an Intellectual-Principle, and has thenceforth its own task, as everything must that exists in the Intellectual Realm.

It looks towards its higher and has intellection; towards itself and orders, administers, governs its lower.

The total of things could not have remained stationary in the Intellectual Cosmos, once there was the possibility of continuous variety, of beings inferior but as necessarily existent as their superiors.

4. So it is with the individual souls; the appetite for the divine Intellect urges them to return to their source, but they have, too, a power apt to administration in this lower sphere; they may be compared to the light attached upwards to the sun, but not grudging its bounty to what lies beneath it. In the Intellectual, then, they remain with the All-Soul, and are immune from care and trouble; in the heavenly sphere, inseparable from the All-Soul, they are administrators with it just as kings, associated with the supreme ruler and governing with him, do not descend from their kingly stations: the souls indeed are thus far in the one place; but there comes a stage at which they descend from the universal to become partial and self-centred; in a weary desire of standing apart they find their way, each to a place of its very own. This state long maintained, the Soul is a deserter from the totality; its differentiation has severed it; its vision is no longer set in the Intellectual; it is a partial thing, isolated, weakened, full of care, intent upon the fragment; severed from the whole, it nestles in one form of being; for this it abandons all else, entering into and caring for only the one, for a thing buffeted about by a worldful of things: thus it has drifted away from the universal and, by an actual presence, it administers the particular; it is caught into contact now, and tends to the outer to which it has become present and into whose inner depths it henceforth sinks far.

With this comes what is known as the casting of the wings, the enchaining in body: the Soul has lost that innocency of conducting the higher which it knew when it stood with the All-Soul, that earlier state to which all its interest would bid it hasten back.

It has fallen: it is at the chain: debarred from expressing itself now through its intellectual phase, it operates through sense; it is a captive; this is the burial, the encavernment, of the Soul.

But in spite of all it has, for ever, something transcendent: by a conversion towards the intellective act, it is loosed from the shackles and soars—when only it makes its memories the starting-point of a new vision of essential being. Souls that take this way have place in both spheres, living of necessity the life there and the life here by turns, the upper life reigning in those able to consort more continuously with the divine Intellect, the lower dominant where character or circumstances are less favourable.

All this is indicated by Plato, without emphasis, where he distinguishes those of the second mixing-bowl, describes them as 'parts', and goes on to say that, having in this way become partial, they must of necessity experience birth.

Of course, where he speaks of God sowing them, he is to be understood as when he tells of God speaking and delivering orations; what is rooted in the nature of the All is figuratively treated as coming into being by generation and creation: stage and sequence are transferred, for clarity of exposition, to things whose being and definite form are eternal.

5. It is possible to reconcile all these apparent contradictions—the divine sowing to birth, as opposed to a voluntary descent aiming at the completion of the universe; the judgement and the cave; necessity and free choice—in fact the necessity includes the choice; embodiment as an evil; the Empedoclean teaching of a flight from God, a wandering away, a sin bringing its punishment; the 'solace by flight' of Heraclitus; in a word, a voluntary descent which is also involuntary.

All degeneration is no doubt involuntary, yet when it has been brought about by an inherent tendency, that submission to the inferior may be described as the penalty of an act.

On the other hand these experiences and actions are determined by an eternal law of nature, and they are due to the movement of a being which in abandoning its superior is running out to serve the needs of another: hence there is no inconsistency or untruth in saying that the Soul is sent down by God; final results are always to be referred to the starting-point even across many intervening stages.

Still there is a twofold flaw: the first lies in the motive of the Soul's descent (its audacity, its Tolma), and the second in the evil it does when actually here: the first is punished by what the Soul has suffered by its descent: for the faults committed here, the lesser penalty is to enter into body after body—and soon to return—by judgement according to desert, the word judgement indicating a divine ordinance; but any outrageous form of ill-doing incurs a proportionately greater punishment administered under the surveillance of chastising daimons.

Thus, in sum, the Soul, a divine being and a dweller in the loftier realms, has entered body: it is a god, a later phase of the divine: but, under stress of its powers and of its tendency to bring order to its next lower, it penetrates to this sphere in a voluntary plunge: if it turns back quickly all is well; it will have taken no hurt by acquiring the knowledge of evil and coming to understand what sin is, by bringing its forces into manifest play, by exhibiting those activities and productions which, remaining merely potential in the unembodied, might as well never have been even there, if destined never to come into actuality, so that the Soul itself would never have known that suppressed and inhibited total.

The act reveals the power, a power hidden, and we might almost say obliterated or non-existent, unless at some moment it became effective: in the world as it is, the richness of the outer stirs us all to the wonder of the inner whose greatness is displayed in acts so splendid.

6. Something besides a unity there must be or all would be indiscernibly buried, shapeless within that unbroken whole: none of the real beings (of the Intellectual Cosmos) would exist if that unity remained at halt within itself: the plurality of these beings, offspring of the unity, could not exist without their own nexts taking the outward path; these are the beings holding the rank of souls.

In the same way the outgoing process could not end with the souls, their issue stifled: every Kind must produce its next; it must unfold from some concentrated central principle as from a seed, and so advance to its term in the varied forms of sense. The prior in its being will remain unalterably in the native seat; but there is the lower phase, begotten to it by an ineffable faculty of its being, native to soul as it exists in the Supreme.

To this power we cannot impute any halt, any limit of jealous grudging; it must move for ever outward until the universe stands accomplished to the ultimate possibility. All, thus, is produced by an inexhaustible power giving its gift to the universe, no part of which it can endure to see without some share in its being.

There is, besides, no principle that can prevent anything from partaking, to the extent of its own individual receptivity, in the nature of Good. If, therefore, Matter has always existed, that existence is enough to ensure its participation in the being which, according to each receptivity, communicates the supreme Good universally: if on the contrary, Matter has come into being as a necessary sequence of the causes preceding it, that origin would similarly prevent it standing apart from the scheme as though it were out of reach of the principle to whose grace it owes its existence.

In sum: the loveliness that is in the sense-realm is an index of the nobleness of the Intellectual sphere, displaying its power and its goodness alike: and all things are for ever linked; the one order Intellectual in its being, the other of sense; one self-existent, the other eternally taking its being by participation in that first, and to the full of its power reproducing the Intellectual nature.

7. The Kind, then, with which we are dealing is twofold, the Intellectual against the sensible: better for the Soul to dwell in the Intellectual, but, given its proper nature, it is under compulsion to participate in the sense-realm also. There is no grievance in its not being, through

and through, the highest; it holds mid-rank among the authentic existences, being of divine station but at the lowest extreme of the Intellectual and skirting the sense-known nature; thus, while it communicates
to this realm something of its own store, it absorbs in turn whenever—
instead of employing in its government only its safeguarded phase—it
plunges in an excessive zeal to the very midst of its chosen sphere; then
it abandons its status as whole soul with whole soul, though even thus
it is always able to recover itself by turning to account the experience
of what it has seen and suffered here, learning, so, the greatness of rest
in the Supreme, and more clearly discerning the finer things by comparison with what is almost their direct antithesis. Where the faculty is
incapable of knowing without contact, the experience of evil brings
the clearer perception of Good.

The outgoing that takes place in the Intellectual-Principle is a
descent to its own downward ultimate: it cannot be a movement to the
transcendent; operating necessarily outwards from itself, wherein it
may not stay inclosed, the need and law of Nature bring it to its
extreme term, to soul—to which it entrusts all the later stages of being
while itself turns back on its course.

The Soul's operation is similar: its next lower act is this universe:
its immediate higher is the contemplation of the Authentic Existences.
To individual souls such divine operation takes place only at one of
their phases and by a temporal process when from the lower in which
they reside they turn towards the noblest; but that soul, which we
know as the All-Soul, has never entered the lower activity, but, immune
from evil, has the property of knowing its lower by inspection, while it
still cleaves continuously to the beings above itself; thus its double task
becomes possible; it takes hence and, since as soul it cannot escape
touching this sphere, it gives hither.

8. And—if it is desirable to venture the more definite statement of
a personal conviction clashing with the general view—even our human
Soul has not sunk entire; something of it is continuously in the Intellectual Realm, though if that part, which is in this sphere of sense, hold
the mastery, or rather be mastered here and troubled, it keeps us blind
to what the upper phase holds in contemplation.

The object of the Intellectual Act comes within our ken only when
it reaches downward to the level of sensation: for not all that occurs at
any part of the Soul is immediately known to us; a thing must, for that
knowledge, be present to the total soul; thus desire locked up within
the desiring faculty remains unknown except when we make it fully
ours by the central faculty of perception, or by deliberate choice, or

by both at once. Once more, every soul has something of the lower on the body side and something of the higher on the side of the Intellectual-Principle.

The Soul of the All, as an entirety, governs the universe through that part of it which leans to the body side, but since it does not exercise a will based on calculation as we do—but proceeds by purely intellectual act as in the execution of an artistic conception—its ministrance is that of a labourless overpoising, only its lowest phase being active upon the universe it embellishes.

The souls that have gone into division and become appropriated to some thing partial have also their transcendent phase, but are preoccupied by sensation, and in the mere fact of exercising perception they take in much that clashes with their nature and brings distress and trouble since the object of their concern is partial, deficient, exposed to many alien influences, filled with desires of its own and taking its pleasure, that pleasure which is its lure.

But there is always the other (the transcendent phase of soul), that which finds no savour in passing pleasure, but holds its own even way.

Ennead V
First Tractate—The Three Initial Hypostases

1. What can it be that has brought the souls to forget the father, God, and, though members of the Divine and entirely of that world, to ignore at once themselves and It?

The evil that has overtaken them has its source in self-will, in the entry into the sphere of process, and in the primal differentiation with the desire for self-ownership. They conceived a pleasure in this freedom and largely indulged their own motion; thus they were hurried down the wrong path, and in the end, drifting further and further, they came to lose even the thought of their origin in the Divine. A child wrenched young from home and brought up during many years at a distance will fail in knowledge of its father and of itself: the souls, in the same way, no longer discern either the divinity or their own nature; ignorance of their rank brings self-depreciation; they misplace their respect, honouring everything more than themselves; all their awe and admiration is for the alien, and, clinging to this, they have broken apart, as far as a soul may, and they make light of what they have deserted; their regard for the mundane and their disregard of themselves bring about their utter ignoring of the Divine.

Admiring pursuit of the external is a confession of inferiority; and nothing thus holding itself inferior to things that rise and perish, nothing counting itself less honourable and less enduring than all else it admires could ever form any notion of either the nature or the power of God.

A double discipline must be applied if human beings in this pass are to be reclaimed, and brought back to their origins, lifted once more towards the Supreme and One and First.

There is the method, which we amply exhibit elsewhere, declaring the dishonour of the objects which the Soul holds here in honour; the second teaches or recalls to the Soul its race and worth; this latter is the leading truth, and, clearly brought out, is the evidence of the other.

It must occupy us now, for it bears closely upon our inquiry (as to the Divine Hypostases) to which it is the natural preliminary: the seeker is soul and it must start from a true notion of the nature and quality by which soul may undertake the search; it must study itself in order to learn whether it has the faculty for the inquiry, the eye for the object proposed, whether in fact we ought to seek; for if the object is alien the search must be futile, while if there is relationship the solution of our problem is at once desirable and possible.

2. Let every soul recall, then, at the outset the truth that soul is the author of all living things, that it has breathed the life into them all, whatever is nourished by earth and sea, all the creatures of the air, the divine stars in the sky; it is the maker of the sun; itself formed and ordered this vast heaven and conducts all that rhythmic motion: and it is a principle distinct from all these to which it gives law and move-ment and life, and it must of necessity be more honourable than they, for they gather or dissolve as soul brings them life or abandons them, but soul, since it never can abandon itself, is of eternal being.

How life was purveyed to the universe of things and to the separate beings in it may be thus conceived:

That great soul must stand pictured before another soul, one not mean, a soul that has become worthy to look, emancipate from the lure, from all that binds its fellows in bewitchment, holding itself in quietude. Let not merely the enveloping body be at peace, body's tur-moil stilled, but all that lies around, earth at peace, and sea at peace, and air and the very heavens. Into that heaven, all at rest, let the great soul be conceived to roll inward at every point, penetrating, permeating, from all sides pouring in its light. As the rays of the sun throwing their brilliance upon a louring cloud make it gleam all gold, so the soul entering the material expanse of the heavens has given life, has given immortality: what was abject it has lifted up; and the heavenly sys-tem, moved now in endless motion by the soul that leads it in wisdom, has become a living and a blessed thing; the soul domiciled within, it takes worth where, before the soul, it was stark body—clay and water—or, rather, the blankness of Matter, the absence of Being, and, as an author says, 'the execration of the Gods.'

The Soul's nature and power will be brought out more clearly, more brilliantly, if we consider next how it envelops the heavenly system and guides all to its purposes: for it has bestowed itself upon all that huge expanse so that every interval, small and great alike, all has been ensouled.

The material body is made up of parts, each holding its own place, some in mutual opposition and others variously separated; the Soul is in no such condition; it is not whittled down so that life tells of a part of the Soul and springs where some such separate portion impinges; each separate life lives by the Soul entire, omnipresent in the likeness of the engendering father, entire in unity and entire in diffused variety. By the power of the Soul the manifold and diverse heavenly system is a unit: through soul this universe is a God: and the sun is a God because it is ensouled; so too the stars: and whatsoever we ourselves may be, it is all in virtue of soul; for 'dead is viler than dung'.

This, by which the gods are divine, must be the oldest God of them all: and our own soul is of that same Ideal nature, so that to consider it, purified, freed from all accruement, is to recognize in ourselves that same value which we have found soul to be, honourable above all that is bodily. For what is body but earth, and even if it be fire (as Stoics think), what (but soul) is its burning power? So it is with all the compounds of earth and fire, even with water and air added to them.

If, then, it is the presence of soul that brings worth, how can a man slight himself and run after other things? You honour the Soul elsewhere; honour then yourself.

3. The Soul once seen to be thus precious, thus divine, you may hold the faith that by its possession you are already nearing God: in the strength of this power make upwards towards Him: at no great distance you must attain: there is not much between.

But over this divine, there is a still diviner: grasp the upward neighbour of the Soul, its prior and source.

Soul, for all the worth we have shown to belong to it, is yet a secondary, an image of the Intellectual-Principle: reason uttered is an image of the reason stored within the Soul, and in the same way soul in an utterance of the Intellectual-Principle: it is even the total of its activity, the entire stream of life sent forth by that Principle to the production of further being; it is the forthgoing heat of a fire which has also heat essentially inherent. But within the Supreme we must see energy not as an overflow but in the double aspect of integral inherence with the establishment of a new being. Sprung, in other words, from the Intellectual-Principle, soul is intellective, but with an intellection operating by the method of reasonings: for its perfecting it must look to that Divine Mind, which may be thought of as a father watching over the development of his child born imperfect in comparison with himself.

Thus its substantial existence comes from the Intellectual-Principle;

and the Reason within it becomes Act in virtue of its contemplation of that prior; for its thought and act are its own intimate possession when it looks to the Supreme Intelligence; those only are soul-acts which are of this intellective nature and are determined by its own character; all that is less noble is foreign (traceable to Matter) and is accidental to the Soul in the course of its peculiar task.

In two ways, then, the Intellectual-Principle enhances the divine quality of the Soul, as father and as immanent presence; nothing separates them but the fact that they are not one and the same, that there is succession, that over against a recipient there stands the Ideal-Form received; but this recipient, Matter to the Supreme Intelligence, is also noble as being at once informed by divine intellect and uncompounded.

What the Intellectual-Principle must be is carried in the single word that Soul, itself so great, is still inferior.

4. But there is yet another way to this knowledge:

Admiring the world of sense as we look out upon its vastness and beauty and the order of its eternal march, thinking of the gods within it, seen and hidden, and the celestial spirits and all the life of animal and plant, let us mount to its archetype, to the yet more authentic sphere: that we are to contemplate all things as members of the Intellectual—eternal in their own right, vested with self-springing consciousness and life—and, presiding over all these, the unsoiled Intelligence and the unapproachable wisdom.

That archetypal world is the true Golden Age, age of Kronos, whose very name suggests (in Greek) Abundance κόρος and Intellect νοῦς. For here is contained all that is immortal: nothing here but is Divine Mind; all is God; this is the place of every soul. Here is rest unbroken: for how can that seek change, in which all is well; what need that reach to, which holds all within itself; what increase can that desire, which stands utterly achieved? All its content, thus, is perfect, that itself may be perfect throughout, as holding nothing that is less than the divine, nothing that is less than intellective. Its knowing is not by search but by possession, its blessedness inherent, not acquired; for all belongs to it eternally and it holds the authentic Eternity imitated by Time which, circling round the Soul, makes towards the new thing and passes by the old. Soul deals with thing after thing—now Socrates; now a horse: always some one entity from among beings—but the Intellectual-Principle is all and therefore its entire content is simultaneously present in that identity: this is pure being in eternal actuality; nowhere is there any future, for every then is a now; nor is there any past, for nothing there has ever ceased to be; everything has taken its stand for ever, an identity well pleased, we might say, to be as it is; and everything, in that entire content, is Intellectual-Principle and Authentic-Existence; and the total of all is Intellectual-Principle entire and Being entire. Intellectual-Principle by its intellective act establishes Being, which in turn, as the object of intellection, becomes the cause of intellection and of existence to the Intellectual-Principle—though, of course, there is another cause of intellection which is also a cause to Being, both rising in a source distinct from either.

Now while these two are coalescents, having their existence in common, and are never apart, still the unity they form is two-sided; there is Intellectual-Principle as against Being, the intellectual agent as against the object of intellection; we consider the intellective act and we have the Intellectual-Principle; we think of the object of that act and we have Being.

Such difference there must be if there is to be any intellection; but similarly there must also be identity (since, in perfect knowing, subject and object are identical).

Thus the Primals (the first 'Categories') are seen to be: Intellectual-Principle; Existence; Difference; Identity: we must include also Motion and Rest: Motion provides for the intellectual act, Rest preserves identity as Difference gives at once a Knower and a Known, for, failing this, all is one, and silent.

So too the objects of intellection (the ideal content of the Divine Mind)—identical in virtue of the self-concentration of the principle which is their common ground—must still be distinct each from another; this distinction constitutes Difference.

The Intellectual Cosmos thus a manifold, Number and Quantity arise: Quality is the specific character of each of these Ideas which stand as the principles from which all else derives.

5. As a manifold, then, this God, the Intellectual-Principle, exists above the Soul here, the Soul which once for all stands linked a member of the divine, unless by a deliberate apostasy.

Bringing itself close to the divine Intellect, becoming, as it were, one with this, it seeks still further: what Being, now, has engendered this God, what is the Simplex preceding this multiple; what the cause at once of its existence and of its existing as a manifold; what the source of this Number, this Quantity?

Number, Quantity, is not primal: obviously before even duality, there must stand the unity.

The Dyad is a secondary; deriving from unity, it finds in unity the determinant needed by its native indetermination: once there is any determination, there is Number, in the sense, of course, of the real (the archetypal) Number. And the Soul is such a number or quantity. For the Primals are not masses or magnitudes; all of that gross order is later, real only to the sense-thought; even in seed the effective reality is not the moist substance but the unseen—that is to say Number (as the determinant of individual being) and the Reason-Principle (of the product to be).

Thus by what we call the Number and the Dyad of that higher realm, we mean Reason Principles and the Intellectual-Principle: but while the Dyad is undetermined—representing, as it were, the underlie (or Matter) of the Intellectual World—the number which rises from the Dyad and The One is always a Form-Idea: thus the Intellectual-Principle is, so to speak, shaped by the Ideas rising within it—or rather, it is shaped in a certain sense by The One and in another sense by itself, since its potential vision becomes actual and intellection is, precisely, an act of vision in which subject and object are identical.

6. But how and what does the Intellectual-Principle see and, especially, how has it sprung from that which is to become the object of its vision?

The mind demands the existence of these Beings, but it is still in trouble over the problem endlessly debated by the most ancient philosophers: from such a unity as we have declared The One to be, how does anything at all come into substantial existence, any multiplicity, dyad, or number? Why has the Primal not remained self-gathered so that there be none of this profusion of the manifold which we observe in existence and yet are compelled to trace to that absolute unity?

In venturing an answer, we first invoke God Himself, not in loud word but in that way of prayer which is always within our power, leaning in soul towards Him by aspiration, alone towards the alone. But if we seek the vision of that great Being within the Inner Sanctuary—self-gathered, tranquilly remote above all else—we begin by considering the images stationed at the outer precincts, or, more exactly to the moment, the first image that appears. How the Divine Mind comes into being must be explained:

Everything moving has necessarily an object towards which it advances; but since the Supreme can have no such object, we may not ascribe motion to it: anything that comes into being after it can be produced only as a consequence of its unfailing self-intention; and, of course, we dare not talk of generation in time, dealing as we are with eternal Beings: where we speak of origin in such reference, it is in the sense, merely, of cause and subordination: origin from the Supreme must not be taken to imply any movement in it: that would make the

Being resulting from the movement not a second principle but a third: the Movement would be the second hypostasis.

Given this immobility in the Supreme, it can neither have yielded assent nor uttered decree nor stirred in any way towards the existence of a secondary.

What happened, then? What are we to conceive as rising in the neighbourhood of that immobility?

It must be a circumradiation—produced from the Supreme but from the Supreme unaltering—and may be compared to the brilliant light encircling the sun and ceaselessly generated from that unchanging substance.

All existences, as long as they retain their character, produce—about themselves, from their essence, in virtue of the power which must be in them—some necessary, outward-facing hypostasis continuously attached to them and representing in image the engendering archetypes: thus fire gives out its heat; snow is cold not merely to itself; fragrant substances are a notable instance; for, as long as they last, something is diffused from them and perceived wherever they are present.

Again, all that is fully achieved engenders: therefore the eternally achieved engenders eternally an eternal being. At the same time, the offspring is always minor: what then are we to think of the All-Perfect but that it can produce nothing less than the very greatest that is later than itself? This greatest, later than the divine unity, must be the Divine Mind, and it must be the second of all existence, for it is that which sees The One on which alone it leans while the First has no need whatever of it. The offspring of the prior to Divine Mind can be no other than that Mind itself and thus is the loftiest being in the universe, all else following upon it—the Soul, for example, being an utterance and act of the Intellectual-Principle as that is an utterance and act of The One. But in soul the utterance is obscured, for soul is an image and must look to its own original: that Principle, on the contrary, looks to the First without mediation—thus becoming what it is —and has that vision not as from a distance but as the immediate next with nothing intervening, close to the One as Soul to it.

The offspring must seek and love the begetter; and especially so when begetter and begotten are alone in their sphere; when, in addition, the begetter is the highest Good, the offspring (inevitably seeking its good) is attached by a bond of sheer necessity, separated only in being distinct.

7. We must be more explicit:

The Intellectual-Principle stands as the image of The One, firstly because there is a certain necessity that the first should have its offspring, carrying onward much of its quality, in other words that there be something in its likeness as the sun's rays tell of the sun. Yet The One is not an Intellectual-Principle; how then does it engender an Intellectual-Principle?

Simply by the fact that in its self-quest it has vision: this very seeing is the Intellectual-Principle. Any perception of the external indicates either sensation or intellection, sensation symbolized by a line, intellection by a circle . . . [corrupt passage].

Of course the divisibility belonging to the circle does not apply to The One; here, to be sure, is a unity, but there the Unity which is the potentiality of all existence.

The items of this potentiality the divine intellection brings out, so to speak, from the unity and knows them in detail, as it must if it is to be an intellectual principle.

It has besides a consciousness, as it were, within itself of this same potentiality; it knows that it can of itself beget an hypostasis and can determine its own Being by the virtue emanating from its prior; it knows that its nature is in some sense a definite part of the content of that First; that it thence derives its essence, that its strength lies there, and that its Being takes perfection as a derivative and a recipient from the First. It sees that, as a member in some sense of the realm of division and part, it receives life and intellection and all else it has and is, from the undivided and partless, since that First is no member of existence, but can be the source of all on condition only of being held down by no one distinctive shape but remaining the undeflected unity.

To be all in itself would place it in the realm of Being. And so the First is not a thing among the things contained by the Intellectual-Principle though the source of all. In virtue of this source things of the later order are essential beings; for from that fact there is determination; each has its form: what has being cannot be envisaged as outside of limit; the nature must be held fast by boundary and fixity; though to the Intellectual Beings this fixity is no more than determination and form, the foundations of their substantial existence.

A being of this quality, like the Intellectual-Principle, must be felt to be worthy of the all-pure: it could not derive from any other than from the first principle of all; as it comes into existence, all other beings must be simultaneously engendered—all the beauty of the Ideas, all the Gods of the Intellectual realm. And it still remains pregnant with this offspring; for it has, so to speak, drawn all within itself again, holding them lest they fall away towards Matter to be brought up in the House of Rhea (in the realm of flux). This is the meaning hidden in the

Mysteries, and in the Myths of the gods: Kronos, as the wisest, exists before Zeus; he must absorb his offspring that, full within himself, he may be also an Intellectual-Principle manifest in some product of his plenty; afterwards, the myth proceeds, Kronos engenders Zeus, who already exists as the (necessary and eternal) outcome of the plenty there; in other words the offspring of the Divine Intellect, perfect within itself, is Soul (the life-principle carrying forward the Ideas in the Divine Mind). The perfection entails the offspring; a power so vast could not remain unfruitful.

Now, even in the Divine the engendered could not be the very highest; it must be a lesser, an image; it will be undetermined, as its progenitor was, but will receive determination, and, so to speak, its shaping idea, from the progenitor.

Yet the offspring of the Intellectual-Principle must be a Reason-Principle, that is to say, a substantial existence (hypostasis) identified with the principle of deliberative thought (in the Timaeus): such then is that (higher Soul) which circles about the Divine Mind, its light, its image inseparably attached to it: on the upper level united with it, filled from it, enjoying it, participant in its nature, intellective with it, but on the lower level in contact with the realm beneath itself, or, rather, generating in turn an offspring which must lie beneath; of this lower we will treat later; so far we deal still with the Divine.

8. This is the explanation of Plato's Triplicity, in the passage where he names as the Primals the Beings gathered about the King of All and establishes a Secondary containing the Secondaries and a Third containing the Tertiaries.

He teaches, also, that there is an author of the Cause, that is of the Intellectual-Principle, which to him is the Creator who made the Soul, as he tells us, in the famous mixing bowl. This author of the causing principle, of the divine mind, is to him the Good, that which transcends the Intellectual-Principle and transcends Being: often too he uses the term 'The Idea' to indicate Being and the Divine Mind. Thus Plato knows the order of generation—from the Good, the Intellectual-Principle; from the Intellectual-Principle, the Soul. These teachings are, therefore, no novelties, no inventions of today, but long since stated, if not stressed; our doctrine here is the explanation of an earlier and can show the antiquity of these opinions on the testimony of Plato himself.

Earlier, Parmenides made some approach to the doctrine in identifying Being with Intellectual-Principle while separating Real Being from the realm of sense.

'Knowing and Being are one thing', he says, and this unity is to

him motionless in spite of the intellection he attributes to it: to preserve its unchanging identity he excludes all bodily movement from it;
and he compares it to a huge sphere in that it holds and envelops all
existence and that its intellection is not an outgoing act but internal.
Still, with all his affirmation of unity, his own writings lay him open
to the reproach that his unity turns out to be a multiplicity.

The Platonic Parmenides is more exact; the distinction is made between the Primal One, a strictly pure Unity, and a secondary One
which is a One-Many and a third which is a One-and-Many; thus he
too is in accordance with our thesis of the Three Kinds.

9. Anaxagoras, again, in his assertion of a Mind pure and unmixed,
affirms a simplex First and a sundered One, though writing long ago he
failed in precision.

Heraclitus, with his sense of bodily forms as things of ceaseless
process and passage, knows the One as eternal and intellectual.

In Empedocles, similarly, we have a dividing principle, 'Strife', set
against 'Friendship'—which is The One and is to him bodiless, while
the elements represent Matter.

Later there is Aristotle; he begins by making the First transcendent
and intellective but cancels that primacy by supposing it to have self-
intellection. Further, he affirms a multitude of other intellective beings
—as many indeed as there are orbs in the heavens; one such principle
as mover to every orb—and thus his account of the Intellectual Realm
differs from Plato's and, failing necessity, he brings in probability;
though it is doubtful whether he has even probability on his side, since
it would be more probable that all the spheres, as contributory to
one system, should look to a unity, to the First.

We are obliged to ask whether to Aristotle's mind all these Intellectual Beings spring from one, and that one their First; or whether the
Principles in the Intellectual are many.

If from one, then clearly the Intellectual system will be analogous
to that of the universe of sense—sphere encircling sphere, with one, the
outermost, dominating all: the First (in the Intellectual) will envelop
the entire scheme and will be an Intellectual (or Archetypal) Cosmos;
and as in our universe the spheres are not empty but the first sphere is
thick with stars and none without them, so, in the Intellectual Cosmos,
those principles of Movement will envelop a multitude of Beings, and
that world will be the realm of the greater reality.

If on the contrary each is a principle, then the effective powers
become a matter of chance; under what compulsion are they to hold
together and act with one mind towards that work of unity, the har-

mony of the entire heavenly system? Again what can make it necessary that the material bodies of the heavenly system be equal in number to the Intellectual moving principles, and how can these incorporeal Beings be numerically many when there is no Matter to serve as the basis of difference?

For these reasons the ancient philosophers that ranged themselves most closely to the school of Pythagoras and of his later followers and to that of Pherecydes, have insisted upon this Nature, some developing the subject in their writings while others treated of it merely in unwritten discourses, some no doubt ignoring it entirely.

10. We have shown the inevitability of certain convictions as to the scheme of things:

There exists a Principle which transcends Being; this is The One, whose nature we have sought to establish in so far as such matters lend themselves to proof. Upon The One follows immediately the Principle which is at once Being and the Intellectual-Principle. Third comes the Principle, Soul.

Now just as these three exist for the system of Nature, so, we must hold, they exist for ourselves. I am not speaking of the material order— all that is separable—but of what lies beyond the sense realm in the same way as the Primals are beyond all the heavens; I mean the corresponding aspect of man, what Plato calls the Interior Man.

Thus our soul, too, is a divine thing, belonging to another order than sense; such is all that holds the rank of soul, but (above the life-principle) there is the Soul perfected as containing Intellectual-Principle with its double phase, reasoning and giving the power to reason. The reasoning phase of the Soul, needing no bodily organ for its thinking but maintaining, in purity, its distinctive Act that its thought may be uncontaminated—this we cannot err in placing, separate and not mingled into body, within the first Intellectual. We may not seek any point of space in which to seat it; it must be set outside of all space: its distinct quality, its separateness, its immateriality, demand that it be a thing alone, untouched by all of the bodily order. That is why we read of the universe, that the Demiurge cast the Soul around it from without—understand that phase of soul which is permanently seated in the Intellectual—and of ourselves that the charioteer's head reaches upwards towards the heights.

The admonition to sever soul from body is not, of course, to be understood spatially—that separation stands made in Nature—the reference is to holding our rank, to use of our thinking, to an attitude of alienation from the body in the effort to lead up and attach to the over-world, equally with the other, that phase of soul seated here and, alone, having to do with body, creating, moulding, spending its care upon it.

11. Since there is a Soul which reasons upon the right and good— for reasoning is an inquiry into the rightness and goodness of this rather than that—there must exist some permanent Right, the source and foundation of this reasoning in our soul; how, else, could any such discussion be held? Further, since the Soul's attention to these matters is intermittent, there must be within us an Intellectual-Principle acquainted with that Right not by momentary act but in permanent possession. Similarly there must be also the principle of this principle, its cause, God. This Highest cannot be divided and allotted, must remain intangible but not bound to space, it may be present at many points, wheresoever there is anything capable of accepting one of its manifestations: thus a centre is an independent unity; everything within the circle has its term at the centre; and to the centre the radii bring each their own. Within our nature is such a centre by which we grasp and are linked and held; and those of us are firmly in the Supreme whose being is concentrated There.

12. Possessed of such powers, how does it happen that we do not lay hold of them, but for the most part, let these high activities go idle—some, even, of us never bringing them in any degree to effect?

The answer is that all the Divine Beings are unceasingly about their own act, the Intellectual-Principle and its Prior always self-intent; and so, too, the Soul maintains its unfailing movement; for not all that passes in the Soul is, by that fact, perceptible; we know just as much as impinges upon the faculty of sense. Any activity not transmitted to the sensitive faculty has not traversed the entire Soul: we remain unaware because the human being includes sense-perception; man is not merely a part (the higher part) of the Soul but the total.

None the less every being of the order of soul is in continuous activity as long as life holds, continuously executing to itself its characteristic act: knowledge of the act depends upon transmission and perception. If there is to be perception of what is thus present, we must turn the perceptive faculty inward and hold it to attention there. Hoping to hear a desired voice we let all others pass and are alert for the coming at last of that most welcome of sounds: so here, we must let the hearings of sense go by, save for sheer necessity, and keep the Soul's perception bright and quick to the sounds from above.

Ennead VI
Ninth Tractate—on the Good, or the One

1. It is in virtue of unity that beings are beings.

This is equally true of things whose existence is primal and of all that are in any degree to be numbered among beings. What could exist at all except as one thing? Deprived of unity, a thing ceases to be what it is called: no army unless as a unity: a chorus, a flock, must be one thing. Even house and ship demand unity, one house, one ship; unity gone, neither remains: thus even continuous magnitudes could not exist without an inherent unity; break them apart and their very being is altered in the measure of the breach of unity.

Take plant and animal; the material form stands a unity; fallen from that into a litter of fragments, the things have lost their being; what was is no longer there; it is replaced by quite other things—as many others, precisely, as possess unity.

Health, similarly, is the condition of a body acting as a co-ordinate unity. Beauty appears when limbs and features controlled by this principle, unity. Moral excellence is of a soul acting as a concordant total, brought to unity.

Come thus to soul—which brings all to unity, making, molding, shaping, ranging to order—there is a temptation to say, 'Soul is the bestower of unity; soul therefore is the unity'. But soul bestows other characteristics upon material things and yet remains distinct from its gift: shape, Ideal-Form, and the rest are all distinct from the giving soul: so, clearly, with this gift of unity; soul to make things unities looks out upon the unity just as it makes man by looking upon Man, realizing in the man the unity belonging to Man.

Anything that can be described as a unity is so in the precise degree in which it holds a characteristic being; the less or more the degree of the being, the less or more the unity. Soul, while distinct from unity's very self, is a thing of the greater unity in proportion as it is of the

261

greater, the authentic, being. Absolute unity it is not: it is soul and one soul, the unity in some sense a concomitant; there are two things, soul and soul's unity, as there is body with body's unity. The looser aggregates such as a choir are furthest from unity, the more compact are the nearer; soul is nearer yet but still a participant.

Is soul to be identified with unity on the ground that unless it were one thing it could not be soul? No; unity is equally necessary to every other thing, yet unity stands distinct from them; body and unity are not identical; body, too, is a participant.

Besides, the soul, even the individual soul, is a manifold, though not composed of parts: it has diverse powers—reasoning, desiring, perceiving—all held together by this chain of unity. Itself a unity, soul confers unity, but also accepts it.

2. It may be suggested that, while in the unities of the partial order the essence and the unity are distinct, yet in collective existence, in Real Being, they are identical, so that when we have grasped Being we hold unity; Real Being would coincide with Unity. Thus, if Essential Being is the Intellectual-Principle, Unity also is the Intellectual-Principle which is at once Primal Being and Pure Unity, purveying, accordingly, to the rest of things something of Being and something, in proportion, of the unity which is itself.

There is nothing (we may be told) with which the unity would be more plausibly identified than with Being; either it is the same as Being—a man and one man are identical—or it will correspond to the Number which rules in the realm of the particular; it will be a number applying to a certain unique thing as the number two applies to others.

Now if Number is a thing among things, then clearly so this unity must be; we would have to discover what thing of things it is. If Number is not a thing but an operation of the mind moving out to reckon, then the unity will not be a thing.

We found that anything losing unity loses its being; we are therefore obliged to inquire whether the unity in particulars is identical with the being, and Unity Absolute identical with Collective Being.

Now the being of the particular is a manifold; unity cannot be a manifold; there must therefore be a distinction between Being and Unity. Thus a man is at once a reasoning living being and a total of parts; his variety is held together by his unity; man therefore and unity are different—man a thing of parts against unity partless. Much more must Collective Being, as container of all existence, be a manifold and therefore distinct from the unity in which it is but participant.

Again, Collective Being contains life and intelligence—it is no dead thing—and so, once more, is a manifold.

If Being is identical with Intellectual-Principle, even at that it is a manifold; all the more so when count is taken of the Ideal-Forms in it; for the Idea, particular or collective, is, after all, a numerable agglomeration whose unity is that of a cosmos.

Above all, unity is The First: but Intellectual-Principle, Ideas, and Being, cannot be so; for any member of the realm of Forms is an aggregation, a compound, and therefore—since components must precede their compound—is a later.

Other considerations also go to show that the Intellectual-Principle cannot be the First. Intellect must be about the Intellectual Act: at least in its higher phase, that not concerned with the outer universe, it must be intent upon its Prior; its introversion is a conversion upon the Principle.

Considered as at once Thinker and Object of its Thought, it is dual, not simplex, not The Unity: considered as looking beyond itself, it must look to a better, to a prior: looking simultaneously upon itself and upon its Transcendent, it is, once more, not a First.

There is no other way of stating Intellectual-Principle than as that which, holding itself in the presence of The Good and First and looking towards That, is self-present also, self-knowing and knowing itself as All-Being: thus manifold, it is far from being The Unity.

In sum: The Unity cannot be the total of beings for so its oneness is annulled; it cannot be the Intellectual-Principle, for so it would be that total which the Intellectual-Principle is; nor is it Being, for Being is the total of things.

3. What then must The Unity be, what nature is left for it?

No wonder that to state it is not easy; even Being and Form are not easy, though we have a way, an approach through the Ideas.

The soul or mind reaching towards the formless finds itself incompetent to grasp where nothing bounds it or to take impression where the impinging reality is diffuse; in sheer dread of holding to nothingness, it slips away. The state is painful; often it seeks relief by retreating from all this vagueness to the region of sense, there to rest as on solid ground, just as the sight distressed by the minute rests with pleasure on the bold.

Soul must see in its own way; this is by coalescence, unification; but in seeking thus to know the Unity it is prevented by that very unification from recognizing that it has found; it cannot distinguish

itself from the object of this intuition. None the less, this is our one
resource if our philosophy is to give us knowledge of The Unity.

We are in search of unity; we are to come to know the principle of
all, the Good and First; therefore we may not stand away from the
realm of Firsts and lie prostrate among the lasts: we must strike for
those Firsts, rising from things of sense which are the lasts. Cleared
of all evil in our intention towards The Good, we must ascend to the
Principle within ourselves; from many, we must become one; only so
do we attain to knowledge of that which is Principle and Unity. We
shape ourselves into Intellectual-Principle; we make over our soul in
trust to Intellectual-Principle and set it firmly in That; thus what That
sees the soul will waken to see: it is through the Intellectual-Principle
that we have this vision of The Unity; it must be our care to bring
over nothing whatever from sense, to allow nothing from that source
to enter into Intellectual-Principle: with Intellect pure, and with the
summit of Intellect, we are to see the All-Pure.

If the quester has the impression of extension or shape or mass
attaching to That Nature he has not been led by Intellectual-Principle
which is not of the order to see such things; the activity has been of
sense and of the judgement following upon sense: only Intellectual-
Principle can inform us of the things of its scope; its competence is
upon its priors, its content, and its issue: but even its content is outside
of sense; and still purer, still less touched by multiplicity, are its
priors, or rather its Prior.

The Unity, then, is not Intellectual-Principle but something higher
still: Intellectual-Principle is still a being but that First is no being but
precedent to all Being: it cannot be a being, for a being has what we
may call the shape of its reality but The Unity is without shape, even
shape Intellectual.

Generative of all, The Unity is none of all; neither thing nor quantity nor quality nor intellect nor soul; not in motion, not at rest, not in
place, not in time: it is the self-defined, unique in form or, better,
formless, existing before Form was, or Movement or Rest, all of which
are attachments of Being and make Being the manifold it is.

But how, if not in movement, can it be otherwise than at rest?

The answer is that movement and rest are states pertaining to
Being, which necessarily has one or the other or both. Besides, anything at rest must be so in virtue of Rest as something distinct: Unity
at rest becomes the ground of an attribute and at once ceases to be a
simplex.

Note, similarly, that when we speak of this First as Cause we are affirming something happening not to it but to us, the fact that we take from this Self-Enclosed: strictly we should put neither a This nor a That to it; we hover, as it were, about it, seeking the statement of an experience of our own, sometimes nearing this Reality, sometimes baffled by the enigma in which it dwells.

4. The main source of the difficulty is that awareness of this Principle comes neither by knowing nor by the Intellection that discovers the Intellectual Beings but by a presence overpassing all knowledge. In knowing, soul or mind abandons its unity; it cannot remain a simplex: knowing is taking account of things; that accounting is multiple; the mind thus plunging into number and multiplicity departs from unity.

Our way then takes us beyond knowing; there may be no wandering from unity; knowing and knowable must all be left aside; every object of thought, even the highest, we must pass by, for all that is good is later than This and derives from This as from the sun all the light of the day.

'Not to be told; not to be written': in our writing and telling we are but urging towards it: out of discussion we call to vision: to those desiring to see, we point the path; our teaching is of the road and the travelling; the seeing must be the very act of one that has made this choice.

There are those that have not attained to see. The soul has not come to know the splendour There; it has not felt and clutched to itself that love-passion of vision known to the lover come to rest where he loves. Or struck perhaps by that authentic light, all the soul lit by the nearness gained, we have gone weighted from beneath; the vision is frustrate; we should go without burden and we go carrying that which can but keep us back; we are not yet made over into unity.

From none is that Principle absent and yet from all: present, it remains absent save to those fit to receive, disciplined into some accordance, able to touch it closely by their likeness and by that kindred power within themselves through which, remaining as it was when it came to them from the Supreme, they are enabled to see in so far as God may at all be seen.

Failure to attain may be due to such impediment or to lack of the guiding thought that establishes trust; impediment we must charge against ourselves and strive by entire renunciation to become emancipate; where there is distrust for lack of convincing reason, further considerations may be applied:

5. Those to whom existence comes about by chance and automatic action and is held together by material forces have drifted far from

God and from the concept of unity; we are not here addressing them but only such as accept another nature than body and have some conception of soul.

Soul must be sounded to the depths, understood as an emanation from Intellectual-Principle and as holding its value by a Reason-Principle thence infused. Next, this Intellect must be apprehended, an Intellect other than the reasoning faculty known as the rational principle; with reasoning we are already in the region of separation and movement: our sciences are Reason-Principles lodged in soul or mind, having manifestly acquired their character by the presence in the soul of Intellectual-Principle, source of all knowing.

Thus we come to see Intellectual-Principle almost as an object of sense: it is perceptible as standing above soul, father to soul, and it is one with the Intellectual Cosmos; we must think of it as a quiet, unwavering motion; containing all things and being all things, it is a multiple but at once indivisible and comporting difference. It is not discriminate as are the Reason-Principles, which can in fact be known one by one: yet its content is not a confusion; every item stands forth distinctly, just as in a science the entire content holds as an indivisible and yet each item is a self-standing verity.

Now a plurality thus concentrated like the Intellectual Cosmos is close upon The First—and reason certifies its existence as surely as that of soul—yet, though of higher sovereignty than soul, it is not The First since it is not a unity, not simplex as unity, principle over all multiplicity, must be.

Before it there is That which must transcend the noblest of the things of Being: there must be a prior to this Principle which aiming towards unity is yet not unity but a thing in unity's likeness. From this highest it is not sundered; it too is self-present: so close to the unity, it cannot be articulated: and yet it is a principle which in some measure has dared secession.

That awesome Prior, The Unity, is not a being, for so its unity would be vested in something else: strictly no name is apt to it, but since name it we must there is a certain rough fitness in designating it as unity with the understanding that it is not the unity of some other thing.

Thus it eludes our knowledge, so that the nearer approach to it is through its offspring, Being: we know it as cause of existence to Intellectual-Principle, as fount of all that is best, as the efficacy which, self-perduring and undiminishing, generates all beings and is not to be counted among these its derivatives, to all of which it must be prior.

This we can but name The Unity, indicating it to each other by a designation that points to the concept of its partlessness while we are in reality striving to bring our own minds to unity. We are not to think of such unity and partlessness as belonging to point or monad; the veritable unity is the source of all such quantity which could not exist unless first there existed Being and Being's Prior: we are not, then, to think in the order of point and monad but to use these—in their simplicity and their rejection of magnitude and partition—as symbols for the higher concept.

6. In what sense, then, do we assert this Unity and how is it to be adjusted to our mental processes?

Its oneness must not be belittled to that of monad and point: for these the mind abstracts extension and numerical quantity and rests upon the very minutest possible, ending no doubt in the partless but still in something that began as a partible and is always lodged in something other than itself. The Unity was never in any other and never belonged to the partible: nor is its impartibility that of extreme minuteness; on the contrary it is great beyond anything, great not in extension but in power, sizeless by its very greatness as even its immediate sequents are impartible not in mass but in might. We must therefore take the Unity as infinite not in measureless extension or numerable quantity but in fathomless depths of power.

Think of The One as Mind or as God, you think too meanly; use all the resources of understanding to conceive this Unity and, again, it is more authentically one than God, even though you reach for God's unity beyond the unity the most perfect you can conceive. For This is utterly a self-existent, with no concomitant whatever. This self-sufficing is the essence of its unity. Something there must be supremely adequate, autonomous, all-transcending, most utterly without need.

Any manifold, anything beneath The Unity, is dependent: combined from various constituents, its essential nature goes in need of unity; but unity cannot need itself; it stands unity accomplished. Again, a manifold depends upon all its factors; and furthermore each of those factors in turn—as necessarily inbound with the rest and not self-standing—sets up a similar need both to its associates and to the total so constituted.

The sovereignly self-sufficing principle will be Unity-Absolute, for only in this unity is there a nature above all need whether within itself or in regard to the rest of things. Unity seeks nothing towards its being or its well-being or its safehold upon existence; cause to all, how can it acquire its character outside of itself or know any good outside?

The good of its being can be no borrowing: This is The Good. Nor has it station; it needs no standing-ground as if inadequate to its own sustaining; what calls for such underpropping is the soulless, some material mass that must be based or fall. This is base to all, cause of universal existence and of ordered station. All that demands place is in need; a First cannot go in need of its sequents: all need is effort towards a first principle; the First, principle to all, must be utterly without need. If the Unity be seeking, it must inevitably be seeking to be something other than itself; it is seeking its own destroyer. Whatever may be said to be in need is needing a good, a preserver; nothing can be a good to The Unity, therefore.

Neither can it have will to anything; it is a Beyond-Good, not even to itself a good but to such beings only as may be of quality to have part with it. Nor has it Intellection; that would comport diversity: nor Movement; it is prior to Movement as to Intellection.

To what could its Intellection be directed? To itself? But that would imply a previous ignorance; it would be dependent upon that Intellection in order to have knowledge of itself; but it is the self-sufficing. Yet this absence of self-knowing, of self-intellection, does not comport ignorance; ignorance is of something outside—a knower ignorant of a knowable—but in the Solitary there is neither knowing nor anything unknown. Unity, self-present, it has no need of self-intellection: indeed this 'self-presence' were better left out, the more surely to preserve the unity; we must eliminate all knowing and all association, all intellection whether internal or external. It is not to be thought of as having but as being Intellection; Intellection does not itself perform the intellective act but is the cause of the act in something else and cause is not to be identified with caused: most assuredly the cause of all is not a thing within that all.

This Principle is not, therefore, to be identified with the good of which it is the source; it is good in the unique mode of being The Good above all that is good.

7. If the mind reels before something thus alien to all we know, we must take our stand on the things of this realm and strive thence to see. But in the looking beware of throwing outward; this Principle does not lie away somewhere leaving the rest void; to those of power to reach, it is present; to the inapt, absent. In our daily affairs we cannot hold an object in mind if we have given ourselves elsewhere, occupied upon some other matter; that very thing, and nothing else, must be before us to be truly the object of observation. So here also; preoccupied by the impress of something else, we are withheld under that

pressure from becoming aware of The Unity; a mind gripped and fastened by some definite thing cannot take the print of the very contrary. As Matter, it is agreed, must be void of quality in order to accept the types of the universe, so and much more must the soul be kept formless if there is to be no infixed impediment to prevent it being brimmed and lit by the Primal Principle.

In sum, we must withdraw from all the extern, pointed wholly inwards; no leaning to the outer; the total of things ignored, first in their relation to us and later in the very idea; the self put out of mind in the contemplation of the Supreme; all the commerce so closely There that, if report were possible, one might become to others reporter of that communion.

Such converse, we may suppose, was that of Minos, thence known as the Familiar of Zeus; and in that memory he established the laws which report it, enlarged to that task by his vision There. Some, on the other hand, there will be to disdain such citizen service, choosing to remain in the higher: these will be those that have seen much.

God—we read—is outside of none, present unperceived to all; we break away from Him, or rather from ourselves; what we turn from we cannot reach; astray ourselves, we cannot go in search of another; a child distraught will not recognize its father; to find ourselves is to know our source.

8. Every soul that knows its history is aware, also, that its movement, unthwarted, is not that of an outgoing line; its natural course may be likened to that in which a circle turns not upon some external but on its own centre, the point to which it owes its rise. The soul's movement will be about its source; to this it will hold, poised intent towards that unity to which all souls should move and the divine souls always move, divine in virtue of that movement; for to be a god is to be integral with the Supreme; what stands away is man still multiple, or beast.

Is then this 'centre' of our souls the Principle for which we are seeking?

We must look yet further: we must admit a Principle in which all these centres coincide: it will be a centre by analogy with the centre of the circle we know. The soul is not a circle in the sense of the geometric figure but in that its primal nature (wholeness) is within it and about it, that it owes its origin to what is whole, and that it will be still more entire when severed from body.

In our present state—part of our being weighed down by the body, as one might have the feet under water with all the rest untouched—we bear ourselves aloft by that intact part and, in that, hold through our own centre to the centre of all the centres, just as the centres of the great circles of a sphere coincide with that of the sphere to which all belong. Thus we are secure.

If these circles were material and not spiritual, the link with the centres would be local; they would lie round it where it lay at some distant point: since the souls are of the Intellectual, and the Supreme still loftier, we understand that contact is otherwise procured, that is by those powers which connect Intellectual agent with Intellectual object; indeed soul is closer to the Supreme than Intellect to its object—such is its similarity, identity, and the sure link of kindred. Material mass cannot blend into other material mass: unbodied beings are not under this bodily limitation; their separation is solely that of otherness, of differentiation; in the absence of otherness, it is similars mutually present.

Thus the Supreme as containing no otherness is ever present with us; we are present with it when we put otherness away. It is not that the Supreme reaches out to us seeking our communion: we reach towards the Supreme; it is we that become present. We are always before it: but we do not always look: thus a choir, singing set in due order about the conductor, may turn away from that centre to which all should attend; let it but face aright and it sings with beauty, present effectively. We are ever before the Supreme—cut off is utter dissolution; we can no longer be—but we do not always attend: when we look, our Term is attained; this is rest; this is the end of singing ill; effectively before Him, we lift a choral song full of God.

Ennead I
Third Tractate—Dialectic

1. What art is there, what method, what discipline to bring us there where we must go?

The Term at which we must arrive we may take as agreed: we have established elsewhere, by many considerations, that our journey is to the Good, to the Primal-Principle; and, indeed, the very reasoning which discovered the Term was itself something like an initiation.

But what order of beings will attain the Term?

Surely, as we read, those that have already seen all or most things, those who at their first birth have entered into the life-germ from which is to spring a metaphysician, a musician, or a born lover, the metaphysician taking to the path by instinct, the musician and the nature peculiarly susceptible to love needing outside guidance.

But how lies the course? Is it alike for all, or is there a distinct method for each class of temperament?

For all there are two stages of the path, as they are making upwards or have already gained the upper sphere.

The first degree is the conversion from the lower life; the second—held by those that have already made their way to the sphere of the Intelligibles, have set as it were a footprint there but must still advance within the realm—lasts until they reach the extreme hold of the place, the Term attained when the topmost peak of the Intellectual realm is won.

But this highest degree must bide its time: let us first try to speak of the initial process of conversion.

We must begin by distinguishing the three types. Let us take the musician first and indicate his temperamental equipment for the task.

The musician we may think of as being exceedingly quick to beauty, drawn in a very rapture to it: somewhat slow to stir of his own impulse, he answers at once to the outer stimulus: as the timid are sensitive to noise so he to tones and the beauty they convey; all that offends against unison or harmony in melodies or rhythms repels him; he longs for measure and shapely pattern.

This natural tendency must be made the starting-point to such a man; he must be drawn by the tone, rhythm, and design in things of sense: he must learn to distinguish the material forms from the Authentic-Existent which is the source of all these correspondences and of the entire reasoned scheme in the work of art: he must be led to the Beauty that manifests itself through these forms; he must be shown that what ravished him was no other than the Harmony of the Intellectual world and the Beauty in that sphere, not some one shape of beauty but the All-Beauty, the Absolute Beauty; and the truths of philosophy must be implanted in him to lead him to faith in that which, unknowing it, he possesses within himself. What these truths are we will show later.

2. The born lover, to whose degree the musician also may attain—and then either come to a stand or pass beyond—has a certain memory of beauty but, severed from it now, he no longer comprehends it: spellbound by visible loveliness he clings amazed about that. His lesson must be to fall down no longer in bewildered delight before some one embodied form; he must be led, under a system of mental discipline, to beauty everywhere and made to discern the One Principle underlying all, a Principle apart from the material forms, springing from another source, and elsewhere more truly present. The beauty, for example, in a noble course of life and in an admirably organized social system may be pointed out to him—a first training this in the loveliness of the immaterial—he must learn to recognize the beauty in the arts, sciences, virtues; then these severed and particular forms must be brought under the one principle by the explanation of their origin. From the virtues he is to be led to the Intellectual-Principle, to the Authentic-Existent; thence onward, he treads the upward way.

3. The metaphysician, equipped by that very character, winged already and not, like those others, in need of disengagement, stirring of himself towards the supernal but doubting of the way, needs only a guide. He must be shown, then, and instructed, a willing wayfarer by his very temperament, all but self-directed.

Mathematics, which as a student by nature he will take very easily, will be prescribed to train him to abstract thought and to faith in the unembodied; a moral being by native disposition, he must be led to make his virtue perfect; after the Mathematics he must be put through a course in Dialectic and made an adept in the science.

4. But this science, this Dialectic essential to all the three classes alike, what, in sum, is it?

It is the Method, or Discipline, that brings with it the power of pronouncing with final truth upon the nature and relation of things—what each is, how it differs from others, what common quality all have, to what Kind each belongs and in what rank each stands in its Kind and whether its Being is Real-Being, and how many Beings there are, and how many non-Beings to be distinguished from Beings.

Dialectic treats also of the Good and the not-Good, and of the particulars that fall under each, and of what is the Eternal and what the not-Eternal—and of these, it must be understood, not by seeming-knowledge ('sense-knowledge') but with authentic science.

All this accomplished, it gives up its touring of the realm of sense and settles down in the Intellectual Cosmos and there plies its own peculiar Act: it has abandoned all the realm of deceit and falsity, and pastures the Soul in the 'Meadows of Truth': it employs the Platonic division to the discernment of the Ideal-Forms, of the Authentic-Existence, and of the First-Kinds (or Categories of Being): it establishes, in the light of Intellection, the affiliations of all that issues from these Firsts, until it has traversed the entire Intellectual Realm: then, by means of analysis, it takes the opposite path and returns once more to the First Principle.

Now it rests: instructed and satisfied as to the Being in that sphere, it is no longer busy about many things: it has arrived at Unity and it contemplates: it leaves to another science all that coil of premises and conclusions called the art of reasoning, much as it leaves the art of writing: some of the matter of logic, no doubt, it considers necessary—to clear the ground—but it makes itself the judge, here as in everything else; where it sees use, it uses; anything it finds superfluous, it leaves to whatever department of learning or practice may turn that matter to account.

5. But whence does this science derive its own initial laws?

The Intellectual-Principle furnishes standards, the most certain for any soul that is able to apply them. What else is necessary Dialectic puts together for itself, combining and dividing, until it has reached perfect Intellection. 'For', we read, 'it is the purest (perfection) of Intellection and Contemplative-Wisdom.' And, being the noblest method and science that exists it must needs deal with Authentic-Existence, The Highest there is: as Contemplative-Wisdom (or true-knowing) it deals with Being, as Intellection with what transcends Being.

What, then, is Philosophy?

Philosophy is the supremely precious.

Is Dialectic, then, the same as Philosophy?

It is the precious part of Philosophy. We must not think of it as the mere tool of the metaphysician: Dialectic does not consist of bare theories and rules: it deals with verities; Existences are, as it were, Matter to it, or at least it proceeds methodically towards Existences, and possesses itself, at the one step, of the notions and of the realities.

Untruth and sophism it knows, not directly, not of its own nature, but merely as something produced outside itself, something which it recognizes to be foreign to the verities laid up in itself; in the falsity presented to it, it perceives a clash with its own canon of truth. Dialectic, that is to say, has no knowledge of propositions—collections of words—but it knows the truth and, in that knowledge, knows what the schools call their propositions: it knows above all the operation of the Soul, and, by virtue of this knowing, it knows, too, what is affirmed and what is denied, whether the denial is of what was asserted or of something else, and whether propositions agree or differ; all that is submitted to it, it attacks with the directness of sense-perception and it leaves petty precisions of process to what other science may care for such exercises.

6. Philosophy has other provinces, but Dialectic is its precious part: in its study of the laws of the universe, Philosophy draws on Dialectic much as other studies and crafts use Arithmetic, though, of course, the alliance between Philosophy and Dialectic is closer.

And in morals, too, Philosophy uses Dialectic: by Dialectic it comes to contemplation, though it originates of itself the moral state or rather the discipline from which the moral state develops.

Our reasoning faculties employ the data of Dialectic almost as their proper possession, for their use of these data commonly involves Matter as well as Form.

And while the other virtues bring the reason to bear upon particular experiences and acts, the virtue of Wisdom (i.e. the virtue peculiarly induced by Dialectic) is a certain super-reasoning much closer to the Universal; for it deals with (such abstract ideas as) correspondence and sequence, the choice of time for action and inaction, the adoption of this course, the rejection of that other: Wisdom and Dialectic have the task of presenting all things as Universals and stripped of matter for treatment by the Understanding.

But can these inferior kinds of virtue exist without Dialectic and philosophy?

Yes—but imperfectly, inadequately.

And is it possible to be a Proficient, a Master in Dialectic, without these lower virtues?

It would not happen: the lower will spring either before or together with the higher. And it is likely that everyone normally possesses the natural virtues from which, when Wisdom steps in, the perfected virtue develops. After the natural virtues, then, Wisdom, and so the perfecting of the moral nature. Once the natural virtues exist, both orders, the natural and the higher, ripen side by side to their final excellence: or as the one advances it carries forward the other towards perfection.

But, ever, the natural virtue is imperfect in vision and in strength—and to both orders of virtue the essential matter is from what principles we derive them.

Ennead V
Eighth Tractate — on the Intellectual Beauty

1. It is a principle with us that one who has attained to the vision of the Intellectual Cosmos and grasped the beauty of the Authentic Intellect will be able also to come to understand the Father and Transcendent of that Divine Being. It concerns us, then, to try to see and say, for ourselves and as far as such matters may be told, how the Beauty of the divine Intellect and of the Intellectual Cosmos may be revealed to contemplation.

Let us go to the realm of magnitudes:—suppose two blocks of stone lying side by side: one is unpatterned, quite untouched by art; the other has been minutely wrought by the craftsman's hands into some statue of god or man, a Grace or a Muse, or if a human being, not a portrait but a creation in which the sculptor's art has concentrated all loveliness.

Now it must be seen that the stone thus brought under the artist's hand to the beauty of form is beautiful not as stone—for so the crude block would be as pleasant—but in virtue of the Form or Idea introduced by the art. This form is not in the material; it is in the designer before ever it enters the stone; and the artificer holds it not by his equipment of eyes and hands but by his participation in his art. The beauty, therefore, exists in a far higher state in the art; for it does not come over integrally into the work; that original beauty is not transferred; what comes over is a derivative and a minor: and even that shows itself upon the statue not integrally and with entire realization of intention but only in so far as it has subdued the resistance of the material.

Art, then, creating in the image of its own nature and content, and working by the Idea or Reason-Principle of the beautiful object it is to produce, must itself be beautiful in a far higher and purer degree since it is the seat and source of that beauty, indwelling in the art, which must naturally be more complete than any comeliness of the external. In the degree in which the beauty is diffused by entering into matter, it is so much the weaker than that concentrated in unity; everything that reaches outwards is the less for it, strength less strong, heat less hot, every power less potent, and so beauty less beautiful.

Then again every prime cause must be, within itself, more powerful than its effect can be: the musical does not derive from an unmusical source but from music; and so the art exhibited in the material work derives from an art yet higher.

Still the arts are not to be slighted on the ground that they create by imitation of natural objects; for, to begin with, these natural objects are themselves imitations; then, we must recognize that they give no bare reproduction of the thing seen but go back to the Reason-Principles from which Nature itself derives, and, furthermore, that much of their work is all their own; they are holders of beauty and add where nature is lacking. Thus Pheidias wrought the Zeus upon no model among things of sense but by apprehending what form Zeus must take if he chose to become manifest to sight.

2. But let us leave the arts and consider those works produced by Nature and admitted to be naturally beautiful which the creations of art are charged with imitating, all reasoning life and unreasoning things alike, but especially the consummate among them, where the moulder and maker has subdued the material and given the form he desired. Now what is the beauty here? It has nothing to do with the blood or the menstrual process: either there is also a colour and form apart from all this or there is nothing unless sheer ugliness or (at best) a bare recipient, as it were the mere Matter of beauty.

Whence shone forth the beauty of Helen, battle-sought; or of all those women like in loveliness to Aphrodite; or of Aphrodite herself; or of any human being that has been perfect in beauty; or of any of these gods manifest to sight, or unseen but carrying what would be beauty if we saw?

In all these is it not the Idea, something of that realm but communicated to the produced from within the producer, just as in works of art, we held, it is communicated from the arts to their creations? Now we can surely not believe that, while the made thing and the Idea thus impressed upon Matter are beautiful, yet the Idea not so alloyed but resting still with the creator—the Idea primal, immaterial, firmly a unity—is not Beauty.

If material extension were in itself the ground of beauty, then the creating principle, being without extension, could not be beautiful: but beauty cannot be made to depend upon magnitude since, whether in a large object or a small, the one Idea equally moves and forms the mind by its inherent power. A further indication is that as long as the object remains outside us we know nothing of it; it affects us by entry; but only as an Idea can it enter through the eyes which are not of scope to take an extended mass: we are, no doubt, simultaneously possessed of the magnitude which, however, we take in not as mass but by an elaboration upon the presented form.

Then again the principle producing the beauty must be, itself, ugly, neutral, or beautiful: ugly, it could not produce the opposite; neutral, why should its product be the one rather than the other? The Nature, then, which creates things so lovely must be itself of a far earlier beauty; we, undisciplined in discernment of the inward, knowing nothing of it, run after the outer, never understanding that it is the inner which stirs us; we are in the case of one who sees his own reflection but not realizing whence it comes goes in pursuit of it.

But that the thing we are pursuing is something different and that the beauty is not in the concrete object is manifest from the beauty there is in matters of study, in conduct and custom; briefly, in soul or mind. And it is precisely here that the greater beauty lies, perceived whenever you look to the wisdom in a man and delight in it, not wasting attention on the face, which may be hideous, but passing all appearance by and catching only at the inner comeliness, the truly personal; if you are still unmoved and cannot acknowledge beauty under such conditions, then looking to your own inner being you will find no beauty to delight you and it will be futile in that state to seek the greater vision, for you will be questing it through the ugly and impure.

This is why such matters are not spoken of to everyone; you, if you are conscious of beauty within, remember.

3. Thus there is in the Nature-Principle itself an Ideal archetype of the beauty that is found in material forms and, of that archetype again, the still more beautiful archetype in Soul, source of that in Nature. In the proficient soul this is brighter and of more advanced loveliness: adorning the soul and bringing to it a light from that greater light which is Beauty primally, its immediate presence sets the soul reflecting upon the quality of this prior, the archetype which has no such entries, and is present nowhere but remains in itself alone, and thus is not even to be called a Reason-Principle but is the creative source of the very first Reason-Principle which is the Beauty to which Soul serves as Matter.

This prior, then, is the Intellectual-Principle, the veritable, abiding and not fluctuant since not taking intellectual quality from outside itself. By what image, thus, can we represent it? We have nowhere to go but to what is less. Only from itself can we take an image of it; that is, there can be no representation of it, except in the sense that we represent gold by some portion of gold—purified, either actually or mentally, if it be impure—insisting at the same time that this is not the total thing gold, but merely the particular gold of a particular parcel. In the same way we learn in this matter from the purified Intellect in ourselves or, if you like, from the gods and the glory of the Intellect in them.

For assuredly all the gods are august and beautiful in a beauty beyond our speech. And what makes them so? Intellect; and especially Intellect operating within them (the divine sun and stars) to visibility. It is not through the loveliness of their corporeal forms: even those that have body are not gods by that beauty; it is in virtue of Intellect that they, too, are gods, and as gods beautiful. They do not veer between wisdom and folly: in the immunity of Intellect unmoving and pure, they are wise always, all-knowing, taking cognizance not of the human but of their own being and of all that lies within the contemplation of Intellect. Those of them whose dwelling is in the heavens are ever in this meditation—what task prevents them?—and from afar they look, too, into that further heaven by a lifting of the head. The gods belonging to that higher Heaven itself, they whose station is upon it and in it, see and know in virtue of their omnipresence to it. For all There is heaven; earth is heaven, and sea heaven; and animal and plant and man; all is the heavenly content of that heaven: and the gods in it, despising neither men nor anything else that is there where all is of the heavenly order, traverse all that country and all space in peace.

4. To 'live at ease' is There; and to these divine beings verity is mother and nurse, existence and sustenance; all that is not of process but of authentic being they see, and themselves in all: for all is transparent, nothing dark, nothing resistant; every being is lucid to every other, in breadth and depth; light runs through light. And each of them contains all within itself, and at the same time sees all in every other, so that everywhere there is all, and all is all and each all, and infinite the glory. Each of them is great; the small is great; the sun, There, is all the stars; and every star, again, is all the stars and sun. While some one manner of being is dominant in each, all are mirrored in every other.

Movement There is pure (as self-caused), for the moving principle
is not a separate thing to complicate it as it speeds.

So, too, Repose is not troubled, for there is no admixture of the
unstable; and the Beauty is all beauty since it is not resident in what is
not beautiful. Each There walks upon no alien soil; its place is its essential self; and, as each moves, so to speak, towards what is Above, it
is attended by the very ground from which it starts: there is no distinguishing between the Being and the Place; all is Intellect, the Principle and the ground on which it stands, alike. Thus we might think
that our visible sky (the ground or place of the stars), lit as it is, produces the light which reaches us from it, though of course this is really
produced by the stars (as it were, by the Principles of light alone, not
also by the ground as the analogy would require).

In our realm all is part rising from part and nothing can be more
than partial; but There each being is an eternal product of a whole
and is at once a whole and an individual manifesting as part but, to
the keen vision There, known for the whole it is.

The myth of Lynceus seeing into the very deeps of the earth tells
us of those eyes in the divine. No weariness overtakes this vision which
yet brings no such satiety as would call for its ending; for there never
was a void to be filled so that, with the fullness and the attainment of
purpose, the sense of sufficiency be induced: nor is there any such in-
congruity within the divine that one Being There could be repulsive
to another: and of course all There are unchangeable. This absence of
satisfaction means only a satisfaction leading to no distaste for that
which produces it; to see is to look the more, since for them to continue
in the contemplation of an infinite self and of infinite objects is but to
acquiesce in the bidding of their nature.

Life, pure, is never a burden; how then could there be weariness
There where the living is most noble? That very life is wisdom, not a
wisdom built up by reasonings but complete from the beginning, suffering no lack which could set it inquiring, a wisdom primal, unbor-
rowed, not something added to the Being, but its very essence. No
wisdom, thus, is greater; this is the authentic knowing, assessor to the
divine Intellect as projected into manifestation simultaneously with it;
thus, in the symbolic saying, Justice is assessor to Zeus.

(Perfect widom:) for all the Principles of this order, dwelling There,
are as it were visible images projected from themselves, so that all
becomes an object of contemplation to contemplators immeasurably
blessed. The greatness and power of the wisdom There we may know
from this, that it embraces all the real Beings, and has made all and all

follow it, and yet that it is itself those beings, which sprang into being with it, so that all is one and the essence There is wisdom. If we have failed to understand, it is that we have thought of knowledge as a mass of theorems and an accumulation of propositions, though that is false even for our sciences of the sense-realm. But in case this should be questioned, we may leave our own sciences for the present, and deal with the knowing in the Supreme at which Plato glances where he speaks of 'that knowledge which is not a stranger in something strange to it'—though in what sense, he leaves us to examine and declare, if we boast ourselves worthy of the discussion. This is probably our best starting-point.

5. All that comes to be, work of nature or of craft, some wisdom has made; everywhere a wisdom presides at a making.

No doubt the wisdom of the artist may be the guide of the work; it is sufficient explanation of the wisdom exhibited in the arts; but the artist himself goes back, after all, to that wisdom in Nature which is embodied in himself; and this is not a wisdom built up of theorems but one totality, not a wisdom consisting of manifold detail co-ordinated into a unity but rather a unity working out into detail.

Now, if we could think of this as the primal wisdom, we need look no further, since, at that, we have discovered a principle which is neither a derivative nor a 'stranger in something strange to it'. But if we are told that, while this Reason-Principle is in Nature, yet Nature itself is its source, we ask how Nature came to possess it; and, if Nature derived it from some other source, we ask what that other source may be; if, on the contrary, the principle is self-sprung, we need look no further: but if (as we assume) we are referred to the Intellectual-Principle we must make clear whether the Intellectual-Principle engendered the wisdom: if we learn that it did, we ask whence; if from itself, then inevitably it is itself Wisdom.

The true Wisdom, then (found to be identical with the Intellectual-Principle), is Real Being; and Real Being is Wisdom; it is wisdom that gives value to Real Being; and Being is Real in virtue of its origin in wisdom. It follows that all forms of existence not possessing wisdom are, indeed, Beings in right of the wisdom which went to their forming, but, as not in themselves possessing it, are not Real Beings.

We cannot, therefore, think that the divine Beings of that sphere, or the other supremely blessed There, need look to our apparatus of science: all of that realm (the very Beings themselves), all is noble image, such images as we may conceive to lie within the soul of the wise —but There not as inscription but as authentic existence. The ancients had this in mind when they declared the Ideas (Forms) to be Beings, Essentials.

6. Similarly, as it seems to me, the wise of Egypt—whether in precise knowledge or by a prompting of nature—indicated the truth where, in their effort towards philosophical statement, they left aside the writing-forms that take in the detail of words and sentences—those characters that represent sounds and convey the propositions of reasoning—and drew pictures instead, engraving in the temple-inscriptions a separate image for every separate item: thus they exhibited the absence of discursiveness in the Intellectual Realm.

For each manifestation of knowledge and wisdom is a distinct image, an object in itself, an immediate unity, not an aggregate of discursive reasoning and detailed willing. Later from this wisdom in unity there appears, in another form of being, an image, already less compact, which announces the original in terms of discourse and unravels the causes by which things are such that the wonder rises how a generated world can be so excellent.

For, one who knows must declare his wonder that this wisdom, while not itself containing the causes by which Being exists and takes such excellence, yet imparts them to the entities produced according to its canons. This excellence, whose necessity is scarcely or not at all manifest to search, exists, if we could but find it out, before all searching and reasoning.

What I say may be considered in one chief thing, and thence applied to all the particular entities:

7. Consider the universe: we are agreed that its existence and its nature come to it from beyond itself; are we, now, to imagine that its maker first thought it out in detail—the earth, and its necessary situation in the middle; water and, again, its position as lying upon the earth; all the other elements and objects up to the sky in due place and order; living beings with their appropriate forms as we know them, their inner organs and their outer limbs—and that having thus appointed every item beforehand, he then set about the execution?

Such designing was not even possible; how could the plan for a universe come to one that had never looked outward? Nor could he work on material gathered from elsewhere as our craftsmen do, using hands and tools; feet and hands are of the later order.

One way, only, remains: all things must exist in something else; of that prior—since there is no obstacle, all being continuous within the realm of reality—there has suddenly appeared a sign, an image, whether given forth directly or through the ministry of soul or of some phase of soul matters nothing for the moment: thus the entire aggregate of existence springs from the divine world, in greater beauty There because There unmingled but mingled here.

From the beginning to end all is gripped by the Forms of the Intellectual Realm: Matter itself is held by the Ideas of the elements and to these Ideas are added other Ideas and others again, so that it is hard to work down to crude Matter beneath all that sheathing of Idea. Indeed since Matter itself is, in its degree, an Idea—the lowest—all this universe is Idea and there is nothing that is not Idea as the archetype was. And all is made silently, since nothing had part in the making but Being and Idea—a further reason why creation went without toil. The Exemplar was the Idea of an All and so an All must come into being.

Thus nothing stood in the way of the Idea, and even now it dominates, despite all the clash of things: the creation is not hindered on its way even now; it stands firm in virtue of being All. To me, moreover, it seems that if we ourselves were archetypes, Ideas, veritable Being, and the Idea with which we construct here were our veritable Essence, then our creative power, too, would toillessly effect its purpose: as man now stands, he does not produce in his work a true image of himself: become man, he has ceased to be the All; ceasing to be man—we read —'he soars aloft and administers the Cosmos entire'; restored to the All he is maker of the All.

But—to our immediate purpose—it is possible to give a reason why the earth is set in the midst and why it is round and why the ecliptic runs precisely as it does, but, looking to the creating principle, we cannot say that because this was the way therefore things were so planned: we can say only that because the Exemplar is what it is, therefore the things of this world are good; the causing principle, we might put it, reached the conclusion before all formal reasoning and not from any premises, not by sequence or plan but before either, since all of that order is later, all reason, demonstration, persuasion.

Since there is a Source, all the created must spring from it and in accordance with it; and we are rightly told not to go seeking the causes impelling a Source to produce, especially when this is the perfectly sufficient Source and identical with the Term: a Source which is Source and Term must be the All-Unity, complete in itself.

8. This then is Beauty primally: it is entire and omnipresent as an entirety; and therefore in none of its parts or members lacking in beauty; beautiful thus beyond denial. Certainly it cannot be anything

(be, for example, Beauty) without being wholly what thing; it can be nothing which it is to possess partially or in which it utterly fails (and therefore it must entirely be Beauty entire).

If this principle were not beautiful, what other could be? Its prior does not deign to be beautiful; that which is the first to manifest itself —Form and object of vision to the intellect—cannot but be lovely to see. It is to indicate this that Plato, drawing on something well within our observation, represents the Creator as approving the work he has achieved: the intention is to make us feel the lovable beauty of the archetype and of the Divine Idea; for to admire a representation is to admire the original upon which it was made.

It is not surprising if we fail to recognize what is passing within us: lovers, and those in general that admire beauty here, do not stay to reflect that it is to be traced, as of course it must be, to the Beauty There. That the admiration of the Demiurge is to be referred to the Ideal Exemplar is deliberately made evident by the rest of the passage: 'He admired; and determined to bring the work into still closer likeness with the Exemplar': he makes us feel the magnificent beauty of the Exemplar by telling us that the Beauty sprung from this world is, itself, a copy from That.

And indeed if the divine did not exist, the transcendently beautiful, in a beauty beyond all thought, what could be lovelier than the things we see? Certainly no reproach can rightly be brought against this world save only that it is not That.

9. Let us, then, make a mental picture of our universe: each member shall remain what it is, distinctly apart; yet all is to form, as far as possible, a complete unity so that whatever comes into view, say the outer orb of the heavens, shall bring immediately with it the vision, on the one plane, of the sun and of all the stars with earth and sea and all living things as if exhibited upon a transparent globe.

Bring this vision actually before your sight, so that there shall be in your mind the gleaming representation of a sphere, a picture holding all the things of the universe moving or in repose or (as in reality) some at rest, some in motion. Keep this sphere before you, and from it imagine another, a sphere stripped of magnitude and of spatial differences; cast out your inborn sense of Matter, taking care not merely to attenuate it: call on God, maker of the sphere whose image you now hold, and pray Him to enter. And may He come bringing His own Universe with all the gods that dwell in it—He who is the one God and all the gods, where each is all, blending into a unity, distinct in powers but all one god in virtue of that one divine power of many facets.

More truly, this is the one God who is all the gods; for, in the coming to be of all those, this, the one, has suffered no diminishing. He and all have one existence, while each again is distinct. It is distinction by state without interval: there is no outward form to set one here and another there and to prevent any from being an entire identity; yet there is no sharing of parts from one to another. Nor is each of those divine wholes a power in fragment, a power totalling to the sum of the measurable segments: the divine is one all-power, reaching out to infinity, powerful to infinity: and so great is God that his very members are infinites. What place can be named to which He does not reach?

Great, too, is this firmament of ours and all the powers constellated within it, but it would be greater still, unspeakably, but that there is inbound in it something of the petty power of body; no doubt the powers of fire and other bodily substances might themselves be thought very great, but in fact, it is through their failure in the true power that we see them burning, destroying, wearing things away, and slaving towards the production of life; they destroy because they are themselves in process of destruction, and they produce because they belong to the realm of the produced.

The power in that other world has merely Being and Beauty of Being. Beauty without Being could not be, nor Being voided of Beauty: abandoned of Beauty, Being loses something of its essence. Being is desirable because it is identical with Beauty; and Beauty is loved because it is Being. How then can we debate which is the cause of the other, where the nature is one? The very figment of Being needs some imposed image of Beauty to make it passable, and even to ensure its existence; it exists to the degree in which it has taken some share in the beauty of Idea; and the more deeply it has drawn on this, the less imperfect it is, precisely because the nature which is essentially the beautiful has entered into it the more intimately.

EARLY CHRISTIAN
THOUGHT

St. Paul, who received his early education at the University town of Tarsus, appears through his writings to have been as well acquainted with the civilization of Rome as he was with the literary products of Greek culture, and particularly does he seem to have been familiar with the philosophy of Stoicism. Yet he remained basically suspicious of the pagan world and single-minded in his emphasis on faith. Our selection from the *Book of Acts*, Chapter 17, presents the pungency of his response to a meeting in Athens with some philosophers.

Justin Martyr (110-165 A.D.) was born in Samaria. He seems to have been well educated and a disciple of Platonic philosophy before his conversion. Abandoning his studies in the schools of the philosophers, he took every opportunity to proclaim the Gospel as the only safe and certain philosophy and way to salvation. The selections from his *Dialogue with Trypho* and from the *Hortatory Address to the Greeks* present a milder form of rejection of Greek philosophy (especially Platonism) as insufficient for man's salvation, and yet showing clearly the impact of his earlier studies on his later views.

We know very little about Minucius Felix except that prior to his conversion to Christianity he had been an advocate at Rome. That Minucius Felix was an actual person we know only indirectly, as assumed by Lactantius [in his *Inst. Div.* V.1, 21] and by Jerome [*De Viris Illustribus*, chap. 58]. The *Octavius*, from which our selection comes, presents an argument between a pagan Roman, Q. Caecilius Natalis, and a Christian, Octavius. The supposed transcriber of the debate is requested to arbitrate the issues raised by the disputants. Caecilius represents the role of the then current paganism, agnostic in outlook, broadly educated, and professing polite but skeptical interest in the speculations and contradictions of rival philosophies. The work itself depicts the cultured and professional classes and the social and religious conditions at Rome at the end of the second century. The transcriber is of course the writer, Minucius Felix; while the remaining figure, Octavius Januarius, is cast for the role of chief speaker and champion of Christian religion. Octavius speaks to men of culture and refinement at a time when paganism was thought to be intellectually bankrupt. He is represented as already dead, and the discourse is seemingly a tribute to his gifts and his memory. Octavius is depicted as brought up in the pagan tradition and a close friend of the author, Minucius.

The *Octavius* serves to show the advance gained by Christianity in social and civil status and how it had become the movement of reform, of intellectual and moral protest. Caecilius is the apologist for paganism: his argument is an appeal to philosophic commonplaces on the precarious results of reasoning processes, referring to the philosophic bruit between those who argue about providence, chance, and fate. Religion in its various forms rests also on the accumulated wisdom of the forefathers in every nation. The argument tries to show that tradition and history represent the sole criterion for the conflicting claims as presented by the philosophers and those who uphold religious beliefs. There follows an attack on the Christians which denounces their hostility to pagan culture. In brief, Caecilius is defending Rome as the symbol of the truths of pagan religion—which have brought world-wide dominion and pre-eminence. The defense of Christianity raises the question of the poverty of Caecilius' argument and closes as an appreciation of the distinctive qualities of the Christian ethos, and of their trust in God. It is interesting to note that the *Octavius,* as a defense of Christianity, is approached from Roman forms of Platonic, Stoic, and Epicurean arguments for providence; the name of Jesus does not once occur.

Clement of Alexandria, who died about 215 A.D., was Athenian born and taught in later life in Alexandria. The selection here from his *Stromata* (or *Miscellanies*) presents a somewhat larger illustration than his importance would seem to warrant. Yet, Clement presents one of the strongest arguments in support of a Christian *gnosis*—an explicit attempt to show the role of philosophy as a preparation for the Christian philosopher. His student, Origen (185-254 A.D.), succeeded Clement as the Master of his school. Origen was known to have been a famous teacher in his own right, although an extreme asceticism prompted him to castrate himself out of his zeal for purity.

Tertullian (160-230 A.D.), the most outspoken in his opposition to philosophy and profane literature, was born in Carthage and became a fiery convert to Christianity about the year 197. His uncompromising attitudes and stubborn and relentless pursuit of his own views led him finally to leave the church to join the Montanists (213 A.D.), a heretical sect. He finally went off to form his own sect. Tertullian is doubtless best known for his insistence that the certainty of faith is demonstrated by its impossibility according to reason. But he was an influential figure in the formation of Christian principles in the Latin language.

St. Paul
Book of Acts

Chapter XVII.

Now when they had passed through Amphipolis and Apollonia, they came to Thessalonica, where there was a synagogue of the Jews. And Paul went in, as was his custom, and for three weeks he argued with them from the scriptures, explaining and proving that it was necessary for the Christ to suffer and to rise from the dead, and saying, "This Jesus, whom I proclaim to you, is the Christ." And some of them were persuaded, and joined Paul and Silas; as did a great many of the devout Greeks and not a few of the leading women. But the Jews were jealous, and taking some wicked fellows of the rabble, they gathered a crowd, set the city in an uproar, and attacked the house of Jason, seeking to bring them out to the people. And when they could not find them, they dragged Jason and some of the brethren before the city authorities, crying, "These men who have turned the world upside down have come here also, and Jason has received them; and they are all acting against the decrees of Caesar, saying that there is another king, Jesus." And the people and the city authorities were disturbed when they heard this. And when they had taken security from Jason and the rest, they let them go.

The brethren immediately sent Paul and Silas away by night to Beroea: and when they arrived they went into the Jewish synagogue. Now these Jews were more noble than those in Thessalonica, for they received the word with all eagerness, examining the scriptures daily to see if these things were so. Many of them therefore believed, with not a few Greek women of high standing as well as men. But when the Jews of Thessalonica learned that the word of God was proclaimed by Paul at Beroea also, they came there too, stirring up and inciting the crowds. Then the brethren immediately sent Paul off on his way to the sea, but Silas and Timothy remained there. Those who conducted Paul brought him as far as Athens: and receiving a command for Silas and Timothy to come to him as soon as possible, they departed.

Now while Paul was waiting for them at Athens, his spirit was provoked within him as he saw that the city was full of idols. So he argued in the synagogue with the Jews and the devout persons, and in the market place every day with those who chanced to be there. Some also of the Epicurean and Stoic philosophers met him. And some said, "What would this babbler say?" Others said, "He seems to be a preacher of foreign divinities"—because he preached Jesus and the resurrection. And they took hold of him and brought him to the Areopagus, saying, "May we know what this new teaching is which you present? For you bring some strange things to our ears; we wish to know therefore what these things mean." Now all the Athenians and the foreigners who lived there spent their time in nothing except telling or hearing something new.

So Paul, standing in the middle of the Areopagus, said: "Men of Athens, I perceive that in every way you are very religious. For as I passed along, and observed the objects of your worship, I found also an altar with this inscription. 'To an unknown god.' What therefore you worship as unknown, this I proclaim to you. The God who made the world and everything in it, being Lord of heaven and earth, does not live in shrines made by man, nor is he served by human hands, as though he needed anything, since he himself gives to all men life and breath and everything. And he made from one every nation of men to live on all the face of the earth, having determined allotted periods and the boundaries of their habitation, that they should seek God, in the hope that they might feel after him and find him. Yet he is not far from each one of us, for

'In him we live and move and have our being';

as even some of your poets have said,

'For we are indeed his offspring.'

Being then God's offspring, we ought not to think that the Deity is like gold, or silver, or stone, a representation by the art and imagination of man. The times of ignorance God overlooked, but now he commands all men everywhere to repent, because he has fixed a day on which he will judge the world in righteousness by a man whom he has appointed, and of this he has given assurance to all men by raising him from the dead."

Now when they heard of the resurrection of the dead, some mocked; but others said, "We will hear you again about this." So Paul went out from among them. But some men joined him and believed, among them Dionysius the Areopagite and a woman named Damaris and others with them.

Justin Martyr
Dialogue with Trypho

Chapter II.—JUSTIN DESCRIBES HIS STUDIES IN PHILOSOPHY

"I will tell you," said I, "what seems to me; for philosophy is, in fact, the greatest possession, and most honourable before God,[1] to whom it leads us and alone commends us; and these are truly holy men who have bestowed attention on philosophy. What philosophy is, however, and the reason why it has been sent down to men, have escaped the observation of most; for there would be neither Platonists, nor Stoics, nor Peripatetics, nor Theoretics,[2] nor Pythagoreans, this knowledge being *one*.[3] I wish to tell you why it has become many-headed. It has happened that those who first handled it [i.e., philosophy], and who were therefore esteemed illustrious men, were succeeded by those who made no investigations concerning truth, but only admired the perseverance and self-discipline of the former, as well as the novelty of the doctrines; and each thought that to be true which he learned from his teacher: then, moreover, those latter persons handed down to *their* successors such things, and others similar to them; and this system was called by the name of him who was styled the father of the doctrine. Being at first desirous of personally conversing with one of these men, I surrendered myself to a certain Stoic; and having spent a consider-

---

1. 𝔅 some omit, and put θεῷ of prev. cl. in this cl., reading so: "Philosophy is the greatest possession, and most honourable, and introduces us to God," etc.

2. Maranus thinks that those who are different from the masters of practical philosophy are called *Theoretics*. I do not know whether they may be better designated *Sceptics* or *Pyrrhonists*.—Otto.

3. Julian, *Orat.* vi., says: "Let no one divide our philosophy into many parts, or cut it into many parts, and especially let him not make many out of *one*: for as truth is one, so also is philosophy."

able time with him, when I had not acquired any further knowledge of God (for he did not know himself, and said such instruction was unnecessary), I left him and betook myself to another, who was called a Peripatetic, and as *he* fancied, shrewd. And this man, after having entertained me for the first few days, requested me to settle the fee, in order that our intercourse might not be unprofitable. Him, too, for this reason I abandoned, believing him to be no philosopher at all. But when my soul was eagerly desirous to hear the peculiar and choice philosophy, I came to a Pythagorean, very celebrated—a man who thought much of his own wisdom. And then, when I had an interview with him, willing to become his hearer and disciple, he said, 'What then? Are you acquainted with music, astronomy, and geometry? Do you expect to perceive any of those things which conduce to a happy life, if you have not been first informed on those points which wean the soul from sensible objects, and render it fitted for objects which appertain to the mind, so that it can contemplate that which is honourable in its essence and that which is good in its essence?' Having commended many of these branches of learning, and telling me that they were necessary, he dismissed me when I confessed to him my ignorance. Accordingly I took it rather impatiently, as was to be expected when I failed in my hope, the more so because I deemed the man had some knowledge; but reflecting again on the space of time during which I would have to linger over those branches of learning, I was not able to endure longer procrastination. In my helpless condition it occurred to me to have a meeting with the Platonists, for their fame was great. I thereupon spent as much of my time as possible with one who had lately settled in our city,[4]—a sagacious man, holding a high position among the Platonists,—and I progressed, and made the greatest improvements daily. And the perception of immaterial things quite overpowered me, and the contemplation of ideas furnished my mind with wings,[5] so that in a little while I supposed that I had become wise; and such was my stupidity, I expected forthwith to look upon God, for this is the end of Plato's philosophy.

---

4. Either Flavia Neapolis is indicated, or Ephesus.—Otto.

5. Narrating his progress in the study of Platonic philosophy, he elegantly employs this trite phrase of Plato's.—Otto.

Justin Martyr
Hortatory Address to the Greeks

Chapter XXXVI.—TRUE KNOWLEDGE NOT HELD BY THE PHILOSOPHERS

And if "the discovery of the truth" be given among them as one definition of philosophy, how are they who are not in possession of the true knowledge worthy of the name of philosophy? For if Socrates, the wisest of your wise men, to whom even your oracle, as you yourselves say, bears witness, saying, "Of all men, Socrates is the wisest"—if he confesses that he knows nothing, how did those who came after him profess to know even things heavenly? For Socrates said that he was on this account called wise, because, while other men pretended to know what they were ignorant of, he himself did not shrink from confessing that he knew nothing. For he said, "I seem to myself to be wisest by this little particular, that what I do not know, I do not suppose I know." Let no one fancy that Socrates ironically feigned ignorance, because he often used to do so in his dialogues. For the last expression of his apology which he uttered as he was being led away to the prison, proves that in seriousness and truth he was confessing his ignorance: "But now it is time to go away, I indeed to die, but you to live. And which of us goes to the better state, is hidden to all but God." Socrates, indeed, having uttered this last sentence in the Areopagus, departed to the prison, ascribing to God alone the knowledge of those things which are hidden from us; but those who came after him, though they are unable to comprehend even earthly things, profess to understand things heavenly as if they had seen them. Aristotle at least—as if he had seen things heavenly with greater accuracy than Plato—declared that God did not exist, as Plato said, in the fiery substance (for this was Plato's doctrine) but in the fifth element, air. And while he demanded that concerning these matters he should be believed on account of the excellence of his language, he yet departed this life because he was overwhelmed with the infamy and disgrace of being unable to discover even the nature of the Euripus in Chalcis.[1] Let not any one, therefore, of sound judgment prefer the elegant diction of these men to his own salvation, but let him, according to that old story, stop his ears with wax, and flee the sweet hurt which these sirens would inflict upon him. For the above-mentioned men, presenting their elegant language as a kind of bait, have sought to seduce many from the right religion, in imitation of him who dared to teach the first men polytheism. Be not persuaded by these persons, I entreat you, but read the prophecies of the sacred writers.[2] And if any slothfulness or old hereditary superstition prevents you from reading the prophecies of the holy men through which you can be instructed regarding the one only God, which is the first article of the true religion, yet believe him who, though at first he taught you polytheism, yet afterwards preferred to sing a useful and necessary recantation—I mean Orpheus, who said what I quoted a little before; and believe the others who wrote the same things concerning one God. For it was the work of Divine Providence on your behalf, that they, though unwillingly, bore testimony that what the prophets said regarding one God was true, in order that, the doctrine of a plurality of gods being rejected by all, occasion might be afforded you of knowing the truth.

---

1. This is now supposed to be fable.
2. Literally, "sacred men."

Minucius Felix
Octavius[1]

Book V.

4. . . . Everyone must feel indignant and annoyed that certain persons—persons untrained in study, uninitiated in letters, ignorant even of the meaner arts—should come to fixed conclusions upon the universe in its majesty, which through the centuries is to this day matter of debate in countless schools of philosophy. And no wonder, seeing that man's limited intelligence is so incapable of exploring God, that neither in the case of things above, suspended aloft in heaven, nor of things below the earth plunged beneath the depths, is it given to him to know, or permitted to scrutinize, without irreverence. Sufficient be it for our happiness, and sufficient for our wisdom if, according to the ancient oracle of the wise man, we learn closer acquaintance with our own selves. But seeing that with mad and fruitless toil we overstep the limits of our humble intelligence, and from our earth-bound level seek, with audacious eagerness, to scale heaven itself and the stars of heaven, let us at least not aggravate our error by vain and terrifying imaginations. . . .

5. Suppose that in the beginning nature gathered the seeds of all things together, and formed them into a mass—what god was here the author? Or suppose that by their fortuitous clashing the elements of the universe combined, took order and shape—what god was the artificer? Fire may have kindled the stars; the nature of its material have suspended heaven on high, founded the earth by its weight, drained moisture into the sea—if so, what ground is there for religion, for terror and superstitious dread? Man and each living thing is born,

---

1. Minucius Felix includes in this dialogue the argument for and against Christianity. This selection is from the speech against Christianity delivered by one of the disputants, Caecilius.

lives, grows up; consists of a spontaneous combination of elements, into which once again man and every living thing is separated, resolved and dispersed; so all things flow back to their source, and return unto themselves without artificer, or arbiter, or author of their being. So by the gathering together of the seeds of fire, new and ever new suns continually shine; so by the exhalation of earth's vapors mists continually grow, and by their condensation and combination clouds rise on high; and as they drop, rains fall, winds blow, hailstorms rattle; as the storm clouds collide, thunders growl, lightning flashes, thunderbolts dart; yes and they fall at random, hurtle down upon the mountains, charge trees, smite without distinction places sacred or profane; strike guilty men or often enough the god-fearing. Why tell of tempests capricious and uncertain, which without rule or rhyme bring havoc in their wake? or how in shipwrecks the fates of the good and of the evil are confounded, and their deserts confused? in fires, of indiscriminate destruction of the innocent and of the guilty? or, when some region of the sky is infected with the blight of pestilence, how all perish without distinction? In the rage and heat of battle, how the better men are first to fall? In peace too, not only does rascality run level with virtue, but wins such respect that half the times one does not know whether to detest their depravity or to envy their good fortune. But if the world were governed by divine providence and the authority of some deity, Phalaris and Dionysius would never have deserved a throne, Rutilius and Camillus exile, or Socrates the hemlock. See, the trees laden with fruit, the corn already white to harvest, the vineyard heavy with wine—ruined by rain or cut with hail. So hidden from our eyes and overlaid is the uncertain truth, or—as seems more credible—lawless chance, with tricky and haphazard accidents, rules over all.

6. Seeing then that either chance is certain, or nature uncertain, how much more reverent and better it is to accept the teaching of our elders as the priest of truth; to maintain the religions handed down to us; to adore the gods, whom from the cradle you were taught to fear rather than to know familiarly; not to dogmatize about divinities, but to believe our forefathers who, in an age still rude, in the world's nativity, were privileged to regard gods as kindly or as kings! Hence it is that throughout wide empires, provinces and towns, we see each people having its own individual rites and worshipping its local gods, the Eleusinians Ceres, the Phrygians the Great Mother, the Epidaurians Aesculapius, the Chaldaeans Bel, the Syrians Astarte, the Taurians Diana, the Gauls Mercury, the Romans one and all. Thus it is that their power and authority has embraced the circuit of the whole

world, and has advanced the bounds of empire beyond the paths of the
sun, and the confines of ocean; while they practice in the field god-
fearing valor, make strong their city with awe of sacred rites, with
chaste virgins, with many a priestly dignity and title; besieged and im-
prisoned within the limits of the Capitol, they still reverenced the gods,
whom others might have spurned as wrath, and through the ranks of
Gauls amazed at their undaunted superstition passed on armed not with
weapons but with godly reverence and fear; in captured fortresses,
even in the first flush of victory, they reverence the conquered deities;
everywhere they entertain the gods and adopt them as their own;[2]
while they raise altars even to the unknown deities, and to the spirits
of the dead. Thus is it that they adopt the sacred rites of all nations,
and withal have earned dominion. Hence the course of worship has
continued without break, not impaired but strengthened by the lapse
of time; for indeed antiquity is wont to attach to ceremonies and to
temples a sanctity proportioned to the length of their continuance.

7. It was not at mere random—though here I might venture to
concede a point and go wrong in good company—that our ancestors
devoted their attention to observing auguries, to consulting entrails, to
instituting sacrifices, or dedicating shrines. Look at the written records;
you will find that all religious rites originated either to secure the
reward of divine approval or to avert impending anger, or to propitiate
its swelling rage and fury. Witness the Idaean Mother who at her
coming vindicated a matron's chastity and freed the city from fear of
the enemy; witness the statues of the horsemen brothers consecrated,
even as they appeared, in the lake waters, who, breathless on their
foaming and smoking steeds, announced the victory over Perses on the
same day on which they had achieved it; witness the revival of the
games in honor of offended Jupiter, thanks to the dream of a common
plebeian; witness the devotion of the Decii, ratified by Heaven; and
witness too Curtius and the gulf, whose yawning mouth horse and rider,
or the honor due to their devotion, closed. Only too often contempt for
the auspices has attested the presence of the gods. So with the Allia of
"ill-omened name"; so with the fleet of Claudius and Junius, not in
action against the Carthaginians, but in disastrous wreck; and did not
Trasimene run red with blood of Romans because Flaminius despised
the auguries? And had we not to reclaim our standards from the Par-
thians because Crassus dared and derided the imprecations of the

---

2. It was the practice, before an enemy's city was attacked, for Roman priests
according to a prescribed formula to invoke its tutelar gods, inviting them to leave
it and to come to Rome, where they would receive equal or fuller worship.

Dread Goddesses? I omit old instances, not a few; I take no account of the songs of the poets touching the births of gods, their gifts and their rewards; I pass predictions of fate conveyed by oracles, for fear of your regarding antique lore as fabulous. Turn your gaze on the temples and shrines of gods by which the commonwealth of Rome is protected and adorned: they owe more to the presence and the tenancy of the deities who dwell therein than to the worship, the decorations and the votive gifts with which they are enriched. Hence it is that prophets, filled and inspired by God, anticipate the future, give warning in perils, healing in disease, hope to the afflicted, help to the wretched, solace in calamity, and in toil alleviation. Even in sleep we see, hear, and recognize the gods, whom by day we impiously deny, reject and mock with false oaths.

8. Therefore, since all nations unhesitatingly agree as to the existence of the immortal gods, however uncertain may be our account of them or of their origin, it is intolerable that any man should be so puffed up with pride and impious conceit of wisdom, as to strive to abolish or undermine religion, so ancient, so useful, and so salutary. He may be a Theodorus of Cyrene, or an earlier Diagoras of Melos, called Atheist by antiquity, who both alike, by asserting that there were no gods, cut at the root of all the fear and reverence by which mankind is governed; yet will they never establish their impious tenets under the name and authority of pretended philosophy.

When Protagoras of Abdera, by way of debate rather than of profanity, discussed the godhead, the men of Athens expelled him from their borders, and burned his writings in the marketplace. Is it not then deplorable that a gang—excuse my vehemence in using strong language for the cause I advocate—a gang, I say, of discredited and proscribed desperadoes band themselves against the gods? Fellows who gather together illiterates from the dregs of the populace and credulous women with the instability natural to their sex, and so organize a rabble of profane conspirators, leagued together by meetings at night and ritual fasts and unnatural repasts, not for any sacred service but for piacular rites, a secret tribe that shuns the light, silent in the open, but talkative in hid corners; they despise temples as if they were tombs; they spit upon the gods; they jeer at our sacred rites; pitiable themselves, they pity (save the mark) our priests; they despise titles and robes of honor, going themselves half-naked! What a pitch of folly! what wild impertinence! present tortures they despise, yet dread those of an uncertain future; death after death they fear, but death in the present they fear not; for them illusive hope charms away terror with assurances of a life to come.

9. Already—for ill weeds grow apace—decay of morals grows from day to day, and throughout the wide world the abominations of this impious confederacy multiply. Root and branch it must be exterminated and accursed. They recognize one another by secret signs and marks; they fall in love almost before they are acquainted; everywhere they introduce a kind of religion of lust, a promiscuous "brotherhood" and "sisterhood" by which ordinary fornication, under cover of a hallowed name, is converted to incest. And thus their vain and foolish superstition makes an actual boast of crime. For themselves, were there not some foundation of truth, shrewd rumor would not impute gross and unmentionable forms of vice. I am told that under some idiotic impulse they consecrate and worship the head of an ass, the meanest of all beasts, a religion worthy of the morals which gave it birth. Others say that they actually reverence the private parts of their director and high priest, and adore his organs as parent of their being. This may be false, but such suspicions naturally attach to their secret and nocturnal rites. To say that a malefactor put to death for his crimes, and wood of the death-dealing cross, are objects of their veneration is to assign fitting altars to abandoned wretches and the kind of worship they deserve. Details of the initiation of neophytes are as revolting as they are notorious. An infant, cased in dough to deceive the unsuspecting, is placed beside the person to be initiated. The novice is thereupon induced to inflict what seem to be harmless blows upon the dough, and unintentionally the infant is killed by his unsuspecting blows; the blood—oh, horrible—they lap up greedily; the limbs they tear to pieces eagerly; and over the victim they make league and covenant, and by complicity in guilt pledge themselves to mutual silence. Such sacred rites are more foul than any sacrilege. Their form of feasting is notorious; it is in everyone's mouth, as testified by the speech of our friend of Cirta. On the day appointed they gather at a banquet with all their children, sisters, and mothers, people of either sex and every age. There, after full feasting, when the blood is heated and drink has inflamed the passions of incestuous lust, a dog which has been tied to a lamp is tempted by a morsel thrown beyond the range of his tether to bound forward with a rush. The tale-telling light is upset and extinguished, and in the shameless dark lustful embraces are indiscriminately exchanged; and all alike, if not in act, yet by complicity, are involved in incest, as anything that occurs by the act of individuals results from the common intention.

10. Much I purposely pass over; I have said more than enough of things most or all of which are true, as is shown by the secrecy of this depraved religion. Why make such efforts to obscure and conceal what-

ever is the object of their worship, when things honorable always rejoice in publicity, while guilt loves secrecy? Why have they no altars,
no temples, no recognized images? Why do they never speak in public,
never meet in the open, if it be not that the object of their worship
and their concealment is either criminal or shameful?

Whence, who, or where is He, the One and only God, solitary, for-
lorn, whom no free nation, no kingdom, no superstition known to Rome
has knowledge of? The miserable Jewish nationality did indeed worship
one God, but even so openly, in temples, with altars, victims, and
ceremonies; yet one so strengthless and powerless that he and his dear
tribe with him are in captivity to Rome. And yet again what monstrous
absurdities these Christians invent about this God of theirs, whom they
can neither show nor see! that he searches diligently into the ways and
deeds of all men, yea even their words and hidden thoughts, hurrying
to and fro, ubiquitously; they make him out a troublesome, restless,
shameless and interfering being, who has a hand in everything that is
done, interlopes at every turn, and can neither attend to particulars
because he is distracted with the whole, nor to the whole because he is
engaged with particulars.

11. Further, they threaten the whole world and the universe and
its stars with destruction by fire, as though the eternal order of nature
established by laws divine could be put to confusion, or as though the
bonds of all the elements could be broken, the framework of heaven
be split in twain, and the containing and surrounding mass be brought
down in ruin. Not content with this insane idea, they embellish and
embroider it with old wives' tales; say that they are born anew after
death from the cinders and the ashes, and with a strange unaccountable
confidence believe in one another's lies; you might suppose they had
already come to life again. One perversion and folly matches the other.
Against heaven and the stars, which we leave even as we found them,
they denounce destruction; for themselves when dead and gone, creatures born to perish, the promise of eternity! Hence no doubt their
denunciation of funeral pyres and of cremation, just as though the
body, even though spared the flame, would not in the course of years
and ages be resolved into dust; and just as though it mattered whether
it is torn to pieces by wild beasts or drowned in the sea, or buried in
the ground, or consumed in the flame; for corpses, if they have sensation, must find all interment painful; while if they have not, speed of
dispatch is the best treatment. Under this delusion they promise themselves, as virtuous, a life of never ending bliss after death; to all others,
as evildoers, everlasting punishment.

Much might be added on this subject, but my discourse must hasten to its end. That they themselves are evildoers I need not labor to prove; I have already shown it; though even if I grant their well-doing, guilt or innocence is usually, I know, attributed to destiny. And here we have your agreement; for all action which others ascribe to fate, you ascribe to God; followers of your sect are moved not by their own free will, but by election; and thus you invent an unjust judge, to punish men for their bad luck, not for their use of will.

Here I should like to ask whether the resurrection is with bodies or without bodies, and if so, with what bodies, their own or made anew? Without a body? That means, so far as I know, neither mind, nor soul, nor life. With the same body? But that has already gone to pieces. With another body? in that case a new man is born, and not the former man renewed. And yet though time has come and gone, and innumerable ages have flowed on, what single individual has ever returned from the lower regions even with the Protesilaus privilege of a few hours' furlough, so that we might have one example to trust? Your figments of diseased imagination and the futile fairy tales invented by poets' fancy to give sweetness to their song have been rehashed by your credulity into the service of your God.

12. You do not anyhow allow your experiences of the present to undeceive your vain desires of promissory expectation. Let present life, poor fools, be your gauge of what happens after death. See how some part of you, the greater and the better part as you say, suffer want, cold, toil, hunger; and yet your God permits and seems to overlook it; he is unwilling or unable to help his own; consequently he is either powerless or unjust. You dream of posthumous immortality; when unnerved by danger, when parched with fever, when racked with pain, can you not be sensible of your condition? recognize your feebleness? against your will, poor fool, you are convicted of weakness, and yet will not admit it!

Things, however, common to all I pass over; but for you there stand in wait punishments, tortures, crosses (crosses not for adoration, but for endurance), yes and the flames which you foretell and fear; where is the God who will succor you in the next life, but in this life cannot? Have not the Romans without your God empire and rule; do they not enjoy the whole world, and lord it over you? Meanwhile in anxious doubt you deny yourselves wholesome pleasures; you do not attend the shows; you take no part in the processions; fight shy of public banquets; abhor the sacred games, meats from the victims, drinks poured in libation on the altars. So frightened are you of the gods whom you deny! You twine no blossoms for the head, grace the body with no perfumes; you reserve your unguents for funerals; refuse garlands even to the graves, pale, trembling creatures, objects for pity— but the pity of our gods! Poor wretches, for whom there is no life hereafter, yet who live not for today.

Well then, if you have any sense or modesty, have done with prying into the regions of the sky, into the destiny and secrets of the universe; enough for the ignorant and uncultured, the rude and boorish, to look at what is under their nose; those who are not privileged to understand things civic are still less qualified to discuss things divine.

13. Yet, if philosophize you must, let any that is equal to the task imitate if he can Socrates, the prince of wisdom. When questioned about things in heaven his famous answer ran, "that which is above us, does not concern us." Well did he deserve the testimonial of the oracle to his superior wisdom. The reason, as he himself divined, why the oracle set him before all others, was not that he had found out the meaning of everything, but that he had learned that he knew nothing; so surely is the confession of ignorance the highest wisdom. From this source flowed the guarded scepticism of Arcesilas, and later of Carneades and most of the Academic school, on all the deepest questions; this is the kind of philosophy in which the unlearned may indulge with caution, the learned with distinction. May we not all admire and follow the hesitation of Simonides, the poet? When Hiero the tyrant asked him what he thought of the being and attributes of the gods, he first begged for a day for consideration, next day for two days more; then, on a new reminder, for yet another. Finally, when the tyrant asked his reasons for so much delay, he replied "because to him, the longer the progress of the search, the more obscure became the truth." To my mind things that are doubtful, as they are, should be left in doubt, and, where so many and such great minds differ, rash and hasty votes should not be cast on either side for fear of countenancing old wives' superstition, or of subverting all religion. . . .

Clement of Alexandria
The Stromata

Book I.

Chapter II.—OBJECTION TO THE NUMBER OF EXTRACTS FROM PHILOSOPHICAL WRITINGS IN THESE BOOKS ANTICIPATED AND ANSWERED

In reference to these commentaries, which contain as the exigencies of the case demand, the Hellenic opinions, I say thus much to those who are fond of finding fault. First, even if philosophy were useless, if the demonstration of its uselessness does good, it is yet useful. Then those cannot condemn the Greeks, who have only a mere hearsay knowledge of their opinions, and have not entered into a minute investigation in each department, in order to acquaintance with them. For the refutation, which is based on experience, is entirely trustworthy. For the knowledge of what is condemned is found the most complete demonstration. Many things, then, though not contributing to the final result, equip the artist. And otherwise erudition commends him, who sets forth the most essential doctrines so as to produce persuasion in his hearers, engendering admiration in those who are taught, and leads them to the truth. And such persuasion is convincing, by which those that love learning admit the truth; so that philosophy does not ruin life by being the originator of false practices and base deeds, although some have calumniated it, though it be the clear image of truth, a divine gift to the Greeks;[1] nor does it drag us away from the faith, as if we were bewitched by some delusive art, but rather, so to speak, by the use of an ampler circuit, obtains a common exercise

---

1. [Noteworthy with his *caveat* about *comparison*. He deals with Greek philosophers as surgeons do with comparative anatomy.]

demonstrative of the faith. Further, the juxtaposition of doctrines, by comparison, saves the truth, from which follows knowledge.

Philosophy came into existence, not on its own account, but for the advantages reaped by us from knowledge, we receiving a firm persuasion of true perception, through the knowledge of things comprehended by the mind. For I do not mention that the *Stromata*, forming a body of varied erudition, wish artfully to conceal the seeds of knowledge. As, then, he who is fond of hunting captures the game after seeking, tracking, scenting, hunting it down with dogs; so truth, when sought and got with toil, appears a delicious thing. Why, then, you will ask, did you think it fit that such an arrangement should be adopted in your memoranda? Because there is great danger in divulging the secret of the true philosophy to those, whose delight it is unsparingly to speak against everything, not justly; and who shout forth all kinds of names and words indecorously, deceiving themselves and beguiling those who adhere to them. "For the Hebrews seek signs," as the apostle says, "and the Greeks seek after wisdom."[2]. . .

Chapter V.—PHILOSOPHY THE HANDMAID OF THEOLOGY

Accordingly, before the advent of the Lord, philosophy was necessary to the Greeks for righteousness. And now it becomes conducive to piety; being a kind of preparatory training to those who attain to faith through demonstration. "For thy foot," it is said, "will not stumble, if thou refer what is good, whether belonging to the Greeks or to us, to Providence."[3] For God is the cause of all good things; but of some primarily, as of the Old and the New Testament; and of others by consequence, as philosophy. Perchance, too, philosophy was given to the Greeks directly and primarily, till the Lord should call the Greeks. For this was a schoolmaster to bring 'the Hellenic mind," as the law, the Hebrews, "to Christ."[4] Philosophy, therefore, was a preparation, paving the way for him who is perfected in Christ.

"Now," says Solomon, "defend wisdom, and it will exalt thee, and it will shield thee with a crown of pleasure."[5] For when thou hast strengthened wisdom with a cope by philosophy, and with right ex-

2. I *Cor.* i. 22.
3. *Prov.* iii. 23.
4. *Gal.* iii. 24.
5. *Prov.* iv. 8, 9.

penditure, thou wilt preserve it unassailable by sophists. The way of truth is therefore one. But into it, as into a perennial river, streams flow from all sides. It has been therefore said by inspiration: "Hear, my son, and receive my words; that thine may be the many ways of life. For I teach thee the ways of wisdom; that the fountains fail thee not,"[6] which gush forth from the earth itself. Not only did He enumerate several ways of salvation for any one righteous man, but He added many other ways of many righteous, speaking thus: "The paths of the righteous shine like the light."[7] The commandments and the modes of preparatory training are to be regarded as the ways and appliances of life.

"Jerusalem, Jerusalem, how often would I have gathered thy children, as a hen her chickens!"[8] And Jerusalem is, when interpreted, "a vision of peace." He therefore shows prophetically, that those who peacefully contemplate sacred things are in manifold ways trained to their calling. What then? He "would," and could not. How often, and where? Twice; by the prophets, and by the advent. The expression, then, "How often," shows wisdom to be manifold; and in every mode of quantity and quality, it by all means saves some, both in time and in eternity. "For the Spirit of the Lord fills the earth." And if any should violently say that the reference is to the Hellenic culture, when it is said, "Give not heed to an evil woman; for honey drops from the lips of a harlot," let him hear what follows: "who lubricates thy throat for the time." But philosophy does not flatter. Who, then, does He allude to as having committed fornication? He adds expressly, "For the feet of folly lead those who use her, after death, to Hades. But her steps are not supported." Therefore remove thy way far from silly pleasure. "Stand not at the doors of her house, that thou yield not thy life to others." And He testifies, "Then shalt thou repent in old age, when the flesh of thy body is consumed." For this is the end of foolish pleasure. Such, indeed, is the case. And when He says, "Be not much with a strange woman,"[9] He admonishes us to use indeed, but not to linger and spend time with, secular culture. For what was bestowed on each generation advantageously, and at seasonable times, is a preliminary training for the word of the Lord. "For already some men, ensnared by the charms of handmaidens, have despised their consort philosophy, and have grown old, some of them in music, some in

6. *Prov.* iv, 10, 11, 21.
7. *Prov.* iv. 18.
8. *Matt.* xxiii. 37 ; *Luke* xiii. 34.
9. *Prov.* v. 2, 3, 5, 8, 9, 11, 20.

geometry, others in grammar, the most in rhetoric."[10] "But as the encyclical branches of study contribute to philosophy, which is their mistress; so also philosophy itself co-operates for the acquisition of wisdom. For philosophy is the study of wisdom, and wisdom is the knowledge of things divine and human; and their causes." Wisdom is therefore queen of philosophy, as philosophy is of preparatory culture. For if philosophy "professes control of the tongue, and the belly, and the parts below the belly, it is to be chosen on its own account. But it appears more worthy of respect and pre-eminence, if cultivated for the honour and knowledge of God."[11] And Scripture will afford a testimony to what has been said in what follows. Sarah was at one time barren, being Abraham's wife. Sarah having no child, assigned her maid, by name Hagar, the Egyptian, to Abraham, in order to get children. Wisdom, therefore, who dwells with the man of faith (and Abraham was reckoned faithful and righteous), was still barren and without child in that generation, not having brought forth to Abraham aught allied to virtue. And she, as was proper, thought that he, being now in the time of progress, should have intercourse with secular culture first (by Egyptian the world is designated figuratively); and afterwards should approach to her according to divine providence, and beget Isaac."[12]

And Philo interprets Hagar to mean "sojourning." For it is said in connection with this, "Be not much with a strange woman."[13] Sarah he interprets to mean "my princedom." He, then, who has received previous training is at liberty to approach to wisdom, which is supreme, from which grows up the race of Israel. These things show that that wisdom can be acquired through instruction, to which Abraham attained, passing from the contemplation of heavenly things to the faith and righteousness which are according to God. And Isaac is shown to mean "self-taught"; wherefore also he is discovered to be a type of Christ. He was the husband of one wife Rebecca, which they translate "Patience." And Jacob is said to have consorted with several, his name being interpreted "Exerciser." And exercises are engaged in by means of many and various dogmas. Whence, also, he who is really "endowed with the power of seeing" is called Israel,[14] having much experience, and being fit for exercise.

---

10. Philo Judæus, *On Seeking Instruction*, 435.

11. Quoted from Philo with some alterations.

12. See Philo, *Meeting to Seek Instruction*.

13. *Prov.* v. 20. Philo, *On Meeting to Seek Knowledge*, near beginning.

14. Philo, in the book above cited, interprets "Israel," "seeing God." From this book all the instances and etymologies occurring here are taken.

Something else may also have been shown by the three patriarchs, namely, that the sure seal of knowledge is composed of nature, of education, and exercise.

You may have also another image of what has been said, in Thamar sitting by the way, and presenting the appearance of a harlot, on whom the studious Judas (whose name is interpreted "powerful"), who left nothing unexamined and uninvestigated, looked; and turned aside to her, preserving his profession towards God. Wherefore also, when Sarah was jealous at Hagar being preferred to her, Abraham, as choosing only what was profitable in secular philosophy, said, "Behold, thy maid is in thine hands: deal with her as it pleases thee";[15] manifestly meaning, "I embrace secular culture as youthful, and a handmaid; but thy knowledge I honour and reverence as true wife." And Sarah afflicted her; which is equivalent to corrected and admonished her. It has therefore been well said, "My son, despise not thou the correction of God; nor faint when thou art rebuked of Him. For whom the LORD loveth He chasteneth, and scourgeth every son whom He receiveth."[16] And the foresaid Scriptures, when examined in other places, will be seen to exhibit other mysteries. We merely therefore assert here, that philosophy is characterized by investigation into truth and the nature of things (this is the truth of which the Lord Himself said, "I am the truth"[17]); and that, again, the preparatory training for rest in Christ exercises the mind, rouses the intelligence, and begets an inquiring shrewdness, by means of the true philosophy, which the initiated possess, having found it, or rather received it, from the truth itself. . . .

Chapter VII.—THE ECLECTIC PHILOSOPHY PAVES THE WAY FOR DIVINE VIRTUE

The Greek preparatory culture, therefore, with philosophy itself, is shown to have come down from God to men, not with a definite direction, but in the way in which showers fall down on the good land, and on the dunghill, and on the houses. And similarly both the grass and the wheat sprout; and the figs and any other reckless trees grow on sepulchres. And things that grow, appear as a type of truths. For they enjoy the same influence of the rain. But they have not the same grace

---

15. *Gen.* xvi. 6.
16. *Prov.* iii. 11, 12; *Heb.* xii. 5, 6.
17. *John* xiv. 6.

as those which spring up in rich soil, inasmuch as they are withered or plucked up. And here we are aided by the parable of the sower, which the Lord interpreted. For the husbandman of the soil which is among men is one; He who from the beginning, from the foundation of the world, sowed nutritious seeds; He who in each age rained down the Lord, the World. But the times and places which received [such gifts], created the differences which exist. Further, the husbandman sows not only wheat (of which there are many varieties), but also other seeds—barley, and beans, and peas, and vetches, and vegetable and flower seeds. And to the same husbandry belongs both planting and the operations necessary in the nurseries, and gardens, and orchards, and the planting and rearing of all sorts of trees.

In like manner, not only the care of sheep, but the care of herds, and breeding of horses, and dogs, and bee-craft, all arts, and to speak comprehensively, the care of flocks and the rearing of animals, differ from each other more or less, but are all useful for life. And philosophy—I do not mean the Stoic, or the Platonic, or the Epicurean, or the Aristotelian, but whatever has been well said by each of those sects, which teach righteousness along with a science pervaded by piety,—this eclectic whole I call philosophy.[18] But such conclusions of human reasonings, as men have cut away and falsified, I would never call divine.

And now we must look also at this, that if ever those who know not how to do well, live well;[19] for they have lighted on well-doing. Some, too, have aimed well at the word of truth through understanding. "But Abraham was not justified by works, but by faith."[20] It is therefore of no advantage to them after the end of life, even if they do good works now, if they have not faith. Wherefore also the Scriptures were translated into the language of the Greeks, in order that they might never be able to allege the excuse of ignorance, inasmuch as they are able to hear also what we have in our hands, if they only wish. One speaks in one way of the truth, in another way the truth interprets itself. The guessing at truth is one thing, and truth itself is another. Resemblance is one thing, the thing itself is another. And the one results from learning and practice, the other from power and faith. For the teaching of piety is a gift, but faith is grace. "For by doing the will of God we know the will of God."[21] "Open, then,"

---

18. [Most important as defining Clement's system, and his use of this word, "philosophy."]

19. Something seems wanting to complete the sense.

20. *Rom.* iv.

says the Scripture, "the gates of righteousness; and I will enter in, and confess to the LORD." But the paths to righteousness (since God saves in many ways, for He is good) are many and various, and lead to the Lord's way and gate. And if you ask the royal and true entrance, you will hear, "This is the gate of the LORD, the righteous shall enter in by it."[22] While there are many gates open, that in righteousness is in Christ, by which all the blessed enter, and direct their steps in the sanctity of knowledge. Now Clemens, in his Epistle to the Corinthians, while expounding the differences of those who are approved according to the Church, says expressly, "One may be a believer; one may be powerful in uttering knowledge; one may be wise in discriminating between words; one may be terrible in deeds."[23] . . .

Book II

Chapter II.—THE KNOWLEDGE OF GOD CAN BE ATTAINED ONLY THROUGH FAITH

"Be not elated on account of thy wisdom," say the Proverbs. "In all thy ways acknowledge her, that she may direct thy ways, and that thy foot may not stumble." By these remarks he means to show that our deeds ought to be conformable to reason, and to manifest further that we ought to select and possess what is useful out of all culture. Now the ways of wisdom are various that lead right to the way of truth. Faith is the way. "Thy foot shall not stumble" is said with reference to some who seem to oppose the one divine administration of Providence. Whence it is added, "Be not wise in thine own eyes," according to the impious ideas which revolt against the administration of God. "But fear God," who alone is powerful. Whence it follows as a consequence that we are not to oppose God. The sequel especially teaches

---

21. *John* vii. 17.
22. *Ps.* cxviii. 19, 20.
23. First Epistle of Clement, chap. xlviii.

clearly, that "the fear of God is departure from evil;" for it is said, "and depart from all evil." Such is the discipline of wisdom ("for whom the Lord loveth He chastens"[24]), causing pain in order to produce understanding, and restoring to peace and immortality. Accordingly, the Barbarian philosophy, which we follow, is in reality perfect and true. And so it is said in the book of Wisdom: "For He hath given me the unerring knowledge of things that exist, to know the constitution of the word," and so forth, down to "and the virtues of roots." Among all these he comprehends natural science, which treats of all the phenomena in the world of sense. And in continuation, he alludes also to intellectual objects in what he subjoins: "And what is hidden or manifest I know; for Wisdom, the artificer of all things, taught me."[25] You have, in brief, the professed aim of our philosophy; and the learning of these branches, when pursued with right course of conduct, leads through Wisdom, the artificer of all things, to the Ruler of all,—a Being difficult to grasp and apprehend, ever receding and withdrawing from him who pursues. But He who is far off has—oh ineffable marvel! —come very near. "I am a God that draws near," says the Lord. He is in essence remote; "for how is it that what is begotten can have approached the Unbegotten?" But He is very near in virtue of that power which holds all things in its embrace. "Shall one do aught in secret, and I see him not?"[26] For the power of God is always present, in contact with us, in the exercise of inspection, of beneficence, of instruction. Whence Moses, persuaded that God is not to be known by human wisdom, said, "Show me Thy glory";[27] and into the thick darkness where God's voice was, pressed to enter—that is, into the inaccessible and invisible ideas respecting Existence. For God is not in darkness or in place, but above both space and time, and qualities of objects. Wherefore neither is He at any time in a part, either as containing or as contained, either by limitation or by section. "For what house will ye build to Me?" saith the Lord.[28] Nay, He has not even built one for Himself, since He cannot be contained. And though heaven be called His throne, not even thus is He contained, but He rests delighted in the creation.

It is clear, then, that the truth has been hidden from us; and if that has been already shown by one example, we shall establish it a

---

24. *Prov.* iii. 5, 6, 7, 12, 23.
25. *Wisd.* vii. 17, 20, 21, 22.
26. *Jer.* xxiii. 23, 24.
27. *Ex.* xxxiii. 18.
28. *Isa.* lxvi. 1.

little after by several more. How entirely worthy of approbation are they who are both willing to learn, and able, according to Solomon, "to know wisdom and instruction, and to perceive the words of wisdom, to receive knotty words, and to perceive true righteousness," there being another [righteousness as well], not according to the truth, taught by the Greek laws, and by the rest of the philosophers. "And to direct judgments," it is said—not those of the bench, but he means that we must preserve sound and free of error the judicial faculty which is within us—"That I may give subtlety to the simple, to the young man sense and understanding. For the wise man," who has been persuaded to obey the commandments, "having heard these things, will become wiser" by knowledge; and "the intelligent man will acquire rule, and will understand a parable and a dark word, the sayings and enigmas of the wise."[29] For it is not spurious words which those inspired by God and those who are gained over by them adduce, nor is it snares in which the most of the sophists entangle the young, spending their time on nought true. But those who possess the Holy Spirit "search the deep things of God,"[30]—that is, grasp the secret that is in the prophecies. "To impart of holy things to the dogs" is forbidden, so long as they remain beasts. For never ought those who are envious and perturbed, and still infidel in conduct, shameless in barking at investigation, to dip in the divine and clear stream of the living water. "Let not the waters of thy fountain overflow, and let thy waters spread over thine own streets."[31] For it is not many who understand such things as they fall in with; or know them even after learning them, though they think they do, according to the worthy Heraclitus. Does not even he seem to thee to censure those who believe not? "Now my just one shall live by faith,"[32] the prophet said. And another prophet also says, "Except ye believe, neither shall ye understand."[33] For how ever could the soul admit the transcendental contemplation of such themes, while unbelief respecting what was to be learned struggled within? But faith, which the Greeks disparage, deeming it futile and barbarous, is a voluntary preconception, the assent of piety—"the subject of things hoped for, the evidence of things not seen," according to the divine apostle. "For hereby," pre-eminently, "the elders obtained a good report. But without faith it is impossible to

29. *Prov.* i. 2-6.
30. I Cor. ii. 10.
31. *Prov.* v. 16.
32. *Hab.* ii. 4.
33. *Isa.* vii. 9.

please God."[34] Others have defined faith to be a uniting assent to an unseen object, as certainly the proof of an unknown thing is an evident assent. If then it be choice, being desirous of something, the desire is in this instance intellectual. And since choice is the beginning of action, faith is discovered to be the beginning of action, being the foundation of rational choice in the case of any one who exhibits to himself the previous demonstration through faith. Voluntarily to follow what is useful, is the first principle of understanding. Unswerving choice, then, gives considerable momentum in the direction of knowledge. The exercise of faith directly becomes knowledge, reposing on a sure foundation. Knowledge, accordingly, is defined by the sons of the philosophers as a habit, which cannot be overthrown by reason. Is there any other true condition such as this, except piety, of which alone the Word is teacher? I think not. Theophrastus says that sensation is the root of faith. For from it the rudimentary principles extend to the reason that is in us, and the understanding. He who believeth then the divine Scriptures with sure judgment, receives in the voice of God, who bestowed the Scripture, a demonstration that cannot be impugned. Faith, then, is not established by demonstration. "Blessed therefore those who, not having seen, yet have believed."[35] The Siren's songs, exhibiting a power above human, fascinated those that came near, conciliating them, almost against their will, to the reception of what was said.

Chapter III.—FAITH NOT A PRODUCT OF NATURE

Now the followers of Basilides regard faith as natural, as they also refer it to choice, [representing it] as finding ideas by intellectual comprehension without demonstration; while the followers of Valentinus assign faith to us, the simple, but will have it that knowledge springs up in their own selves (who are saved by nature) through the advantage of a germ of superior excellence, saying that it is as far removed from faith as the spiritual is from the animal. Further, the followers of Basilides say that faith as well as choice is proper according to every interval; and that in consequence of the supramundane selection mundane faith accompanies all nature, and that the free gift of faith is comformable to the hope of each. Faith, then, is no longer the direct result of free choice, if it is a natural advantage.

34. *Heb.* xi. 1, 2, 6.
35. *John* xx. 29.

Nor will he who has not believed, not being the author [of his unbelief], meet with a due recompense; and he that has believed is not the cause [of his belief]. And the entire peculiarity and difference of belief and unbelief will not fall under either praise or censure, if we reflect rightly, since there attaches to it the antecedent natural necessity proceeding from the Almighty. And if we are pulled like inanimate things by the puppet-strings of natural powers, willingness and unwillingness, and impulse, which is the antecedent of both, are mere redundancies. And for my part, I am utterly incapable of conceiving such an animal as has its appetencies, which are moved by external causes, under the dominion of necessity. And what place is there any longer for the repentance of him who was once an unbeliever, through which comes forgiveness of sins? So that neither is baptism rational, nor the blessed seal, nor the Son, nor the Father. But God, as I think, turns out to be the distribution to men of natural powers, which has not as the foundation of salvation voluntary faith.

Chapter IV.—FAITH THE FOUNDATION OF ALL KNOWLEDGE

But we, who have heard by the Scriptures that self-determining choice and refusal have been given by the Lord to men, rest in the infallible criterion of faith, manifesting a willing spirit, since we have chosen life and believe God through His voice. And he who has believed the Word knows the matter to be true; for the Word is truth. But he who has disbelieved Him that speaks, has disbelieved God.

"By faith we understand that the worlds were framed by the word of God, so that what is seen was not made of things which appear," says the apostle. "By faith Abel offered to God a fuller sacrifice than Cain, by which he received testimony that he was righteous, God giving testimony to him respecting his gifts; and by it he, being dead, yet speaketh," and so forth, down to "than enjoy the pleasures of sin for a season."[36] Faith having, therefore, justified these before the law, made them heirs of the divine promise. Why then should I review and adduce any further testimonies of faith from the history in our hands? "For the time would fail me were I to tell of Gideon, Barak, Samson, Jephtha, David, and Samuel, and the prophets," and what follows.[37] Now, inasmuch as there are four things in which the truth resides—

---

36. *Heb.* xi. 3, 4, 25.
37. *Heb.* xi. 32.

Sensation, Understanding, Knowledge, Opinion,—intellectual apprehension is first in the order of nature; but in our case, and in relation to ourselves, Sensation is first, and of Sensation and Understanding the essence of Knowledge is formed; and evidence is common to Understanding and Sensation. Well, Sensation is the ladder to Knowledge; while Faith, advancing over the pathway of the objects of sense, leaves Opinion behind, and speeds to things free of deception, and reposes in the truth.

Should one say that Knowledge is founded on demonstration by a process of reasoning, let him hear that first principles are incapable of demonstration; for they are known neither by art nor sagacity. For the latter is conversant about objects that are susceptible of change, while the former is practical solely, and not theoretical. Hence it is thought that the first cause of the universe can be apprehended by faith alone. For all knowledge is capable of being taught; and what is capable of being taught is founded on what is known before. But the first cause of the universe was not previously known to the Greeks; neither, accordingly, to Thales, who came to the conclusion that water was the first cause; nor to the other natural philosophers who succeeded him, since it was Anaxagoras who was the first who assigned to Mind the supremacy over material things. But not even he preserved the dignity suited to the efficient cause, describing as he did certain silly vortices, together with the inertia and even foolishness of Mind. Wherefore also the Word says, "Call no man master on earth."[38] For knowledge is a state of mind that results from demonstration; but faith is a grace which from what is indemonstrable conducts to what is universal and simple, what is neither with matter, nor matter, nor under matter. But those who believe not, as to be expected, drag all down from heaven, and the region of the invisible, to earth, "absolutely grasping with their hands rocks and oaks," according to Plato. For, clinging to all such things, they asseverate that that alone exists which can be touched and handled, defining body and essence to be identical: disputing against themselves, they very piously defend the existence of certain intellectual and bodiless forms descending somewhere from above from the invisible world, vehemently maintaining that there is a true essence. "Lo, I make new things," saith the Word, "which eye hath not seen, nor ear heard, nor hath it entered into the heart of man."[39] With a new eye, a new ear, a new heart, whatever can be seen and heard is to be apprehended, by the faith and understanding of

38. *Matt.* xxiii. 9.
39. *Isa.* lxiv. 4; I *Cor.* ii. 9.

the disciples of the Lord, who speak, hear, and act spiritually. For there is genuine coin, and other that is spurious; which no less deceives unprofessionals, that it does not the money-changers; who know through having learned how to separate and distinguish what has a false stamp from what is genuine. So the money-changer only says to the unprofessional man that the coin is counterfeit. But the reason why, only the banker's apprentice, and he that is trained to this department, learns.

Now Aristotle says that the judgment which follows knowledge is in truth faith. Accordingly, faith is something superior to knowledge, and is its criterion. Conjecture, which is only a feeble supposition, counterfeits faith; as the flatterer counterfeits a friend, and the wolf the dog. And as the workman sees that by learning certain things he becomes an artificer, and the helmsman by being instructed in the art will be able to steer; he does not regard the mere wishing to become excellent and good enough, but he must learn it by the exercise of obedience. But to obey the Word, whom we call Instructor, is to believe Him, going against Him in nothing. For how can we take up a position of hostility to God? Knowledge, accordingly, is characterized by faith; and faith, by a kind of divine mutual and reciprocal correspondence, becomes characterized by knowledge.

Epicurus, too, who very greatly preferred pleasure to truth, supposes faith to be a preconception of the mind; and defines preconception to be a grasping at something evident, and at the clear understanding of the thing; and asserts that, without preconception, no one can either inquire, or doubt, or judge, or even argue. How can one, without a preconceived idea of what he is aiming after, learn about that which is the subject of his investigation? He, again, who has learned has already turned his preconception into comprehension. And if he who learns, learns not without a preconceived idea which takes in what is expressed, and that man has ears to hear the truth. And happy is the man that speaks to the ears of those who hear; as happy certainly also is he who is a child of obedience. Now to hear is to understand. If, then, faith is nothing else than a preconception of the mind in regard to what is the subject of discourse, and obedience is so called, and understanding and persuasion; no one shall learn aught without faith, since no one [learns aught] without preconception. Consequently there is a more ample demonstration of the complete truth of what was spoken by the prophet, "Unless ye believe, neither will ye understand." Paraphrasing this oracle, Heraclitus of Ephesus says, "If a man hope not, he will not find that which is not hoped for, seeing it is inscrutable and inaccessible." Plato the philosopher, also, in *The Laws,* says, "that he who would be blessed and happy, must be straight from the beginning a partaker of the truth, so as to live true for as long a period as possible; for he is a man of faith. But the unbeliever is one to whom voluntary falsehood is agreeable; and the man to whom involuntary falsehood is agreeable is senseless; neither of which is desirable. For he who is devoid of friendliness, is faithless and ignorant." And does he not enigmatically say in *Euthydemus,* that this is "the regal wisdom"? In *The Statesman* he says expressly, "So that the knowledge of the true king is kingly; and he who possesses it, whether a prince or private person, shall by all means, in consequence of this act, be rightly styled royal." Now those who have believed in Christ both are and are called *Chrestoi* (good), as those who are cared for by the true king are kingly. For as the wise are wise by their wisdom, and those observant of law are so by the law; so also those who belong to Christ the King are kings, and those that are Christ's Christians. Then, in continuation, he adds clearly, "What is right will turn out to be lawful, law being in its nature right reason, and not found in writings or elsewhere." And the stranger of Elea pronounces the kingly and statesmanlike man *"a living law."* Such is he who fulfils the law, "doing the will of the Father,"[40] inscribed on a lofty pillar, and set as an example of divine virtue to all who possess the power of seeing. The Greeks are acquainted with the staves of the Ephori at Lacedæmon, inscribed with the law on wood. But my law, as was said above, is both royal and living; and it is right reason. "Law, which is king of all—of mortals and immortals," as the Bœotian Pindar sings. For Speusippus,[41] in the first book against Cleophon, seems to write like Plato on this wise: "For if royalty be a good thing, and the wise man the only king and ruler, the law, which is right reason, is good;" which is the case. The Stoics teach what is in conformity with this, assigning kinghood, priesthood, prophecy, legislation, riches, true beauty, noble birth, freedom, to the wise man alone. But that he is exceedingly difficult to find, is confessed even by them. . . .

---

40. *Matt.* xxi. 31.
41. Plato's successor.

Book VI

Chapter VII.—WHAT TRUE PHILOSOPHY IS, AND WHENCE SO CALLED

As we have long ago pointed out, what we propose as our subject is not the discipline which obtains in each sect, but that which is really philosophy, strictly systematic Wisdom, which furnishes acquaintance with the things which pertain to life. And we define Wisdom to be certain knowledge, being a sure and irrefragable apprehension of things divine and human, comprehending the present, past, and future, which the Lord hath taught us, both by His advent and by the prophets. And it is irrefragable by reason, inasmuch as it has been communicated. And so it is wholly true according to [God's] intention, as being known through means of the Son. And in one aspect it is eternal, and in another it becomes useful in time. Partly it is one and the same, partly many and indifferent—partly without any movement of passion, partly with passionate desire—partly perfect, partly incomplete.

This wisdom, then—rectitude of soul and of reason, and purity of life—is the object of the desire of philosophy, which is kindly and lovingly disposed towards wisdom, and does everything to attain it.

Now those are called philosophers, among us, who love Wisdom, the Creator and Teacher of all things, that is, the knowledge of the Son of God; and among the Greeks, those who undertake arguments on virtue. Philosophy, then, consists of such dogmas found in each sect (I mean those of philosophy) as cannot be impugned, with a corresponding life, collected into one selection; and these, stolen from the Barbarian God-given grace, have been adorned by Greek speech. For some they have borrowed, and others they have misunderstood. And in the case of others, what they have spoken, in consequence of being moved, they have not yet perfectly worked out; and others by human conjecture and reasoning, in which also they stumble. And they think that they have hit the truth perfectly; but as we understand them, only partially. They know, then, nothing more than this world. And it is just like geometry, which treats of measures and magnitudes and forms, by delineation on plane-surfaces; and just as painting appears to take in the whole field of view in the scenes represented. But it gives a false description of the view, according to the rules of the art, employing the signs that result from the incidents of the lines of vision. By this means, the higher and lower points in the view, and those between, are preserved; and some objects seem to appear in the foreground, and others in the background, and others to appear in some other way, on the smooth and level surface. So also the philosophers copy the truth, after the manner of painting. And always in the case of each one of them, their self-love is the cause of all their mistakes. Wherefore one ought not, in the desire for the glory that terminates in men, to be animated by self-love; but loving God, to become really holy with wisdom. If, then, one treats what is particular as universal, and regards that, which serves, as the Lord, he misses the truth, not understanding what was spoken by David by way of confession: "I have eaten earth [ashes] like bread."[42] Now, self-love and self-conceit are, in his view, earth and error. But if so, science and knowledge are derived from instruction. And if there is instruction, you must seek for the master. Cleanthes claims Zeno, and Metrodorus Epicurus, and Theophrastus Aristotle, and Plato Socrates. But if I come to Pythagoras, and Pherecydes, and Thales, and the first wise men, I come to a stand in my search for their teacher. Should you say the Egyptians, the Indians, the Babylonians, and the Magi themselves, I will not stop from asking their teacher. And I lead you up to the first generation of men; and from that point I begin to investigate Who is their teacher. No one of men; for they had not yet learned. Nor yet any of the angels: for in the way that angels, in virtue of being angels, speak, men do not hear; nor, as we have ears, have they a tongue to correspond; nor would any one attribute to the angels organs of speech, lips I mean, and the parts contiguous, throat, and windpipe, and chest, breath and air to vibrate. And God is far from calling aloud in the unapproachable sanctity, separated as He is from even the archangels.

And we also have already heard that angels learned the truth, and their rulers over them; for they had a beginning. It remains, then, for us, ascending to seek their teacher. And since the unoriginated Being is one, the Omnipotent God; one, too, is the First-begotten, "by whom all things were made, and without whom not one thing ever was made."[43] "For one, in truth, is God, who formed the beginning of all things;" pointing out "the first-begotten Son," Peter writes, accurately comprehending the statement, "In the beginning God made the heaven

---

42. *Ps.* cii. 9.
43. *John* i. 3.

and the earth."[44] And He is called Wisdom by all the prophets. This is He who is the Teacher of all created beings, the Fellow-counsellor of God, who foreknew all things; and He from above, from the first foundation of the world, "in many ways and many times,"[45] trains and perfects; whence it is rightly said, "Call no man your teacher on earth."[46]

You see whence the true philosophy has its handles; though the Law be the image and shadow of the truth: for the Law is the shadow of the truth. But the self-love of the Greeks proclaims certain men as their teachers. As, then, the whole family runs back to God the Creator;[47] so also all the teaching of good things, which justifies, does to the Lord, and leads and contributes to this.

But if from any creature they received in any way whatever the seeds of the Truth, they did not nourish them; but committing them to a barren and rainless soil, they choked them with weeds, as the Pharisees revolted from the Law, by introducing human teachings,— the cause of these being not the Teacher, but those who choose to disobey. But those of them who believed the Lord's advent and the plain teaching of the Scriptures, attain to the knowledge of the law; as also those addicted to philosophy, by the teaching of the Lord, are introduced into the knowledge of the true philosophy: "For the oracles of the Lord are pure oracles, melted in the fire, tried in the earth, purified seven times."[48] Just as silver often purified, so is the just man brought to the test, becoming the Lord's coin and receiving the royal image. Or, since Solomon also calls the "tongue of the righteous man gold that has been subjected to fire."[49] intimating that the doctrine which has been proved, and is wise, is to be praised and received, whenever it is amply tried by the earth: that is, when the gnostic soul is in manifold ways sanctified, through withdrawal from earthy fires. And the body in which it dwells is purified, being appropriated to the pureness of a holy temple. But the first purification which takes place in the body, the soul being first, is abstinence from evil things, which some consider perfection, and is, in truth, the perfection of the common believer—Jew and Greek. But in the case of the Gnostic, after that which is reckoned

44. *Gen.* i. 1.
45. *Heb.* i. 1.
46. *Matt.* xxiii. 8-10.
47. *Eph.* iii. 14, 15.
48. *Ps.* xii. 6.
49. *Prov.* x. 20.

perfection in others, his righteousness advances to activity in well-doing. And in whomsoever the increased force of righteousness advances to the doing of good, in his case perfection abides in the fixed habit of well-doing after the likeness of God. For those who are the seed of Abraham, and besides servants of God, are "the called;" and the sons of Jacob are the elect—they who have tripped up the energy of wickedness.

If, then, we assert that Christ Himself is Wisdom, and that it was His working which showed itself in the prophets, by which the gnostic tradition may be learned, as He Himself taught the apostles during His presence; then it follows that the *gnosis,* which is the knowledge and apprehension of things present, future, and past, which is sure and reliable, as being imparted and revealed by the Son of God, is wisdom.

And if, too, the end of the wise man is contemplation, that of those who are still philosophers aims at it, but never attains it, unless by the process of learning it receives the prophetic utterance which has been made known, by which it grasps both the present, the future, and the past—how they are, were, and shall be.

And the *gnosis* itself is that which has descended by transmission to a few, having been imparted unwritten by the apostles. Hence, then, knowledge or wisdom ought to be exercised up to the eternal and unchangeable habit of contemplation. . . .

Chapter X.—THE GNOSTIC AVAILS HIMSELF OF THE HELP OF ALL HUMAN KNOWLEDGE

For to him knowledge (*gnosis*) is the principal thing. Consequently, therefore, he applies to the subjects that are a training for knowledge, taking from each branch of study its contribution to the truth. Prosecuting, then, the proportion of harmonies in music; and in arithmetic noting the increasing and decreasing of numbers, and their relations to one another, and how the most of things fall under some proportion of numbers; studying geometry, which is abstract essence, he perceives a continuous distance, and an immutable essence which is different from these bodies. And by astronomy, again, raised from the earth in his mind, he is elevated along with heaven, and will revolve with its revolution; studying ever divine things, and their harmony with each other; from which Abraham starting, ascended to the knowledge of Him who created them. Further, the Gnostic will avail himself of dialectics, fixing on the distinction of genera into species, and will master the distinction of existences, till he come to what are primary and simple.

But the multitude are frightened at the Hellenic philosophy, as children are at masks, being afraid lest it lead them astray. But if the faith (for I cannot call it knowledge) which they possess be such as to be dissolved by plausible speech, let it be by all means dissolved, and let them confess that they will not retain the truth. For truth is immoveable; but false opinion dissolves. We choose, for instance, one purple by comparison with another purple. So that, if one confesses that he has not a heart that has been made right, he has not the table of the money-changers or the test of words. And how can he be any longer a money-changer, who is not able to prove and distinguish spurious coin, even offhand?

Now David cried, "The righteous shall not be shaken for ever;"[50] neither, consequently, by deceptive speech nor by erring pleasure. Whence he shall never be shaken from his own heritage. "He shall not be afraid of evil tidings;"[51] consequently neither of unfounded calumny, nor of the false opinion around him. No more will he dread cunning words, who is capable of distinguishing them, or of answering rightly to questions asked. Such a bulwark are dialectics, that truth cannot be trampled under foot by the Sophists. "For it behoves those who praise in the holy name of the Lord," according to the prophet, "to rejoice in heart, seeking the Lord. Seek then Him, and be strong. Seek His face continually in every way."[52] "For, having spoken at sundry times and in divers manners,"[53] it is not in one way only that He is known.

It is, then, not by availing himself of these as virtues that our Gnostic will be deeply learned. But by using them as helps in distinguishing what is common and what is peculiar, he will admit the truth. For the cause of all error and false opinion, is inability to distinguish in what respect things are common, and in what respects they differ. For unless, in things that are distinct, one closely watch speech, he will inadvertently confound what is common and what is peculiar. And where this takes place, he must of necessity fall into pathless tracts and error.

The distinction of names and things also in the Scriptures them- ▸

---

50. *Ps.* cxii. 6.
51. *Ps.* cxii. 7.
52. *Ps.* cv. 3, 4.
53. *Heb.* i. 1.

selves produces great light in men's souls. For it is necessary to understand expressions which signify several things, and several expressions when they signify one thing. The result of which is accurate answering. But it is necessary to avoid the great futility which occupies itself in irrelevant matters; since the Gnostic avails himself of branches of learning as auxiliary preparatory exercises, in order to the accurate communication of the truth, as far as attainable and with as little distraction as possible, and for defence against reasonings that plot for the extinction of the truth. He will not then be deficient in what contributes to proficiency in the curriculum of studies and the Hellenic philosophy; but not principally, but necessarily, secondarily, and on account of circumstances. For what those labouring in heresies use wickedly, the Gnostic will use rightly.

Therefore the truth that appears in the Hellenic philosophy, being partial, the real truth, like the sun glancing on the colours both white and black, shows what like each of them is. So also it exposes all sophistical plausibility. Rightly, then, was it proclaimed also by the Greeks:—

"Truth the queen is the beginning of great virtue."[54]

Book VII

Chapter II.—THE SON THE RULER AND SAVIOUR OF ALL

To know God is, then, the first step of faith; then, through confidence in the teaching of the Saviour, to consider the doing of wrong in any way as not suitable to the knowledge of God.

So the best thing on earth is the most pious man; and the best thing in heaven, the nearer in place and purer, is an angel, the partaker of the eternal and blessed life. But the nature of the Son, which is nearest to Him who is alone the Almighty One, is the most perfect, and most holy, and most potent, and most princely, and most kingly, and most beneficent. This is the highest excellence, which orders all things in accordance with the Father's will, and holds the helm of the universe in the best way, with unwearied and tireless power, working all things in which it operates, keeping in view its hidden designs. For

---

54. Pindar.

from His own point of view the Son of God is never displaced; not being divided, not severed, not passing from place to place; being always everywhere, and being contained nowhere; complete mind, the complete paternal light; all eyes, seeing all things, hearing all things, knowing all things, by His power scrutinizing the powers. To Him is placed in subjection all the host of angels and gods; He, the paternal Word, exhibiting the holy administration for Him who put [all] in subjection to Him.

Wherefore also all men are His; some through knowledge, and others not yet so; and some as friends, some as faithful servants, some as servants merely. This is the Teacher, who trains the Gnostic by mysteries, and the believer by good hopes, and the hard of heart by corrective discipline through sensible operation. Thence His providence is in private, in public, and everywhere.

And that He whom we call Saviour and Lord is the Son of God, the prophetic Scriptures explicitly prove. So the Lord of all, of Greeks and of Barbarians, persuades those who are willing. For He does not compel him who (through choosing and fulfilling, from Him, what pertains to laying hold of it the hope) is able to receive salvation from Him.

It is He who also gave philosophy to the Greeks by means of the inferior angels. For by an ancient and divine order the angels are distributed among the nations.[55] But the glory of those who believe is "the Lord's portion." For either the Lord does not care for all men; and this is the case either because He is unable (which is not to be thought, for it would be a proof of weakness), or because He is unwilling, which is not the attribute of a good being. And He who for our sakes assumed flesh capable of suffering, is far from being luxuriously indolent. Or He does care for all, which is befitting for Him who has become Lord of all. For He is Saviour; not [the Saviour] of some, and of others not. But in proportion to the adaptation possessed by each, He has dispensed His beneficence both to Greeks and Barbarians, even to those of them that were predestinated, and in due time called, the faithful and elect. Nor can He who called all equally, and assigned special honours to those who have believed in a specially excellent way, ever envy any. Nor can He who is the Lord of all, and serves above all the will of the good and almighty Father, ever be hindered by another. But neither does envy touch the Lord, who without beginning was impassible; nor are the things of men such as to be envied by the Lord. But it is another, he whom passion hath touched, who envies.

55. *Deut.* xxxii. 8, 9.

And it cannot be said that it is from ignorance that the Lord is not willing to save humanity, because He knows not how each one is to be cared for. For ignorance applies not to the God who, before the foundation of the world, was the counsellor of the Father. For He was the Wisdom "in which" the Sovereign God "delighted."[56] For the Son is the power of God, as being the Father's most ancient Word before the production of all things, and His Wisdom. He is then properly called the Teacher of the beings formed by Him. Nor does He ever abandon care for men, by being drawn aside from pleasure, who, having assumed flesh, which by nature is susceptible of suffering, trained it to the condition of impassibility. . . .

Chapter X.—STEPS TO PERFECTION

For knowledge (*gnosis*), to speak generally, a perfecting of man as man, is consummated by acquaintance with divine things, in character, life, and word, accordant and conformable to itself and to the divine Word. For by it faith is perfected, inasmuch as it is solely by it that the believer becomes perfect. Faith is an internal good, and without searching for God, confesses His existence, and glorifies Him as existent. Whence by starting from this faith, and being developed by it, through the grace of God, the knowledge respecting Him is to be acquired as far as possible.

Now we assert that knowledge (*gnosis*) differs from the wisdom σοφία, which is the result of teaching. For as far as anything is knowledge, so far it is certainly wisdom; but in as far as aught is wisdom, it is not certainly knowledge. For the term wisdom appears only in the knowledge of the uttered word.

But it is not doubting in reference to God, but believing, that is the foundation of knowledge. But Christ is both the foundation and the superstructure, by whom are both the beginning and the ends. And the extreme points, the beginning and the end—I mean faith and love—are not taught. But knowledge, conveyed from communication through the grace of God as a deposit, is entrusted to those who show themselves worthy of it; and from it the worth of love beams forth from light to light. For it is said, "To him that hath shall be given:"[57] to faith, knowledge; and to knowledge, love; and to love, the inheritance.

---

56. *Prov.* viii. 30.
57. *Luke* xix. 26.

And this takes place, whenever one hangs on the Lord by faith, by knowledge, by love, and ascends along with Him to where the God and guard of our faith and love is. Whence at last (on account of the necessity for very great preparation and previous training in order both to hear what is said, and for the composure of life, and for advancing intelligently to a point beyond the righteousness of the law) it is that knowledge is committed to those fit and selected for it. It leads us to the endless and perfect end, teaching us beforehand the future life that we shall lead, according to God, and with gods; after we are freed from all punishment and penalty which we undergo, in consequence of our sins, for salutary discipline. After which redemption the reward and the honours are assigned to those who have become perfect; when they have got done with purification, and ceased from all service, though it be holy service, and among saints. Then become pure in heart, and near to the Lord, there awaits them restoration to everlasting contemplation; and they are called by the appellation of gods, being destined to sit on thrones with the other gods that have been first put in their places by the Saviour.

Knowledge is therefore quick in purifying, and fit for that acceptable transformation to the better. Whence also with ease it removes [the soul] to what is akin to the soul, divine and holy, and by its own light conveys man through the mystic stages of advancement; till it restores the pure in heart to the crowning place of rest; teaching to gaze on God, face to face, with knowledge and comprehension. For in this consists the perfection of the gnostic soul, in its being with the Lord, where it is in immediate subjection to Him, after rising above all purification and service.

Faith is then, so to speak, a comprehensive knowledge of the essentials; and knowledge is the strong and sure demonstration of what is received by faith, built upon faith by the Lord's teaching, conveying [the soul] on to infallibility, science, and comprehension. And, in my view, the first saving change is that from heathenism to faith, as I said before; and the second, that from faith to knowledge. And the latter terminating in love, thereafter gives the loving to the loved, that which knows to that which is known. And, perchance, such an one has already attained the condition of "being equal to the angels."[58] Accordingly, after the highest excellence in the flesh, changing always duly to the better, he urges his flight to the ancestral hall, through the holy septenniad [of heavenly abodes] to the Lord's own mansion; to be a light, steady, and continuing eternally, entirely and in every part immutable. . . .

---

58. *Luke* xx. 36.

Origen
On First Principles
Book III

Chapter V.—THAT THE WORLD TOOK ITS BEGINNING IN TIME

And now, since there is one of the articles of the Church which is held principally in consequence of our belief in the truth of our sacred history, viz., that this world was created and took its beginning at a certain time, and, in conformity to the cycle of time decreed to all things, is to be destroyed on account of its corruption, there seems no absurdity in rediscussing a few points connected with this subject. And so far, indeed, as the credibility of Scripture is concerned, the declarations on such a matter seem easy of proof. Even the heretics, although widely opposed on many other things, yet on this appear to be at one, yielding to the authority of Scripture.

Concerning, then, the creation of the world, what portion of Scripture can give us more information regarding it, than the account which Moses has transmitted respecting its origin? And although it comprehends matters of profounder significance than the mere historical narrative appears to indicate, and contains very many things that are to be spiritually understood, and employs the letter, as a kind of veil, in treating of profound and mystical subjects; nevertheless the language of the narrator shows that all visible things were created at a certain time. But with regard to the consummation of the world, Jacob is the first who gives any information, in addressing his children in the words: "Gather yourselves together unto me, ye sons of Jacob, that I may tell you what shall be in the last days," or "after the last days."[1] If, then, there be "last days," or a period "succeeding the last days," the days

1. *Gen.* xlix. 1.

which had a beginning must necessarily come to an end. David, too, declares: "The heavens shall perish, but Thou shalt endure; yea, all of them shall wax old as doth a garment: as a vesture shalt Thou change them, and they shall be changed: but Thou art the same, and Thy years shall have no end."[2] Our Lord and Saviour, indeed, in the words, "He who made them at the beginning, made them male and female,"[3] Himself bears witness that the world was created; and again, when He says, "Heaven and earth shall pass away, but My word shall not pass away."[4] He points out that they are perishable, and must come to an end. The apostle, moreover, in declaring that "the creature was made subject to vanity, not willingly, but by reason of Him who hath subjected the same in hope, because the creature itself also shall be delivered from the bondage of corruption into the glorious liberty of the children of God,"[5] manifestly announces the end of the world; as he does also when he again says, "The fashion of this world passeth away."[6] Now, by the expression which he employs, "that the creature was made subject to vanity," he shows that there was a beginning to this world: for if the creature were made subject to vanity on account of some hope, it was certainly made subject from a cause; and seeing it was from a cause, it must necessarily have had a beginning; for, without some beginning, the creature could not be subject to vanity, nor could that creature hope to be freed from the bondage of corruption, which had not begun to serve. But any one who chooses to search at his leisure, will find numerous other passages in holy Scripture in which the world is both said to have a beginning and to hope for an end.

Now, if there be any one who would here oppose either the authority or credibility of our Scriptures, we would ask of him whether he asserts that God can, or cannot, comprehend all things? To assert that He cannot, would manifestly be an act of impiety. If then he answer, as he must, that God comprehends all things, it follows from the very fact of their being capable of comprehension, that they are understood to have a beginning and an end, seeing that which is altogether without any beginning cannot be at all comprehended. For however far understanding may extend, so far is the faculty of comprehending illimitably withdrawn and removed when there is held to be no beginning.

2. *Ps.* cii. 26, 27.
3. *Matt.* xix. 4.
4. *Matt.* xxiv. 35.
5. *Rom.* viii. 20, 21.
6. *I Cor.* vii. 31.

But this is the objection which they generally raise: they say, "If the world had its beginning in time, what was God doing before the world began? For it is at once impious and absurd to say that the nature of God is inactive and immoveable, or to suppose that goodness at one time did not do good, and omnipotence at one time did not exercise its power." Such is the objection which they are accustomed to make to our statement that this world had its beginning at a certain time, and that, agreeably to our belief in Scripture, we can calculate the years of its past duration. To these propositions I consider that none of the heretics can easily return an answer that will be in conformity with the nature of their opinions. But we can give a logical answer in accordance with the standard of religion, when we say that not then for the first time did God begin to work when He made this visible world; but as, after its destruction, there will be another world, so also we believe that others existed before the present came into being. And both of these positions will be confirmed by the authority of holy Scripture. For that there will be another world after this, is taught by Isaiah, who says, "There will be new heavens, and a new earth, which I shall make to abide in my sight, saith the LORD";[7] and that before this world others also existed is shown by Ecclesiastes, in the words: "What is that which hath been? Even that which shall be. And what is that which has been created? Even this which is to be created: and there is nothing altogether new under the sun. Who shall speak and declare, Lo, this is new? It hath already been in the ages which have been before us."[8] By these testimonies it is established both that there were ages before our own, and that there will be others after it. It is not, however, to be supposed that several worlds existed at once, but that, after the end of this present world, others will take their beginning; respecting which it is unnecessary to repeat each particular statement, seeing we have already done so in the preceding pages.

This point, indeed, is not to be idly passed by, that the holy Scriptures have called the creation of the world by a new and peculiar name, terming it καταβολή, which has been very improperly translated into Latin by "constitutio"; for in Greek καταβολή signifies rather "dejicere," i.e., to cast downwards,—a word which has been, as we have already remarked, improperly translated into Latin by the phrase "constitutio mundi," as in the Gospel according to John, where the Saviour says, "And there will be tribulation in those days, such as was not since

---

7. *Isa.* lxvi. 22.
8. *Eccles.* i. 9, 10.

the beginning of the world";[9] in which passage καταβολή is rendered by beginning (*constitutio*), which is to be understood as above explained. The apostle also, in the Epistle to the Ephesians, has employed the same language, saying, "Who hath chosen us before the foundation of the world";[10] and this foundation he calls καταβολή, to be understood in the same sense as before. It seems worth while, then, to inquire what is meant by this new term; and I am, indeed, of opinion that, as the end and consummation of the saints will be in those ages which are not seen, and are eternal, we must conclude (as frequently pointed out in the preceding pages), from a contemplation of that very end, that rational creatures had also a similar beginning. And if they had a beginning such as the end for which they hope, they existed undoubtedly from the very beginning in those ages which are not seen, and are eternal. And if this is so, then there has been a descent from a higher to a lower condition, on the part not only of those souls who have deserved the change by the variety of their movements, but also on that of those who, in order to serve the whole world, were brought down from those higher and invisible spheres to these lower and visible ones, although against their will—"Because the creature was subjected to vanity, not willingly, but because of Him who subjected the same in hope";[11] so that both sun, and moon, and stars, and angels might discharge their duty to the world, and to those souls which, on account of their excessive mental defects, stood in need of bodies of a grosser and more solid nature; and for the sake of those for whom this arrangement was necessary, this visible world was also called into being. From this it follows, that by the use of the word καταβολή, a descent from a higher to a lower condition, shared by all in common, would seem to be pointed out. The hope indeed of freedom is entertained by the whole of creation—of being liberated from the corruption of slavery—when the sons of God, who either fell away or were scattered abroad, shall be gathered together into one, or when they shall have fulfilled their other duties in this world, which are known to God alone, the Disposer of all things. We are, indeed, to suppose that the world was created of such quality and capacity as to contain not only all those souls which it was determined should be trained in this world, but also all those powers which were prepared to attend, and serve, and assist them. For it is established by many declarations that all

---

9. *Matt.* xxiv. 21.
10. *Eph.* i. 4.
11. *Rom.* viii. 20, 21.

rational creatures are of one nature; on which ground alone, could the justice of God in all His dealings with them be defended, seeing every one has the reason in himself, why he has been placed in this or that rank in life.

This arrangement of things, then, which God afterwards appointed (for He had, from the very origin of the world, clearly perceived the reasons and causes affecting those who, either owing to mental deficiencies, deserved to enter into bodies, or those who were carried away by their desire for visible things, and those also who, either willingly or unwillingly, were compelled, by Him who subjected the same in hope, to perform certain services to such as had fallen into that condition), not being understood by some, who failed to perceive that it was owing to preceding causes, originating in free will, that this variety of arrangement had been instituted by God, they have concluded that all things in this world are directed either by fortuitious movements or by a necessary fate, and that nothing is within the power of our own will. And, therefore, also they were unable to show that the providence of God was beyond the reach of censure.

But as we have said that all the souls who lived in this world stood in need of many ministers, or rulers, or assistants; so, in the last times, when the end of the world is already imminent and near, and the whole human race is verging upon the last destruction, and when not only those who were governed by others have been reduced to weakness, but those also to whom had been committed the cares of government, it was no longer such help nor such defenders that were needed, but the help of the Author and Creator Himself was required to restore to the one the discipline of obedience, which had been corrupted and profaned, and to the other the discipline of rule. And hence the only-begotten Son of God, who was the Word and the Wisdom of the Father, when He was in the possession of that glory with the Father, which He had before the world was, divested Himself of it, and, taking the form of a servant, was made obedient unto death, that He might teach obedience to those who could not otherwise than by obedience obtain salvation. He restored also the laws of rule and government which had been corrupted, by subduing all enemies under His feet, that by this means (for it was necessary that He should reign until He had put all enemies under His feet, and destroyed the last enemy—death) He might teach rulers themselves moderation in their government. As He had come, then, to restore the discipline, not only of government, but of obedience, as we have said, accomplishing in Himself first what He desired to be accomplished by others, He became obedient to the

Father, not only to the death of the cross, but also, in the end of the world, embracing in Himself all whom He subjects to the Father, and who by Him come to salvation, He Himself, along with them, and in them, is said also to be subject to the Father; all things subsisting in Him, and He Himself being the Head of all things, and in Him being the salvation and the fulness of those who obtain salvation. And this consequently is what the apostle says of Him: "And when all things shall be subjected to Him, then shall the Son also Himself be subject to Him that put all things under Him, that God may be all in all."

I know not, indeed, how the heretics, not understanding the meaning of the apostle in these words, consider the term "subjection" degrading as applied to the Son; for if the propriety of the title be called in question, it may easily be ascertained from making a contrary supposition. Because if it be not good to be in subjection, it follows that the opposite will be good, viz., not to be in subjection. Now the language of the apostle, according to their view, appears to indicate by these words, "And when all things shall be subdued unto Him, then shall the Son also Himself be subject unto Him that put all things under Him,"[12] that He, who is not now in subjection to the Father, will become subject to Him when the Father shall have first subdued all things unto Him. But I am astonished how it can be conceived to be the meaning, that He who, while all things are not yet subdued to Him, is not Himself in subjection, should—at a time when all things have been subdued to Him, and when He has become King of all men, and holds sway over all things—be supposed then to be made subject, seeing He was not formerly in subjection; for such do not understand that the subjection of Christ to the Father indicates that our happiness has attained to perfection, and that the work undertaken by Him has been brought to a victorious termination, seeing He has not only purified the power of supreme government over the whole of creation, but presents to the Father the principles of the obedience and subjection of the human race in a corrected and improved condition. If, then, that subjection be held to be good and salutary by which the Son is said to be subject to the Father, it is an extremely rational and logical inference to deduce that the subjection also of enemies, which is said to be made to the Son of God, should be understood as being also salutary and useful; as if, when the Son is said to be subject to the Father, the perfect restoration of the whole of creation is signified, so also, when enemies are said to be subjected to the Son of God, the salvation of

---

12. I *Cor.* xv. 28.

the conquered and the restoration of the lost is in that understood to consist.

This subjection, however, will be accomplished in certain ways, and after certain training, and at certain times; for it is not to be imagined that the subjection is to be brought about by the pressure of necessity (lest the whole world should then appear to be subdued to God by force), but by word, reason, and doctrine; by a call to a better course of things, by the best systems of training, by the employment also of suitable and appropriate threatenings, which will justly impend over those who despise any care or attention to their salvation and usefulness. In a word, we men also, in training either our slaves or children, restrain them by threats and fear while they are, by reason of their tender age, incapable of using their reason; but when they have begun to understand what is good, and useful, and honorable, the fear of the lash being over, they acquiesce through the suasion of words and reason in all that is good. But how, consistently with the preservation of freedom of will in all rational creatures, each one ought to be regulated, i.e., who they are whom the word of God finds and trains, as if they were already prepared and capable of it; who they are whom it puts off to a later time; who these are from whom it is altogether concealed, and who are so situated as to be far from hearing it; who those, again, are who despise the word of God when made known and preached to them, and who are driven by a kind of correction and chastisement to salvation, and whose conversion is in a certain degree demanded and extorted; who those are to whom certain opportunities of salvation are afforded, so that sometimes, their faith being proved by an answer alone,[13] they have unquestionably obtained salvation;— from what causes or on what occasions these results take place, or what the divine wisdom sees within them, or what movements of their will leads God so to arrange all these things, is known to Him alone, and to His only-begotten Son, through whom all things were created and restored, and to the Holy Spirit, through whom all things are sanctified, who proceedeth from the Father,[14] to whom be glory for ever and ever. Amen.

---

13. By a profession of faith in baptism.

14. It was not until the third Synod of Toledo, A.D. 589, that the "filioque" clause was added to the Creed of Constantinople—this difference forming, as is well known, one of the dogmatic grounds for the disunion between the Western and Eastern Churches down to the present day, the latter Church denying that the Spirit proceedeth from the Father *and the Son*.

Chapter VI.—ON THE END OF THE WORLD

Now, respecting the end of the world and the consummation of all things, we have stated in the preceding pages, to the best of our ability, so far as the authority of holy Scripture enabled us, what we deem sufficient for purposes of instruction; and we shall here only add a few admonitory remarks, since the order of investigation has brought us back to the subject. The highest good, then, after the attainment of which the whole of rational nature is seeking, which is also called the end of all blessings, is defined by many philosophers as follows: The highest good, they say, is to become as like to God as possible. But this definition I regard not so much as a discovery of theirs, as a view derived from holy Scripture. For this is pointed out by Moses, before all other philosophers, when he describes the first creation of man in these words: "And God said, Let Us make man in Our own image, and after Our likeness";[15] and then he adds the words: "So God created man in His own image: in the image of God created He him; male and female created He them, and He blessed them."[16] Now the expression, "In the image of God created He him," without any mention of the word "likeness," conveys no other meaning than this, that man received the dignity of God's image at his first creation; but that the perfection of his likeness has been reserved for the consummation,—namely, that he might acquire it for himself by the exercise of his own diligence in the imitation of God, the possibility of attaining to perfection being granted him at the beginning through the dignity of the divine image, and the perfect realization of the divine likeness being reached in the end by the fulfillment of the necessary works. Now, that such is the case, the Apostle John points out more clearly and unmistakably, when he makes this declaration: "Little children, we do not yet know what we shall be; but if a revelation be made to us from the Saviour, ye will say, without any doubt, we shall be like Him."[17] By which expression he points out with the utmost certainty, that not only was the end of all things to be hoped for, which he says was still unknown to him, but also the likeness to God, which will be conferred in proportion to the completeness of our deserts. The Lord Himself, in the Gospel, not only declares that these same results are future, but that they are to be brought about by His own inter-

15. *Gen.* i. 26.
16. *Gen.* i. 27, 28.
17. *John* iii. 2.

cession, He Himself deigning to obtain them from the Father for His disciples, saying, "Father, I will that where I am, these also may be with Me; and as Thou and I are one, they also may be one in Us."[18] In which the divine likeness itself already appears to advance, if we may so express ourselves, and from being merely similar, to become the same, because undoubtedly in the consummation or end God is "all and in all." And with reference to this, it is made a question by some whether the nature of bodily matter, although cleansed and purified, and rendered altogether spiritual, does not seem either to offer an obstruction towards attaining the dignity of the divine likeness, or to the property of unity, because neither can a corporeal nature appear capable of any resemblance to a divine nature, which is certainly incorporeal; nor can it be truly and deservedly designated one with it, especially since we are taught by the truths of our religion that that which alone is one, viz., the Son with the Father, must be referred to a peculiarity of the divine nature.

Since, then, it is promised that in the end God will be all and in all, we are not, as is fitting, to suppose that animals, either sheep or other cattle, come to that end, lest it should be implied that God dwelt even in animals, whether sheep or other cattle; and so, too, with pieces of wood or stones, lest it should be said that God is in these also. So, again, nothing that is wicked must be supposed to attain to that end, lest, while God is said to be in all things, He may also be said to be in a vessel of wickedness. For if we now assert that God is everywhere and in all things, on the ground that nothing can be empty of God, we nevertheless do not say that He is now "all things" in those in whom He is. And hence we must look more carefully as to what that is which denotes the perfection of blessedness and the end of things, which is not only said to be God in all things, but also "all in all." Let us then inquire what all those things are which God is to become in all.

I am of opinion that the expression, by which God is said to be "all in all," means that He is "all" in each individual person. Now He will be "all" in each individual in this way: when all which any rational understanding, cleansed from the dregs of every sort of vice, and with every cloud of wickedness completely swept away, can either feel, or understand, or think, will be wholly God; and when it will no longer behold or retain anything else than God, but when God will be the measure and standard of all its movements; and thus God will be "all," for there will no longer be any distinction of good and evil, seeing evil nowhere exists; for God is all things, and to Him no evil is

18. *John* xvii. 24; 21.

near; nor will there be any longer a desire to eat from the tree of the knowledge of good and evil, on the part of him who is always in the possession of good, and to whom God is all. So then, when the end has been restored to the beginning, and the termination of things compared with their commencement, that condition of things will be re-established in which rational nature was placed, when it had no need to eat of the tree of the knowledge of good and evil; so that when all feeling of wickedness has been removed, and the individual has been purified and cleansed, He who alone is the one good God becomes to him "all," and that not in the case of a few individuals, or of a considerable number, but He Himself is "all in all." And when death shall no longer anywhere exist, nor the sting of death, nor any evil at all, then verily God will be "all in all." But some are of opinion that that perfection and blessedness of rational creatures, or natures can only remain in that same condition of which we have spoken above, i.e., that all things should possess God, and God should be to them all things, if they are in no degree prevented by their union with a bodily nature. Otherwise they think that the glory of the highest blessedness is impeded by the intermixture of any material substance. But this subject we have discussed at greater length, as may be seen in the preceding pages.

And now, as we find the apostle making mention of a spiritual body, let us inquire, to the best of our ability, what idea we are to form of such a thing. So far, then, as our understanding can grasp it, we consider a spiritual body to be of such a nature as ought to be inhabited not only by all holy and perfect souls, but also by all those creatures which will be liberated from the slavery of corruption. Respecting the body also, the apostle has said, "We have a house not made with hands, eternal in the heavens,"[19] i.e., in the mansions of the blessed. And from this statement we may form a conjecture, how pure, how refined, and how glorious are the qualities of that body, if we compare it with those which, although they are celestial bodies, and of most brilliant splendor, were nevertheless made with hands, and are visible to our sight. But of that body it is said, that it is a house not made with hands, but eternal in the heavens. Since, then, those things "which are seen are temporal, but those things which are not seen are eternal,"[20] all those bodies which we see either on earth or in heaven, and which are capable of being seen, and have been made with hands, but are not eternal, are far excelled in glory by that which is not visible, nor

---

19. 2 *Cor.* v. 1.
20. 2 *Cor.* iv. 18.

made with hands, but is eternal. From which comparison it may be conceived how great are the comeliness, and splendor, and brilliancy of a spiritual body; and how true it is, that "eye hath not seen, nor ear heard, nor hath it entered into the heart of man to conceive, what God hath prepared for them that love him."[21] We ought not, however, to doubt that the nature of this present body of ours may, by the will of God, who made it what it is, be raised to those qualities of refinement, and purity, and splendor (which characterize the body referred to), according as the condition of things requires, and the deserts of our rational nature shall demand. Finally, when the world required variety and diversity, matter yielded itself with all docility throughout the diverse appearances and species of things to the Creator, as to its Lord and Maker, that He might educe from it the various forms of celestial and terrestrial beings. But when things have begun to hasten to that consummation that all may be one, as the Father is one with the Son, it may be understood as a rational inference, that where all are one, there will no longer be any diversity.

The last enemy, moreover, who is called death, is said on this account to be destroyed, that there may not be anything left of a mournful kind when death does not exist, nor anything that is adverse when there is no enemy. The destruction of that last enemy, indeed, is to be understood, not as if its substance, which was formed by God, is to perish, but because its mind and hostile will, which came not from God, but from itself, are to be destroyed. Its destruction, therefore, will not be its non-existence, but its ceasing to be an enemy, and to be death. For nothing is impossible to the Omnipotent, nor is anything incapable of restoration to its Creator; for He made all things that they might exist, and those things which were made for existence cannot cease to be. For this reason also will they admit of change and variety, so as to be placed, according to their merits, either in a better or worse position; but no destruction of substance can befall those things which were created by God for the purpose of permanent existence. For those things which agreeably to the common opinion are believed to perish, the nature either of our faith or of the truth will not permit us to suppose to be destroyed. Finally, our flesh is supposed by ignorant men and unbelievers to be destroyed after death, in such a degree that it retains no relic at all of its former substance. We, however, who believe in its resurrection, understand that a change only has been produced by death, but that its substance certainly remains;

---

21. I *Cor.* ii. 9; cf. *Isa.* lxiv. 4.

and that by the will of its Creator, and at the time appointed, it will be restored to life; and that a second time a change will take place in it, so that what at first was flesh formed out of earthly soil, and was afterwards dissolved by death, and again reduced to dust and ashes ("For dust thou art,"[22] it is said, "and to dust shalt thou return"), will be again raised from the earth, and shall after this, according to the merits of the indwelling soul, advance to the glory of a spiritual body.

Into this condition, then, we are to suppose that all this bodily substance of ours will be brought, when all things shall be re-established in a state of unity, and when God shall be all in all. And this result must be understood as being brought about, not suddenly, but slowly and gradually, seeing that the process of amendment and correction will take place imperceptibly in the individual instances during the lapse of countless and unmeasured ages, some outstripping others, and tending by a swifter course towards perfection, while others again follow close at hand, and some again a long way behind; and thus, through the numerous and uncounted orders of progressive beings who are being reconciled to God from a state of enmity, the last enemy is finally reached, who is called death, so that he also may be destroyed, and no longer be an enemy. When, therefore, all rational souls shall have been restored to a condition of this kind, then the nature of this body of ours will undergo a change into the glory of a spiritual body. For as we see it not to be the case with rational natures, that some of them have lived in a condition of degradation owing to their sins, while others have been called to a state of happiness on account of their merits; but as we see those same souls who had formerly been sinful, assisted, after their conversion and reconciliation to God, to a state of happiness; so also are we to consider, with respect to the nature of the body, that the one which we now make use of in a state of meanness, and corruption, and weakness, is not a different body from that which we shall possess in incorruption, and in power, and in glory; but that the same body, when it has cast away the infirmities in which it is now entangled, shall be transmuted into a condition of glory, being rendered spiritual, so that what was a vessel of dishonor may, when cleansed become a vessel unto honor, and an abode of blessedness. And in this condition, also, we are to believe, that by the will of the Creator, it will abide for ever without any change, as is confirmed by the declaration of the apostle, when he says, "We have a

---

22. *Gen.* iii. 19.

house, not made with hands, eternal in the heavens." For the faith of
the Church does not admit the view of certain Grecian philosophers,
that there is besides the body, composed of four elements, another fifth
body, which is different in all parts, and diverse from this our present
body; since neither out of sacred Scripture can any produce the slightest suspicion of evidence for such an opinion, nor can any rational
inference from things allow the reception of it, especially when the
holy apostle manifestly declares, that it is not new bodies which are
given to those who rise from the dead, but that they receive those
identical ones which they had possessed when living, transformed from
an inferior into a better condition. For his words are: "It is sown an
animal body, it will rise a spiritual body: it is sown in corruption,
it will arise in incorruption: it is sown in weakness, it will
arise in power: it is sown in dishonor, it will arise in glory."[23] As,
therefore, there is a kind of advance in man, so that from being first
an animal being, and not understanding what belongs to the Spirit of
God, he reaches by means of instruction the stage of being made a
spiritual being, and of judging all things, while he himself is judged
by no one; so also, with respect to the state of the body, we are to
hold that this very body which now, on account of its service to the
soul, is styled an animal body, will, by means of a certain progress,
when the soul, united to God, shall have been made one spirit with
Him (the body even then ministering, as it were, to the spirit), attain
to a spiritual condition and quality, especially since, as we have often
pointed out, bodily nature was so formed by the Creator, as to pass
easily into whatever condition he should wish, or the nature of the case
demand.

The whole of this reasoning, then, amounts to this: that God
created two general natures,—a visible, i.e., a corporeal nature; and an
invisible nature, which is incorporeal. Now these two natures admit of
two different permutations. That invisible and rational nature changes
in mind and purpose, because it is endowed with freedom of will, and
is on this account found sometimes to be engaged in the practice of
good, and sometimes in that of the opposite. But this corporeal nature
admits of a change in substance; whence also God, the arranger of all
things, has the service of this matter at His command in the molding,
or fabrication, or retouching of whatever He wishes, so that corporeal
nature may be transmuted, and transformed into any forms or species
whatever, according as the deserts of things may demand; which the

23. I *Cor.* xv. 28.

prophet evidently has in view when he says, "It is God who makes and transforms all things."[24]

And now the point for investigation is whether, when God shall be all in all, the whole of bodily nature will, in the consummation of all things, consist of one species, and the sole quality of body be that which shall shine in the indescribable glory which is to be regarded as the future possession of the spiritual body. For if we rightly understand the matter, this is the statement of Moses in the beginning of his book, when he says, "In the beginning God created the heavens and the earth."[25] For this is the beginning of all creation: to this beginning the end and consummation of all things must be recalled, i.e., in order that that heaven and that earth may be the habitation and resting place of the pious; so that all the holy ones, and the meek, may first obtain an inheritance in that land, since this is the teaching of the law, and of the prophets, and of the Gospel. In which land I believe there exist the true and living forms of that worship which Moses handed down under the shadow of the law; of which it is said, that "they serve unto the example and shadow of heavenly things"[26]—those, viz., who were in subjection in the law. To Moses himself also was the injunction given, "Look that thou make them after the form and pattern which were showed thee on the mount."[27] From which it appears to me, that as on this earth the law was a sort of schoolmaster to those who by it were to be conducted to Christ, in order that, being instructed and trained by it, they might more easily, after the training of the law, receive the more perfect principles of Christ; so also another earth, which receives into it all the saints, may first imbue and mold them by the institutions of the true and everlasting law, that they may more easily gain possession of those perfect institutions of heaven, to which nothing can be added; in which there will be, of a truth, that Gospel which is called everlasting, and that Testament, ever new, which shall never grow old.

In this way, accordingly, we are to suppose that at the consummation and restoration of all things, those who make a gradual advance, and who ascend in the scale of improvement, will arrive in due measure and order at that land, and at that training which is contained in it, where they may be prepared for those better institutions to which no addition can be made. For, after His agents and servants,

24. *Ps.* cii. 25, 26.
25. *Gen.* i. 1.
26. *Heb.* viii. 5.
27. *Ex.* xxv. 40.

the Lord Christ, who is King of all, will Himself assume the kingdom; i.e., after instruction in the holy virtues, He will Himself instruct those who are capable of receiving Him in respect of His being wisdom, reigning in them until He has subjected them to the Father, who has subdued all things to Himself, i.e., that when they shall have been made capable of receiving God, God may be to them all in all. Then accordingly, as a necessary consequence, bodily nature will obtain that highest condition to which nothing more can be added. Having discussed, up to this point, the quality of bodily nature, or of spiritual body, we leave it to the choice of the reader to determine what he shall consider best. And here we may bring the third book to a conclusion.

Tertullian
Prescription against Heretics

Chapter VII.—PAGAN PHILOSOPHY THE PARENT OF HERESIES. THE CONNECTION BETWEEN DEFLECTIONS FROM CHRISTIAN FAITH AND THE OLD SYSTEMS OF PAGAN PHILOSOPHY

These are "the doctrines" of men and "of demons" produced for itching ears of the spirit of this world's wisdom: this the Lord called "foolishness," and "chose the foolish things of the world" to confound even philosophy itself. For (philosophy) it is which is the material of the world's wisdom, the rash interpreter of the nature and the dispensation of God. Indeed heresies are themselves instigated by philosophy. From this source came the æons, and I know not what infinite forms, and the trinity of man in the system of Valentinus, who was of Plato's school. From the same source came Marcion's better god, with all his tranquillity; he came of the Stoics. Then, again, the opinion that the soul dies is held by the Epicureans; while the denial of the restoration of the body is taken from the aggregate school of all the philosophers; also, when matter is made equal to God, then you have the teaching of Zeno; and when any doctrine is alleged touching a god of fire, then Heraclitus comes in. The same subject-matter is discussed over and over again by the heretics and the philosophers; the same arguments are involved. Whence comes evil? Why is it permitted? What is the origin of man? and in what way does he come? Besides the question which Valentinus has very lately proposed—Whence comes God? Which he settles with the answer: From *enthymesis* and *ectroma*. Unhappy Aristotle! who invented for these men dialectics, the art of building up and pulling down; an art so evasive in its propositions, so farfetched in its conjectures, so harsh, in its arguments, so productive of contentions—embarrassing even to itself, retracting everything, and really treating of nothing! Whence spring those "fables and endless genealogies," and "unprofitable questions," and "words which spread like a cancer?" From all these, when the apostle would restrain us, he expressly names *philosophy* as that which he would have us be on our guard against. Writing to the Colossians, he says, "See that no one beguile you through philosophy and vain deceit, after the tradition of men, and contrary to the wisdom of the Holy Ghost." He had been at Athens, and had in his interviews (with its philosophers) become acquainted with that human wisdom which pretends to know the truth, whilst it only corrupts it, and is itself divided into its own manifold heresies, by the variety of its mutually repugnant sects. What indeed has Athens to do with Jerusalem? What concord is there between the Academy and the Church? what between heretics and Christians? Our instruction comes from "the porch of Solomon," who had himself taught that "the Lord should be sought in simplicity of heart." Away with all attempts to produce a mottled Christianity of Stoic, Platonic, and dialectic composition! We want no curious disputation after possessing Christ Jesus, no inquisition after enjoying the gospel! With our faith, we desire no further belief. For this is our palmary faith, that there is nothing which we ought to believe besides.

Chapter VIII.—CHRIST'S WORD, "SEEK AND YE SHALL FIND,"
NO WARRANT FOR HERETICAL DEVIATIONS FROM
THE FAITH. ALL CHRIST'S WORDS TO THE JEWS ARE
FOR US, NOT INDEED AS SPECIFIC COMMANDS,
BUT AS PRINCIPLES TO BE APPLIED

I come now to the point which is urged both by our own brethren and by the heretics. Our brethren adduce it as a pretext for entering on curious inquiries, and the heretics insist on it for importing the scrupulosity of their unbelief. It is written, they say, "Seek, and ye shall find."[1] Let us remember at what time the Lord said this. I think it was at the very outset of His teaching when there was still a doubt felt by all whether He were the Christ, and when even Peter had not yet declared Him to be the Son of God, and John Baptist had actually ceased to feel assurance about Him. With good reason, therefore, was it then said, "Seek, and ye shall find," when inquiry was still to be

_____
1. *Matt.* vii. 7.

made of Him who was not yet become known. Besides, this *was said* in respect of the Jews. For it is to them that the whole matter of this reproof pertains, seeing that they had a revelation where they might seek Christ. "They have," says He, "Moses and Elias,"[2]—in other words, the law and the prophets, which preach Christ; as also in another place He says plainly, "Search the Scriptures, in which ye expect to find salvation; for they testify of me";[3] which will be the meaning of "Seek, and ye shall find." For it is clear that the next words also apply to the Jews: "Knock, and it shall be opened unto you."[4] The Jews had formerly been in covenant with God; but being afterwards cast off on account of their sins, they began to be without God. The Gentiles, on the contrary, had never been in covenant with God; they were only as "a drop from a bucket," and "as dust from the threshing floor,"[5] and were ever outside the door. Now, how shall he who was always outside knock at the place where he never was? What door does he know of, when he has passed through none, either by entrance or ejection? Is it not rather he who is aware that he once lived within and was thrust out, that probably found the door and knocked thereat? In like manner, "Ask, and ye shall receive,"[6] is suitably said to one who was aware from whom he ought to ask,—by whom also some promise had been given; that is to say, "the God of Abraham, of Isaac, and of Jacob." Now, the Gentiles knew nothing either of Him, or of any of His promises. Therefore it was to Israel that he spake when He said, "I am not sent but to the lost sheep of the house of Israel."[7] Not yet had He "cast to the dogs the children's bread";[8] not yet did He charge them to "go into the way of the Gentiles."[9] It is only at the last that He instructs them to "go and teach all nations, and baptize them,"[10] when they were so soon to receive "the Holy Ghost, the Comforter, who should guide them into all the truth."[11] And this, too, makes towards the same conclusion. If the apostles, who were ordained to be teachers to the Gentiles, were themselves to have the Comforter for their teacher, far more needless

---

2. *Luke* xvi. 29.
3. *John* v. 39.
4. *Matt.* vii. 7.
5. *Isa.* xl. 15.
6. *Matt.* vii. 7.
7. *Matt.* xv. 24.
8. *Ver.* 26.
9. *Matt.* x. 5.
10. *Matt.* xxviii. 19.
11. *John* xvi. 13.

was it to say to us, "Seek, and ye shall find," to whom was to come, without research, our instruction by the apostles, and to the apostles themselves by the Holy Ghost. All the Lord's sayings, indeed, are set forth for all men; through the ears of the Jews have they passed on to us. Still most of them were addressed to *Jewish* persons; they therefore did not constitute instruction properly designed for ourselves, but *rather* an example.

Chapter IX.—THE RESEARCH AFTER DEFINITE TRUTH ENJOINED ON US. WHEN WE HAVE DISCOVERED THIS, WE SHOULD BE CONTENT

I now purposely relinquish this ground of argument. Let it be granted, that the words, "Seek, and ye shall find," were addressed to all men equally. Yet even here one's aim is carefully to determine the sense of the words consistently with that reason, which is the guiding principle in all interpretation. Now no divine saying is so unconnected and diffuse, that its *words* only are to be insisted on, and their *connection* left undetermined. But at the outset I lay down this position that there is some one, and therefore definite, thing taught by Christ, which the Gentiles are by all means bound to believe, and for that purpose to "seek," in order that they may be able, when they have "found" it, to believe. However, there can be no indefinite seeking for that which has been taught as one only definite thing. You must "seek" until you "find," and believe when you have found; nor have you anything further to do but to keep what you have believed, provided you believe this besides, that nothing else is to be believed, and therefore nothing else is to be sought, after you have found and believed what has been taught by Him who charges you to seek no other thing than that which He has taught. When, indeed, any man doubts about this, proof will be forthcoming, that we have in our possession that which was taught by Christ. Meanwhile, such is my confidence in our proof, that I anticipate it, in the shape of an admonition to certain persons, not "to seek" anything beyond what they have believed—that this is what they ought to have sought, how to avoid interpreting, "Seek, and ye shall find," without regard to the rule of reason.

Chapter X.—ONE HAS SUCCEEDED IN FINDING DEFINITE TRUTH, WHEN HE BELIEVES. HERETICAL WITS ARE ALWAYS OFFERING MANY THINGS FOR VAIN DISCUSSION, BUT WE ARE NOT TO BE ALWAYS SEEKING

Now the reason of this saying is comprised in three points: in the matter, in the time, in the limit. In the matter, so that you must consider *what it is* you have to seek; in the time, *when* you have to seek; in the limit, *how long*. What you have "to seek," then, is that which Christ has taught, and you must go on seeking of course for such time as you fail to find,—until indeed you find it. But you have succeeded in finding when you have believed. For you would not have believed if you had not found; as neither would you have sought except with a view to find. Your object, therefore, in seeking *was* to find; and your object in finding *was* to believe. All further delay for seeking and finding you have prevented by believing. The very fruit of your seeking has determined for you this limit. This boundary has He set for you Himself, who is unwilling that you should believe anything else than what He has taught, or, therefore, even seek for it. If, however, because so many other things have been taught by one and another, we are on that account bound to go on seeking, so long as we are able to find anything, we must at that rate be ever seeking, and never believe anything at all. For where shall be the end of seeking? where the stop in believing? where the completion in finding? Shall it be with Marcion? But even Valentinus proposes to us the maxim, "Seek, and ye shall find." Then shall it be with Valentinus? Well, but Apelles, too, will assail me with the same quotation; Hebion also, and Simon, and all in turn, have no other argument wherewithal to entice me, and draw me over to their side. Thus I shall be nowhere, and still be encountering that challenge, "Seek, and ye shall find," precisely as if I had no resting-place; as if indeed I had never found that which Christ has taught—that which ought to be sought, that which must needs be believed.

Chapter XI.—AFTER WE HAVE BELIEVED, SEARCH SHOULD CEASE; OTHERWISE IT MUST END IN A DENIAL OF WHAT WE HAVE BELIEVED. NO OTHER OBJECT PROPOSED FOR OUR FAITH

There is impunity in erring, if there is no delinquency; although indeed to err it is itself an act of delinquency. With impunity, I repeat, does a man ramble, when he purposely deserts nothing. But yet, if I have believed what I was bound to believe, and then afterwards think that there is something new to be sought after, I of course expect that there is something else to be found, although I should by no means entertain such expectation, unless it were because I either had not believed, although I apparently had become a believer, or else have ceased to believe. If I thus desert my faith, I am found to be a denier thereof. Once for all I would say, No man seeks, except him who neither ever possessed, or else has lost what he sought. The old woman in the Gospel had lost one of her ten pieces of silver, and therefore she sought it;[12] when, however, she found it, she ceased to look for it. The neighbor was without bread, and therefore he knocked; but as soon as the door was opened to him, and he received the bread, he discontinued knocking.[13] The widow kept asking to be heard by the judge, because she was not admitted; but when her suit was heard, thenceforth she was silent.[14] So that there is a limit both to seeking, and to knocking, and to asking. "For to every one that asketh," says He, "it shall be given, and to him that knocketh it shall be opened, and by him that seeketh it shall be found."[15] Away with the man who is ever seeking because he never finds; for he seeks there where nothing can be found. Away with him who is always knocking because it will never be opened to him; for he knocks where there is none to open. Away with him who is always asking because he will never be heard; for he asks of one who does not hear.

Chapter XII.—A PROPER SEEKING AFTER DIVINE KNOWLEDGE, WHICH WILL NEVER BE OUT OF PLACE OR EXCESSIVE, IS ALWAYS WITHIN THE RULE OF FAITH

As for us, although we must still seek, and *that* always, yet where ought our search to be made? Amongst the heretics, where all things are foreign and opposed to our own verity, and to whom we are forbidden to draw near? What slave looks for food from a stranger, not to say an enemy of his master? What soldier expects to get bounty

12. *Luke* xv. 8.
13. *Luke* xi. 5.
14. *Luke* xviii. 2, 3,
15. *Luke* xi. 9.

and pay from kings who are unallied, I might almost say hostile—unless forsooth he be a deserter, and a runaway, and a rebel? Even that old woman searched for the piece of silver within her own house. It was also at his neighbor's door that the persevering assailant kept knocking. Nor was it to a hostile judge, although a severe one, that the widow made her appeal. No man gets instruction from that which tends to destruction. No man receives illumination from a quarter where all is darkness. Let our "seeking," therefore be in that which is our own, and from those who are our own, and concerning that which is our own,—that, and only that, which can become an object of inquiry without impairing the rule of faith.

Chapter XIII.—SUMMARY OF THE CREED, OR RULE OF FAITH. NO QUESTIONS EVER RAISED ABOUT IT BY BELIEVERS. HERETICS ENCOURAGE AND PERPETUATE THOUGHT INDEPENDENT OF CHRIST'S TEACHING

Now, with regard to this rule of faith—that we may from this point acknowledge what it is which we defend—it is, you must know, that which prescribes the belief that there is one only God, and that He is none other than the Creator of the world, who produced all things out of nothing through His own Word, first of all sent forth; that this Word is called His Son, *and,* under the name of God, was seen "in diverse manners" by the patriarchs, heard at all times in the prophets, at last brought down by the Spirit and Power of the Father into the Virgin Mary, was made flesh in her womb, and, being born of her, went forth as Jesus Christ; thenceforth He preached the new law and the new promise of the kingdom of heaven, worked miracles; having been crucified, He rose again the third day; then, having ascended into the heavens, He sat at the right hand of the Father; sent instead of Himself the Power of the Holy Ghost to lead such as believe; will come with glory to take the saints to the enjoyment of everlasting life and of the heavenly promises, and to condemn the wicked to everlasting fire, after the resurrection of both these classes shall have happened, together with the restoration of their flesh. This rule, as it will be proved, was taught by Christ, and raises amongst ourselves no other questions than those which heresies introduce, and which make men heretics.

Chapter XIV.—CURIOSITY OUGHT NOT RANGE BEYOND THE RULE OF FAITH. RESTLESS CURIOSITY, THE FEATURE OF HERESY

So long, however, as its form exists in its proper order, you may seek and discuss as much as you please, and give full rein to your curiosity, in whatever seems to you to hang in doubt, or to be shrouded in obscurity. You have at hand, no doubt, some learned brother gifted with the grace of knowledge, some one of the experienced class, some one of your close acquaintance who is curious like yourself; although with yourself, a seeker, he will, after all, be quite aware that it is better for you to remain in ignorance, lest you should come to know what you ought not, because you have acquired the knowledge of what you ought to know. "Thy faith," He says, "hath saved thee"[16] not *observe* your skill in the Scriptures. Now, faith has been deposited in the rule; it has a law, and in the observance thereof salvation. Skill, however, consists in curious art, having for its glory simply the readiness that comes from knack. Let such curious art give place to faith; let such glory yield to salvation. At any rate, let them either relinquish t'.eir noisiness, or else be quiet. To know nothing in opposition to the rule of faith, is to know all things. Suppose that heretics were not enemies to the truth, so that we were not forewarned to avoid them, what sort of conduct would it be to agree with men who do themselves confess that they are still seeking? For if they are still seeking, they have not as yet found anything amounting to certainty; and therefore, whatever they seem for a while to hold, they betray their own skepticism, whilst they continue seeking. You therefore, who seek after their fashion, looking to those who are themselves ever seeking, a doubter to doubters, a waverer to waverers, must needs be "led, blindly by the blind, down into the ditch."[17] But when, for the sake of deceiving us, they pretend that they are still seeking, in order that they may palm their essays upon us by the suggestion of an anxious sympathy,—when, in short, after gaining an access to us they proceed at once to insist on the necessity of our inquiring into such points as they were in the habit of advancing, then it is high time for us in moral obligation to repel them, so that they may know that it is not Christ, but themselves, whom we disavow. For since they are still seekers, they have no fixed tenets yet; and being not fixed in tenet, they have not yet believed; and being not yet believers, they are not Christians. But even though

---

16. *Luke* xviii. 42.
17. *Matt.* xv. 14.

they have their tenets and their belief, they still say that inquiry is necessary in order to discussion. Previous, however, to the discussion, they deny what they confess not yet to have believed, so long as they keep it an object of inquiry. When men, therefore, are not Christians even on their own admission, how much more do they fail to appear such to us! What sort of truth is that which they patronize, when they commend it to us with a lie? Well, but they actually treat of the Scriptures and recommend their opinions out of the Scriptures! To be sure they do. From what other source could they derive arguments concerning the things of the faith, except from the records of the faith?

Chapter XV.—HERETICS NOT TO BE ALLOWED TO ARGUE OUT OF THE SCRIPTURES. THE SCRIPTURES, IN FACT, DO NOT BELONG TO THEM

We are therefore come to the gist of our position; for at this point we were aiming, and for this we were preparing in the preamble of our address which we have just completed,—so that we may now join issue on the contention to which our adversaries challenge us. They put forward the Scriptures, and by this insolence of theirs they at once influence some. In the encounter itself, however, they weary the strong, they catch the weak, and dismiss waverers with a doubt. Accordingly, we oppose to them this step above all others, of not admitting them to any discussion of the Scriptures.

If in these lie their resources, before they can use them, it ought to be clearly seen to whom belongs the possession of the Scriptures, that none may be admitted to the use thereof who has no title at all to the privilege.

Tertullian
On The Soul

Chapter I.—IT IS NOT TO THE PHILOSOPHERS
THAT WE RESORT FOR INFORMATION ABOUT
THE SOUL BUT TO GOD

Having discussed . . . the origin of the soul, . . . that the soul consisted rather in an adaptation of matter than of the inspiration of God,
I now turn to the other questions incidental to the subject; and (in
my treatment of these) I shall evidently have mostly to contend with
the philosophers. In the very prison of Socrates they skirmished about
the state of the soul. I have my doubts at once whether the time was
an opportune one for their (great) master—(to say nothing of the
place), although *that* perhaps does not much matter. For what could
the soul of Socrates then contemplate with clearness and serenity?
The sacred ship had returned (from Delos), the hemlock draft to
which he had been condemned had been drunk, death was now present
before him: (his mind) was, as one may suppose, naturally excited at
every emotion; or if nature had lost her influence, it must have been
deprived of all power of thought. Or let it have been as placid and
tranquil so you please, inflexible, in spite of the claims of natural duty,
at the tears of her who was so soon to be his widow, and at the sight
of his thenceforward orphan children, yet his soul must have been
moved even by its very efforts to suppress emotion; and his constancy
itself must have been shaken, as he struggled against the disturbance
of the excitement around him. Besides, what other thoughts could any
man entertain who had been unjustly condemned to die, but such as
should solace him for the injury done to him? Especially would this
be the case with that glorious creature, the philosopher, to whom in-
jurious treatment would not suggest a craving for consolation, but
rather the feeling of resentment and indignation. Accordingly, after his

sentence, when his wife came to him with her effeminate cry, O Socrates, you are unjustly condemned! he seemed already to find joy in answering, Would you then wish me justly condemned? It is therefore not to be wondered at, if even in his prison, from a desire to break the foul hands of Anytus and Meletus, he, in the face of death itself, asserts the immortality of the soul by a strong assumption such as was wanted to frustrate the wrong (they had inflicted upon him). So that all the wisdom of Socrates, at that moment, proceeded from the affectation of an assumed composure, rather than the firm conviction of ascertained truth. For by whom has truth ever been discovered without God? By whom has God ever been found without Christ? By whom has Christ ever been explored without the Holy Spirit? By whom has the Holy Spirit ever been attained without the mysterious gift of faith? Socrates, as none can doubt, was actuated by a different spirit. For they say that a demon clave to him from his boyhood—the very worst teacher certainly, notwithstanding the high place assigned to it by poets and philosophers—even next to, (nay, along with) the gods themselves. The teachings of the power of Christ had not yet been given— (that power) which alone can confute this most pernicious influence of evil that has nothing good in it, but is rather the author of all error, and the seducer from all truth. Now if Socrates was pronounced the wisest of men by the oracle of the Pythian demon, which, you may be sure, neatly managed the business for his friend, of how much greater dignity and constancy is the assertion of the Christian wisdom, before the very breath of which the whole host of demons is scattered! This wisdom of the school of heaven frankly and without reserve denies the gods of this world, and shows no such inconsistency as to order a "cock to be sacrificed to Æsculapius:"[1] no new gods and demons does it introduce, but expels the old ones; it corrupts not youth, but instructs them in all goodness and moderation; and so it bears the unjust condemnation not of one city only, but of all the world, in the cause of that truth which incurs indeed the greater hatred in proportion to its fulness: so that it tastes death not out of a (poisoned) cup almost in the way of jollity; but it exhausts it in every kind of bitter cruelty, on gibbets and in holocausts. Meanwhile, in the still gloomier prison of the world amongst your Cebeses and Phædos, in every investigation concerning (man's) soul, it directs its inquiry according to the rules of God. At all events, you can show us no more powerful expounder of the soul than the Author thereof. From God you may learn about that

---

1. The allusion is to the *inconsistency* of the philosopher, who condemned the gods of the vulgar, and died offering a gift to one of them.

which you hold of God; but from none else will you get this knowledge, if you get it not from God. For who is to reveal that which God has hidden? To that quarter must we resort in our inquiries whence we are most safe even in deriving our ignorance. For it is really better for us not to know a thing, because He has not revealed it to us, than to know it according to man's wisdom, because *he* has been bold enough to assume it.

Chapter II.—THE CHRISTIAN HAS SURE AND SIMPLE KNOWLEDGE CONCERNING THE SUBJECT BEFORE US

Of course we shall not deny that philosophers have sometimes thought the same things as ourselves. The testimony of truth is the issue thereof. It sometimes happens even in a storm, when the boundaries of sky and sea are lost in confusion, that some harbour is stumbled on (by the labouring ship) by some happy chance; and sometimes in the very shades of night, through blind luck alone, one finds access to a spot, or egress from it. In nature, however, most conclusions are suggested, as it were, by that common intelligence wherewith God has been pleased to endow the soul of man. This intelligence has been caught up by philosophy, and, with the view of glorifying her own art, has been inflated (it is not to be wondered at that I use this language) with straining after that facility of language which is practised in the building up and pulling down of everything, and which has greater aptitude for persuading men by speaking than by teaching. She assigns to things their forms and conditions; sometimes makes them common and public, sometimes appropriates them to private use; on certainties she capriciously stamps the character of uncertainty; she appeals to precedents, as if all things are capable of being compared together; she describes all things by rule and definition, allotting diverse properties even to similar objects; she attributes nothing to the divine permission, but assumes as her principles the laws of nature. I could bear with her pretensions, if only she were herself true to nature, and would prove to me that she had a mastery over nature as being associated with its creation. She thought, no doubt, that she was deriving her mysteries from sacred sources, as men deem them, because in ancient times most authors were supposed to be (I will not say godlike, but) actually gods: as, for instance, the Egyptian Mercury to whom Plato paid very great deference;[2] and the Phrygian Silenus, to whom Midas lent his long ears, when the shepherds brought him to him; and Hermotimus, to whom the good people of Clazomenæ built a temple after his death; and Orpheus; and Musæus; and Pherecydes, the master of Pythagoras. But why need we care, since these philosophers have also made their attacks upon those writings which are condemned by us under the title of apocryphal, certain as we are that nothing ought to be received which does not agree with the true system of prophecy, which has arisen in this present age; because we do not forget that there have been false prophets, and long previous to them fallen spirits, which have instructed the entire tone and aspect of the world with cunning knowledge of this (*philosophic*) cast? It is, indeed, not incredible that any man who is in quest of wisdom may have gone so far, as a matter of curiosity, as to consult the very prophets; (*but be this as it may*), if you take the philosophers, you would find in them more diversity than agreement, since even in their agreement their diversity is discoverable. Whatever things are true *in their systems*, and agreeable to prophetic wisdom, they either recommend as emanating from some other source, or else perversely apply in some other sense. This process is attended with very great detriment to the truth, when they pretend that it is either helped by falsehood, or else that falsehood derives support from it. The following circumstance must needs have set ourselves and the philosophers by the ears, especially in this present matter, that they sometimes clothe sentiments which are common to both sides, in arguments which are peculiar to themselves, but contrary in some points to our rule and standard of faith; and at other times defend opinions which are especially their own, with arguments which both sides acknowledge to be valid, and occasionally conformable to their system of belief. The truth has, at this rate, been well-nigh excluded by the philosophers, through the poisons with which they have infected it; and thus, if we regard both the modes of coalition *which we have now mentioned*, and which are equally hostile to the truth, we feel the urgent necessity of freeing, on the one hand, the sentiments held by us in common with them from the arguments of the philosophers, and of separating, on the other hand, the arguments which both parties employ from the opinions of the same philosophers. *And this we may do* by recalling all questions to God's inspired standard, with the obvious exception of such simple cases as being free from the entanglement of any preconceived conceits, one may fairly admit on mere *human* testi-

---

2. See his *Phaedrus*, c. lix. (p. 274) ; also Augustin, *De. Civ. Dei,* viii, 11; Euseb. *Praep. Evang.* ix. 3.

mony; because plain evidence of this sort we must sometimes borrow from opponents, when our opponents have nothing to gain from it. Now I am not unaware what a vast mass of literature the philosophers have accumulated concerning the subject before us, in their own commentaries thereon—what various schools of principles there are, what conflicts of opinion, what prolific sources of questions, what perplexing methods of solution. Moreover, I have looked into Medical Science also, the sister (as they say) of Philosophy, which claims as her function to cure the body, and thereby to have a special acquaintance with the soul. From this circumstance she has great differences with her sister, pretending as the latter does to know more about the soul, through the more obvious treatment, as it were, of her in her domicile *of the body.* But never mind all this contention between them for preeminence! For extending their several researches on the soul, Philosophy, on the one hand, has enjoyed the full scope of her genius; while Medicine, on the other hand, has possessed the stringent demands of her art and practice. Wide are men's inquiries into uncertainties; wider still are their disputes about conjectures. However great the difficulty of adducing proofs, the labour of producing conviction is not one whit less; so that the gloomy Heraclitus was quite right, when, observing the thick darkness which obscured the researches of the inquirers about the soul, and wearied with their interminable questions, he declared that he had certainly not explored the limits of the soul, although he had traversed every road *in her domains.* To the Christian, however, but few words are necessary for the clear understanding of the whole subject. But in the few words there always arises certainty to him; nor is he permitted to give his inquiries a wider range than is compatible with their solution; for "endless questions" the apostle forbids.[3] It must however, be added, that no solution may be found by any man, but such as is learned from God; and that which is learned of God is the sum and substance of the whole thing.

Chapter III.—THE SOUL'S ORIGIN DEFINED OUT OF THE SIMPLE WORDS OF SCRIPTURE

Would to God that no "heresies had been ever necessary, in order that they which are approved may be made manifest!"[4] We should

3. *Tim.* i. 4.
4. I *Cor.* x. 19.

then be never required to try our strength in contests about the soul with philosophers, those patriarchs of heretics, as they may be fairly called.[5] The apostle, so far back as his own time, foresaw, indeed, that philosophy would do violent injury to the truth.[6] This admonition *about false philosophy* he was induced to offer after he had been at Athens, had become acquainted with that *loquacious* city[7], and had there had a taste of its huckstering wiseacres and talkers. In like manner is the treatment of the soul according to the sophistical doctrines of men which "mix their wine with water."[8] Some of them deny the immortality of the soul; others affirm that it is immortal, and something more. Some raise disputes about its substance; others about its form; others, again, respecting each of its several faculties. One school of philosophers derives its state from various sources, while another ascribes its departure to different destinations. *The various schools reflect the character of their masters,* according as they have received their impressions from the dignity of Plato, or the vigor of Zeno, or the equanimity of Aristotle, or the stupidity of Epicurus, or the sadness of Heraclitus, or the madness of Empedocles. The fault, I suppose, of the divine doctrine lies in its springing from Judæa[9] rather than from Greece. Christ made a mistake, too, in sending forth fishermen to preach, rather than the sophist. Whatever noxious vapours, accordingly, exhaled from philosophy, obscure the clear and wholesome atmosphere of truth, it will be for Christians to clear away, both by shattering to pieces the arguments which are drawn from the principles of things—I mean those of the philosophers—and by opposing to them the maxims of heavenly wisdom—that is, such as are revealed by the Lord; in order that both the pitfalls wherewith philosophy captivates the heathen may be removed, and the means employed by heresy to shake the faith of Christians may be repressed. . . .

---

5. Compare Tertullian's *Adv. Hermog.* c. viii.
6. *Col.* ii. 8.
7. Linguatem civitatem. Compare *Acts* xvii. 21.
8. *Isa.* i. 22.
9. *Isa.* ii. 3.

BIBLIOGRAPHY

¶ I. THE HELLENISTIC BACKGROUND

James Mark Baldwin, *Dictionary of Philosophy and Psychology* (New York, 1905), Vol. III.

E. R. Bevan, "Hellenism," *Encyclopaedia Britannica* (Chicago, 11th ed., 1909-10).

J. H. Breasted, *Ancient Times* (New York, rev. ed., 1935), especially Parts IV and V.

A. and M. Croiset, *Histoire de la litterature grecque* (Paris, 1928), Vol. V.

Friedrich Ueberwegs *Grundriss der Geschichte der Philosophie,* Vol. I of *Die Philosophie des Altertums* (Berlin, 12th. ed., 1926).

B. A. G. Fuller, *History of Greek Philosophy* (New York, rev. ed., 1945, 3 vols.).

Wilhelm Kroll and Kurt Witte (eds.), *Paulys Real-Encyclopädie der classischen Altertumsurissenschaft* (Stuttgart, 1903).

Gilbert Murray, *A History of Ancient Greek Literature* (New York, 1915), especially Ch. 18.

M. I. Rostovtzeff, *A History of the Ancient World* (Oxford, 1926-27, 2 vols.).

————, *Social and Economic History of the Hellenistic World* (Oxford, 1941, 3 vols.).

W. W. Tarn, *Hellenistic Civilisation* (London, 3rd rev. ed., 1952).

Paul Wendland, *Die hellenistisch-römische Kultur in ihren Beziehungen zu Judentum und Christentum* (Tübringen, rev. ed., 1912).

¶ II. GENERAL WORKS ON HELLENISTIC PHILOSOPHY

Alfred W. Benn, *The Greek Philosophers* (New York, 2nd. ed., 1914).

Emile Bréhier, *Histoire de la philosophie* (Paris, 1960), Vol. I.

F. W. Bussell, *School of Plato* (London, 1896).

Cicero, *De finibus, De natura deorum, De officiis* ("Loeb Classical Library," Cambridge, 1961), an excellent translation of Greek philosophy into Roman terms.

Samuel Dill, *Roman Society from Nero to Marcus Aurelius* (New York, 1956).

Diogenes Laertuis, *Lives of Eminent Philosophers*, trans. by R. D. Hicks (Cambridge, 1959, 2 vols.).

T. R. Glover, *Conflict of Religions in the Early Roman Empire* (New York, 3rd. ed., 1909).

Paul Elmer More, *Hellenistic Philosophies* (Princeton, 1923).

Walter Pater, *Marius the Epicurean* (New York n.d.).

Plutarch, *Moralia* ("Loeb Classical Library," Cambridge, 15 vols.), a most interesting picture of Greek culture in the first century A.D.

Eduard Zeller, *Outlines of the History of Greek Philosophy*, trans. by L. R. Palmer, (New York, 13th ed., 1959).

¶ III. EPICUREANISM

Cyril Bailey, (ed. and trans.), *Epicurus* (Oxford, 1926).

Diogenes Laertius, *Lives* . . . (see above), Book X.

André J. M. Festugière, *Epicurus and His Gods*, trans. by C. W. Chilton (Cambridge, 1956).

R. D. Hicks, *Stoic and Epicurean* (New York, 1962).

Lucretius, *On the Nature of the Universe*, trans. by R. Latham (Baltimore, 1958).

J. Masson, *Lucretius, Epicurean and Poet* (London, 1907-09).

W. J. Oates, *The Stoic and Epicurean Philosophers* (New York, 1957).

Walter Pater, *Marius the Epicurean* (see above), the most sympathetic reading of Epicurus in English.

George Santayana, *Three Philosophical Poets* (New York, 1910).

A. E. Taylor, *Epicurus* (New York, 1910).

Hermann Usener, (ed.), *Epicurea* (Leipzig, 1887), the standard collection of sources.

¶ IV. STOICISM

J. von Arnim, *Stoicorum veterum fragmenta* (Leipzig, 1905-24, 4 vols.).

E. V. Arnold, *Roman Stoicism* (New York, 1958)

E. R. Bevan, *Stoics and Sceptics* (New York, 1959).

F. W. Bussell, *Marcus Aurelius and the Later Stoics* (Edinburgh, 1910).

J. Christensen, *An Essay on the Unity of Stoic Philosophy* (Copenhagen, 1962).

R. D. Hicks, *Stoic and Epicurean* (see above).

B. Mates, *Stoic Logic* (Berkeley, 1953).

Paul Elmer More, *Hellenistic Philosophies* (see above).

W. J. Oates, *The Stoic and Epicurean Philosophers* (see above).

Gilbert Murray, *The Stoic Philosophy* (London, 1915).

M. Pohlenz, *Die stoa* (Göttingen, 1959, 2 vols.).

S. Sambursky, *Physics of the Stoics*, (London, 1959).

Seneca, *Epistolae morales*, trans. by R. M. Gummere ("Loeb Classical Library," Cambridge, 1917-53, 3 vols., Vols. II and III revised).

Eduard Zeller, *Stoics, Epicureans, and Skeptics*, trans. by O. J. Reichel (New York, rev. ed., 1962).

¶ V. SKEPTICISM

E. R. Bevan, *Stoics and Sceptics* (see above).

V. C. L. Brochard, *Les sceptiques grecs* (Paris, 1959), excellent.

Cicero, *De natura deorum, academica* (see above).

M. Croiset, *La vie et les oeuvres de Lucien* (Paris, 1882).

Diogenes Laertius, *Lives* . . . (see above), "Pyrrho" and "Timon" in Book IX.

A. Goedeckemeyer, *Die Geschichte des griechischen Skeptizismus* (Leipzig, 1905).

Philip Hallie, *Scepticism, Man and God* (Middletown, Conn., 1964), selections from the major writings of Sextus Empiricus.

R. D. Hicks, *Stoic and Epicurean* (see above). Despite the title, this book contains a clear summary of Skepticism in Chs. 8, 9, and 10.

Lucian, *The Works of Lucian Samosata*, trans. by H. W. Fowler (Oxford, 1905), complete with exceptions specified in preface.

————, *Selected Works*, trans. with an introduction by Bryan P. Reardon (New York, 1965).

Norman MacColl, *The Greek Sceptics, Pyrrho to Sextus* (London, 1869).

M. M. Patrick, *The Greek Sceptics* (New York, 1929).

Léon Robin, *Pyrrhon et le scepticisme grec* (Paris, 1944).

Sextus Empiricus, *Sextus Empiricus*, trans. by R. G. Bury, ("Loeb Classical Library," Cambridge, 1933-53, 4 vols.).

Eduard Zeller, *Stoics, Epicureans, and Sceptics* (see above).

¶ VI. ALEXANDRIAN JUDAISM AND NEOPLATONISM

Alfred W. Benn, *The Greek Philosophers* (see above), Ch. 14.

Charles Bigg, *Neoplatonism* (New York, 3rd ed., 1895).

Emile Bréhier, *Les idées philosophiques et religieuses de Philon d'Alexandrie* (Paris, 3rd ed., 1950).

————, *The Philosophy of Plotinus*, trans. by Joseph Thomas (Chicago, 1958).

————, (ed. and trans.), *Plotinus* (Budé, 1929-38, 7 vols.).

F. W. Bussell, *School of Plato* (London, 1896), an excellent account of the transition to Alexandrian Platonism.

F. H. Colson, *The Works of Philo* ("Loeb Classical Library," Cambridge, 1929-, 11 vols. with 2 vol. supp.).

Finkelstein, Louis (ed.), *The Jews* (New York, 3rd ed., 1960).

T. R. Glover, *Conflict of Religions in the Early Roman Empire* (see above).
George F. Moore, *Judaism in the First Centuries of the Christian Era, The Age of the Tannaim* (Cambridge, 1927-30, 3 vols.).
Gilbert Murray, *Five Stages of Greek Religion* (New York, 1955).
Plotinus, *The Enneads*, trans. by Stephen MacKenna, introduction by Paul Henry, S. J. (New York, 3rd ed. rev., n.d.).
M. I. Rostovtzeff, *Social and Economic History of the Roman Empire* (Oxford, rev. ed., 1957, 2 vols.).
G. Scholem, *Major Trends in Jewish Mysticism* (New York, 1954).
————, *Jewish Gnosticism* (New York, 1960).
W. W. Tarn, *Hellenistic Civilization* (see above).
H. A. Wolfson, *Philo* (Cambridge, rev. ed., 1962), foundations of religious philosophy in Judaism, Christianty, and Islam.
Eduard Zeller, *Outlines of the History of Greek Philosophy*, (see above), especially good on Jewish-Greek philosophy; see also the section on the Neo-Pythagoreans.

¶ VII. ALEXANDRIAN PLATONISM AND THE FORMATION OF CHRISTIAN THOUGHT

Ante-Nicene Fathers (Buffalo, 1885-96; reprinted by William B. Eerdmans, Grand Rapids, 1956), contains documents of Justin Martyr, Minucius Felix, Clement of Alexandria, Origen, and Tertullian.
Edwyn Bevan, "Hellenism" (see above, particularly the section "Hellenism and Christianity").
Charles Bigg, *The Church's Task under the Roman Empire* (Oxford, 1905).
————, *Origins of Christianity* (Oxford, 1909).
Cambridge Ancient History, (New York, 1923-39, 12 vols. with 5 vols. of plates, especially the chapters on philosophy and religion and the excellent bibliographies.
W. D. Davies, *Paul and Rabbinic Judaism* (London, 1948).
Martin Dibelius, *Studies in the Acts of the Apostles* (New York, 1956).
Morton Scott Enslin, *Christian Beginnings: Parts I and II* (New York, 1938).
André J. M. Festugière, and Pierre Fabre, *Le monde greco-romain au temps de Notre-Seigneur*, (Paris, 1935), Vol. II.
F. J. Foakes-Jackson and K. Lake, *The Beginnings of Christianity*, Pt. I: *The Acts of the Apostles* (London, 1920, 5 vols.).
T. R. Glover, *Conflict of Religions in the Early Roman Empire* (see above), on Tertullian.
Robert M. Grant, *Gnosticism and Early Christianity* (New York, 1959).
Adolf Harnack, *Lehrbuch der Dogmengeschichte* (Freiburg, 4th ed., 1909), Vol. I; English ed. (*History of Dogma*) trans. by Neil Buchanan.
Edwin Hatch, *The Influence of Greek Ideas on Christianity* (New York, 1957).

Hans Jonas, *The Gnostic Religion* (Boston, 1958).

P. de Labriolle, *La reáction païenne: Etude sur la prolemique antichretienne du 1er au 6e siècles* (Paris, 1934).

Arthur Darby Nock, *Early Gentile Christianity and Its Hellenistic Background* (New York, 1964).

Simone Petrement, *Le dualisme chez Platon, les Gnostiques, et les Manichéens* (Paris, 1947).

Richard Reitzenstein, *Die hellenistischen Mysterienreligionen* (Leipzig, 3rd ed., 1927).

Johannes Weiss, *Earliest Christianity: A History of the Period* A.D. *30-150* (New York, 1937, 1959), Vol. I.

Paul Wendland, *Die hellenistisch-romïsche Kultur* (see above).

INDEX